D0022493

The Lorette Wilmot Library
Nazareth College of Rochester

DEMCO

Inside Language

Inside Language

VIVIAN COOK

ARNOLD

A member of the Hodder Headline Group
LONDON • NEW YORK • SYDNEY • AUCKLAND

WITHDRAWN

LORETTE WILMOT LIBRARY
NAZARETH COLLEGE

First published in Great Britain in 1997 by
Arnold, a member of the Hodder Headline Group.
338 Euston Road, London NW1 3BH
175 Fifth Avenue, New York, NY 10010

Distributed exclusively in the USA by
St Martin's Press Inc.,
175 Fifth Avenue,
New York, NY 10010

© 1997 Vivian Cook

All rights reserved. No part of this publication may be reproduced or transmitted in
any form or by any means, electronically or mechanically, including photocopying,
recording or any information storage or retrieval system, without either prior
permission in writing from the publisher or a licence permitting restricted copying. In
the United Kingdom such licences are issued by the Copyright Licensing Agency: 90
Tottenham Court Road, London W1P 9HE.

British Library Cataloguing in Publication Data
A catalogue entry for this book is available from the British Library

Library of Congress Cataloging-in-Publication Data
A catalog record for this book is available from the Library of Congress

ISBN 0 340 60761 0 (Pb)
ISBN 0 340 69270 7 (Hb)

Composition by J&L Composition Ltd, Filey, North Yorkshire
Printed and bound in Great Britain by J W Arrowsmith Ltd, Bristol.

Contents

Contents

Structure of the book

Chapter Two   Pronouns and the Language System

The language system. Pronoun systems: speech role and number (first to third to nth persons); status (*tu* and *vous*); missing pronouns (*Love you baby*); pronouns and gender (*The patient must keep to the time of his? her? his or her? their? appointment*), non-sexist pronouns (*hizer* to *per*); case forms of pronouns (*between you and me/I*); English pronoun systems (Old English, Middle English, New Forest, British Jamaican); pronouns and reference (*She gave it to her/herself*).

Chapter Three   Basic Grammar

Grammatical words and content words (*the* vs. *table*); malapropisms (*a supercilious knowledge of accounts*). Grammatical inflections (*jump/jumps/jumped* etc); beginners' English grammar in textbooks. The order of Subject, Verb, and Object (*Here's looking at you kid* vs. *Such place Eternal Justice had prepar'd*). Phrase structure and the mind. Movement and principles of language (*Casablanca is hot.* vs. *Is Casablanca hot?*).

Chapter Four   The Sound System of Language

Sounds and meanings. Intonation and its functions (*John?* vs. *John!*). Producing the sounds of speech: vowels and consonants. Air and speech. Combining sounds into syllables (possible *Bliff* vs. impossible *Bnill*). How to make speech sounds. Sounds and phonemes (*peak* vs. *beak*). Alternatives to speech sounds (whistles, drums and sign language).

Chapter Five   Words and Meanings

The dictionary in the mind (how many things do you know about the word *help*?). Colours and linguistic relativity (the 11 basic colour terms). Levels of meaning (*furniture* vs. *table* vs. *coffee table*). Language and thinking (do speakers of different languages see the world differently?). Components of meaning (*tea* [+hot] [+liquid], *cola* [−hot] [+liquid]); cookery terms. Words and the mind (the tip-of-the-tongue sensation). The structure of content words (*horrorshow kick-boots*).

Chapter Six   The Writing Systems of Language

Signs and language (*£ $ % 3 . . .*). Non-sound-based writing systems (Chinese and Japanese characters). Direction in writing (right to left, top to bottom, alternate, etc). Sound-based writing systems (Korean Han'gul). Alphabet-based writing systems; consonant-based systems (Arabic/Hebrew); consonant and vowel systems (Greek, English). A brief history of the letter A. English spelling – problems and patterns (*in* vs. *inn*). Spoken and written English (*the NCP long-term off-airport car park courtesy pick-up point*).

Chapter Seven   Children Acquiring Language

Perceiving and producing speech sounds (*par* and *bar*). Acquiring words (*I have a tummy ache in my head*). Acquiring early grammar: missing grammatical morphemes (*there trunk*). How to work out MLU (Mean Length of Utterance). Rules of two-word speech (*want high*). Sentences without subjects (pro-drop) (*want car*). Babytalk in different languages: (*bowwow, wan wan* (Japanese), *hawhaw* (Moroccan Arabic), *uu* (Swahili) . . .). Modifications in language spoken to children. Three views of language acquisition: associationist, interactionist, Universal Grammar.

Chapter Eight   Varieties of Language

Gender (*Absolutely gorgeous, isn't it!!!*). Age (*Turn on the wireless*). Region, dialect, and standard language; r-dropping in British English; what to call your grandmother. Status and accents: dialect words (*chook* and *chicken*). Dialect grammar; pronouns (*Howyeh* and *Howyiz*); negation (*no I never*). R-dropping and class. H-dropping in English. Novelists' spelling of English accents (*I 'eard 'e corled 'isself somefink else*). Ne-dropping in French. Class and women's language (*fightin'* vs. *fighting*). Style (*Well?/How are you?/What's the verdict then?*).

Chapter Nine   When Language Goes Wrong

Language and disability (Down's Syndrome, autism). Specific Language Impairment in development. Deficiency in grammar (*That boy climbing a rope to get to the top the rope*). Genetic causes of deficiency (the KE family)? Deficiency and working memory. Aphasia in adults; Broca's aphasia (*it was the where you make all the food, you make it all up today the keep it 'til the next day*); Wernicke's aphasia (*well, we were trying the best that we could while another time it was with the beds over there the same thing*). Difficulty with vocabulary (*fung* for *fork*). Difficulty with grammar (*The child was laddering*). Principles of reading in children's development: logographic (words as wholes, *cat, zoo*); alphabetic (learning correspondances between letters and sounds); orthographic (words as shapes, and letter combinations). Children's invented spellings (YUTS A LADE YET FEHEG AD HE KOT FLEPR). Problems with reading (developmental dyslexia). The e-cancellation test.

Chapter Ten   Language Change

Historical development of languages. The Romance languages. Trees and Language families. Changes in English noun inflections (*cyningas>kinggis> kings*). Survivals from Old English (*geese, woke, tight*). Changes from contact between languages: pidgins and creoles. Changes within the language from social change. The Great Vowel Shift in English. Language in decline? Stopping change. Forcing change: language and discrimination (*chairman, Gorilla Girls*).

Chapter Eleven   Universal Grammar

Universal Grammar – language built-in to the mind. Principles and parameters theory (prepositions vs. postpositions). Principles and parameters of movement (why you can't say *Is Sam is the cat that black?*). Vocabulary (why you can't say *Samson fainted Delilah*). Universal Grammar and language acquisition. The 'black box' metaphor of language acquisition. Innateness of language. Acquisition of parameter-settings. Second-language learning and Universal Grammar.

Acknowledgements

I am very grateful for the comments and help of many friends and colleagues, including Chris and Nicky Andrews, Enam Al-Wer, Philip Brew, David Britain, Pam Cook, Mike Jones, Penny Dukes, Iggy Roca, David Singleton, Andrew Spencer, Leslie Trask, Peter Trudgill, Ron Wardhaugh and Steven Widdows. The book would not have come into being without the vital help and support of the many students from different countries who provided information about their languages. Nor would the book have appeared without the background help of Sidney Bechet, Keith Jarrett and Ornette Coleman. The extract from BBC Radio 4's *Today*, 2 February 1994 on pp. 132–33 is by permission of the BBC; the extract from the newspaper article 'True Hospital waiting lists "double official figures"' by Chris Mihill on pp. 133–4 by permission of *The Guardian* © 1994.

1 Introduction

While many people express an interest in language, they know less about it than about almost any other aspects of their lives. We use language almost every moment of the waking day for every imaginable purpose. We declare war and negotiate peace through language; we propose marriage and vow undying love through language; we use it in shops for buying, in schools for teaching, in churches for praying; we listen to soap operas, sonnets and pop songs; we sue each other in court about what we have said; we think about the meaning of life and we plan what we will have for supper; we write countless books, newspapers, diaries, prescriptions, e-mails and memos. Almost every human activity involves language, directly or indirectly.

Yet most people are as unaware of their language as they are of the beating of their hearts. The only aspect that strikes their conscious attention is how certain language forms show that their speakers belong to particular social groups – this person is old because they say *wireless* not *radio*, working-class because they say *'at* not *hat*, a man because they say *walkin'* rather than *walking*, American because they pronounce the 'r' in *third*, and so on.

The study of language has probably made advances in the twentieth century as great as those of physics or psychiatry. Yet its basic concepts are still hardly known outside academic circles. The concepts of physics and psychiatry have slipped into everyday use; everyone has some idea of the nature of an electron, a black hole, or a phobia. Very few people can say what a phoneme or a morpheme is. Yet in English both 'phoneme' (a unit of sound) and 'electron' date from the 1890s, 'morpheme' (a unit of grammar) from 1896, compared to 'black hole' from 1968. Phonemes and morphemes are as basic to language as electrons and black holes are to physics, and, needless to say, just as controversial.

This book tries to introduce some of the basic ideas about language that have been developed this century, which are as important to people's lives as any concepts from physics or psychiatry. Some are recent; some are comparatively old. The overall aim is to give an idea of the fascination, complexity and importance of language. The book does not present a single linguistic theory nor advance a unified argument, partly because many areas of language study are locked in controversy. To quote Walt Whitman, 'Do I contradict myself? Very well then I contradict myself (I am large; I contain multitudes).' All the diversity of language still cannot be contained within a single framework.

Much of this book uses the English language as a departure point not only because the reader's knowledge of English can be taken for granted but also because many ideas about language started from the study of English. However, a fair proportion of the languages spoken in the world have now been described, revealing not only their idiosyncratic features but also what they have in common. Indeed, this book mentions some 80 languages ranging from Albanian to Zulu. An appendix on pages 273–6 lists the features of forty-odd languages.

Like any serious area of discussion, some abstractions and technicalities are needed from time to time. In this book they tend to cluster in Chapter 3 on the grammar of language, in Chapter 4 on the sound system, and in Chapter 11 on the Universal Grammar theory. A brief glossary of technical terms is provided on pages 277–85. The main danger is often not so much the new technical terms for describing language as the terms that have meanings that differ slightly from their use in everyday speech, such as 'grammar', or 'subject'.

Language data

Language is all around us. The book does not use examples that have been hunted high and low or chosen from the best or most amusing writers but relies on ordinary pieces of language that can be found any day in the newspaper, on the radio, in conversation, in the works of Terry Pratchett or Doug Coupland, in the lyrics of *Camelot* or Lloyd Charmer. Our environment is incredibly rich in language data, tens of thousands of words passing by us each day.

The study of language does not usually require a vast and expensive laboratory, simply the world around us. The data for settling many issues can be found by turning on the radio, by listening to people on the 73 bus, by talking to one's children or one's parents. Some language research is indeed beyond the capabilities of an ordinary individual because it involves complex electronic equipment, observations of large numbers of people over many years, or recordings of millions of words. Much of it, however, means using your ears and your eyes to establish the facts of language all around you but completely taken for granted. A speaker of any language can often contradict the expert on many topics out of their own experience. For example, reference books give the past tense of *dive* as *dived* in British English, *dove* in American English. The *Inside Language* questionnaire described below revealed, surprisingly, that 10 per cent of British people use *dove*. The sheer complexity of language, the variation in the ways that individuals use language, and the large areas of language of which little is known mean anybody can contribute something of their own to its study.

However useful the language all around us may be, this source can never reveal what people do *not* say. The standard alternative used by linguists is to invent examples of language to see if people accept them. Is *bliff* a possible word of English? Is *mrah*? The reason why *mrah* looks wrong and *bliff* looks right will be discussed in Chapter 4. The phrase *a big book* sounds acceptable, but *a book big* does not. Why not? The order would be acceptable in a Spanish phrase, for instance *un libro grande* ('a book big'). Would you say *Anthony fainted*? Would you say *Anthony fainted John*? Would you say *Is the teacher who on leave is Jones*? Again, the reasons for these preferences are explained in Chapters 3 and 11. Making up sentences is a game anyone can play: readers can easily invent their own examples to challenge particular points as the book proceeds. Investigating why certain things feel right, and others do not, leads to interesting insights into language that could not be gathered in any other way.

To check on some of the issues, a small panel of English people were asked to fill in the *Inside Language* questionnaire, the results of which will be reported from time to time. The questionnaire is on pages 5–7 following this introduction. Readers can fill it in themselves now if they want to test their own unbiased reactions before they are influenced by the content of the book. The panel consisted of 48 people mostly living in the town of Colchester in Essex, 50 miles east of London, and connected to education as students or teachers; they therefore chiefly come from Essex or East

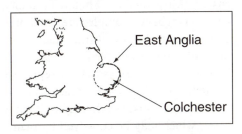

Anglia. (Note: the maps used from time to time are thumbnail sketches that give approximate areas rather than precise locations.) Their age was between 15 and 64, most being in the 18–24 band. Readers from different backgrounds, ages or regions can compare their answers with those of the panel. In addition the University of Essex in Colchester, where I work, is fortunate to have students of 106 different nationalities. Many of the examples from languages as diverse as Japanese, Swahili and Greek come from their help.

The overall message of this book is straightforward. Language is so vital in our lives that everybody needs to know at least as much about it as they do about their diet, their health, the signs of the zodiac or the policies of the current government. Without this basic knowledge about language, people are at the mercy, on the one hand, of their unconscious reactions to people and events based on language and, on the other, of those who try to establish a particular form of society through language, in particular through attitudes to language deliberately imposed upon the educational or political system. The study of language is a scientific discipline; decisions about language need as much to be based on evidence rather than opinion as are those made about the environment, the economy or nuclear physics.

Outline of the book

Chapter 2 gives a quick overview of one area, pronouns, to illustrate the different ways in which language affects our lives and societies. Chapters 3–6 look at the basic components of the language system: grammar, speech, vocabulary and writing. The remaining chapters look at various consequences of these basic aspects of language: how children acquire language (Chapter 7); how language varies from person to person and place to place (Chapter 8); what can go wrong with language (Chapter 9); and how languages change (Chapter 10). Chapter 11 develops some of the concepts of the Universal Grammar theory, a central model in current study of language.

Several resources in this book can be dipped into when the reader likes. One is the *Inside Language* questionnaire that follows. At the end of the book there are a short glossary of technical terms, a list of the main languages referred to in the text with some details about them, and a reference chart of phonetic symbols.

A book about language runs into unique problems because it has to use language to talk about language. Various conventions have to be adopted to distinguish language examples from text and to differentiate the aspects of language that are being discussed. Most of these should be unobtrusive. The convention here is usually that written language examples are cited in italics, e.g. *fish* or *April is the cruellest month*. This distinguishes them from quotations on the subject of language, which are given in single quotation marks, as in the quotation from Edmund Spenser on p. 20. Sometimes it is necessary to represent the sounds of spoken language examples through slanted or square brackets /fɪʃ/ or [fɪʃ], as explained in Chapter 4. Finally, sometimes an abstract element of meaning has to be referred to, i.e. the idea of 'fishiness', which may be conveyed by many different words in different languages. This is indicated by single quotes, 'fish', or is given as a translation in brackets, e.g. *poisson* ('fish'). However, because of the problems intrinsic to using language as a means of describing language, these conventions change slightly in different sections of this book.

Inside Language Questionnaire

This is an adapted form of the questionnaire that was used with the *Inside Language* panel. A reader who wants to check their own responses should answer it *before* reading the parts of the book that deal with a particular topic. Or it can be used to test other people to see how their responses compare with those mentioned in the book.

Personal information

In which part of the world and area did you acquire English as a child or as a second
   language? ....

Which age-group are you?   1–17 18–24 25–49 50–64 65+
Which sex are you?   M   F

1. *What's the first word that comes into your mind when you think of:*
         — bird   ....
         — apple   ....
         — tea   ....

2. *Choose one of the alternatives in each sentence:*
   The patient must keep to the time of his/her/his or her/their appointment.
   The child put on his/her/its hat.
   Between you and I/me, he's an idiot.
   John and I/me didn't quarrel, did we?

3. *Which English words fit the following definitions? If you can't remember the exact
   word, give the nearest one that comes to mind:*
   a navigational instrument used in measuring angular distances, especially
      the altitude of sun, moon, and stars at sea

   ....
   semi-circular or many-sided recess, with an arched or domed roof

   ....
   an underground conduit for drainage, a common sewer

   ....
   a fragrant drug, that melts almost like wax, commonly of a greyish or ash
      colour, used both as a perfume and as a cordial

   ....
   a small boat with oars that is used especially in China

   ....

4. *Suppose that in some language you do not know that one of the objects below is called a 'pling' and the other a 'plung'.*

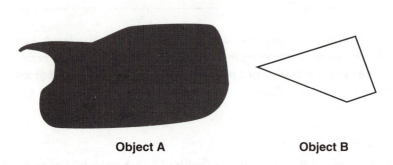

Object A   **Object B**

Which of these objects is called a plung? A or B?

5. *What is the sex of the speakers of each of these sentences?*
Absolutely gorgeous!!!   M   F
Where did you get your accent from? It's so soothing.   M   F
Jane's walkin' to work.   M   F
It's nice, isn't it?   M   F
One question I'd like to ask you know I'm a larger type you know and
   I've got one heck of a job to buy clothes from anywhere . . .   M   F

6. *Which class – Middle Class (MC)/Working Class (WC) – and age group are the speakers of these likely to be?*

A tranny.	MC	WC	1–17	18–24	25–49	50–64	65+
A mush.	MC	WC	1–17	18–24	25–49	50–64	65+
A nice chap.	MC	WC	1–17	18–24	25–49	50–64	65+
A wireless.	MC	WC	1–17	18–24	25–49	50–64	65+
It is I.	MC	WC	1–17	18–24	25–49	50–64	65+
A good bloke.	MC	WC	1–17	18–24	25–49	50–64	65+
A pleasant guy.	MC	WC	1–17	18–24	25–49	50–64	65+
A radio.	MC	WC	1–17	18–24	25–49	50–64	65+
He lost his 'at.	MC	WC	1–17	18–24	25–49	50–64	65+

7. *Tick which of these words you have heard in language spoken by adults to children:*

pussy	mummy	sweetie	gee gee	puff-puff
bow-wow	bunny	wops (wasp)	peepee	tummy

Any others?

....

8. *Your own speech*

   Which word would you use to address your mother? (Mother, Mum, Mummy, etc.)

   ....

   Which word would you use to address your grandmother? (Granny, Granma, Gran, etc.)   ....

   What do you call the children's game in which one child chases all the others?

   ....

   Do you pronounce the 'r' at the end of words such as door *as an 'r' or not?*
   Yes   No

   Do you say Russia is big *with an 'r' after 'Russia'?*   Yes   No

   Do you pronounce better *with a 'glottal stop' (similar to a cough) rather than with a 't'?*   Yes   No

   Do you pronounce beautiful *with a 'w'-like sound at the end rather than an 'l'?*
   Yes   No

   Is the past tense of dive: dived, dove, *or* doved? ....

   Choose one of the alternatives in each sentence:
   Lecturer to student: A very good essay, Jones/Mr Jones/Mike.
   Student to lecturer: Thank you, Smith/Mr Smith/Bill.

9. *Are these sentences possible in English?*

Peter is the student who is absent.	Yes	No
Who did John ask what fixed?	Yes	No
Who did Mary think John saw?	Yes	No
Is the teacher who on leave is Jones?	Yes	No

10. *In each sentence, ring round which is doing the chasing, the cat(s) or the dog(s):*

The cat chases the dog.	the cat(s)	the dog(s)
The dogs are eager to chase.	the cat(s)	the dog(s)
The cats chase the dog.	the cat(s)	the dog(s)
The cats the dogs chase.	the cat(s)	the dog(s)
The dogs are easy to chase.	the cat(s)	the dog(s)
Chase the cats the dogs.	the cat(s)	the dog(s)
The cat the dogs chase.	the cat(s)	the dog(s)
The cats the dogs chase.	the cat(s)	the dog(s)

11. *English has 26 letters in writing, but how many sounds are there in the spoken language?*   ....

    In English the usual order of the sentence is Subject Verb Object as in 'Mary likes John'. Why do you think this is so? ....

    Is there anything wrong in saying To boldly go where no man has gone before?

    ....

2 Pronouns and the Language System

A cat is stalking some blackbirds in the garden. A girl calls out to her brother *The cat is chasing the birds*. Mundane and unremarkable as this use of language may be, something very complex lies between the girl seeing the cat and making the remark, and between her brother hearing it and understanding it. This chapter tries to give some awareness of the language system which enables speakers to carry out this activity, first sketching its outline and then tackling personal pronouns to explore some of its ramifications.

I The language system

To start with, the girl needs a reason for speaking: perhaps she wants to warn her brother to protect the birds, or is commenting on the cat's wicked ways. But knowing what she wants to say is not enough to let her say it, if she does not know the right words and how to construct the sentence. Taking vocabulary first, words need to be found for what she wants to say. As a speaker of English, the girl calls one creature a *bird*, another a *cat*; the cat's movement is called *chase*. The appropriate nouns and verb are automatically sorted out from the thousands of English words stored in her mind, without any conscious attention. A speaker of French would just as easily find the words *chat* ('cat'), *oiseau* ('bird') and *poursuivre* ('chase'); an Irish speaker *ritheann* ('chase'), *cat* ('cat') and *éan* ('bird').

A speaker of any language has a large store of vocabulary at their beck and call, usually available without any effort. Everyone possesses a mental dictionary that works with great speed. How long does it take to decide if the word *glash* is English? How long would it take to look up in a dictionary or even a spelling checker? The speed with which speakers can tap their mental stock of words is so fast that they are seldom aware of the process at all; ordinary speech has a speed of 150 words a minute: that is to say, a speaker has to find a word about two and a half times a second. Searching through a printed dictionary not only takes vastly longer but also requires conscious effort. Much of the language system consists of words and their meanings, kept in a vast internal dictionary with virtually instantaneous access, to be described in Chapter 5.

The girl's words have also to be put together in a way that makes sense and fits what she wants to say. Speakers of English know that, to express the situation that she has in mind, the subject *cat* needs to come first in the sentence, followed by the verb *chase*, followed by the object *bird*, i.e. *cat chase bird*, not the reverse order, *bird chase cat*, as this order of elements would completely change who was chasing whom. The English speaker finds it natural that things should be this way – that the subject comes first, the verb second, the object last. The *Inside Language* panel were asked why the usual order in English is subject – verb – object (Q11). One panel member answered, 'Because it is a logical progression', another, 'It is a very logical format', a third, 'It's easy to understand'.

A speaker of Japanese, however, finds it just as natural that the subject comes first in the sentence, the object second, and the verb last: *Neko ga tori wo oitsuiteiru*, i.e *neko* ('cat'), *tori* ('bird'), *oitsuiteiru* ('chase'). An Irish speaker, on the other hand, takes it for granted that the verb comes first, the subject second and the object last, *Ritheann an cat i ndiaidh an éan* – *ritheann* ('chase'), *cat* ('cat'), *éan* ('bird'). Indeed, all the possible permutations of subject, object, and verb can be found somewhere in the languages of the world, as will be seen in the next chapter.

The basic sentence still has to be fleshed out with fuller meanings. One particular cat is involved, so the article *the* is needed in English to make the phrase *the cat*; there are several birds involved, so *-s* has to be added to *bird* to get *birds*; the event is happening right now, so *is* has to be put before *chase* and the ending *-ing* has to be added to *chase* to get *is chasing*. All of these additions strictly obey the word order of English. There is no choice whatsoever about putting *the* before *cat* to get *the cat* rather than *cat the*, or adding *-s* to the end of *bird* to get *birds* rather than to the beginning to get *sbird*. The speaker is rarely conscious of putting words in a particular order or of choosing word-endings; it is simply the way things *are* in English. But this order is not necessarily true for other languages. The Japanese sentence *Neko ga tori wo oitsuiteiru* needed the particles *ga* and *wo* added to fill out the meaning of the sentence by showing the subject and object of the sentence, as automatic to Japanese as the word-ending *-s* is to English but a very different way of handling the situation.

The girl also has to know the sounds of English to be able to produce the sequence of sounds in *The cat's chasing the birds*. Producing the 'th' sound in *the* involves breathing out, making the vocal cords in the throat vibrate, and putting the tip of the tongue in contact with the back of the upper teeth, as is seen in more detail in Chapter 4. Equally complicated procedures are needed for all the other sounds in the sentence. William Levelt claims that speaking 'is probably man's most complex motor skill', involving 'the coordination of approximately 100 muscles'. The sounds of Japanese, Irish or any other language involve operations as complex in their own ways as those for producing English. All speakers know the sounds of their own language in the sense that they can produce them unthinkingly. Some of these sounds may be peculiar to their own language; some may have universal characteristics common to all languages.

This knowledge of the sounds of language is far from conscious. Everyone is aware that there are 26 letters in the English writing system, plus a few special symbols like & and %, but few people can state how many distinct *sounds* there are in spoken English. Guesses from the *Inside Language* panel ranged from 30 to hundreds to 'loads' and 'too many to count' (Q11). The correct answer, of around 44 for British speakers (the precise number depending on the accent), is only known by those who have studied language academically. Even though some of the panel were linguistics undergraduates, only 17 per cent had an answer in the 40s. As seen in the next chapter, the vagueness of the term 'sound' in the question means the answers may not be accurate. Nevertheless the results demonstrate that most people are unaware of basic aspects of the spoken language. The meanings a speaker wants to convey through language cannot be communicated to another person without being transformed into sequences of sounds or letters.

So, putting a sentence together requires speakers not only to put the words in the right order, *cat chase bird*, and in the right combination, *is chasing*, but also to express additional meanings through word-endings and changes to their form – *birds*, *chasing*, and so on. All of this intricate knowledge is instantly available in their minds. How long does it take to decide whether the following sentence is correct English? *Cat the is chasing the birds*. Again, compare this process with how long it takes to check in an English grammar book whether the article *the* follows a noun like *cat* rather than precedes it. The time and effort in the conscious search is quite out of proportion to that required for the instant, unthinking response. The mind has a powerful system for ordering and combining words in particular ways. Apart from the initial impetus to speak, little of this process is under conscious control.

Many animals such as dogs use a range of noises to express feelings such as fear, hunger or aggression. Bees dance in a particular way to show where they have found honey. Dogs and bees indeed have communication systems, but, at least to our current knowledge, they have no system like human language. From the first moment that children start to use more than one word at a time, they put words in a definite order. English children say *little girl*, not *girl little*, *me buy birdie* not *buy birdie me*; their sentences have a consistent word order, different as their speech may be from that of adults in many other respects. Human beings have a built-in propensity to create a language system with particular characteristics, as will be seen here time and again.

II The pronoun system

Later chapters split the language system up into separate parts. This chapter treats language more broadly by taking the topic of personal pronouns, and seeing the many areas in which they are involved – how people conceive of the speech situation, how they assert power over others through class or gender, whether it is correct to say *between you and I*, and how pronouns relate to nouns. The language system is a complex interaction of many parts, many of which are revealed in the use of such everyday words as *he* and *you*.

Pronouns like *I* and *they* differ from nouns like *Miles Davis* or *trumpet* because they can refer to something different every time they are used. In the sentence *Miles Davis played the trumpet*, the noun *Miles Davis* refers to a particular person, *trumpet* to a particular type of instrument. These words have the same meaning in any other sentence, *Miles Davis's best album is 'Kind of Blue'*, *The trumpet is a lead instrument* and so on. In the sentence *He supports conservation*, however, the pronoun *he* might refer to the Prince of Wales, to Bill Gates, or to Mickey Mouse: in short, *he* may refer to any male being whether real or imaginary. In other sentences *he* might refer to totally different people, say in the Dylan Thomas line *He put on his clothes and stepped out and he died*, the proverb *He who hesitates is lost*, or any of the millions of sentences produced in London today. The pronoun *he* varies in the person it refers to from one sentence to another, limited only by masculine gender. Its reference is fixed to a given individual only when the full speech situation is known. Pronouns are like the *x* in algebra: what they stand for depends on the context in which they occur.

1 Pronouns: speech role and number

This section starts with an analysis of pronouns in terms of person and number, which may already be familiar from school grammar lessons. Speech is like a script for a play with a shifting cast of three or more people, not all of whom are necessarily present at the same time. Whenever someone speaks, it takes place at a particular moment of time in a particular place – the 'speech situation'. Pronouns spell out the particular roles that people take in this situation, called 'persons'. The first person pronoun *I* identifies the person who is speaking:

I like bananas; the second person *you* identifies the person who is being addressed: *You like bananas*; and the third person such as *she* identifies people or things that are not involved as listener or speaker in the actual act of speaking *She/he/it/they like(s) bananas*. Constructing any sentence of English means taking these three basic roles into account – who is speaking, who is addressed, and anyone else who is not involved in the actual speaking but needs to be mentioned. Any pronoun has to take one of these three persons.

English pronouns also specify how many people are involved in each role, the concept called 'number', whether 'one', as in the singular *I*, *he*, *she*, and *it*: *She likes bananas*, or 'more than one', as in the plural *we* and *they*: *They like bananas*. The second person in English has the same pronoun *you* for both singular and plural, even if it goes with a plural verb form such as *are*. It is impossible to tell from *You like bananas* whether one or more than one person is being spoken to. The number contrast between singular and plural affects not only pronouns but also nouns (*book/books*) and verbs (*like/likes*).

So English has the familiar six-way pronoun system made up of three persons (first, second, third) and two numbers (singular, plural). English uses person to mark out the participants in the conversation from one other, and number to show whether one or more people are involved. The speaker has to choose the relevant pronoun from the six cells in the grid. To someone brought up in English, these obvious facts about pronouns hardly seem worth mentioning. They are familar from school lessons about German or Latin, if not English: everyone knows that there are six alternatives.

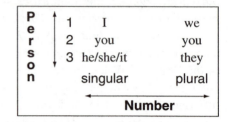

P			
e	1	I	we
r	2	you	you
s	3	he/she/it	they
o			
n		singular	plural

Number

As is so often the case with 'facts' that are taken for granted about language, the ideas of person and number are not, however, common sense but come out of a schoolteaching tradition going back to the Latin grammars of 100 BC. Because of their origin in classical languages, three persons and two numbers fail to do full justice to English, nor do they necessarily fit languages that are unrelated to Latin, say Chinese. For instance, while all languages have pronouns, they vary in how *many* persons and numbers they have. Navaho, an indigenous American language, signals a *fourth* person: when a third person pronoun has already been mentioned in a conversation, a fourth person is used to refer to anybody else.

1st
2nd
3rd
4th
Person
in Navaho

Furthermore, while number in English pronouns is a two-way choice between singular and plural, many languages interpose a *third* distinction for 'two people' – the 'dual' number. The contrast is between one person, two people, and more than two people. Old English, the period of English spoken before 1100 AD, had such a three-way system; the first person was the singular *ic* (I), the dual *wit*, and the plural *we*, with similar choices for the other persons in the pronoun system.

singular	dual	plural

Number in Old English

Other languages still have a three-way choice of number. For example Tok Pisin, spoken in Papua New Guinea and partly derived from English, has first person singular *mi*, dual *mitupela* and plural *yupela*. Tongan has three first person forms – singular *kita*, dual *kitaua* and plural *kitautolu*. Languages exist with even more number contrasts. Fijian has pronouns for singular, dual, trial (three)

singular	dual	trial	plural

Number in Fijian

and plural as well as four persons. The two-way choice between singular 'one' and plural 'more than one' is by no means the only possibility for languages.

Nor does the English six-way system exhaust all the possibilities in the first person plural. The English plural *we* may either include or exclude the person addressed. Suppose Judy says to Richard *We're going out tonight*. This sentence might mean that Judy is announcing to Richard that she and Anne are going out or it may be that Judy is reminding Richard that she and Richard are going out together as a couple; one meaning excludes the listener from *we*, the other includes them. This distinction is signalled in Melanesian Pidgin English by two different pronouns: *yumi* (you + me) and *mipela* (me + someone else). Palaung, a language spoken in Burma, has both a dual/plural distinction and a distinction between inclusive and exclusive pronouns for 'we': /yar/ (two people, not including the hearer), /ar/ (two people, including the hearer), /yɛ/ (more than two, not including the hearer) and /ɛ/ (more than two people, including the hearer).

2 *Pronouns and status*

So, once you know what persons and numbers are used in a language, you should be able to choose the right pronoun to fit a particular speech situation. However, pronouns illustrate something that is true of many aspects of language: once a distinction has been established for one reason, it can be exploited for another. The apparently straightforward concept of singular and plural number can be overlaid with other meanings. Standard Modern English makes no difference between singular and plural *you*, apart from a few marginal survivals of *thou* and *ye*, even if some dialects of Irish English distinguish singular *you* and plural *youse*.

Other languages, however, regularly make a distinction between singular and plural second person that does not depend on the number of people involved. In French, individuals who are close to the speaker socially are addressed with the singular second person *tu*: *Tu joues bien* ('you play well'); individuals who are more distant from the speaker are addressed with the plural form *vous*: *Vous jouez bien* ('you play well'). The difference between *tu* and *vous*, ostensibly one between singular and plural number, is nothing of the kind: a single individual can be referred to by a plural pronoun. The chief modern use of singular *tu* is to act as a sign of closeness between friends, fellow-students, colleagues, and particularly members of the family. Switching from addressing someone as *vous* to calling them *tu* shows a change in the relationship of the speaker and listener or in the circumstances of speaking. Mountain climbers are said to change from *vous* to *tu* above a certain altitude when the common danger brings them closer together. In addition, *tu* has demonstrated political solidarity between speaker and listener since at least the days when the French Revolution insisted that all citizens addressed each other as *tu*. At a French-speaking academic conference in the 1980s, the only form used in the talks and public discussions was *tu*, still a sign of social solidarity.

A second use of *tu* is for talking down to another person, say a child or an animal; *tu* is a sign that the speaker has a higher social status than the person addressed.

Teachers, for example, assert their authority by calling their pupils *tu*. The sign of this power relation is that the use of *tu* is not reciprocated; that is to say, one speaker says *tu*, the other *vous*. If the person addressed with *tu* is the speaker's equal, he or she may respond with the singular, *tu*; if inferior, the plural, *vous*, is used. A survey in French-speaking Canada showed that children addressed grandparents, priests and employers with *vous*, but these adults answered them with *tu*. So it is not just what you call other people that defines the relationship but what they call *you*. The social status function of *tu* has diminished in recent years, being partly undermined by the use of *tu* to show solidarity.

In French, therefore, reciprocated *tu* may show either social closeness or solidarity with other people. This use of the second person number distinction for status and solidarity is common in different languages, and is known as the T/V system, after the Latin *tu* (T) and *vos* (V). Other languages in Europe as well as French use singular T to show social closeness/solidarity and plural V to show social distance/status. The Spanish T form is *tu*, the V form *Usted*; the German T form is *du*, the V form *Sie*; the Russian T form is *ty*, the V form *vy*; and so on. In some languages, such as Spanish, the V form is the same as a singular third person pronoun, *Usted*; in others, such as German, it is the same as a third person plural, *Sie*. In all of these languages T and V pronouns are used to fit the social relationships between speaker and listener, with slightly different overtones in each language. In the German version of the good guy/bad guy police interrogation technique, the good guy allegedly uses the V form *Sie* as a sign of politeness, the bad guy uses the T form *du* to assert power over the suspect. Often the written form of the V pronoun has a capital letter, as in German T *du* versus V *Sie* and Italian T *tu* versus V *Lei*. Speakers of these languages find it puzzling that English capitalizes the first person singular *I* rather than the second person *you*.

There has been much speculation about how the plural came to suggest distance and high status, the singular familiarity and solidarity. One idea is that it is an extension of the royal *we*; the claim of kings to be plural established the plural as a sign of power and status, and this usage percolated down to other levels of society. Another is that during the fourth century AD when there were two Roman emperors at the same time, one in Rome and one in Constantinople, it was diplomatic to address the emperor in the plural, and so power came to be associated with the plural form.

These reasons cannot, however, explain why this T/V system occurs in languages unconnected to Latin. For the use of the plural for status also occurs in Turkish, Basque and Bengali. Nor is it necessarily status and solidarity alone that are involved in the choice between T and V. In Russian, choosing the appropriate T *ty* or V *vy* form depends *inter alia* on the topic of conversation, the age, generation and sex of the speaker, and the precise family relationship.

Some languages use them to reflect a complex range of social roles. In Japanese, the choice between different pronoun forms is dictated by complex social relationships between speaker and listener. The first person singular 'I' can be either *watakushi*, *watashi*, *boku*, *ore* or *atashi*, according to the relative status and sex of the speaker and listener. *Watakushi* is the most formal form, used, say, to a social superior. The pronoun *watashi* is more neutral. Next come *boku*, which is the norm for men under 21, and *ore*, used only to close friends. In 1957 the Japanese Ministry of Education approved *boku* for men students but recommended they switched to *watashi* when they graduated. The choice of Japanese pronoun marks off the speaker and listener on a social scale. One first person form, *chin*, used to be used only by the Emperor. A further complication is the difference between the sexes. Men use the first person pronouns *watakushi*, *boku* or *ore*; either sex uses *watashi*; but only women use *atashi*, which, from a man, would be a sign of gayness. There are therefore difficulties for male English students who are taught Japanese by a woman and never hear the male status pronouns used naturally.

Japanese is not the only language to signal sex and status through choice of the first person pronoun. In Thai the correct first person singular for addressing a stranger is *phǒm* from a man (see Chapter 4 for an explanation of the tone marks above the letters), *dǐchǎn* from a woman; in informal conversation with family and friends, it is *chǎn* but *kān* if all the speakers are the same sex; a child speaking to an adult uses *nǔu*. Other first person forms are needed for addressing the king, *kramòm* coming from a man, *kramòmchǎn* from a woman. Thai speakers in fact have around 25 different first person pronouns to choose from in everyday circumstances.

Languages, then, use pronouns to reflect diverse social relationships between the participants. Until Japanese speakers know the social relationship between them and the other participants, they do not know which pronouns to use to refer to themselves or to the others. The concept of social relationship is also important in European languages like Polish. Anna Wierzbicka, a Polish linguist living in Australia, tells of two expatriate Poles who had only talked English to each other for many years suddenly having to talk in Polish and not knowing which pronouns to use because they had never before had to think of each other in terms of the Polish pronoun system. To an English speaker, the crucial aspects of the speech situation are person and number. Other languages treat various social roles as being just as important.

3 'Missing' pronouns

The use of English as a starting-point conceals another important fact about pronouns in other languages: they do not necessarily have to be present at all. Many languages in effect leave the subject pronoun out of the sentence and let the listener work out the situational roles from the rest of the sentence or from the context. For example, an Italian can say *Sono di Torino* ('am from Turin') and the listener knows from the verb *sono* that the speaker is talking in the first person singular even though no pronoun is present. Or the speaker could say *Vende* ('sells') with no third person pronoun, but the ending of the verb *-e* reveals that the third person singular is intended. Languages like Italian in which the sentence does not require a subject are technically called 'pro-drop' languages.

To an extent, the different endings of the Italian verb for person and number provide the clues to the missing subject. Since English has only a few verb-endings, there is no way of telling from the verb *speak* whether the absent subject is *I*, *you*, *we* or *they*. English is therefore an example of a 'non-pro-drop' language in which subjects are compulsory in the sentence. This puts English in a minority of around 7 per cent of the world's languages, along with German and French.

The pronoun system described above left out a crucial dimension for languages – whether the subject pronoun is actually present in the sentence or not. The pronoun does not necessarily *have* to be left out in pro-drop languages; there is usually a choice whether to put it in or leave it out. However, this choice opens up another potential way of conveying meaning through the pronoun system. If it is usual to have no subject in a pro-drop language, putting it in adds an extra meaning to the sentence, which is absent from non-pro-drop languages.

So, in Spanish, another pro-drop language, the first person *yo*, for instance, is sometimes used to underline the person's responsibility as in *Yo espero* ('I am waiting') compared with *Espero*. In Greek, omission of the second person in greetings shows that the speaker is closer to the listener than leaving it in; *Ya!* ('hello') shows a friendlier relationship than including either the T *su* as in *Ya su!* or the V *sa* as in *Ya sa!* In pro-drop languages the T/V system in a sense includes a third possibility – absence of pronoun: it is a three-way T/V/Ø system.

4 Pronouns and gender

A widespread contrast in human languages is called 'gender'. Some German nouns, for example, are masculine – *der Tisch* ('table') goes with the masculine pronoun *er* ('he'). Other nouns are feminine – *die Tür* ('door') goes with the feminine pronoun *sie* ('she'). Others are neuter – *das Haus* ('house') goes with the neuter pronoun *es* ('it'). The chief manifestation of gender in many languages is how pronouns are allocated to nouns, grouped into masculine, feminine or neuter.

Some languages do not have pronouns with gender, for example Persian, Turkish and Hungarian. In English, gender only affects some pronouns, affecting the third person singular *he*, *she* and *it*, but not *I*, *you*, *we* or *they*. The choice between *he*, *she*, and *it* depends on sex; a woman is *she*, a man is *he*, something without sex is *it*. English is therefore said to have 'biological' or 'natural' gender, as the noun groups of masculine, feminine and neuter correspond to the real-world categories male, female and non-sexed. The exceptions beloved by English grammar books are personifications of things as people. Often these are feminine, as in the case of large moving machines such as *ships, planes, cars*. Less commonly they are masculine, as in rivers: *That old man river, he keeps on rolling along*. Even these few metaphorical uses of gender seem to be declining: up to the 1930s the *Times* newspaper invariably referred to countries as *she*, as in *Canada and her great neighbour*, but by the 1980s the use of *she* had waned to less than 10 per cent.

Other languages also have natural gender, such as Tamil. Many languages taught in English schools, however, use a system called 'arbitrary' gender, meaning that the gender of nouns is linked arbitrarily to pronouns without reference to their actual sex. In German, for instance, *das Mädchen* ('girl') is neuter but *der Tisch* ('table') is masculine. In French *la table* ('table') is feminine, *le toit* ('roof') is masculine, and there is no neuter.

It is hard to find a rationale for the gender of nouns in arbitrary gender languages. The way that nouns are grouped into genders is often based on the sounds with which the word ends rather than on their meaning. In French, 94 per cent of nouns ending in *-age* /ʒ/ such as *voyage* ('journey') are masculine, and 90 per cent of endings in /z/ such as *heureuse* ('happy') are feminine. In Italian nouns ending in *-o* are usually masculine, as in *vino* ('wine'), and nouns ending in *-a* usually feminine, e.g. *casa* ('house'). Such groupings have nothing to do with biological sex.

The celebrated issue in English does not concern gender so much as sex. A natural gender language needs a way of deciding which pronouns should go with nouns that refer to members of *both* sexes. How should an everyday notice in a doctor's surgery be worded, for example? *The patient must keep to the time of his? her? his or her? their? appointment.* A practical issue which affects every page of this book is which pronoun to use to refer to a single speaker of indeterminate sex, as in *A speaker of English knows that he/she/he or she/they ought to feel guilty about splitting infinitives. He* suggests that the writer is ignoring women. *She* may imply that the writer is falling over backwards to be politically correct or is treating women as a subordinate group; for instance, books for teachers by male writers that call all teachers or children *she* can have a patronising feel. One linguistics book not only calls all speakers *he*, all hearers *she*, but also, when there are two or more speakers in the conversation, has the first one male, the second female, surely as discriminatory as the uses it is trying to avoid. The combination *he or she* is cumbersome and soon becomes irritating. *It* seems ruled out as denying people's humanity, even if Wordsworth could write *A simple Child . . . What should it know of death?*

The *Inside Language* panel were asked whether people would use *his/her/his or her/their* in the sentence *The patient must keep to the time of ___ appointment* (Q2). The most popular answer was the joint *his or her* with 46 per cent; *their* trailed behind with 29 per cent; *his* had 10 per cent, and *her* only 4 per cent. People are then genuinely divided in their choice of pronoun, even if they try to avoid pronouns that commit them to a single sex. The questionnaire also asked them to insert a pronoun into the sentence *The child put on ___ hat.* The favourite answer was *its* with 48 per cent, followed by *his* with 38 per cent, while *her* had 2 per cent. Apparently people feel happier about using *it* to refer to a child than might have been expected.

The soft option is to put the noun in the plural, *Patients must keep to the time of their appointments*, since this enables the non-gender form *they* to be used. This usage is clearly impossible when a single individual is being talked about. My own preference wherever possible is to use my natural spoken form *they* with the singular noun and let the fact that *they* is plural go by the board, as in the third paragraph of this chapter, *A speaker of any language has a large store of vocabulary at their beck and call.* This was anathema to the Fowlers in *The King's English*: it 'is the popular solution; it sets the literary man's teeth on edge'.

The use of *they* for the singular mixed gender was nevertheless the most common form in English till the eighteenth century, and was in fact used by Shakespeare in *Much Ado*: *God send everyone their heart's desire!* It has been supported by a minority ever since, going from the grammarian Henry Sweet in 1891 to the American writers Casey Miller and Kate Swift in 1977. The concept of number is not taken literally in many languages but is overridden by considerations of social role, as in the T/V contrast seen above. If there is a conflict between number and gender in English pronouns, the easiest solution is to override number. Nevertheless *they* may continue to be obtrusive in some styles of written English, and the Fowlers' advice 'to give the same meaning in some entirely different way' may still be sound.

An alternative is to propose a new third person singular pronoun that can be coined for humans but has no gender. The proposals started with *ne* in 1850 and went through *thon* (1884), *hizer* (1891), *heesh* (1940), *tey* (1972), *hann* (1984) and many others. The most natural-seeming coinage is perhaps *per*, first used by the psychologist Donald McKay in 1972 and used most memorably in Marge Piercy's science fiction novel *Woman on the Edge of Time*, as in *We lower per to the ground*, *It's per way*, and *It's time for per to die.*

How people use language must relate to the way that their minds work in some respects, as will be discussed in Chapter 11. So, if mixed-sex groups such as doctors are always treated as masculine, this usage may indeed marginalize women by permanently associating these roles with men in people's minds. However, blaming language for sexism is to some extent blaming the messenger for the message; it is primarily the thinking that is wrong.

Trying to change language consciously by, say, adopting a new gender system has often had mixed results on language. The Archbishop of Canterbury in a 1996 radio interview can still blithely say *The school only has a child for a fifth of his time*. The split infinitive *to commonly believe* was regarded as un-English by Henry Alford in 1864: 'surely this is a practice entirely unknown to English speakers and writers.' Most commentators ever since have recommended that it should be avoided wherever possible. Yet split infinitives are still as healthy as ever. The *Inside Language* questionnaire panel were asked if there was anything wrong in saying *To boldly go where no man has gone before* (Q11), the notorious motto from *Star Trek*. Twenty-five per cent found nothing at all wrong with it; 46 per cent commented on the split infinitive, though 19 per cent said it didn't matter; 6 per cent commented on the sexism of *man* in this context! The version of the motto in the third generation of *Star Trek* is now *To boldly go where no one has gone before.*

Yet the attempts to reform English pronouns seem to have had surprisingly potent effects. One study of written American English found that the frequency of *he* and *man* fell by about 75 per cent between 1971 and 1979. Many would nevertheless dispute cause and effect: altering people's language may not so much change their ways of thinking as make them sound as if they have changed. The proof will be whether the apparent decline of *he* indeed leads to a drop in sexism apart from language usage. Other parts of the pronoun system that have been described here may have similar effects on people's attitudes in other languages. It would be fascinating to test how speakers' ideas of number are affected in T/V languages, how the concept of self is affected in languages with multiple first person pronouns like Japanese and Thai, and how the role of men in France is affected by the fact that there is a single pronoun for both *he* and *it*!

Gender is only one of the possible ways of dividing up nouns into classes, familiar to speakers of English because of its use with English pronouns and its presence in neighbouring languages such as French, German and Spanish. In Bahasa Melayu, the chief language of Malaysia, there are no gender or number differences. *Orang* means not only 'man/men' but also 'woman/women' (the English word *orang-utan* therefore in Bahasa Melayu meant 'person of the forest'). However, the classical language has a complex system of around 40 'classifiers' that go with particular nouns. A long, stick-like object needs the classifier *batang* as in *sebatang rokok* ('a cigarette'); if it is ring-shaped, it needs *bentuk* as in *sebentuk cincin* ('a ring'); if it is broad, it needs *bidang,* as in *sebidang tanah* ('a stretch of land'); if it is a type of house, it needs *tangga,* as in *setangga rumah Melayu* ('a Malaysian house', lit. 'a house Malaysian'). Systems of classifiers are widespread in languages. An English parallel is the phrases used to count 'uncountable' nouns – *two loaves of bread,* not *two breads,* and *three sheets of paper,* not *three papers.*

5 Case forms of pronouns

The English first person singular pronoun does not just have the form *I*, but can also be *me, my, mine, myself,* etc.; the third person singular is *he, him, his, himself,* etc. These different forms signal the role that the pronoun plays in the sentence. *I* has the role of the subject of the sentence, as in *I like Jane*; *me* has the role of the object in *Jane likes me*. This difference is known as 'case'– signalling roles in the sentence through changes in the form of words, again a traditional analysis going back to classical languages.

In English the case system applies only to pronouns. It distinguishes subject pronouns *I, she, they* and so on from object pronouns *me, her, them* and the like, and from possessive pronouns *my, her, their* and so on. Other languages have case systems for nouns as well as pronouns and have a greater range of cases. Latin, for example, has six cases, affecting nouns and pronouns (though, as a pro-drop language, it may also of course leave pronouns out). Let us take the noun *amor* ('love'). Using the traditional terms, Latin has nominative (subject) case *amor*, accusative (object) case *amorem*, and genitive (possessive) case *amoris*. In addition to these three cases that overlap with English, Latin expresses the roles of the person who receives something, the dative case (indirect object) *amori*, and the role of the person something is done by, the ablative case, *amore*. Some Latin nouns have a further case for addressing people, the vocative: *Kennedy's Latin Primer* informs one quaintly that *anne* means 'o year'.

nominative
vocative
accusative
genitive
dative
ablative

Case in Latin

Old English had an ampler case system than modern English, involving both pronouns and nouns, like Latin. The third person singular masculine, for example, had four cases, *he* (subject), *hine* (object), *his* (possessive) and *him* (dative), with parallel forms for the neuter (*hit, hit, his, him*), and for the feminine (*heo, hi, hire, hire*). Modern Finnish has an even more complex system of 15 cases.

Simple as the modern English case system may be, it nevertheless provides problems for its users. In the early stages of language acquisition, children are not apparently aware of the difference between first and second person subject pronouns: *John like honey* means 'I like honey'; *Mummy like teddy* means 'You like teddy'. Nor do they use the adult case system for pronouns, preferring the object forms for the subject role, *Me got bean* or *Him gone*. Children have to learn that English pronouns have three persons and that they have different forms for the object and subject cases.

In English the verb *to be* is followed by the object case, like other verbs. The pronoun *him* in *It is him* has the same form as in *I saw him*. Latin, however, puts the noun that follows the verb *to be* in the subject case. Traditional grammar books have taken this to be a model that English should follow. William Cobbett in 1819, for instance, said *It was me* ought to be *It is I*. It is, however, dangerous to apply the system of one language selectively to another language. Latin is a pro-drop language which leaves the subject out altogether. Those who support *It is I* on the model of Latin should therefore also recommend that English speakers say *Is raining* rather than *It is raining* or answer *Do* rather than *I do* in the marriage ceremony. There is no logical reason why some features of Latin should take precedence over the English forms, others not; languages are independent of each other, however much they have in common beneath the surface. Already in 1580, Edmund Spenser was asking, 'Why a gods name may not we, as else the Greeks, have the kingdome of our owne Language?'

The pressure from the Latin-based school tradition has succeeded, if not in changing people's behaviour – who says *It is I* naturally? – at least in making them acutely self-conscious. Lois Lane remarks to Superman Junior in an episode of a TV series, *There is you; there is I; there is no we*. In the film *Camelot* Lancelot du Lac proclaims *C'est moi, 'Tis I*, showing that whatever inhibitions scriptwriters have about *'Tis me* in English, they have no such qualms about French *C'est moi* ('It's me'). The *Inside Language* panel were asked to give the class and age of people who would say *It is I* (Q6). Seventy-nine per cent thought they would be over 50 years old, 81 per cent that they would be middle-class. Lois and Lancelot are apparently trying hard to sound like middle-aged members of the middle class.

The problem of choosing the appropriate case form has also affected pronouns linked by *and*, for instance *My dog and I went for a walk* versus *My dog and me went for a walk.* My own natural spoken form is *my dog and me*, but I could never deliberately use it in writing. The *Inside Language* panel were asked whether *I* or *me* was best in *John and __ didn't quarrel, did we?* (Q2). Ninety-two per cent said *I*, 6 per cent *me*, suggesting that subject *me* is still a minority quirk among speakers of English.

The choice of case form is also an issue after prepositions such as *to, for* or *between*. Usually in English prepositions are followed by the object case: *He looked at me*, rather than *He looked at I*. The difficulty arises when pronouns are linked together with *and*, particularly when *between* is involved – *between you and I* or *between you and me*? The *Inside Language* panel were asked whether they would use *I* or *me* in *Between you and __, he's an idiot* (Q2). Eighty-three per cent chose *me*, 15 per cent *I*; the preferred choice is still the traditional *me* form after a preposition, at least consciously. Yet *between you and I* with the subject case *I* is now widely heard, and this usage appears to be spreading to other contexts. A political commentator on the television news, for instance, said *Sadly the money is coming from you and I via the government.* At a recent international conference of English teachers the keynote speaker said, *One of the things that helped my wife and I was . . .* According to a survey, the aspect of English that listeners to the BBC were most sensitive about was the use of subject rather than object forms of pronouns.

A plausible reason for moving towards *I* rather than *me* is called 'hypercorrection': if you are uncertain what to say, it is better to *over*do it than *under*do it. A person who speaks another dialect of English but is trying to adopt the prestige British accent may not know when to stop. They might, depending on their background, pronounce the 'h' in *hour* if they do not usually have 'h' sounds, pronounce *Thames* with the 'th' sound in *think* if they do not have 'th' sounds, or pronounce *gas* to rhyme with *pass*. These are signs of people adapting speech for social reasons overreaching the mark they are aiming at. *Between you and I* looks like the same phenomenon of the speaker playing safe for social reasons. Hypercorrection will be described further in Chapter 8.

The forms of pronouns can also be felt to assert political power over people, in a similar way to gender. Rastafarians prefer the object form *I* rather than *mi* because they feel *mi* puts them in a subservient object position rather than a subject position. The refrain of a song by Lloyd Charmer, for example, is *Rasta never fail I yet*.

6 Pronouns and reference

The next issue about pronouns is who the third person pronoun refers to. The reference of the first and second persons is usually dictated by the roles in the speech

Some English pronoun systems
(only the subject form is given for each)

Old English (pre-1100 AD)

	Singular	Dual	Plural
1st	ic	wit	we
2nd	þu	git	ge
3rd	he heo hit	–	hi

(The symbol þ is equivalent to modern voiced /ð/ in *there*.)

Middle English (pre-1500)

	Singular	Plural
1st	ich (i)	we
2nd	þu	ye
3rd	he sche hit (it)	þey

(The forms in brackets are not stressed, and lead to the modern forms.)

New Forest dialect (1913) (West Country in Hampshire)

	Singular	Plural
1st	ei, oi	wee
2nd	dhee, ee	yu, yee, ee
3rd	hee shee it 't	dhay

New Forest

(In the author's system, *ee* is the long 'i' sound, *dh* the 'th' sound; i.e. most of the forms are closer to standard English than they appear at first sight, apart from *'t*, *yee*, and *ee*.)

British Jamaican Creole (1982)

	Singular	Plural
1st	me, a	wi
2nd	yu	unu
3rd	im, i	dem

(*Sources*: Wilson, *The Dialect of the New Forest*; Sutcliffe, *British Black English*, etc.)

situation itself. It is usually obvious who is speaking (*I*) and who is being addressed (*you*). The third person is trickier, since by definition it refers to anybody or anything *not* involved as speaker or listener. This section gives a quick overview of the complex area of language study called 'binding theory', to give some flavour of the approach to the language system used by many linguists today, which will be described in greater depth in Chapter 11.

In a sentence such as *They liked the performance*, the third person pronoun *they* refers to some people obvious from the speech situation – the critics, the audience, the stage-hands, etc. – either because they have just been mentioned or because they are already well known to the speaker and listener. In a sentence like *John is afraid that he will have to leave*, however, the pronoun *he* could refer to two different people, either someone identified by the noun *John* earlier in the sentence, or someone else not mentioned in the sentence at all – Fred, Frank Sinatra, etc. In an actual speech situation, this problem usually takes care of itself and it is obvious who is meant. However, the sentence itself does not make clear whether the third person pronoun *he* refers to someone already mentioned or to somebody completely new.

Linguists have been interested in seeing how the organization of the sentence can resolve who the pronoun refers to. Take the pronouns *him* and *himself*. In *John voted for him* the listener knows that, whoever the pronoun *him* may refer to, it can*not* be John: something stops *him* linking to *John*. In the sentence *John voted for himself*, on the contrary, the listener knows that the reflexive pronoun *himself must* refer to John and can refer to nobody else: something forces *himself* to link to *John*. Speakers of English know that *him* and *himself* link to nouns in the sentence in totally opposite ways. They have a system for deciding which pronoun goes with which noun, again so obvious and automatic that people are surprised it needs mentioning.

The system can be seen better in more complicated sentences. In *John said Peter voted for him*, the listener knows that Peter voted for John (or for someone else not mentioned) but did not vote for himself.

John said Peter voted for him.

The pronoun *him* is linked to the noun *John*, if not to some unknown.

In the apparently similar sentence *John said Peter voted for himself,* the listener is just as convinced that Peter voted for himself, *not* for John.

John said Peter voted for himself.

Now *himself* is linked to *Peter* within the sentence, not to *John* or anyone outside.

The vital difference is the position where the pronoun occurs in the sentence. The pronoun *himself* must link to a noun inside a limited section of the sentence, in fact within the clause *Peter voted for himself*.

John said Peter voted for himself.
←———— clause ————→

Him, on the other hand, has to go with a noun outside this limited area, that is to say, within the whole sentence *John said Peter voted for him*.

John said Peter voted for him.
←———————— sentence ————————→

The difference is that *himself* links to a noun that must be *inside* the limited area of the clause, whereas *him* must link to a noun *outside* this limited area altogether.

Speakers of English know how *him* or *himself* link to nouns. Straight pronouns like *him* link to nouns within the sentence; reflexive pronouns like *himself* link to nouns within the smaller confines of the clause. Using this clue enables listeners to work out who *himself* refers to in *John said that Peter voted for himself* and who *him* refers to in *Peter discovered John's report on him*. These sentences formed part of an experiment whose purpose was to see whether English people, who had never probably thought about it in their lives before, would agree about the links between pronouns and nouns in a range of sentences. In fact they were in about 90 per cent agreement about whether *him* or *himself* went with *John* or *Peter* in most sentences.

In other words, the rule about *him* and *himself* is not just an arbitrary invention by linguists but is something all speakers of English already know, even if they are completely unaware of it. The language system in their minds includes some highly abstract elements of language, way below their conscious attention but manifest in the answers they come to. The rules given so far are just a pale approximation of this complex knowledge, as we see in later chapters. For example, the division into clause and sentence is too rough and ready to work perfectly.

The different links between *him* and *himself* and nouns become more interesting when other languages are taken into account and have led to the specialized area of research called 'binding theory'– how noun phrases are 'bound' to pronouns – to be discussed in Chapter 11. The language system can seldom be understood properly by looking at just one language. The modern study of language is often concerned with abstract properties that go across languages – how pronouns link to nouns – rather than peculiarities of a single language – how *him* links to *John* in English. It is not just the facts of English that are important, or those of any language in particular, but the general properties of the language system in the human mind, like the general properties of vision that, say, allow us to turn a succession of 24 frames a second into a moving picture. Hence many of the exciting issues about language today are at a high level of abstraction, based on years of developing theories of language and looking at wider and wider ranges of languages. Though this abstraction can cause some difficulty to start with, it leads to far more powerful ideas about language, rather like Newton proposing a theory of gravity rather than a theory of how apples drop to the ground.

III Grammar and the language system

This chapter has explored a range of issues involving pronouns, most of which could be expanded indefinitely. Later chapters will describe how pronouns are involved in the use of language in society, in the acquisition of language by children, and in the loss of language through injury. The main issues are not the actual sounds of language, nor even the meanings of the words, but the system that organizes sounds and meaning through number, person, 'binding' and so on. This has been called the 'computational system' of language by Noam Chomsky – the bridge between sounds and meanings.

The more usual word for it, which has been avoided up to here, is 'grammar'. To most people, grammar is a memory of their school years. Their experience of grammar is of the traditional English grammar handed down by the eighteenth century, rather than anything more recent. The idea of grammar makes many people uncomfortable, as it is a threat to social status; English speakers fear they are unwittingly giving things away about themselves by splitting infinitives, using *between you and I*, and so on.

However, this system of grammatical organization is what gives language its power. Language is not possible without a grammar. While the grammars of human languages vary in many ways, they all *have* a grammar with many common characteristics. This is not a grammar of the type that is traditionally learnt at school with its lists of parts of speech, rules, and exceptions, but the dynamic system that allows one person to organize a sentence *The cat is chasing the birds*, another *Neko ga tori wo oitsuiteiru*. The interesting questions about language are how this central computational system works, and how such a complex system is acquired by every human child within a few years of birth.

Sources and further reading

General background

General books on language that are both readable and based on current views include: D. Crystal, *The Cambridge Encyclopedia of Language* (Cambridge: CUP, 1987); S. Pinker, *The Language Instinct* (Harmondsworth: Penguin, 1995).

Pronouns

Much of the general information on pronouns here is based on: P. Mühlhäusler and R. Harré, *Pronouns and People: The Linguistic Construction of Social and Personal Identity* (Oxford: Blackwell, 1990); P. Mühlhäusler, 'Babel revisited', *UNESCO Courier*, 16 Feb. 1994, 16–32; B. Comrie (ed.), *The Major Languages of East and South-East Asia* (London: Routledge, 1990).

Speech role and number

Details of person and number are chiefly taken from: G. Corbett, *Gender* (Cambridge: CUP, 1991); R. Burling, *Man's Many Voices* (New York: Holt, Rinehart & Winston, 1970).

Pronouns and status

The classic article on pronouns and status is: R. Brown and A. Gilman, 'The pronouns of power and solidarity', originally published in T.A. Sebeok (ed.), *Style in Language* (Cambridge, MA: MIT Press, 1960), 253–76, but reprinted many times, e.g. in P.P. Giglioli (ed.), *Language and Social Context* (Harmondsworth: Penguin, 1972), 252–81.

Canadian French is reported in W.E. Lambert and G.R. Tucker, *Tu Vous Usted: A Social-Psychological Study of Address Patterns* (Rowley, MA: Newbury House, 1976). A useful starting book is: A. Wierzbicka, *Semantics, Culture, and Cognition* (Cambridge: CUP, 1992).

Missing pronouns (pro-drop)

The pro-drop parameter is described in most recent books on grammar, e.g. V.J. Cook and M. Newson, *Chomsky's Universal Grammar: An Introduction* (Oxford: Blackwell, 1996).

Gender

A full treatment of gender can be found in: G. Corbett, *Gender* (Cambridge: CUP, 1991), from which many of the language examples are taken. The *Times* example comes from L. Bauer, *Watching English Change* (London: Longman, 1994). The link between pronunciation and gender in French is discussed in G.R. Tucker, W.E. Lambert and A.A. Rigault, *The French Speaker's Skill with Grammatical Gender* (The Hague: Mouton, 1977). The problem of gender and English pronouns is dealt with in many sources, such as: D. Cameron, *Feminism and Linguistic Theory* (Basingstoke: Macmillan, 1985); J. Coates, *Women, Men, and Language* (London: Longman, 1986). Male speakers and female hearers feature in W. Levelt, *Speaking* (Cambridge, MA: MIT Press, 1989). The many attempts to coin a non-sexist pronoun are documented in: D. Baron, *Grammar and Gender* (New Haven, CT: Yale University Press, 1986); M. Piercy, *Woman on the Edge of Time* (London: Women's Press, 1979). See also C. Miller and K. Swift, *Words and Women: New Language in New Times* (Anchor Press, 1977). The sources on style are: H.W. and F.G. Fowler, *The King's English* (Oxford: Clarendon Press, 1918). The BBC survey is cited in D. Crystal, *The English Language* (Harmondsworth: Penguin, 1988).

Pronoun systems

The sources consulted for the English pronouns are: (Old and Middle English) any history of English, say, Strang, *A History of English* (London: Methuen, 1970); (New Forest) J. Wilson,

The Dialect of the New Forest (Oxford: OUP, 1913); (British Jamaican) D. Sutcliffe, *British Black English* (Oxford: Blackwell, 1982).

Pronoun reference (binding theory)

Any standard introduction to grammar covers binding, e.g. Cook and Newson, *Chomsky's Universal Grammar* (see above).

3 Basic Grammar

Conveying a message more complex than *Help!* or *Sh!* involves combining words in various ways. It is one thing to say *The patients sued the doctor*, another *The doctor sued the patients*, another *The patient sues the doctors*, another *Patients sue doctors*. The changes in word order show whether it is the patients or the doctor who are suing. The changes in word-ending show whether it has already happened (*sued*) or happens as a matter of custom (*patients sue . . .*) and whether there is one patient or several (*patients*). The omission of the article *the* (*patients* rather than *the patients*) turns the interpretation of the sentence away from a particular situation to situations in general. None of these meanings would be conveyed without grammar.

This chapter takes up the idea of grammar as the central computational system in language from Chapter 2 and introduces some basic concepts that are central to the understanding of the language system and which will be drawn on in later chapters. It starts by distinguishing grammatical words from content words. This leads into the crucial concepts of word order and phrase structure. Finally it discusses the ideas of structure within the current theory of Universal Grammar.

I Grammatical words and content words

This section introduces a major division between words that belong in the dictionary and words that belong in the grammar. The entry for the word *cup* in a dictionary gives a list of its meanings – 'small vessel', 'chalice' and several more. However, the entry for the word *and* in the COBUILD English dictionary looks rather different. Five of its twelve paragraphs describe how *and* links parts of the sentence together, whether words *Jack and Jill* or clauses *Jack fell down and Jill came tumbling after*. Seven paragraphs describe how *and* can introduce a change of topic – *And there's more* was a comedian's catchphrase in the 1980s – and is used in arithmetic – *Two and two are four* and so on. Unlike the dictionary entry for the word *cup*, the entry for *and* does not give its meanings so much as state its connecting function in the sentence, that is to say, its role in grammar.

Words like *cup* or *sue* are known as 'content' or 'lexical' words; they can be best defined in terms of meaning; they are numbered in their thousands. Words like *the* and *and* are 'grammatical' words, best defined in terms of grammar; they number 200 or so in English. The most frequent words of a language like English are not the content words that belong in the dictionary but the grammatical words that form part of the grammar system. Every sentence an English speaker says has to make use of personal pronouns such as *I* and *you* because these reflect how English grammar locates the speaker and hearer within the speech situation, as we saw in Chapter 2. Nor can *a* and *the* be avoided; nouns in English have to have either *a/an* (*a mop*), *the* (*the mop*) or zero article (i.e. no article at all, *mops*). These words form part of everything that can be expressed through English, whatever it may be. Grammatical words are high in frequency because they are necessary to every sentence of English. All of the top 30 words in Jane Austen's dialogues are grammatical words. About 45 of the top 50 words in children's writing are grammatical words, the exceptions being *went*, *said*, *came*, *saw* and *home*. The top 72 words from Japanese students of English are all grammatical words, as are the top 46 from the COBUILD Project.

It is sometimes said that 50 words make up 45 per cent of everything that is said. On the COBUILD figures, the top 50 words of English in fact account for rather less, 2 211 644 out of 18 000 000, that is to say 12 per cent, still a striking figure. A similar proportion is found in French: 44 per cent of a text is made up of 32 grammatical words such as *nous* ('we') and *où* ('where').

There are many other differences between content words and grammatical words in English. Membership of the group of content words is open in that new words can arrive all the time, whether into the individual's vocabulary or into the language itself, for instance, *fax* and *modem*. The group of grammatical words is closed and new members are not admitted. Content words are usually pronounced in only a single way. The word *house* is /haʊs/, *perpendicular* is /pəpəndikjʊlə:/ every time they are spoken (if the phonetic script is not transparent, the system is described in the next chapter and tables for English sounds are provided on pages 64, 65 and 70). But the same person may pronounce the grammatical word *have* as /həv/ with one vowel in *Yes I have,* /hæv/ with another vowel in *Have you seen him?,* as /əv/ without the /h/ in *I would have gone* or as /v/ alone in *I've been to Paris.* Grammatical words often vary in pronunciation from the 'full' pronunciation to the most 'reduced', from /hæv/ to /v/ for *have*. One English sound is effectively reserved for the beginning of grammatical words, namely the voiced 'th' sound /ð/ of *this, the, they, them, thence,* etc., which never occurs at the beginning of content words, only at the end, as in *breathe* or in the middle, *smother*. In writing, too, there are differences between grammatical and content words. Grammatical words may be as short as one or two letters – *I, an, we, in, by, to.* Content words, however, must have three or more letters – *eye, Ann, wee, inn, buy, two.*

English pronouns have two or more pronunciations according to whether they are stressed or unstressed. *You* varies between /jə/ with the /ə/ vowel of <u>a</u>bout, sometimes written as *yer* to show non-standard speech in cartoons, /jʊ/ with the short /ʊ/ vowel of *good* when unstressed *I'll give it you in a moment*, and /ju:/ with the long /u:/ vowel of *moon* when stressed *If <u>you</u> were the only girl in the world*. The pronoun *he* similarly varies between having the /i:/ of *bean* and the short /ɪ/ of *bin*, /hi:/ and /hɪ/, and in keeping or losing its 'h', /hɪ/ and /ɪ/, as seen in Chapter 8.

A mistake with a content word is likely to consist of putting another content word in its place; I asked in a pub for a *tuna shandy* rather than a *tuna sandwich*. This type of mistake forms the basis for the kind of humour named 'malapropism' after Sheridan's Mrs Malaprop, who would like a young lady to be 'instructed in geometry so that she might know something of the contagious countries'. When a Member of Parliament complained to the Speaker of the House of Commons that his letters had been delayed, she denied that she was responsible for the activities of *Paddington Bear*, to be reminded by other MPs that she actually meant *Postman Pat*. A mistake with a function word is more likely to consist of leaving it out altogether, say, *Give me biscuit*, rather than *Give me a biscuit*. Seldom is one function word substituted for another, *Give me but biscuit*. The exception is the occasional substitution of one preposition for another, as in *applause that you'd expect from* (for) *the leading soprano* and *the vision of speaking computers on* (in) *science fiction*. (In fact prepositions are sometimes considered content words as we see in Chapter 11.) The lack of mistakes with grammatical words is not, however, true of spelling: some common spelling confusions are between pairs of grammatical words such as *to/too*, *were/where*, *of/off* and *their/there*.

The difference between grammatical and content words shows up from time to time in the pauses of spontaneous speech. Content words are more likely to be preceded by a pause than grammatical words. So a speaker may say *The – government are likely to – win the next – election*, pausing before the lexical words *government*, *win* and *election*, but not before the grammatical words *are*, *to* and *the*. As the number of grammatical words is limited compared to lexical words and they are largely predictable from the structure of the sentence, speakers do not have to work hard to find them in their mental dictionary. The number of content words, however, is vast; the choice of the right verb or noun takes longer than the choice of the right article; hence speakers hesitate slightly longer before saying *election* than before *the*. The difference between lexical words and grammatical words recurs throughout the discussion of grammar, particularly in children's acquisition (Chapter 7) and aphasia (Chapter 9).

To sum up, grammatical words such as *to* and *the* are the skeleton of the sentence, necessary whatever is being talked about. Content words such as *cup* and *help* reflect the speakers' interests and the topics they want to talk about, which vary from moment to moment and person to person. Content words take part in systems of meaning, grammatical words in systems of grammar.

Some malapropisms (using the wrong content word)

The original – Mrs Malaprop (1775)

I would by no means wish a daughter of mine to be a progeny of learning . . . I would send her at nine years old to a boarding-school, in order to learn a little ingenuity and artifice. Then, sir, she should have a supercilious knowledge of accounts . . . but above all she should be mistress of orthodoxy that she might not mis-spell.

A rival – Nell Sims, a housekeeper in a Perry Mason novel (1946)

It's a case of one man's poison being another's meat.
Food preservation is the first law of nature.
A stitch in time is worth a pound of cure.
An eavesdropper gathers no moss.
Just a case of absence making the heart grow fonder of the bird in hand.

The authentic – real-life mistakes reported in A. Cutler (ed.) (1982)

We have a lovely Victorian condom set (condiment)
although murder is a form of suicide
as long as I'm in my own little nit (niche)
he was offered an engineering degree (job)
list of advertisements and Peter General's the only one (applicants)

The psychological – examples from Freud (1901): some slips of the tongue arise from 'elements which are not intended to be uttered'

A patient said she only saw her uncle *in flagranti*, meaning *en passant*.
A doctor said that in a sanatorium they can *umbringen* (put an end to) every type of patient, meaning *unterbringen* (take in).
A woman said that her new English teacher showed that he would like to give her private lessons *durch die Bluse* (through the blouse) rather than *durch die Blume* (through flowers, i.e. indirectly).

II Grammatical inflections

The second crucial element of grammar is inflections, for example the endings -*s* and -*ed* that are added to English words, as in *books* and *jumped*. This section first defines what grammatical inflections are, then looks at how they are used in English and other languages and finally describes alternative systems used in other languages.

English nouns like *books* can be split up into two elements, *book* plus the inflection *-s*. Verbs like *jumped* can be split into *jump* plus the inflection *-ed*. In these cases the inflections have the grammatical function of indicating the plural and the past tense respectively. Words like *teacher*, on the other hand, can also be taken apart into two units, a verb *teach* plus an *-er* ending; words like *appearance* can be decomposed into the verb *appear* plus the ending *-ance*. Here the endings do not so much have a grammatical function as turn one word into another with a related meaning. Inflections like *-s* resemble the grammatical words seen in the last section; endings like *-er* are more closely related to content words.

The blocks out of which words are made are called 'morphemes', a term as basic to grammar as 'stimulus' is to psychology or 'electron' to physics. A morpheme can be defined as the smallest unit of meaning: *books* is one morpheme, *book* with a clear dictionary meaning, plus a second morpheme *-s* with the grammatical meaning of 'plural'. A complementary definition of 'morpheme' is the smallest unit of grammar; the word *teacher* has two morphemes, *teach* and *-er*, that have meanings and can be treated independently as part of the grammar.

Morphemes such as *book* are called 'free' because they are words in their own right and can occur on their own without any props. Morphemes like *dis-* and *-s* only appear when attached to other morphemes – *displeased* or *cups* – and are called 'bound' morphemes. Words can be built up out of many morphemes, as seen in the terms for chemical substances such as drugs; I take *beclomethasone diproprionate*, for example, and one of my family was on *trifluoperazine* last year. Other languages take the incorporation of morphemes within the word to dizzier heights than English. Siberian Yupik, an Inuit language, has a single word *Angya-ghlla-ng-yug-tuq* which translates into English as *He wants to get a big boat*.

Chapter 5 will discuss how new words can be built from morphemes. This chapter concerns the bound morphemes involved in the grammar, technically called 'grammatical inflections'. The English plural morpheme *-s* seen in *books* is one example of a grammatical inflection, the past tense *-ed* in *jumped* another. A grammatical inflection does not necessarily have a single form. In writing, the spelling of the plural *-s* morpheme in English varies twofold between *-s*, *locks* and *-es*, *ditches*. In speech, the same morpheme varies three ways between /s/ *locks*, /ɪz/ *ditches* and /z/ *keys*. The difference hinges on the sound that precedes the inflection: if the preceding sound is a 'sibilant' such as /z/, the form of the plural morpheme is /ɪz/ as in /dɪtʃɪz/ (*ditches*); if the preceding sound is a voiceless consonant such as /k/, it is a voiceless /s/ as in /lɒks/ (*locks*); if the preceding sound is a voiced consonant or a vowel, it is a voiced /z/ as in /k:ɪz/ (*keys*). (The process of speech production is explained in the next chapter.)

Spoken English is not particularly rich in grammatical inflections compared to other languages, having only two for nouns and four for verbs:

- the plural *-s* for nouns, as in *books*
- the genitive *'s* for nouns, as in *John's*

- the third person singular *-s* for verbs as in *likes*
- the past tense *-ed* for verbs as in *liked*
- the past participle form of some verbs, usually *-ed*, as in *followed*, sometimes *-en* as in *seen*,
- the continuous participle *-ing* for verbs as in *is liking*.

All these inflections are compulsory in the sense that an adult speaker of standard English cannot say, except by accident, *He like me*, *three boat* or *I am go*, even if these are perfectly comprehensible. But, as can be seen from the qualifications 'adult' and 'standard', children and speakers of other varieties of English do not necessarily have the same restrictions. Children often go through an early stage of language acquisition without inflections, saying for example *Pig go in* and *Man drive truck*, as will be seen in Chapter 7. Speakers of East Anglian dialect may say *He like her* or *She want some* with no *-s*.

Other languages rely on grammatical inflections to a greater extent than English. In Russian, for example, the word *gazeta* (newspaper) has five other endings in the singular (*gazetu, gazeti, gazete, gazetoi, gazete*) and five more in the plural (*gazeti, gazet, gazetam, gazetami, gazetax*). These distinguish the different 'cases', that is to say the way that the noun fits in to the structure of the sentence, as mentioned in Chapter 2, as the subject of the sentence *gazeta*, as the object *gazetu*, and so on. Ukrainian distinguishes seven case endings in the singular, seven in the plural; Finnish has fifteen. Such cases are dormant in English, with the exception of pronoun forms such as *he/him/his*, even if they were abundant in Old English (and left English with the spelling problem of silent *e*, as we see in Chapter 10).

The same applies to the verb. English has one inflection, *-s*, in the present tense *I/you/we speak* versus *he/she/it speaks*, Moroccan Arabic has seven. In Finnish, a verb can have 4000 different forms. The record is probably held by Archi, a language spoken in Russia, in which a single verb could have over a million forms.

like	1st/2nd sing/plur, 3rd plur
likes	3rd sing

English present tense forms

At the opposite pole from Arabic and Finnish are languages that have no grammatical inflections at all. The following sentence of Vietnamese means 'though poor he likes to help his friends', with the word-by-word translation underneath:

Tuy	*nghèo,*	*nhu'ng*	*anh*	*thích*	*giúp*	*bạn*
though	poor	yet	he	like	help	friend

Anh (he) has only a single form where English has a choice of *he/him/his* and so on; *thích* (like) has no other forms or endings, compared with *likes/liked/liking*; and *bạn* (friend) is the same in the singular and the plural, compared with *friend/friends*. Each word in the sentence is a whole item of its own and cannot be divided up or have different forms.

Languages like Vietnamese are sometimes known as isolating languages because each word is 'isolated' rather than combined with inflections; they have no bound grammatical inflections. The consequences for these languages are considerable. From one perspective, Russian packs three times as much into every word as Vietnamese; from another, the average Russian word is longer than the average word of Vietnamese. The average number of morphemes per word is 1.06 for Vietnamese, 1.68 for English and 3.33 for Russian. (Vietnamese does not score a perfect 1.0 because it does have some derivational morphemes for constructing vocabulary items, even if it has no grammatical inflections.)

Given a sentence with three nonsense words, *I ordered some flugs,* a *couple of blits, and three snutches*, speakers of English will almost invariably pronounce the nouns as *flugs* with a final /z/, *blits* with a /s/ and *snutches* with an /ɪz/ even though they have never said these words before. The plural of *Häagen Dazs* is undoubtedly pronounced /ɪz/. The plural of *poorochondria* (Doug Coupland's term for 'hypochondria derived from not having medical insurance') must be *poorochondrias* with a /z/. The same applies to computer jargon; *an e-mail/two e-mails* – /z/; *a fax/two faxes* – /ɪz/; *a gigabit/two gigabits* – /s/. Speakers' unconscious knowledge of English automatically adds the appropriate form of plural *-s* to old words or to new. Their minds store a general rule which they can always apply, not just information about particular words such as *book*. So remote is this knowledge from conscious attention that I had to check the information about sibilants and /ɪz/ in a reference book, even though I doubtless make use of it in virtually every sentence I speak.

The plural morpheme in English is often referred to as plural *-s* after its most common forms. Other less regular variations of the plural morpheme are:

- a vowel at the end of the noun, *gladioli*
- a change of vowel or vowels in the word itself, *women* /wɪmɪn/ and *teeth* /tiːθ/
- no change at all, as in *two sheep* and *some fish*.

The plural morpheme includes these different forms. Most of the odder variants have historical explanations based either on the inflections of other languages with which English has been in contact, such as Latin, *gladioli*, or on earlier forms of English, *sheep*, to be seen in Chapter 10. For modern speakers, these exceptions are isolated words which are learnt one by one rather than by the general rule of how to form 'regular' *-s*, even though some form small subgroups such as *calf/calves, half/halves*.

Other languages make greater use of vowel-changing for showing morphemes than English. Words in Semitic languages have a root consisting of consonants with variable vowels. The morphemes for tense in Moroccan Arabic consist of vowel replacements, with other changes to the consonants. The root *k*t*b* means 'write'; the different tense morphemes fill this skeleton out with vowels to get *katab* ('he wrote'), *sayaktub* ('he will write'), *maktoub* ('written'), *kitaaba* ('the writing') and many more. An English parallel is the vowel and consonant changes in *he leaves* /liːvz/ versus *he left* /left/. Classical Arabic morphemes are conveyed by the successive vowels of the word, such as the *a-a* of *katab* ('wrote') and the *a-ou* of *maktoub* ('written'); past tense consists of a basic /a/ for the first vowel slot in the root which is then 'spread' to later vowel slots. The root can also be combined with other morphemes to get further combinations like *kteb* ('made someone write') and *takaatabu* ('they kept up a correspondence'). The consequences of this type of morphology for Arabic writing are discussed in Chapter 6.

The grammatical words like *to* and the grammatical inflections like plural *-s* are known collectively as 'grammatical morphemes'. This group is particularly important to modern theories of language acquisition, language disability and language history, as will be seen in later chapters.

Grammar for beginners

To illustrate the basic grammar of English, here are the forms taught to beginners learning English as a foreign language (EFL). The list is based on the elements of English grammar common to lessons 1–5 of three modern beginners' books for adult learners.

present of *to be*:	It's in Japan.
	I'm Mark.
	He's Jack Kennedy's nephew.
articles *a/an*:	I'm a student.
	She is an old woman.
	It's an exciting place.
Subject pronouns:	She's Italian.
	I've got two brothers and a sister.
	Do you have black or white coffee?
in/from with places:	You ask a woman in the street, the time.
	I'm from India.
	She lives in London.
noun plurals:	boys
	parents
	sandwiches

Essentially these are grammatical morphemes, whether bound inflections or free words, and obviously vital to the simple conversations that the students can engage in at this stage. The example sentences make clear that other crucial forms, though not on the list itself, are the pronouns.

A theme of this section has been the difference between regular and irregular forms of grammatical inflections. The regular forms of a morpheme are not only applied to words the speakers already know, *one brick*, *two bricks*, but also to words they have never heard before, *one blick*, *two blicks*. The minds of English speakers have a powerful rule for expressing plural -*s* that enables them to deal with both old words and new. The irregular forms of the language may form little subgroups, for instance words that take -*i* such as *croci* or *alumni* or words that have no change, *two deer* or *three swine*. These minor forms are applied to new words only when they can be clearly linked to existing groups. The plural of a newly invented word *blick* is unlikely to be *blicki* or *blick*, but a word *blickus* could conceivably have the plural *blicki*. Indeed, English science fiction names sometimes use irregular Latinate plurals, for example *Oankali*, *Eladeldi* and *Tyrenni*. A question that has been recently studied is which forms are used with irregular words used in new ways. My son had a *Walkman* for Christmas; this means he now possesses two *Walkmans*, not two *Walkmen*. My computer has a *mouse* and I have a second one in a box, but I hesitate over saying *two mouses* or *two mice*. Regular and irregular forms are claimed to reflect two different forms of language in the mind and are therefore acquired in different ways, as we see in Chapter 8.

The morphemes of language form a complex area of linguistics called 'morphology'. Languages differ in the overall ways they deal with grammatical morphemes, ranging between having no inflections, as in Vietnamese, using grammatical inflections, like English, and having internal vowel changes, as in Arabic. Learning grammatical morphemes is an important aspect of the acquisition of both first and second languages, as seen in Chapter 7, and they are one of the aspects that disappears in language loss, as seen in Chapter 9.

III The order of Subject, verb and Object

The importance of word order to grammar has already been mentioned. In most languages, though not all, the main elements of the sentence come in a particular order. *Cathy loved Heathcliff* means something different from *Heathcliff loved Cathy*. *Was Reagan a good president?* means something different from *Reagan was a good president*. Even *the little red hen* suggests something subtly different from *the red little hen*.

This section, then, explores the major variation between languages in the order of the grammatical elements of the sentence, Subject (S), verb (V) and Object (O), first establishing what these terms mean and then looking at the word order of English and the major word orders found in the languages of the world. The terms 'Subject', 'verb' and 'Object' have a history in traditional grammar going back to the analysis of classical languages. To show what they mean today, let us take the English sentence *I love Paris* as an example. This sentence divides up into a Subject (S) *I*, a verb (V) *love* and an Object (O) *Paris*.

SUBJECT	VERB	OBJECT
S	V	O
I	*love*	*Paris*

Similarly the sentence *Mary had a little lamb* has a Subject *Mary*, a verb *had* and an Object *a little lamb*, as do, setting aside extra elements, *Here's looking at you, kid* (Subject *here*, verb *is looking at*, Object *you*), *I saw a host of golden daffodils* (Subject *I*, verb *saw*, Object *a host of golden daffodils*), *I have a dream* (Subject *I*, verb *have*, Object *a dream*), and so on.

SUBJECT	VERB	OBJECT
S	V	O
Mary	*had*	*a little lamb*
Here	*'s looking at*	*you*
I	*saw*	*a host of golden daffodils*
I	*have*	*a dream*

1 The order Subject, verb, Object in English

English sentences typically have the three elements in the order Subject–verb–Object (SVO). The Subject *I* is followed by the verb *love*, which is followed by the Object *Paris*, as November is followed by December. To the English speaker, other orders than Subject–verb–Object would be bizarre or incomprehensible: *Love I Paris*, *Paris love I*, although *Paris I love* is possible in certain circumstances.

This SVO order may be disguised, because each of the main elements can be expanded in various ways into phrases consisting of several words rather than a single word. The Object, for example, can be a noun phrase consisting of one word *me*, two words *a dream* or several words *a host of golden daffodils*. Take a sentence at random from today's paper: *The first in this new series introduces a host of characters who live on a rubbish dump and have many different tales to tell.* While the verb is a single word *introduces,* the Subject is a complex phrase *the first in this new series* and the Object is *a host of characters who live on a rubbish dump and have many different tales to tell,* which includes another clause complete with its own Subject *who,* two verbs *live* and *have* and a complex Object *many different tales to tell.* Nevertheless its skeleton is still the SVO order. English is then an SVO language, unlike its ancestor, Old English, or its neighbour, German.

When other word orders than SVO are used in English, they signal particular types of sentence with distinctive meanings. A sentence without a Subject, i.e. verb–Object

(VO) or verb (V), is usually a command: *Play it again, Sam, Beware the ides of March* or *Beam me up, Scotty*. A sentence in which the verb precedes the Subject (VSO) is usually a question: *Will you marry me?*, *Can you see land?* or *Is this a dagger that I see before me?* Moving *will* or *is* or any other auxiliary verb to the beginning of the sentence signals a different meaning from the straightforward 'declarative' order, *You will marry me*, *You can see land* and *This is a dagger that I see before me*.

There are odd exceptions in English where the Subject apparently comes after the verb. One type is sentences with *there*: *There is a fly in my soup/ there are some flies in my soup*. The verb agrees with the noun phrase that comes after it in number rather than with the *there* that comes before it: a dummy Subject *there* fills the Subject position without forcing the verb to be singular or plural. Nevertheless *there* is still the Subject, although it carries no meaning or number. Another exception is exclamations with verbs of motion: *Here comes the sun!/Into the pit lane to make his stop comes the race leader Damon Hill* (TV commentary). In these the verb unexpectedly agrees in number with the following noun phrase rather than with the phrase that comes before it, as can be seen by making them plural *Here come the suns/Into the pit lane come the Ferraris*. Saying that English is an SVO language does not therefore mean that all English sentences have SVO order but that this is the usual order in straightforward sentences. The typical order for a language is known as the 'canonical order'.

2 *The order of Subject, verb and Object in other languages*

Subject–verb–Object (SVO) is the everyday canonical order in many other languages, such as French, Yoruba and Russian. The speakers of an SVO language assume that this order corresponds to the logical order of events. A Subject has to come first because it tells you what the sentence is about – *I*; a verb has to come second because it tells you what the Subject does – *love*; an Object has to be last because it refers to the thing that is affected by the verb – *Paris*. At least so many of the people who filled in the *Inside Language* questionnaire believe (Q11). Some said that SVO 'makes the sentence clear to understand' because 'the Subject is more important than the Object'. They felt the reason is that the SVO order introduces 'the main Subject first' and the 'Object receiving the action at the end'. They find SVO a 'logical progression', 'a logical format', 'clarity, simplicity', 'the most reasonable order', 'because that's the way it has evolved' or just 'common sense'.

SVO is only one of the canonical orders found in the languages of the world. In Japanese the sentence *watashi-wa yume-o mita* ('I had a dream') has the order Subject *watashi* ('I'), followed by Object *yume* ('dream'), followed by verb *mita* ('had') (plus two particles *wa* and *o* that show the grammatical roles of Subject and Object). So the Japanese verb comes last of the three elements rather than in the middle, Subject–Object–verb (SOV) order. Other SOV languages are Persian, Basque and Navaho.

SUBJECT	OBJECT	VERB
S	O	V
watashi-wa	yume-o	mita
(I	dream	had)

This SOV order is as much a matter of common sense to the Japanese speaker as SVO is to the speaker of English. Obviously it is logical to describe the main participants in the sentence, namely the Subject and the Object, before stating the relationship between them, the verb. Speakers of SOV languages can boast that SOV languages outnumber SVO languages by 45 per cent to 42 per cent of the world's languages, as calculated by Russell Tomlin from a base of 402 representative languages.

In Welsh, however, the sentence *Mary saw the dog* is *Gwelodd Mair y ci*. The verb *gwelodd* ('saw') comes before the Subject *Mair* ('Mary'), which comes before the Object *y ci* (the dog). Welsh therefore has the canonical order verb–Subject–Object (VSO).

VERB	SUBJECT	OBJECT
V	S	O
Gwellod	Mair	y ci
(saw	Mary	the dog)

Other VSO languages are Classical Arabic and Maori. Doubtless VSO speakers find it highly logical to state the relationship before specifying the two entities involved, the order used in the logic-based computer language PROLOG. In fact, 9 per cent of languages have VSO order.

The three word orders SVO, SOV and VSO together account for 96 per cent of the world's languages. Setting aside the verb, English SVO, Japanese SOV and Arabic VSO all have the Subject preceding the Object. All three can be captured by a single formula: (V) S (V) O (V). Perhaps Subjects have to come before Objects – SO – in all human languages. Speakers of SO languages can instantly rationalize the logical necessity for the Subject to precede the Object. As one of the *Inside Language* panel commented, 'The Subject is going to need less description than the complement of the verb which comes later in the sentence.'

But the SO speakers' mother tongues may be misleading guides. For 3 per cent of languages have the canonical order verb–Object–Subject (VOS), with the Object preceding the Subject, for example Tagalog and Tongan. It is not necessary for the Subject to come before the Object in all languages, even if the OS order is rare.

Still, none of the languages discussed so far has the Object *first* in the sentence preceding both verb and Subject. Until recently it was considered an absolute rule that

Subjects came before Objects. The orders OSV and OVS were thought to be impossible in human languages. Then, in the 1970s, languages were discovered that filled the missing gaps: Hixkaryana has Object–verb–Subject (OVS) and Apurinã has Object–Subject–verb (OSV). Doubtless their speakers find it equally natural that Objects come first in the sentence. None of the possible orders of the three main elements S, V and O is therefore ruled out, even if the orders SOV, SVO and VSO are by far the most common.

All the Object-initial languages that have been discovered so far, such as Hixkaryana and Apurinã, are in fact spoken within a few hundred miles of each other in the Amazon basin in Brazil. Their geographical closeness nevertheless seems to be an odd coincidence, since these languages belong to different language families, other members of which have the more usual Subjects before Objects. Though these Object-first languages now have only a few speakers, the Indian population of the area used to be 100 times its present size.

Frequency of Subject, Object and verb canonical word orders in the languages of the world

SOV	45%	Basque, Burmese, Hindi, Hungarian, Japanese, Korean, Latin, Navajo, Persian, Punjabi, Tamil, Turkish . . .
SVO	42%	Albanian, Czech, English, Finnish, French, Hebrew, Indonesian, Russian, Serbian, Swahili, Thai, Yoruba, Zulu . . .
VSO	9%	Arabic (Classic), Chinook, Hawaiian, Maori, Scots Gaelic, Tahitian, Welsh . . .
VOS	3%	Tagalog, Tongan . . .
OVS	1%	Hixkaryana . . .
OSV	<1%	Apurinã . . .

Sources: Tomlin, *Basic Word Order*; Hawkins, *Word Order Universals*.

To sum up, human languages have three basic elements S, O and V, which they combine in various ways to arrive at the six possible orders. As always, there are languages that are difficult to place into any scheme. Some have fairly free word order. For example, while Latin is classified as an SOV language, in poetry it has free order: Virgil's oft-cited tag *amor vincit omnia* ('love conquers all') SVO could also be *omnia vincit amor* OVS or *vincit omnia amor* VOS, with no more than a slight change of emphasis.

This freedom for poetical effect has been preserved to a minor extent in poetic English. The opening lines of Milton's *Paradise Lost* are *Of Man's First Disobedience* . . .

sing Heav'nly Muse (Object–verb–Subject, with four lines of verse intervening). A few lines later comes *Him the Almighty Power hurled headlong flaming from th'Etherial Skie . . .* (OSV); slightly later, *Such place Eternal Justice had prepar'd* (OSV). Milton would have found it easy to adapt to life on the River Amazon, grammatically speaking – but of course he also wrote in Latin.

IV Phrase structure

One of the most distinctive properties of language is that it has 'structure'. This section looks at the nature of phrase structure and its reality in the human mind. The systems of grammatical morphemes and word order are not enough in themselves to describe all the properties of the sentence. Words fit together in phrases. Take the sentence *A girl opened the door*. The word *a* seems to go with *girl* and *the* with *door* in a way that *girl* does not go with *opened* or *opened* with *the*. *The door* is a possible answer to the question *What did she open?*; but *Girl opened* or *Opened the* are not answers to any possible question (other than *What are the second and third words of the sentence?*). So *a girl* and *the door* are phrases constructed around the nouns *girl* and *door*, hence called 'noun phrases', as their 'heads' are nouns. *Opened the door* also belongs together as a phrase. It, too, is a possible answer to a question: *What did she do? Opened the door*. As this phrase is constructed around the verb *opened*, it is known as a 'verb phrase' after its head verb.

The usual way of representing how the words of a phrase belong together is through a tree diagram, which lays out the component parts to show their connections. The noun phrase *a girl* can be shown as:

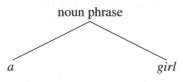

The verb phrase *opened the door* is slightly more complex since it has a noun phrase within it:

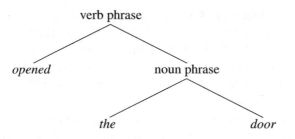

Put together, this makes up a tree diagram for the whole sentence *A girl opened the door.*

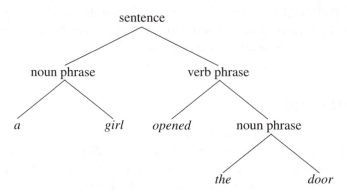

This tree shows that *a* goes with *girl* to produce a noun phrase, *the* with *door* to get another; *opened* goes with *the door* to produce a verb phrase *opened the door*; *a girl* goes with *opened the door* to produce the whole sentence, *A girl opened the door.* When a sentence or a phrase is said to have structure, it means that the words and phrases are connected together in this way.

The concept of phrases has already slipped into the discussion of word order above, since many of the Subjects, verbs and Objects that were discussed were in fact phrases rather than single words: *a little lamb*, the Object in *Mary had a little lamb*, is a noun phrase not a noun, as are *a dream* and *a host of golden daffodils*. A step forward from this definition is to see the Subject of the sentence in terms of the phrase structure of the sentence rather than through word order, case and so on. In any language the Subject is the noun phrase that occurs in the top level of the sentence alongside the verb phrase, regardless of whether it comes before or after it. The Subject noun phrase plays a particular role in the structure of the sentence. Its agreement with the verb, its place in the order of the sentence and its case are all spin-offs from its grammatical role in the sentence.

Phrase structure and the mind

This phrase structure might seem to exist only on the pages of grammar books rather than having reality in our minds. One way of showing its psychological importance is to substitute pronouns for different bits of the sentence. So the phrase *the girl* is replaced by *she* to produce *She opened the door*, and *the door* with *it* to produce *She opened it*. Even the phrase *opened the door* can be replaced with the verb *did*: *Who opened the door? She did.* But there is no way in which *opened the* can be replaced with a pronoun. Phrases can often be detected by this pronoun substitution test: if several words can be replaced by one word then they must somehow form a whole in our minds, not just in the grammar book.

Phrase structure is sometimes reflected in the pauses of speech. A speaker who pauses when reading the sentence aloud is likely to do so in between the phrases: *a girl . . . opened the door* or *a girl . . . opened . . . the door*, not in the middle of the phrases: *a . . . girl opened the . . . door*. Pausing is not a very reliable guide to phrase structure, however, as there is the opposing tendency in spontaneous speech to pause before content words, as we saw earlier: *Well you see it was like this a . . . girl opened the erm . . . er door.*

A series of experiments in the 1960s derived from the work of Thomas Bever showed the influence of the phrase structure on sentence perception. People were played a sentence such as: *That he was happy was evident from the way that he smiled*, to which a clicking noise was added in different places. The major phrase boundary is between the Subject *that he was happy* and the verb phrase *was evident from the way that he smiled*.

That he was happy ‖ *was evident from the way that he smiled.*

What happens if a click is played at the same moment as the word *was*, some way before the boundary?

That he was happy ‖ *was evident from the way that he smiled*
      ↑

In fact people tend to believe that the click has been said at the actual phrase boundary, not within the phrase itself.

That he was happy ‖ *was evident from the way that he smiled.*
    ↑·········►

They do not 'hear' the click where it actually occurs, but displace it to the nearest convenient phrase boundary. The same happens with clicks that occur after the boundary, say on *evident*; people believe that they occur at the boundary:

That he was happy ‖ *was evident from the way that he smiled.*
      ◄·········↑

The only time that the click is not displaced is when it occurs at the boundary itself.

Recently, attempts have been made to establish how the brain itself is involved in grammar through a technique called event-related potentials (ERP), which measures the electrical activity in the brain of people listening to sentences that have normal English phrase structure, e.g. *The man admired Max's proof of the theorem*, and sentences with the incorrect phrase structure, e.g. *The man admired Max's of proof the theorem*. When the listeners hit the problem part of the sentence, the activity in the left side of their brain changed. Problems with phrase structure affect a particular area of the brain, as will be seen in Chapter 9.

Phrases are not therefore artificial creations for linguists to analyse sentences, but have a reality in the minds and even the brains of speakers. Chapter 7 shows that they form one of the bases for children's language acquisition.

V Movement and principles of language

The types of grammar seen so far are not unfamiliar. In a way they look like school grammar with more careful definitions and a few trimmings. However, in the past forty years the study of grammar has reached a much greater depth, chiefly due to the work of Noam Chomsky. This section introduces some concepts from Chomsky's theory of Universal Grammar, which is expanded in Chapter 11. It will be immediately apparent that these deal with language at a high level of abstraction, as physics deals with principles of motion or entropy. Nevertheless they do have precise consequences for our everyday language system, and underlie the ease and speed with which children acquire language.

The core of human language is structure, in a broader sense than the phrase structure dealt with in the last section. To see what this means, let us see how English questions such as *Is Casablanca hot?* are formed. It seems natural to think of the verb *is* 'moving' to the front of the sentence to get the question; this is the traditional analysis of such sentences. Movement can be shown as:

> *Casablanca is hot.*
>
> *Is Casablanca hot?*

Many languages, though not all, form questions by 'moving' part of the sentence to the beginning in this way.

This is not to say that speakers produce questions by starting with the plain statements and then moving bits about – actually thinking *Casablanca is hot* before turning the sentence into *Is Casablanca hot?* The unmoved form is an underlying form rather than an actual sentence, like the underlying unwritten constitution of the UK compared to the actual laws passed by Parliament. Movement is a metaphor for the relationship between this hidden form of the sentence in the mind and what actually occurs, not an actual process of moving things around.

Movement in English affects not only questions but also passive sentences such as *The policeman was hit by a car*, which comes from an underlying structure similar to *A car hit the policeman*.

> *A car hit the policeman.*
>
> *The policeman was hit by a car.*

The underlying Object *the policeman* has become the Subject (and other things have changed as well). Movement in grammar means relating a sentence to the underlying structure in which the elements are in a different place, usually closer to the form of a straightforward statement rather than a question or a passive.

But *what* is moved? In *Is Casablanca hot?* obviously the word *is* has moved. How does the speaker know that *is* should be moved, not *hot*? Perhaps the rule for making questions is: move the second word to the front, i.e. *is*. But, if this movement were tried with the slightly expanded sentence *Romantic Casablanca is hot*, the question would be *Casablanca romantic is hot*, which is obviously wrong. The question rule cannot be phrased in terms of moving the first word, second word and so on. Instead English questions involve moving particular types of word, such as *will*, *is* and *can*, known as 'auxiliaries'. A better version of the rule for forming questions is then: move the auxiliary to the front (and, if there isn't one, substitute a dummy auxiliary by using *do*). Given a sentence such as *Romantic Casablanca, bustling Arabic-speaking port on the Atlantic, will be hot*, English speakers can unerringly form the question *Will romantic Casablanca, bustling Arabic-speaking port on the Atlantic, be hot?*

Suppose the sentence has more than one auxiliary, how do speakers of English know which one to move? Take the sentence *Sam is the cat that is black*. The rule that an auxiliary has to be moved will lead to the question *Is Sam the cat that is black?*, accepted by 100 per cent of the people in one experiment of mine. But the same rule would now lead to the question *Is Sam is the cat that black?*, rejected by 99.6 per cent. The sheer unanimity, unparalleled for most questions about language, shows not just that this is an unusual sentence that they have not heard before, but that there is something very wrong with it.

Perhaps the question rule should be that only the first auxiliary *is* should be moved. While this solution would certainly work for this sentence, it would not cover *The cat that is black is Sam* where the question would be *Is the cat that black is Sam?* Of the *Inside Language* panel, 100 per cent rejected the equivalent *Is the teacher who on leave is Jones?* (Q9), which moves the first *is*. So the rule cannot simply specify that the first or the second auxiliary *is* has to be moved; movement seems to depend on something else.

The solution is that the only *is* that can be moved is the one in the main clause of the sentence *Sam is the cat . . .* rather than the one in the relative clause *. . . that is black*.

main clause   relative clause   main clause   relative clause

Sam is the cat that is black   *Sam is the cat that is black*

✓**Possible**   ✗**Impossible**

Is Sam the cat that is black?   *Is Sam is the cat that black?*

In other words, the element to be moved has to come from a particular place in the phrase structure of the sentence. This is called the 'principle of structure-dependency'. The rules of English for questions, passives, indeed any movement, all depend on structure. They operate with parts of the structure of the sentence, not just by counting words from the left.

But this is true of all languages, not just English; movement must be structure-dependent; that is to say, the elements of the sentence that are moved in passives, questions and so on are always in a particular position in the structure, not just a particular point in the sequence of words. So German passives such as *Hans wurde von Marie gesehen* ('Hans was seen by Mary') or questions such as *Wurde Hans von Maria gesehen?* ('Was Hans seen by Maria?') are also formed by movement that depends on structure, as is the Greek passive *O giatros didachttike Angliká apo ton Peter* ('The doctor was taught English by Peter') or the French question *Où sont les neiges d'antan?* ('Where are the snows of yesteryear?'). Structure-dependency is all-pervasive; all languages observe it for movement, as well as in other areas of grammar such as the principles of binding mentioned in the last chapter. Of course the principle only applies to languages which form passives and questions by movement; Japanese and Bahasa Melayu, for example, form questions by adding particles and keeping the order of the sentence the same, and so do not need structure-dependency for movement.

There is no logical reason why movement should have to depend on structure-dependency. Computer languages do not have this restriction built into them for instance, nor do mathematical equations. It is simply a fact about human languages that movement depends on structure. How children could acquire this abstract principle is mysterious. One possibility is that structure-dependency is built into the human mind; we all possess it potentially in our minds. This explains why neither children learning a first language nor adults learning a second *ever* make the mistake of asking questions like *Is Sam is the cat that black?* Foreign adults learning English were almost as good as natives in my experiment, Finns scoring 100 per cent and Japanese 97 per cent, such high scores again being unusual for non-native speakers. The question of the innateness of principles such as structure-dependency will be explored in Chapter 11.

Structure-dependency is then one example of the abstract principles that underlie the computational system of language. As well as the features that easily catch the eye such as word order or forms of pronouns, grammar also has powerful abstract systems. Such principles are found in all languages. Or, to be more precise, as we have seen with structure-dependency, they are not *broken* in any language. There is in fact no structure-dependency for movement in Japanese, but the reason is that there is no movement in Japanese, not that Japanese breaks the principle.

Much of the interest of grammar arises not from looking at one language in isolation but by comparing how different languages utilize the same resources in different ways. Linguists learn about English inflections by comparing them with, on the one hand, Latin, on the other, Vietnamese. Their knowledge of English word order is improved by comparing it with Japanese and with Hixkaryana. The nature of the Subject of the sentence can be discovered by seeing how the English reliance on word order compares with Italian and Japanese. The Universal Grammar approach adopts the working principle that studying the same grammatical phenomena across several languages can reveal what all human beings have in common. Structure-dependency is a scientific hypothesis about the nature of human language in general. It tells us something, not about English or Italian, but about how the mind creates language

Chomsky's sentences

To give some idea of the range of topics covered in recent grammar, here are some of the crucial pairs of sentences invented by Noam Chomsky to test his theory of Universal Grammar as it developed. Try to spot the differences between each pair.

Colourless green ideas sleep furiously.
Furiously sleep ideas green colourless.
The book seems interesting.
The child seems sleeping. (1957)
John is eager to please.
John is easy to please.
The boy may frighten sincerity.
Sincerity may frighten the boy. (1965)
It seems to each other that they are happy.
They seem to each other to be happy.
They spoke angrily to John.
John was spoken angrily to. (1981)
John reads often to his children.
John reads often books. (1995)

The reason why some of these are grammatical, others ungrammatical, requires an entire book on Universal Grammar.

within it. The hypothesis may, of course, be wrong. Tomorrow someone may discover a language that has movement without structure-dependency, just as they discovered a language with Object Subject order (Hixkaryana). Part of the progress in linguistics has come from trying out the same set of principles with more and more languages, seeing if they work and, if they fail, abandoning them or modifying them in some way.

This chapter has gone from grammatical words to inflections to principles of grammar. While some aspects of grammar are consciously available to the speakers of a language, some are so deeply buried in their minds that they take them as much for granted as they take their breathing or digestion. The impossible sentences violating principles of language may strike them as absurd; why on earth should anybody bother to point out something so obviously wrong? But this reaction is in itself a sign that they are not behaving rationally. The sentences are odd precisely because they go against the deep-seated knowledge of language in human minds. It is by making up such 'impossible' sentences that the outlines of the principles of language in the mind can be made out.

The progression in this chapter also shows how grammar is a major component in the human mind. The grammatical inflections, the phrases, the principles are not just superficial frills on top of the basic communication: they are the way in which the human mind organizes the messages it wants to send and the messages it hears. Far from being the dry subject of the school tradition, endlessly going over the parts of speech handed down by the Romans, always on the lookout for new mistakes to condemn, grammar brings together many sides of language in a system that is unique. Studying grammar gives us a window into the human mind itself.

Sources and further reading

There are many introductions to grammar from a linguistics perspective, for example J. Hurford, *Grammar: A Student's Guide* (Cambridge: CUP, 1994).

Grammatical words and content words

The sources for word frequency are: for children, D. Reid, *Word for Word: The Top 2,000 Words Used by 7 and 8 Year Olds* (Wisbech, Cambs.: Learning Development Aids, 1989); for the COBUILD figures, J. Sinclair, *Corpus, Concordance, Collocation* (Oxford: OUP, 1991); for Jane Austen, J.F. Burrows, *Computation into Criticism: A Study of Jane Austen's Novels and an Experiment in Method* (Oxford: Clarendon Press, 1987); the Japanese figures are my own, derived from the Longman Corpus of Learner English.

The sources of malapropisms are: R.B. Sheridan, *The Rivals* (1775); E.S. Gardner, *The Case of the Drowsy Mosquito* (1946); A. Cutler (ed.), *Slips of the Tongue* (The Hague: Mouton, 1982); S. Freud, *The Psychopathology of Everyday Life*, trans. A. Tyson (London: Hogarth Press, 1960).

Grammatical inflections

The treatment of morphology in general, from which many examples have been taken, can be found in L. Bauer, *Introducing Linguistic Morphology* (Edinburgh: EUP, 1988); A. Spencer, *Morphology* (Oxford: Blackwell, 1994); B. Comrie, 'Linguistic typology', in F. Newmeyer (ed.), *Linguistics: The Cambridge Survey* I: *Linguistics Theory: Foundations* (Cambridge: CUP, 1988), 447–61.

The distinction between regular and irregular is expanded in S. Pinker, *The Language Instinct* (Harmondsworth: Penguin, 1995).

The basic EFL grammar is derived from: J. Garton-Sprenger and S. Greenall, *Flying Colours* I (London: Heinemann, 1990); M. Swan and C. Walters, *The Cambridge English Course* (Cambridge: CUP, 1984); S. Mohamed and R. Acklam, *The Beginners' Choice* (Harlow: Longman, 1992).

The order of Subject, verb and Object

The idea of word order is found in any grammar book. One influential approach is in: J.A. Hawkins, *Word Order Universals* (New York: Academic Press, 1983); J.A. Hawkins, 'On implicational and distributional universals of word order', *Journal of Linguistics* 16 (1980): 193–235.

Canonical order is described in D.I. Slobin and T.G. Bever, 'Children use canonical sentence schemas: a crosslinguistic study of word order and inflection', *Cognition* 12 (1982): 229–65.

The figures for frequency of word orders are taken from R.S. Tomlin, 'The frequency of basic constituent orders', *Papers in Linguistics* 17 (1984): 163–96; R.S. Tomlin, *Basic Word Order: Functional Principles* (London: Croom Helm, 1986).

Hixkaryana is described in D.C. Derbyshire and G.K. Pullum, 'Object-initial languages', *International Journal of American Linguistics* 47 (1981): 192–214.

Phrase structure

The classic experiment with clicks is described in J. Fodor and T. Bever, ' The psychological reality of linguistic segments', *JVLVB* 4 (1965): 414–20; a general account can be found in J.A. Fodor, T. Bever and M. Garrett, *The Psychology of Language* (New York: McGraw-Hill, 1974).

The ERP experiment is described in H. Neville, J.L. Nichol, A. Barss, K.I. Forster and M.F. Garrett, 'Syntactically based sentence processing classes: evidence from event-related brain potentials', *Journal of Cognitive Neuroscience* 3(2) (1991): 151–65.

Movement

Syntactic movement in the sense used here can be found in textbooks with a UG slant, such as V.J. Cook and M. Newson, *Chomsky's Universal Grammar: An Introduction* (Oxford: Blackwell, 1996).

Structure-dependency is also covered in Cook and Newson, and in many of Chomsky's more popular books, such as *Language and Problems of Knowledge: The Managua Lectures* (Cambridge, MA: MIT Press, 1988).

4 The Sound System of Language

Why do people speaking English and French sound so different when the languages look so similar in writing, apart from a few accents? This chapter looks at some of the properties of sound systems that languages have in common and some of the ways in which they differ; Chapter 6 will outline the properties of the writing systems of language. This chapter starts by discussing the ways in which languages use the pitch variation of intonation, goes on to the mechanisms by which speech sounds are produced and then turns to how sounds are organized in speech. Its theme is the diverse ways in which languages make use of the same resources for producing speech.

The pronunciation of English is taken as a starting-point. However, this decision immediately raises the problem of selecting one out of the many accents of English. Most textbooks choose the variety of English called RP originally taken from 'Received Pronunciation', now mostly known simply by the initials RP on their own. Usually RP is thought of as the accent of educated British speakers of English, which does not vary according to region within England, though it differs from other world accents such as General American English. RP accent is then a different concept from the standard language of English, which has a consistent grammar and vocabulary almost everywhere it is spoken, apart from a few well-known local peculiarities.

Choosing RP as a reference point is not to suggest that more than a small minority of people in England speak it, on one estimate 3 per cent. In general the majority of educated speakers in England nowadays have a 'modified RP' with some regional forms. The *Today* news programme on BBC Radio 4, for instance, has a range of English speakers each day. In a recording of a typical programme, although about two-thirds of the speakers were within the general bounds of RP accent, most of them had some regional forms. The continuity

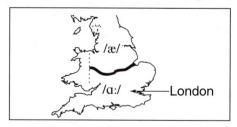

announcer, for instance, said *fastest* with the short 'a' sound of *lass* /æ/ rather than the long 'ah' sound of *last* /ɑː/, showing she probably comes from north of an east–west line from Wales to the Wash, rather than from the south. The weatherman pronounced *throughout* with an initial 'f', showing a feature often associated with a London accent. Variations in English accent will be dealt with in Chapter 8.

RP is used as a reference point, not because of its intrinsic superiority to other accents but because everyone is familiar with it, in the rest of the world as well as in England, particularly through the media. It has been used as the model for teaching English as a Foreign Language in countries where British English is taught rather than American. RP also carries social prestige, as popular terms for it such as 'BBC English' and 'Oxford English' suggest. For centuries versions of RP have been the accent of a particular 'class' rather than a particular region, the south of England having an increased proportion of RP speakers because of its comparative prosperity. The social pressure in the UK is still towards the RP accent, as numerous newspaper discussions and pronouncements by ministers of education proclaim each year. Successive generations of British students have assured me that they have nothing against regional accents – but most of them say so in modified RP accents that belie their good intentions. Hence, other things being equal, RP is still the most useful accent to describe. More practically, however, RP has been studied in greater depth than any other accent and so more is known about its peculiarities.

I Sounds and meanings

This section looks at whether there is a logical link between the sounds of speech and meanings or whether the relationship is purely arbitrary. In a sense there is no reason why a particular speech sound should convey a particular meaning; a rose by any other name would indeed smell as sweet. But could *Romeo* in fact be called *Fred*? *Juliet*, *Gertie*? Or *Gertrude*, *Tracey*? Partly the naturalness of the names is due to our long familiarity with the characters these portray. What could *Gussie Fink-Nottle* be called instead of *Gussie Fink-Nottle*? *Anna Karenina*? *James Bond*? *Irma Prunesquallor*? *John F. Kennedy*? Why do rose-growers prefer to name roses *Ingrid Bergman* or *Queen Elizabeth* rather than *Olive Oyl*?

However, the sounds in a handful of words do fit their meanings better than chance would suggest. Take the objects in Fig. 4.1. Suppose that in an unknown language one of these objects is called a *pling*, the other a *plung*: which is which? 71 per cent of the *Inside Language* panel thought Object A was a *plung*, only 25 per cent calling it a *pling* (Q4). Something about the vowel 'u' conveys a sense of 'large and dark' – *plung*: something about the vowel 'i' conveys a sense of 'small and light' – *pling*.

Several English words with low vowels like 'u' in *cut* or 'a' indeed suggest something 'large' or 'dark': *huge, large, vast, enormous*. Others with 'high' vowels such as 'i' mean something 'small' or 'light': *little, teeny, wee, titchy, mini, pygmy, Lilliput, thin, itsy-bitsy teeny-weeny polka-dot bikini*. In French 'small' is *petit*, 'big' is *grand*,

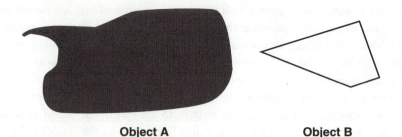

Object A   **Object B**

Fig. 4.1 Names for arbitrary shapes

in Greek *mikro* and *megalo*, in Spanish *chico* and *gordo*, in Dyirbal, an Australian Aboriginal language, /midi/ and /bulgan/, and in Mandarin Chinese *xiaǒ* and *dà*.

John Ohala has explained this phenomenon through the 'Frequency Code'. Vowels with high frequencies such as 'i' go with small size and sharpness – *pling*. Vowels with low frequencies such as 'u' go with large size and softness – *plung*. The Frequency Code hypothesis claims that low sounds in general go with aggressiveness and assertion of power, not just vowels: Margaret Thatcher is believed to have had speech lessons to deepen her voice. The Frequency Code applies across languages and indeed across species: dogs threaten with a low-pitched growl, but submit with a high-pitched yelp. However, in practical terms, the Frequency Code difference between high and low vowels works for only a handful of words in each language. It is, after all, contradicted by the vowels in the very words *big* and *small* themselves!

Not only individual sounds but also certain combinations of sounds tend to go together with certain meanings. The *sn* combination in English often suggests something to do with breathing noises and the nose: *sniff, sneeze, snout, snot, sneer, snuff, snorkel, snooze, snore, snicker, snivel, snort, snuffle*. A person who goes round with their nose in the air might be *snooty*, *snub* people and a bit of a *snob*. Other combinations in English that suggest particular associations are:

- the *ip* words for 'light blows' (*nip, clip, dip, pip, yip*, etc.)
- the *sq* words connected with 'unpleasantness', 'liquid' and 'pressure' (*squeeze, squash, squishy, squelch* and, in my English, *squabby*)
- the *ous* words for 'smacking the lips' (*luscious, delicious, scrumptious, voluptuous*).

A group of 'ion' words is popular in the rhymes of reggae songs, *revolution, generation, appreciation, consideration, nation*, though it is not clear why this sound combination should be attractive. Indeed, academic speakers often share this preference; a recent talk emphasized *marketization, negotiation* and *theorization*.

Some idea of which sounds English speakers consider pleasant and unpleasant can be obtained from the names that science fiction writers invent for aliens. Classical hostile aliens have short aggressive names like *Kryptons*, *Vatch*, *Rull*, *Glotch* or *Perks*. Neutral-seeming or friendly aliens have polysyllabic names like *Alaree*, *animaloids*, *Osnomians*, *Voltiscians* and *Eladeldi*.

Nevertheless, despite the evocative role of sounds in poetry or indeed television advertising, direct or indirect links between sound and meaning are rare, as those who try to learn another language soon discover. Given the Persian words *mard* and *zan*, can you tell which means 'man' and which 'woman'? In fact *mard* is 'man', *zan* 'woman'. Of the Japanese words *minikui* and *kirei*, which means 'ugly' and which 'beautiful'? In fact *kirei* is 'beautiful'. The vast majority of the sounds of language have no necessary connection with the meaning of the words in which they are used.

Animal noises

One of the areas in which speech sounds might be expected to be closest to their meaning is when they are linked to actual noises. Here is a sample of familiar domestic and barnyard noises as portrayed in different languages:

	Cats	*Dogs*	*Sheep*	*Cows*	*Roosters*
English	meow	woof woof	baa	moo	cockadoo-dloo
Japanese	nyanya (*adult*) nyn-nyn (*kitten*)	oue-oue	mee	moo	kokekokou
Persian	meyu	wag-wag	baʔ baʔ	mâ mâ	gogoligogo
Hokkien	meow	wo-wo	meeehh	moo	kok-kok
Thai	meow	bog-bog (*little*) hong-hong (*big*)	bae	mor	ek-i-ek-ek
Greek	yiau	jav jav	bee	muu	cucuricuu
Spanish	miau	guau-guau	mee	muu	quíquiriqúi
Turkish	meau	hæv hæv	mee	moo	–
Dholuo	ywak	guu guu	meee	mboo	kokorioko
French	miaou	ouah ouah	bêêêh	meuh	cocorico
Korean	yow-ong	mong mong	meh-eh-eh	um-meh	cork-eeyo
German	miau-miau	wau-wau	baa-baa	muh-muh	kikeriki

Note: as these are mostly written in the Roman alphabet, they do not necessarily represent the spoken sounds accurately. Some, however were supplied with some phonetic letters to give a closer approximation.

Source: mostly Essex University students and staff.

LORETTE WILMOT LIBRARY
NAZARETH COLLEGE

II Intonation and its functions

However, despite the emotional overtones conveyed by a handful of speech sounds, the aspect of sound that is most associated with emotion is the intonation pattern – the way that the pitch of the voice rises or falls. Most people probably do not even consider intonation to be part of the sound system of language; it seems the natural way of speaking and conveying one's attitudes. Yet this resource is used in very different ways in different languages, which can cause serious misunderstandings between their speakers. This section looks at part of the intonation system of English, comparing it with the system in languages like Chinese.

1 The nuclear tones of English

The main element in intonation is the chief change of pitch, called the 'nuclear tone'. Let us start with the nuclear tones of RP English, using monosyllabic words. One possibility is for the pitch to start at a high level within the speaker's normal range and to fall to a low level over one or more syllables.

This is called a 'high-fall' tone and is represented for the purposes of analysing English by the tone-mark `, as in `yes. A high-fall tone often makes the speaker sound interested and involved in what he or she is saying:

A: Would you like a coffee?
B: `Yes!

Alternatively the pitch may rise from the bottom or middle to the top of the speaker's range – a high-rise tone, ', as in 'yes.

This might be an incredulous repetition:

A: Well he proposed and I said yes.
B: ʹYes?

There are also a pair of rise and fall tones in the lower part of the speaker's pitch range. A low-fall, ˎ, starts from the middle of the range and falls to low, as in ˎyes:

This often sounds definite and serious:

A: Am I all right, doctor?

B: ﹅Yes.

A low-rise, ′, on the other hand, starts low and rises to the middle of the speaker's range, as in ′*yes*:

This sounds cool and perhaps indifferent:

A: Can you help me?

B: ′Yes?

English has two more tones that change pitch direction rather than going continuously up or down. One is the sceptical-sounding fall-rise ˇ, as in ˇ*yes*.

y   s
    e

A: Do you agree?

B: ˇYes. There may be something in what you say.

The other is the enthusiastic-sounding rise-fall, ^, as in ^*yes*:

   e
y   s

A: Do you want to go to the Bahamas for Christmas?

B: ^Yes!

Finally there is a level mid or high tone, ˉ, which occurs less frequently than the others and is typically used for calling people, as in ˉ*cooee*.

cooee

This might be a mother calling a child from the garden.

Needless to say, a full account of English needs many features of intonation apart from these seven tones. In particular, it needs to describe the system for choosing which syllable to put the tone on, such as the difference between *Susan liked* ﹅*Joan*, *Susan* ﹅*liked Joan* and ﹅*Susan liked Joan*. Nor is there agreement that seven tones is the actual number required, some linguists reducing the seven tones to a two-way contrast between rise and fall, some elaborating them with additional patterns, such as the fall-rise-fall or the mid fall.

The ways in which speakers use these tones is even harder to pin down. A particular tone often goes with a particular grammatical type of sentence. `Jones with a high-fall is an answer to a question:

A: Who's that?
B: `Jones.

ʹJones with a low-rise is a polite 'checking' question:

A: ʹJones? You're next.

Sometimes, however, the tone forces the other person to reply in a particular way, as in 'tag' questions such as *did he?* or *aren't you?* added to sentences in conversation. *You're Peter,* `aren't you? has a high-fall on the tag `aren't you? which invites the person addressed to agree. *You're Peter,* ʹaren't you? with a high-rise on the tag ʹaren't you? leaves it open to them to agree or disagree.

Falling tones often suggest that what the person is talking about is accomplished fact. Consequently, in most languages, falls tend to be used at the end of the sentence. Rising tones suggest, on the other hand, that what the speaker is saying is still open to debate, and so they are less common towards the end of the sentence. English often shows continuity, i.e. that the sentence is *not* ending, by using a low-rise for phrases or clauses within the sentence and a high-fall to finish the sentence off: *On* ʹTuesday *I went to* `London has a low-rise on ʹTuesday at the end of the phrase but a high-fall on `London at the end of the sentence.

In many languages, rises are associated with questions, that is to say with uncertainty; indeed, the chief way of making a question in Greek and Portuguese is to use a statement with rising intonation. The almost universal tendency in human languages to regard falling tones as final and rising tones as tentative has been linked to the Frequency Code. In one experiment 92 per cent of listeners thought a steep final fall was more dominant. The lesson to be drawn is that speakers who want to sound authoritative should not use many rises or an overall high pitch.

In RP English, statements do not usually have rising tones. It is almost inconceivable to introduce oneself with a rising tone – *My name's* ʹPeter rather than *My name's* `Peter – as the rise would suggest doubts about one's very existence. Other accents of English, such as Belfast, Tyneside and New Zealand, however, use rises for factual statements without overtones of doubt. Indeed such rises with statements have started to be used by teenagers in Australia and the USA and by some 20-year-olds in London.

Often, however, English intonation has more to do with the speaker's attitude to what they are saying than with the sentence type. The explanations of the different intonation patterns of *yes* given above took advantage of this feature by ascribing particular emotional qualities to tones – interested high-fall `yes, incredulous high-rise ʹyes and so on. These emotional labels work reasonably well with some aspects of English intonation; yet clearly there is far more to expressing emotions than the choice of tone.

These patterns can be regularly heard in news bulletins. A typical news on the local radio had mostly falling tones, reflecting the factual nature of the news, ranging from the excited high-fall ˋ*Four people died* to the matter-of-fact low-fall *Tonight's top* ˎ*stories*. There were also examples of the rise-fall used for enthusiasm, *Hicks made an unbeaten* ˆ*century* and a succession of fall-rises used to show warning or emphasis, *Rush hour* ˇ*roads. The latest on the* ˇ*fires raging around Essex for the* ˇ*third day running*. The low-rise also occurred several times in the middle of the sentence, to link the parts together. Two of the above examples were preceded by low-rises: *England are bowled out for four hundred and* ˌ*forty but Hicks made an unbeaten* ˆ*century* – low-rise on ˌ*forty*, rise-fall on ˆ*century*; *Investigators investigated a light airplane*

Reading the football results

Newsreaders giving the results of football matches on UK television use a set pattern of intonation, presumably to help the viewers check their football pools coupon. The result of the match, whether a home win, an away win or a draw, can be guessed before the reader hears the score for the second team. Here are three incomplete readings: what was the outcome of each match? Home teams are read first.

A. ˋEverton ˌ1 ˋLiverpool . . .

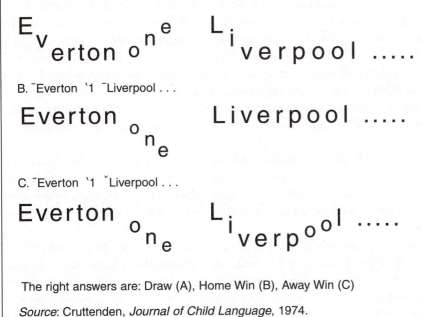

B. ˇEverton ˋ1 ˉLiverpool . . .

C. ˉEverton ˋ1 ˇLiverpool . . .

The right answers are: Draw (A), Home Win (B), Away Win (C)

Source: Cruttenden, *Journal of Child Language*, 1974.

crash in Hampshire in which ʹfour people died – low-rise on ʹHampshire, high-fall on ˋfour. Even if speakers of English are unconscious of it, the choice of intonation is crucial to the meaning they convey to others.

2 *Intonation across languages*

When learning another language, the emotional overtones of intonation often create difficulties. Speakers use intonation without thinking, and it seems to them the natural way of expressing their emotions. Though there are similarities across languages such as the rise/fall distinction, each language has an intonation system of its own. Certain intonation patterns are dangerous in that they convey something different in another language.

A person learning a second language may produce a perfectly plausible intonation for the new language but convey the wrong emotion. An overseas student used to say *Goodʹbye* to me with a dramatic high-fall, suggesting that she had been mortally offended. Similarly, ʹthank you with a low-rise may suggest that L2 speakers are casual and offhand when it is simply the normal polite intonation for saying 'thank you' in their own language.

While there are many other attributes to national stereotypes, intonation certainly makes a contribution. To the English, for example, Germans are serious, Italians are excitable, reflecting how they would react to an English person who spoke with their characteristic intonation patterns – high pitch by Italians, low-falls by Germans. An English newspaper finds, for instance, that Arnold Schwarzenegger speaks in a 'flat Austrian monotone'. In these cases the listener is interpreting the intonation as conveying the emotion that an English speaker would intend rather than as the transfer of features from a different intonation system. Unfortunately, native speakers of a language do not interpret a mistake in intonation as a foreigner's mistake, but regard it as a deliberate attempt to convey a particular emotion. Despite having taught intonation, I only realised *Goodʹbye* was an intonation mistake when the student said it every week.

For the most part, English intonation adds an overtone to a word rather than forming an integral part of it. ʹYes is *yes* plus polite interest; ʹJones is *Jones* plus polite query; ˋaren't you is *aren't you* plus demand for agreement. The meaning of the word itself does not change with the intonation pattern; *yes* is still *yes* whether it has a high-rise or a low-fall.

The function of intonation in 'tone' languages like Yoruba or Chinese is very different. In the Songjiang dialect of Chinese, for example, the syllable *di* can be pronounced with three different tones. ˋdi with a high-fall means 'low'; ˉdi with a level tone means 'bottom'; ʹdi with a high-rise means 'emperor'. The same sequence of sounds is three distinct words, depending on the tone used. The Chinese tone is an integral part of the word which distinguishes it from other words, rather than something that is tacked on to give a grammatical or emotional extra.

The fact that intonation in tone languages like Chinese shows differences between words rather than emotions and attitudes inevitably poses problems when its speakers come to learn a language such as English. Chinese learners may have difficulty in using intonation to convey emotional overtones in English, and hence their English may sound unvarying in emotion. Going the other way, English speakers may easily say the wrong Chinese word if they use the wrong tone: a person who went to a shop and asked for 'li zi (rising tone) would get pears; ˇli zi (fall-rise) would get plums and 'li zi (falling) chestnuts.

III Producing the sounds of speech

This section outlines the complex ways in which speech sounds are made, starting with vowels and going on to consonants. As some parts are unavoidably dense, it can partly be used as a reference source for later chapters rather than read straight through.

Even in languages with a writing system based on sounds, the letters of the alphabet reflect the sounds of speech rather poorly. English has a single *th* spelling in *thing* and *then* but two different 'th' sounds. It is therefore necessary to use a phonetic script that reflects the different sounds of speech more accurately than the usual written forms. So the English word *thing* is transcribed with a phonetic symbol for the 'th' sound /θ/, plus one for the vowel /ɪ/ and one for the final /ŋ/, i.e. /θɪŋ/. The word *then*, however, starts with the other 'th' sound /ð/, followed by an /e/, followed by a different nasal /n/, i.e. /ðen/.

The symbols of phonetic transcription are usually distinguished from normal writing by being put within slanted lines or square brackets: /kiː/ versus *key* or /men/ versus *men* (see pp. 79–80 for the difference between / / and [ ]). Since the reference point here is mostly English, the phonetic symbols are those conventionally used by linguists for describing English, found with slight variation in most dictionaries and guides to English pronunciation. While the context should usually make clear what the symbols refer to, lists of the phonetic symbols for English sounds are given on page 64 (vowels), 65 (diphthongs) and 69–70 (consonants). One minor difficulty is that British and American linguists have alternative symbols for some of the sounds of English, for example /a/ versus /ɒ/ for the vowel of *hot* and /š/ versus /ʃ/ for the first consonant of *shed*.

The symbols for English ultimately relate to the phonetic alphabet laid down by the International Phonetic Association (IPA), which was devised 100 years ago to provide a means of writing down the sounds of all languages in a consistent fashion and has been revised many times since. A chart of the full IPA system is given on page 286 to refer to for non-English sounds. The figures for the languages of the world in this chapter are based on those calculated by Ian Maddiesen from a sample of 317 representative languages in the UCLA Segment Inventory Database (UPSID). The percentages for particular features refer to this sample rather than to all the languages known to exist.

The major division of speech sounds is between the ways in which vowels and consonants are produced. In vowel sounds, the air comes out of the mouth without any obstruction from the tongue, lips, etc. – the /ɑ:/ in *spa* or the /i:/ in *tea*. In consonant sounds, the smooth air-flow through the mouth is obstructed in some way by the tongue or lips – the /t/ of *tie* or the /f/ and /ʃ/ of *fish*. This definition of vowels as unobstructed and consonants as obstructed works for most speech sounds, though it leaves a few doubtful cases, such as the /w/ in *win,* which is produced like a vowel without obstruction but acts like a consonant in occurring at the beginning of the syllable rather than in the middle.

1 Vowels

As well as having smoothly flowing air, a vowel involves 'voice' produced by the 'vocal cords' in the throat. These are flaps in the larynx which open and close rapidly during speech to let out puffs of air, producing a basic vibrating noise, in much the same way as a saxophone reed is vibrated by blowing through it. How fast the vocal cords vibrate affects the pitch of the sound; the individual vibrations can be felt in very slow speech. This subsection deals with 'pure' vowels which have a continuous sound; 'diphthongs', in which the sound changes, are described in later sections.

The two dimensions of tongue position

The sound produced by vibration is modified by the size and shape of the air spaces through which it then passes. A baritone saxophone produces a deeper note than a soprano saxophone because its internal air space is far larger. The characteristic sound can be changed within limits by making temporary adjustments to the permanent air space; saxophone players alter the length of the air space inside the saxophone tube with their fingering to change the note that comes out.

In the same way, speaking modifies the space inside the mouth by altering the position of the tongue. When the tongue is towards the front of the mouth, the empty space takes a particular overall shape, thus affecting the sound. The sounds produced with the tongue towards the front of the mouth are called 'front' vowels, for instance /e/ (*men*) and /æ/ (*man*). When the tongue is moved towards the back of the mouth, a different-shaped air space is created, producing 'back' vowels, such as /u:/ (*loot*) or /ɒ/ (*lot*). In between the front and back positions of the tongue come 'central' sounds, such as the /ə:/ vowel (*bird*). All vowels vary in a dimension from the front to the back of the mouth.

The 'height' of the tongue also affects the air space in the mouth. The /ɪ/ in *sit*, the /e/ in *set* and the /æ/ in *sat* are all front sounds but differ in height. When the tongue is raised towards the roof of the mouth, a 'high' vowel is produced like /ɪ/ (*sit*) and /u:/ (*root*). When the tongue is lowered towards the bottom of the mouth, 'low' vowels are produced such as /æ/ (*sat*). In between come 'mid' vowels such as /e/ (*Ben*) or /ə:/ (*firm*). Much of the variation in vowels amounts to changes in the position of the tongue in the two dimensions from front to back and from high to low.

The space inside the mouth can be represented abstractly as a box with two dimensions. To describe a vowel means deciding on the highest point of the tongue as specified by these two dimensions: /u:/ (*moon*) is a back high vowel as the tongue is highest at the back: /æ/ (*cat*) is a front low vowel because the highest point of the tongue is at the front and slightly above the bottom; /ə:/ (*fur*) is a mid central vowel because the tongue is in the middle in both dimensions; and so on. It is not just the maximum height that affects the sound but the whole modification of the air space within the mouth that this entails. While the point of maximum height is a convenient reference point for specifying any vowel, this specifies the shape of the whole mouth cavity rather than itself being crucial.

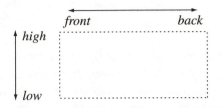

All vowels can be located somewhere within this two-dimensional space.

Often, to make the description easier, the two dimensions are each divided into three areas and the front of the diagram is slanted to correspond better to the shape at the front of the mouth:

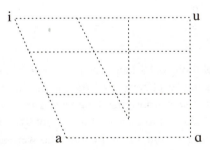

To make the locations within this space precise, the different points on the perimeter are assigned 'cardinal vowels', rather like the points of the compass. The cardinal vowels are theoretical rather than having an actual existence in any language. The most extreme close and high vowel that the human mouth could possibly produce is cardinal [i], the most extreme close and back (and rounded) vowel is cardinal [u], the extreme front and open is cardinal [a] and the extreme back and open is cardinal [ɑ]. Other cardinal vowels are provided for each of the reference points on the perimeter and for rounded versus unrounded vowels. Thus any vowel in any language can be located with reference to this grid. English /i:/ *bee* for example is near to cardinal /i/ while English /ɒ/ *dog* is at the back, a fraction above cardinal /ɑ/. The diagram shown below also gives the approximate positions of the RP /u:/ (*moon*) and /æ/ (*pat*). The

RP 'pure' vowels are given in full in the diagram in the box on page 65. This diagram is as abstract as representing the solar system as rings round the Sun.

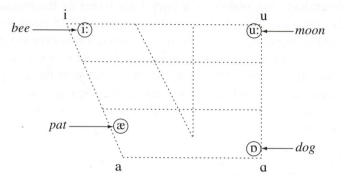

A language needs to make its different vowels contrast by spreading them around these two dimensions. The greatest contrast is between vowels that are as close as possible to the opposite corners of the vowel space – as far back or front as possible and as high or low as possible. The minimal vowel system for a language takes advantage of these contrasts by having three vowels, one high front vowel /i/, one high back vowel /u/ and one central low vowel /a/ (closest perhaps to the starting-point of the English diphthongs /aɪ/ *buy* and /aʊ/ *cow*), which can be shown in a triangular shape, with the two-dimensional box now understood rather than drawn.

i   u

a

Counting 'pure' vowels rather than diphthongs, 18 languages in UPSID have *only* three vowels, mostly conforming to this triangular pattern of /i/, /u/ and /a/, for example Arabic, Greenland Inuit and Dyirbal, an Australian Aboriginal language. The vast majority of languages incorporate these three vowels within their sound system; 91.5 per cent have an /i/ sound, 88 per cent an /a/ and 83.9 per cent an /u/. People who were asked to distinguish /i/ from /u/ in an experiment only made two mistakes out of 10 000 attempts, suggesting that these two sounds are indeed as different as they could possibly be.

Going from the minimum number of vowels to the maximum, some languages have up to 24 vowels; 13 languages in UPSID have 17 or more. The most common number of vowels in a language is in fact five. Greek, like many languages, gets five by adding two mid vowels to the three-vowel triangle: /i/ *zari* ('dice'), /u/ *uranós* ('sky'), /a/ *agapi* ('pure love'), /e/ *erhome* ('come'), /o/ *violi* ('violin'). Other languages with a five-vowel system of similar types are Japanese, Spanish, Zulu and Basque.

i   u

e   o

a

Lip shape in vowels

Changing the shape of the lips is another way of modifying the sound that comes out. English front vowels like /i:/ (*see*) are made with unrounded lips, while back vowels like /u:/ (*ooze*) require the lips to be rounded. Though there is no logical reason why back vowels should be rounded and front vowels should not, front vowels are in fact unrounded in 94 per cent of languages, back vowels rounded in 93.5 per cent. Even by the age of 4 months, babies are able to tell that /i/ requires spread lips and /u/ rounded lips.

Two familiar exceptions are the rounded front vowels in the /y/ vowel of French *rue* ('street') and the German vowel /y:/ *Hüte* ('hat'). It is an odd coincidence that French and German from different branches of European languages both have this rare feature found in only 6 per cent of languages, at least one excuse for the difficulty they pose for English students.

Length

The sounds of speech also differ in terms of how long they take to produce – 'length'. A long sound is indicated in phonetic script by a following colon :. In a few languages consonants differ in terms of length. For example, in Slovak *vrch* /vr̥x/ ('summit') has a short /r/ but *vŕšok* /vr̥:ʃok/ ('hill') has a long /r:/. In Finnish short /l/ as in /veli/ ('brother') differs from long /l:/ as in /vel:i/ ('gruel').

More commonly, languages use length to distinguish vowels. The /i:/ of *bean* is long while the /ɪ/ of *bin* is short: the /u:/ of *moon* long but the /ʊ/ of *wood* short. Length effectively doubles the number of potential vowels by having pairs of long and short at a particular point in the vowel space. A five-vowel triangular system becomes a ten-vowel system by using length as an additional factor, for example in Hawaiian.

Other factors are often tied in with length. In the long /i:/ of English *beat*, the tongue position is also slightly higher and fronter than in its short counterpart, the /ɪ/ of *bit*, and the muscles of the lips and tongue are slightly more tense. Similar slight differences are found in other long/short pairs such as the long relaxed /ɔ:/ in *dawn* versus the short tense /ɒ/ in *don*, one reason why different symbols are used for the two vowels /i:/ *beat* and /ɪ/ *bit* as well as the length marker :.

The vowels that have been described so far are all stationary in that the tongue keeps more or less the same position however long they are said. Technically the name for this is a 'pure' vowel. Some languages have more pure vowels, some fewer. Korean has 18 vowels, 16 of which are pairs of long and short; !Xu, a southern African language spoken in the Kalahari desert region, has no fewer than 24 pure vowels. RP has 11 or 12 pure vowels, depending whether the long /ə:/ of *bird* is counted as a different vowel from the short /ə/ of *asleep*, known as 'schwa', which only occurs in unstressed syllables. Indeed in some transcription systems the vowel of *bird* is given a separate symbol /ɜ:/.

English 'pure' vowels (RP)

	Short, tense	Long, relaxed
Front high	/ɪ/ *kin*	/iː/ *keen*
Back high	/ʊ/ *foot*	/uː/ *boot*
Back mid	/ɒ/ *boss*	/ɔː/ *bore*
Mid front	/e/ *bet*	
Mid central	/ə/ <u>*about*</u>	/əː/ *bird* (sometimes given as /ɜː/)
Front low	/æ/ *bat*	
Low central	/ʌ/ *but*	
Low back		/ɑː/ *bath*

Diphthongs

Diphthongs are a type of vowel in which the tongue moves from one vowel position to another while the vowel is being produced. The vowel sound is not the same at the beginning as at the end. The method of describing diphthongs is to state their starting-point and the destination towards which they move (but do not necessarily reach). In the English /ɔɪ/ of *toy* the starting-point of the tongue is the back mid position, the destination towards the front high /ɪ/ position, as in:

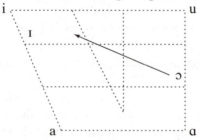

In the English /əʊ/ of *go*, however, the tongue starts centrally and moves back and up towards the /ʊ/ position.

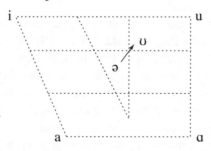

Because diphthongs involve movement, it is impossible to produce them continuously; the listener ends up hearing only the second vowel. RP has seven or eight diph-

English diphthongs

Moving towards front high /ɪ/	/eɪ/ *lane*	/aɪ/ *line*	/ɔɪ/ *loin*
Moving towards back high /ʊ/	/əʊ/ *cone*	/aʊ/ *cow*	
Moving towards central /ə/	/ɪə/ *beer*	/ɛə/ *bear*	/ʊə/ *sure* (in some people's speech)

thongs, depending whether a speaker pronounces words like *poor* with a diphthong /ʊə/ or with the same /ɔ:/ sound as in *paw*.

While the figures for diphthongs in the world's languages are not very certain, the commonest seem to be /eɪ/ and /aʊ/, the rarest /ɔɪ/. The language with the highest number is !Xu with 22.

Pure vowels and diphthongs are two varieties of vowel that differ only in whether the tongue moves. Despite its overtones in ordinary language, the word 'pure' is in phonetics a technical term for a continuous sound made without the tongue moving and without other obstruction. Indeed some 'posh' British accents tend to turn pure vowels into diphthongs; *bed* is /beᵊd/ with a suggestion of an *er* /ə/ coming in rather than /bed/, *bad* is /baᵊd/ and so on.

English vowels around the world

Here are the vowels of RP English located within the cardinal vowels diagram. The vowels outside the figure are the cardinal vowels themselves.

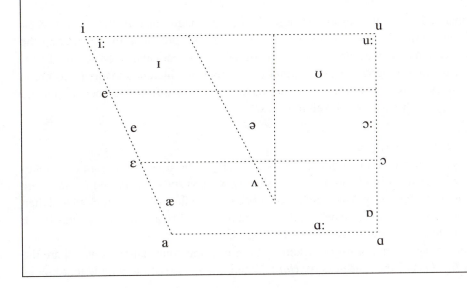

The following chart comparing the RP vowels with other accents of English is based on John Wells, *Accents of English*. It gives the pronunciation for various test words having 'pure' vowels in the different accents; it disguises many differences in pronunciation, particularly the effects of /r/, to be discussed in Chapter 8.

	UK RP	Australia	South Africa	Jamaica	Ireland	General American	Canada
fleece	/iː/	/iː/	/iː/	/iː/	/iː/	/i/	/i/
kit	/ɪ/	/ɪ/	/ɪ/ /ə/	/ɪ/	/ɪ/	/ɪ/	/ɪ/
dress	/e/	/e/	/e/	/ɛ/	/ɛ/	/ɛ/	/ɛ/
trap	/æ/	/æ/	/æ/	/a/	/æ/	/æ/	/æ/
strut	/ʌ/	/ʌ/	/ʌ/	/ʌ/	/ʌ/	/ʌ/	/ʌ/
nurse	/ə/	/ə/	/ə/	/ʌ/ /ʌr/ /ər/	/ʌr/ /ɛr/	/ər/	/ər/
bath	/ɑː/	/aː/	/ɑː/	/aː/	/æ/ /aː/	/æ/	/æ/
palm	/ɑː/	/aː/	/ɑː/	/aː/	/aː/	/ɑ/	/ɑ/
lot	/ɒ/	/ɒ/	/ɒ/	/a/ /ɒ/	/ɒ/	/ɑ/	/ɑ/
cloth	/ɒ/	/ɒ/	/ɒ/	/aː/ /ɔː/	/ɒ/ /ɔː/	/ɔ/	/ɑ/
thought	/ɔː/	/ɔː/	/ɔː/	/aː/ /ɔː/	/ɔː/	/ɔ/	/ɑ/
foot	/ʊ/	/ʊ/	/ʊ/	/ʊ/	/ʊ/	/ʊ/	/ʊ/
goose	/uː/	/uː/	/uː/	/uː/	/uː/	/u/	/u/

Source: Wells, *Accents of English*

2 Consonants

Consonants differ from vowels because the lips or tongue disturb the stream of air rather than letting it flow out smoothly. Since they are produced by obstructing the air, this section describes where the obstruction is – lips, teeth and so on –, what forms the obstruction – tongue, lips, etc. –, and the manner in which it is made. In common with vowels, consonants may, but do not have to, use voice from the vocal cords and may be said with tense or relaxed muscles.

Plosive consonants

One method of producing a consonant is to interrupt the flow of air from the mouth by blocking it for a brief moment. Consonants such as /b/ in *brain* and /k/ in *crane* are known as 'stop' or 'plosive' consonants because the flow of air is stopped and then 'explodes' abruptly out from behind the obstruction. English plosive consonants block the air at three different places, shown in Fig. 4.2.

When the air is temporarily blocked by both lips, the consonants produced are the voiced /b/ (*lab*) or the voiceless /p/ (*lap*). When it is the tip of the tongue that blocks

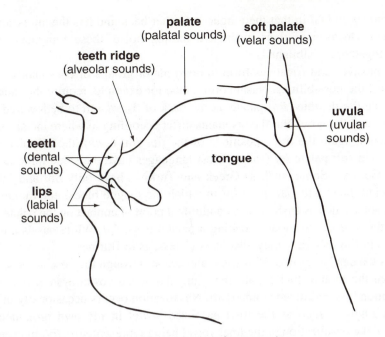

Fig. 4.2 Reference points for the production of consonants

the air by contacting the ridge behind the teeth (the 'alveolar ridge'), the consonants are the voiced /d/ (*dime*) or voiceless /t/ (*time*). Placing the back of the tongue against the back of the roof of the mouth (the 'soft palate' or 'velum') produces the voiced sound /g/ (*get*) or the voiceless /k/ (*kid*).

The six English plosives come in three pairs of voiced and voiceless /t/ /d/, /k/ /g/, /p/ /b/. The voiceless member of the pair is usually said more energetically than the voiced member. So the /b/ in *Bart* is not only voiced compared to the /p/ in *part* but is also said with less energy. The English plosives use three points of contact – the lips, the alveolar ridge behind the teeth and the soft palate. According to UPSID, all languages have at least two of these contacts for plosives and 98.4 per cent of languages have all three. A few languages use other contact points: Tamil has a dental plosive using the teeth rather than the more usual teeth ridge, Arabic a uvular plosive /q/ at the far back of the mouth as in *qal* /qa:l/ ('he said').

Fricatives and other consonants
The second major method of producing consonants is to let the air escape through a narrow gap rather than blocking it completely – 'fricative' sounds. English fricatives involve three of the same places of contact as plosives: the lips and teeth, /v/ (*live*) and /f/ (*life*), the back of the teeth, /ð/ (*this*) and /θ/ (*thick*) and the teeth ridge, /z/ (*rise*) and /s/ (*sip*). In addition the fricatives /ʒ/ (*garage*) and /ʃ/ (*fish*) use the teeth ridge, but

differ from /z/ and /s/ in that the tongue is further back and lets the air escape over a larger area. Because of their distinctive hissing noise, these four are sometimes grouped together as 'sibilants'.

While plosives and fricatives form the two major groups of consonants, this does not exhaust the possibilities. Nasal consonants, for example, require the mouth to be blocked and the flexible 'soft palate' at the back of the mouth to be lowered to force air out through the nose. Nasal consonants differ according to where the air is held up in the mouth, again the three positions of the lips /m/ (*sum*), the alveolar ridge /n/ (*sun*) and the soft palate /ŋ/ (*sung*). Most languages have the same three nasals, for example German. Some, such as Greek and Turkish, have only /m/ and /n/; a few, such as Inuit, have a uvular nasal /N/ in which the tongue blocks the mouth right at the back; some, such as Irish, have an additional point of contact on the palate halfway back on the roof of the mouth, making a palatal nasal /ɲ/. While nasals are usually voiced, as in English, they may also be voiceless, as in Burmese.

Vowels too can be 'nasalized' if some air escapes through the nose at the same time as through the mouth. In Bengali, the triangular seven-vowel system is doubled at each position by a nasalized counterpart. Nasalization occurs occasionally in isolated words of English, such as the final nasalized vowel in my own pronunciation of *restaurant*, the nasalization in the final vowel being represented as /õ/. In French such vowels are far more frequent. Syllable-final /n/ was lost in many French words but replaced by nasalization of the final vowel of the syllable – *fin* ('end'), *son* ('his'), *rien* ('nothing').

So it is not just the English plosives that make use of the same four points but also the fricatives and nasals. All the points of contact have two or more of the sounds that are possible, divided into pairs of voiced and voiceless, apart from the nasals. Laying out the English sounds in four columns, however, shows up some gaps. For example, there is no pair of voiced and voiceless velar fricatives at the soft palate to parallel those at the other three places. German fills this gap with the fricative sound /x/ in *Tuch* ('towel'); Greek with the /x/ sound of /efxaristo/ ('thank you').

The four columns of the table conceal further possible sounds that do not happen to occur in English. The English fricatives /f/ and /v/ involve the bottom lip and the upper teeth (labiodental) rather than both lips together (bilabial): so the fricatives /f/ and /v/ do not match the lip plosives /p/ and /b/ in the same way that the fricatives /s/ and /z/ match the plosives /t/ and /d/. So, not surprisingly, some languages have bilabial fricatives. Greek, for instance, has a voiced fricative /β/ involving both lips in words like *biblio* ('book').

The other possibility concealed by the English chart is the existence of a fifth column for sounds made on the roof of the mouth itself, the 'palate'. Many languages have such palatal consonants. Greek has a palatal fricative /ç/ in words like /stiço/ ('ghost'). French has a palatal nasal /ɲ/ in /aɲo/ *agneau* ('lamb'). Irish has both a fricative palatal /ç/ in /içə/ *oíche* ('night') and a nasal palatal in words such as /aɲir/ *ainir* ('maiden').

The main English consonants

	Voice	**Lips** (labial sounds)	**Teeth** (dental sounds)	**Teeth ridge** (alveolar sounds)	**Soft palate** (velar sounds)
Plosive	−voice	/p/ *pan*		/t/ *tar*	/k/ *can*
	+ voice	/b/ *buy*		/d/ *die*	/g/ *guy*
Fricative	−voice	/f/ *fin*	/θ/ *thin*	/s/ *seal* /ʃ/ *shin*	
	+ voice	/v/ *van*	/ð/ *than*	/z/ *zeal* /ʒ/ *garage*	
Nasal	+ voice	/m/ *lame*		/n/ *lane*	/ŋ/ *long*

The missing fricatives occasionally occur in isolated words of English, either in words like *loch* or in foreign words such as *Bach*. Sometimes they occur as an accidental combination of consonants in words like *huge* or *Hume,* where the /h/ and the /j/ can coalesce as a single palatal fricative [ç]. English has not always lacked these fricatives. Up to around 1400 AD there was a velar fricative /x/ in words such as *daughter* and *through*. The *gh* letter combination that stood for this sound has posed a problem for English spelling ever since /x/ was lost from the spoken language.

A sixth column is also required for sounds that are made by tongue contact even further back in the mouth, 'uvular' sounds. One example is the voiceless plosive /q/ found in Arabic *qal* /qaːl/ ('he said').

The English four-column layout also implies that dental fricatives like the English /ð/ and /θ/ in *this* and *third* are typical. In fact this pair are found in comparatively few languages, unvoiced /θ/ in 18 per cent and voiced /ð/ in 21 per cent of the UPSID sample. Hence they pose a problem for nearly all overseas students of English.

As well as these main types of consonant, there are several minor types, illustrated in English by:

- the 'lateral' /l/ of *lust*, made by keeping the tongue in contact with one side of the teeth ridge only – the only English case where the left/right third dimension matters for speech sounds. Most languages have a single lateral sound, like English; some have two, one at the alveolar ridge, one at the palate, for example Italian and Brazilian Portuguese. Japanese has no laterals, hence the confusion of /l/ and /r/ *lubbish* for *rubbish* by Japanese speakers of English. A Japanese student at Essex university explained to his neighbours 'I'm a Buddhist. Do you mind if I pray at the same time each day?'; a few weeks later they asked him why they never heard the sound of his flute if, as a flautist, he was playing it every day. Welsh has two types of /l/, one a voiceless fricative /ɬ/ as in *pill* (piece of poetry), the other a voiced lateral /l/ as in *pel* ('ball').

- the 'affricates' /tʃ/ (*cheat*) and /dʒ/ (*just*), which combine a plosive and a sibilant fricative, i.e. the /tʃ/ of *cheat* is a combination of the /t/ of *tin* with the /ʃ/ of *shin*.
- the complex /r/ sounds in *red* and *very*. In RP these are often like vowels in that they involve little or no tongue contact. They are idiosyncratic compared to many languages of the world which have varieties of /r/ that are rolled and trilled or that involve contact between the tongue and the roof or back of the mouth, such as the uvular /ʁ/ found in French *rouge* ('red'). The use of /r/ varies from one dialect of English to another, particularly between England and the United States, as we see in Chapter 8. Hence, unlike most other phonetic symbols, /r/ refers to a 'family' of related sounds rather than uniquely referring to a single sound.
- the peculiar fricative /h/ of *hot*, made by breathing out noisily before a vowel. The sound of /h/ then varies according to the vowel that follows it. Pronouncing words like *hat* with an /h/ as /hæt/ rather than as /æt/ is a marker of class in England, though not in most of the rest of the English-speaking world, again to be discussed in Chapter 8.
- the 'approximants' /w/ (*wish*) and /j/ (*yet*). These behave like consonants in coming at the beginning of syllables but are produced like vowels without contact.
- the cough-like glottal stop [ʔ] produced by keeping the vocal cords shut for a moment, thus creating a plosive. In some accents of English a glottal stop is an alternative form of /t/ between vowels. *Better* in my own speech is often /beʔə/ rather than /betə/, as it is for 27 per cent of the *Inside Language* panel (Q8). The glottal stop functions as a fully-fledged sound in many languages rather than an alternative pronunciation, for example in Hebrew and Burmese.

The consonants of English

	Voice	**Labial**	**Dental**	**Alveolar**	**Velar**	**Other**
Plosives:	– voice	/p/ pin		/t/ tin	/k/ kin	
	+ voice	/b/ bin		/d/ din	/g/ gun	
Fricatives:	– voice	/f/ fun	/θ/ think	/ʃ/ shut /s/ seal		/h/ hit
	+ voice	/v/ vista	/ð/ that	/ʒ/ rouge /z/ zeal		
Affricates:	– voice			/tʃ/ church		
	+ voice			/dʒ/ judge		
Nasals:	+ voice	/m/ man		/n/ nice	/ŋ/ rang	
Lateral:						/l/ lip
Approximants:						/j/ yes
						/w/ wet
r sounds						/r/ red

Putting all these together, English has 24 consonants, close to the average 22.8 for a language. The proportion of consonants to vowels is 1.27 to one, slightly low compared to the world average of 2.5 to one; that is to say, proportionately English has rather more vowels than the average.

IV Air and speech

So far this chapter has taken it for granted that the air for speech is produced by the lungs breathing out. In order for speech to be regular, this lung air has to come out at a fairly constant pressure, regulated by complex muscles in the diaphragm and the ribcage. Otherwise speech would be high in pitch just after speakers breathe in and would tail away to low pitch as they go on – this effect can easily be seen if you try reading a long sentence aloud on one breath.

No languages seem to use indrawn breath for normal speech. There are, however, occasions when it is used to disguise the speaker's voice. Suitors serenading their loves are said to use indrawn air in some parts of the Philippines and in German-speaking Switzerland in order to preserve their anonymity. English has a minor non-speech use of indrawn breath in the sound made when one burns oneself accidentally.

The lungs are not the only source of moving air. Southern African languages such as Nama and Zulu use sounds called 'clicks' produced by the tongue sucking air into the mouth; they will be familiar to listeners to music from this region such as the Xhosa click songs of Miriam Makeba. English has some marginal non-speech clicks, for instance the *giddyup* noise made to horses or the *tut-tut* noise of disapproval.

Timing of voice in consonants

Voice has been treated thus far in a simplified fashion as either 'on' or 'off': either the vocal cords vibrate, as in /ʃ/ (*ship*) or they do not, as in /t/ (*tip*). A crucial factor, however, is the moment at which voicing starts during the production of the consonant.

Take the voiced plosive /g/ in *gate* and its voiceless counterpart /k/ in *Kate*. The precise moment when voicing starts is called the 'Voice Onset Time' or VOT, timed in milliseconds (msec) relative to the actual moment of release of the air. Thus voice can start *before* the moment when the consonant is released, termed negative or −VOT, *at* the moment of release, 0 VOT, or *after* the moment of release, positive or +VOT. The Voice Onset Time for English /g/ therefore varies from about −88 msec before the stop is released to nearly the same moment as the release, −21 msec. The sound /g/ is heard as voiced so long as the speaker starts voicing within these time limits (see Figures 4.3 and 4.4).

Tongue-twisters

The point of a tongue-twister is to confuse the language system in the mind by repeating related sounds over and over again.

Mrs Pipple Popple popped a pebble in poor Polly Pepper's eye.
Charlie chooses cheese and cherries.
Old oily Ollie oils oily automobiles.
He ran from the Indes to the Andes in his undies.
Rubber baby buggy bumpers.
Shave a cedar shingle thin.
This thistle seems like that thistle.
Unique New York!
Miss Ruth's red roof thatch.
Peggy Babcock.
Toy boat.
Any noise annoys an oyster but a noisy noise annoys an oyster most.

Tongue-twisters in different languages

Tres tristes tigres trillaron trigo en un trigal. (Spanish: 'Three sad tigers threshed wheat in a wheatfield')
Nama-mugi, nama-gome, nama-tamago. (Japanese: 'Raw wheat, raw rice, raw eggs')
Le ver vert va vers le verre vert. (French: 'The green grub goes to the green glass')
Nie pieprz wieprza pieprzem. (Polish: 'Do not pepper the hog with pepper')
Un limon, mezzo limon (Italian: 'One lemon, half a lemon')

Surrealistic aphorisms by Marcel Duchamp

Abominables fourrures abdominales. ('Abominable abdominal furs')
My niece is cold because my knees are cold.
Etrangler l'étranger. ('Strangle the stranger')

Examples invented for a competition by 9-year-old children in Ardleigh, a village in Essex

Supersonic sausages.
The stranger strangles Susey with some long stretchy string.
Tongue-twisters give me blisters.
Bob and Bill brought bits.
My monkey mistakes my mum's messy mixture for a monkey.
Trees with green leaves.

Clearly not all the children have understood how a tongue-twister works.

Main source: A. Schwartz, *A Twister of Twists*, . . .

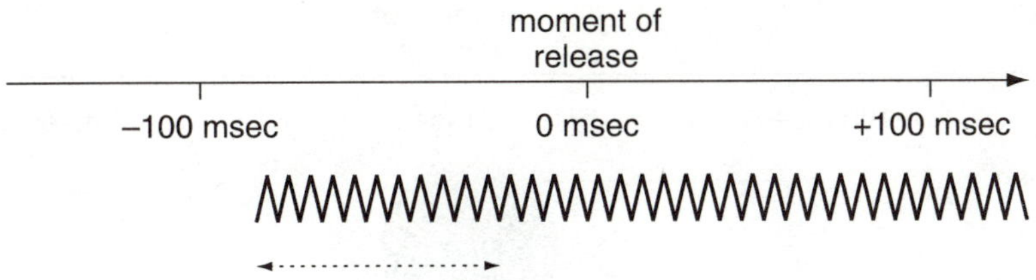

moment of
release

−100 msec   0 msec   +100 msec

MWWWWWWWWWWWWWWWWWW

◄·····················►

Fig. 4.3 Voice Onset Time in English /g/

In the voiceless English plosive /k/, voicing starts around +80 msec *after* the stop is released, that is to stay voicing does not start till a fraction of a second after the release, thus creating a characteristic puff of air after the consonant before the next vowel starts, known as 'aspiration'.

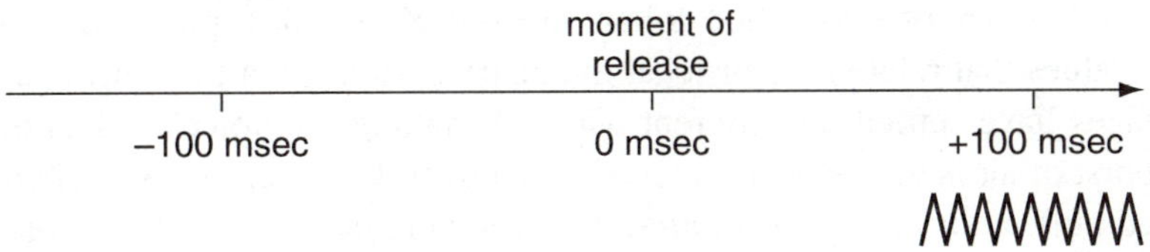

moment of
release

−100 msec   0 msec   +100 msec

MWWWWM

Fig. 4.4 Voice Onset Time in English /k/

A stop with a delay in voicing of +80 msec will be heard as voiceless. An early VOT makes the listener hear a voiced plosive, a late VOT a voiceless plosive. Voice Onset Time varies between languages. A Spanish /g/ such as *gato* ('cat') resembles an English /g/ in that voicing starts earlier than for /k/ with a Voice Onset Time of −108 msec. But the voiceless /k/ *queso* ('cheese') has a Voice Onset Time simultaneous with the release, +29 msec, rather than much after it, +80 msec (see Figs. 4.5 and 4.6).

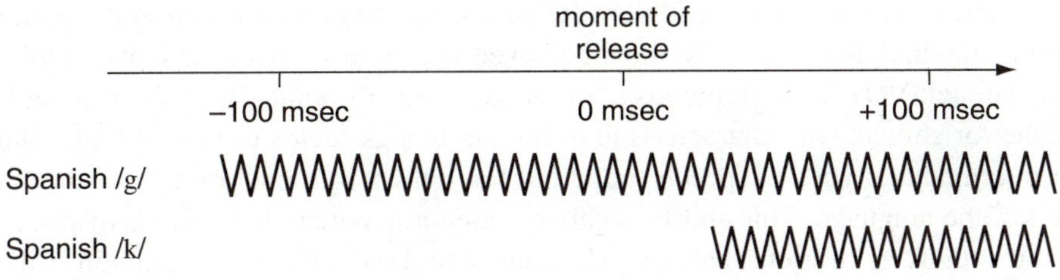

moment of
release

−100 msec   0 msec   +100 msec

Spanish /g/   MWWWWWWWWWWWWWWWWWWWWWWW

Spanish /k/   MWWWWWWWWM

Fig. 4.5 Voice Onset Time in Spanish stops (/g/ and /k/)

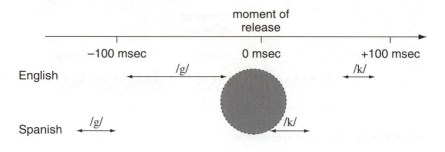

Fig. 4.6 Overlap of English /g/ and Spanish /k/

Consequently Spanish does not have the wide tolerance in VOT for /g/ allowed in English. An English person may take a Spanish /k/ to be a /g/; a Spanish person take some English /g/s to be /k/s, seen in the overlap in Fig. 4.6.

The two languages both use voice to distinguish sounds but they use it differently, just as, while there are objects called dollars in Hong Kong, Singapore and New York, these have values that relate to their local monetary systems, not to a universal value. The languages have settled on different ways of making the voice distinction. This voiceless burst of air is in a sense accidental in English. A /p/ before a vowel will have an aspirated puff of air after it, as in *pit*; a /p/ following /s/ may not, as in *spit*. Using too much aspiration or too little will not interfere with the meaning of the sentence.

However, in languages such as Hindi there are two different sounds, one with, one without aspiration – /pʰəl/ (fruit) and /pəl/ (moment). Potentially there is a three-way distinction between early VOT, 0 VOT and late VOT, rather than the two-way choice of late and early VOT found in Spanish. Thai and Burmese also have three distinct sounds at the dental position.

The idea that speakers of a language divide up sounds into either/or distinctions leads to a general characteristic of languages: speakers perceive speech sounds as distinct categories rather than as continuous variation. A sound is either a /g/ or a /k/, never something in between. Experiments have tested how people perceive synthesized sounds that gradually increase in VOT. It is not that there are two areas within which people are certain of which sound is involved and a grey area in the middle where they are uncertain. Instead they are committed to one sound up to the particular point at which they switch to the other, even if they differ over the location of this point. Though VOT is a continuous scale, it has a cut-off point where the listener has an either/or choice. One characteristic of human beings seems to be that they cannot hear intermediate types of speech sound but force them into one or other of the categories of the language. This ability is called 'categorial perception', that is to say, perceiving sounds as discrete 'categories' rather than as a continuous variation. Like a piano defining 85 notes from a vast range, the human mind perceives sounds as separate items.

How to make speech sounds

To make most (i.e. not all) speech sounds:

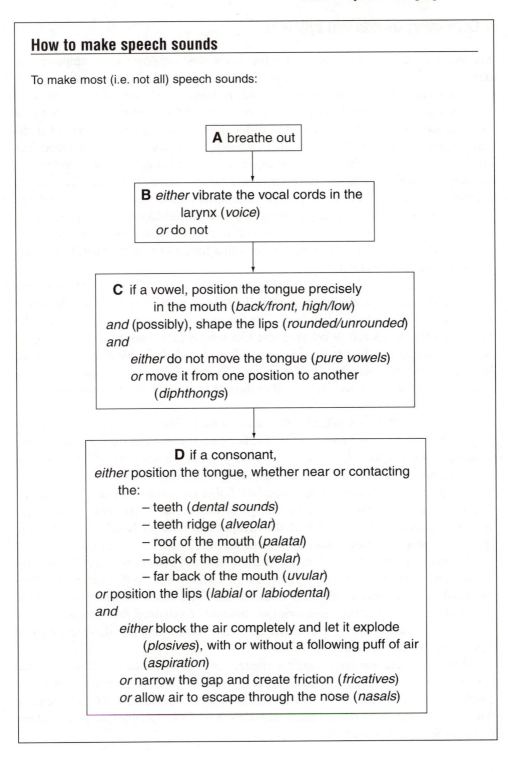

A breathe out

B *either* vibrate the vocal cords in the larynx (*voice*)
or do not

C if a vowel, position the tongue precisely
in the mouth (*back/front, high/low*)
and (possibly), shape the lips (*rounded/unrounded*)
and
either do not move the tongue (*pure vowels*)
or move it from one position to another
(*diphthongs*)

D if a consonant,
either position the tongue, whether near or contacting
the:
– teeth (*dental sounds*)
– teeth ridge (*alveolar*)
– roof of the mouth (*palatal*)
– back of the mouth (*velar*)
– far back of the mouth (*uvular*)
or position the lips (*labial* or *labiodental*)
and
either block the air completely and let it explode
(*plosives*), with or without a following puff of air
(*aspiration*)
or narrow the gap and create friction (*fricatives*)
or allow air to escape through the nose (*nasals*)

V Combining sounds into syllables

Suppose you had to decide on a name for a new washing powder. A computer produces a list of possible names: *Mrah, Bliff, Bnill*. Which would you choose?

Though each of the sounds in these words is English, only one of the words is in fact possible, namely *Bliff*. For this is the only one of the three that conforms to the rules for making English syllables. The differences between the words are not in the actual sounds, all of which are possible in English, but in how they are combined. The crucial element for combining sounds together is the syllable. This section looks at the ways in which syllables are constructed, which varies from one language to another. Syllables have centres, usually vowels; they have beginnings and endings, usually consonants. Sounds vary between the more vowel-like ones that occur in the centre of the syllable where the airstream is least obstructed and the more consonant-like ones that occur at the beginning or end that have most obstruction, technically called the 'sonority hierarchy'.

In English the centre of every syllable must be a vowel (V), including both pure vowels and diphthongs. So the minimal syllable is a vowel V on its own – the /aɪ/ of *eye* or the /ə/ of the article *a* in *a book*. The few exceptions without a vowel are syllables where the nasals and /l/ behave more like vowels than consonants by occupying complete syllables of their own, as in *bottom* /bɒtm̩/ or *bubble* /bʌbl̩/; hence these are known as 'syllabic consonants'. Most languages indeed require a syllable to have a vowel. Slovak, however, uses /r/ and /l/ as the centre of syllables, for example in *vrch* /vr̩x/ ('summit') and *vlk* /vl̩k/ ('wolf').

All languages also have syllables with a Consonant–Vowel (CV) structure, whether English *buy*, French *toit* ('roof') or Arabic /la:/ ('no'). These can build up words with sequences of CV syllables, English CVCVCV *banana*, French CVCVCVCV *réparations* ('repairs'), Arabic CVCV /ʃæmi/ (Syrian/Damascene).

In some languages all syllables consist of this consonant–vowel CV structure. Think of familiar Japanese brand-names such as *Toyota, Mitsubishi, Yamaha*. All Japanese syllables must be CV, with the exception of final 'syllabic' /n/, as in *san* (a respectful form of address) and doubled consonants, as in *Nippon* (Japan). That is to say, Japanese syllables may *not* start with more than one consonant and must *not* have a final consonant: they are all CV rather than CCV or CVC. To the foreigner, Japanese words seem comparatively easy to make out. Train announcements allow one to work out the name of stations in a series of obvious CV syllables, for example *Shimokitazawa* or *Akasakamitsuke*. Sumo wrestlers have names that are also quite easy to recognize, e.g. *Takanohana* or *Kyonoumi*.

Other languages, however, permit a greater range of syllables by allowing a final consonant, that is to say consonant–vowel–consonant CVC. English not only has V syllables like /aɪ/ (*I*) and CV syllables like /baɪ/ (*buy*), but also has CVC syllables like /tɒm/ (*Tom*) and /bɪt/ (*bit*). French similarly has CVC syllables in *femme* /fam/ (*woman*) and *tête* /tɛt/ (*head*).

The final or initial consonant in the syllable can either be restricted to single consonants C or can be two or more consonants CC, CCC and so on. English has some CCV syllables with two initial consonants, as in *stay* /steɪ/ or *play* /pleɪ/; French has /tr/ as in *travail* ('work') or /st/ in *stylo* ('pen'). There are, however, strict rules about which consonants can go together, some which apply to all languages, some only to the sound system of a single language. For example /pn/ and /ps/ are possible CC combinations in French, as in *psychologie* ('psychology') and *pneu* ('tyre'), but are not allowed in English, which has /s/ and /n/ in the parallel words *psychology* and *pneumatic*. Leaving aside combinations with /s/, only four consonants can occur as the second part of an English initial two-consonant CC cluster: /l/ as in *please*, /r/ as in *trip*, /j/ as in *tune* and /w/ as in *quick* (the last two being 'approximants' rather than true consonants). Many combinations like *fmooth* and *ptick* are therefore ruled out. While /s/ can precede several second consonants, as in /st/ in *sting*, /sw/ in *Swede* or /sp/ in *spin*, it cannot be followed by a fricative; there is no word like *sfang* (with the possible exception of *sphere*). Other possible combinations do not actually occur, perhaps for accidental reasons, for instance /sb/ as in *sbang* or /tl/ as in *tlun*. Some combinations are rare: /vj/, for example, occurs only in *view*, /lj/ in *lute*, /sj/ in a few words in some people's speech, such as *suit* and *assume*.

A particular language may also restrict which single consonants can occur in the initial or final C position of the syllable. The English sound /ŋ/ cannot occur at the beginning of a syllable: *sing* or *ringer* or *incredible* are possible but not *ngis* /ŋɪs/ or *nging* /ŋɪŋ/. The English /h/ only occurs at the beginning of the syllable, as in *hot* or *perhaps*, never at the end, despite its occasional presence in the spelling. That is to say, there are no English words pronounced as *toh* /təʊh/ and *perpah* /pəpa:h/. The absence of final /h/ seems obvious to an English speaker. After all, how can one hear a sound that is just air breathed out if nothing follows it? It is equally obvious to a speaker of Persian that the word /mah/ ('moon') differs from the word /ma/ ('us') and that /jɒh/ ('position') differs from /jɒ/ ('place'); Persians have no problems in hearing a final /h/.

English-speaking science fiction writers have the problem of inventing names for aliens from other worlds that seem both plausible and exotic. One possibility is to scatter a few apostrophes to indicate some non-English sound, presumably a click, for example *Halyan't'a*. Another common approach creates possible, but nonexistent, English words out of ordinary sound combinations, such as *Krondaku*, *ezwal* or *Ondods*. Or English sounds are put in unusual combinations, *tnuctipun*, *Kdatlyno*, *Kzinti*; villainous races can also usually be identified by the plosive sounds in their names.

The English consonant combinations that exceed two consonant CC combinations are very restricted. In syllable-initial combinations, the first consonant must be /s/, the second /p/, /t/, /f/ or /k/, and the third /l/, /r/, /j/ or /w/, as in *splinter* /spl/ or *scream* /skr/. Even then certain combinations do not exist, say /stw/ in *stweel* or /spw/ in *spweet*.

While the end of the English syllable can go up to four consonants (CCCC) these also consist of only a few combinations, usually ending in /s/, for the simple reason that English grammar adds /s/ to the end of words to show number of nouns (book<u>s</u>) and verbs (sit<u>s</u>) and possession of nouns (John'<u>s</u>), leading to /lfθs/ in *twelfths*, /mpts/ in *prompts* and /ksts/ in *texts*. Because of the problems of saying such sequences, English speakers often simplify them by leaving one or more of the consonants out, i.e. /twelθs/ for *twelfths* without an /f/. The absolute maximum for English is claimed to be the final five-consonant cluster /mpfst/ in *Thou triumphst!*, if, that is, the speaker says -*mphst* with a /p/.

V	/aɪ/	*aye*
CV	/baɪ/	*buy*
VC	/aɪl/	*isle*
CVC	/baɪt/	*bite*
CCV.	/braɪt/	*bright*
CCCV.	/straɪk/	*strike*
.VCC	/baɪts/	*bites*
.VCCC	/sɔːlts/	*salts*
.VCCCC	/prɒmpts/	*prompts*

Possible English syllables

How do people cope with combinations that are not found in their own language? Science fiction names like *tnuctipun* or *fnool* in fact pose little problem: the impossible CC /tn/ and /fn/ combinations are padded out to be a separate CVC syllable of English by adding a vowel /ə/ to get /tən/ and /fən/. The same happens to foreign names that do not conform to English rules; *Rwanda* often gets an extra /ə/ to produce CVC at the beginning, /rəwændə/, as shown for instance in a notice outside a Bodyshop: *This branch has collected £200 for relief for Rawanda.* The Jaffa orange box labelled *Tnuport Produce of Israel* is doubtless called /tənuːpɔːt/ by those who handle it.

People learning English as a foreign language use the same strategy when a syllable does not conform to the pattern of their first language. As Arabic is a CV language, it has no CC combinations. So speakers of Arabic turn English *plastic* into *belastic* and *translate* into *tiransilate*. Maori speakers similarly turn *milk* into *miraka* and *bridge* into *periki* to avoid the CC combinations /lk/ and /br/. And it is fairly obvious which English words the following Tok Pisin words are based on: *bilak, bulu, sikin, pilum*.

In Japanese the attempt to make English syllables conform to the CV structure makes English words almost unrecognizable. To discover which English words are the basis of the Japanese *sutoraiki, sumaato* and *sutandoba*, delete the Vs which are padding out the CC clusters, to get *s.t.rik.e, s.maat.* ('smart') and *s.tand.bar* (i.e. a bar where you don't sit down). English people similarly add a vowel to make the German *kn* sequence conform to the English pattern in words such as *Knorr* /kənɔː/.

To sum up, the sequences of sounds in a language are tightly restricted in terms of the combinations of consonant that can occur at the beginning or ending of the syllable. Speakers feel uncomfortable with syllables that do not occur in their own language, and attempt to make them conform to their expectations in various ways.

VI Sounds and phonemes

The vague word 'sound' has been used up to this point to talk about speech. But there are different levels of speech sound. One level is the actual description of the sounds themselves as sheer 'sound', studied in the branch of linguistics called 'phonetics'. The next level is the sound system of a particular language. English or French or Japanese use a small selection of the sounds possible in human languages, the subject matter of 'phonology'. The present section looks at this next level, namely how particular languages use sounds within their own phonological systems.

What does it mean to say English has 44 sounds? There are several distinct ways of pronouncing /p/ in English – after /s/ as in *spy*, before a vowel as in *pat* and at the end of a word as in *sap*, the sound that precedes or follows it influencing the VOT. How can the sounds of a language be counted when any sound can have all these variations?

The solution is a second level of sounds, called 'phonemes'. These are the sounds that the native speakers of a particular language use to distinguish different words, i.e. are part of its phonological system. If speakers of English hear someone say /pi:k/ (*peak*) and /bi:k/ (*beak*), they recognize that /p/ is not /b/; in other words they hear two different words with different meanings, *peak* and *beak*. When they hear the /p/ sounds in *pit*, *spit*, *split* and *stop*, however, they still recognize the sound as a /p/ despite the differences.

The sounds /p/ and /b/ are therefore phonemes of English because they potentially distinguish words such as *peak* and *beak*. The distinction between the sheer sounds of speech and the phonemes of a particular language is often shown in phonetic transcript by enclosing sheer sounds in square brackets [t] and the phonemes of a particular language in slanting brackets /t/.

Hindi has two words /p^{h}ik/ and /pi:k/, one with, one without the following puff of air, symbolized by ^{h}. That is to say, Hindi has two /p/ sounds, one with 0 VOT, one with +VOT; both of them are distinct phonemes. The same difference occurs in English in the [p] of *spit* and the [p^h] of *pit* but it is heard by English speakers as two variants of one phoneme, /p/. The technical term for the different ways in which a phoneme can be pronounced is 'allophone'. A particular language may use a sound difference to distinguish two phonemes or may ignore it and treat them as the same phoneme: /p^h/ and /p/ are two phonemes in Hindi, two allophones of one phoneme in English. Indeed Hindi has an aspirated counterpart to add to the English pair at each of the positions for plosives, /p^h/ /t^h/ /k^h/ as well as /p/ /t/ /k/ and /b/ /d/ /g/. English people may be able to tell the difference between /p^h/ and /p/ but the difference does not matter to the English sound system, since it never in itself marks the sole difference between two words.

A further example is the English lateral /l/ in *leap*. One type of English /l/, called 'clear' [l], is the syllable-initial pronunciation in *leap*. A second type, called 'dark' [l] and transcribed as [ɫ], is the syllable-final pronunciation in *peal*. Syllable-initial clear [l] sounds like a front vowel because, apart from the tip of the tongue touching the teeth ridge, the tongue has the configuration of a front vowel with the front part raised. Syllable-final dark [ɫ] sounds like a back vowel because the tongue has the configuration of a back vowel with the back of the tongue raised. A characteristic of Irish English is the lack of difference between clear and dark [l]s.

Many British people nowadays have yet a third variety of /l/, namely a back vowel similar to the initial sound /w/ of *woman* and lacking the tongue contact with the roof of the mouth typical of /l/. The comedian Michael Barrymore has a catchphrase *Awright* /ɔːwaɪʔ/. In my own speech *full* is pronounced closer to /fuw/ than to

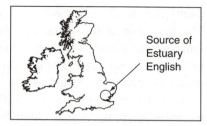

Source of Estuary English

/ful/, a characteristic of the variety of English often now known as Estuary English after the Thames Estuary where it is allegedly spoken. Fifteen per cent of the *Inside Language* panel owned up to this vocalic /l/ (Q8), 77 per cent denied it.

The three [l] sounds are not phonemes of English because the difference is never important to the understanding of speech: an /l/ is an /l/ whichever way it is pronounced. The difference between clear and dark [l]s is entirely predictable from their position in the syllable, and never distinguishes two words. Yet, in Polish, *lata* with a clear [l] means 'year' and *lata* with a dark [ɫ] means 'patch'; the two lateral sounds are different phonemes, not allophones, and so the two words have different meanings.

The type of transcript used in this chapter for English is then based on the phoneme: it is a 'phonemic' transcription showing the significant contrasting sounds in the phonology of a language, not a 'phonetic' transcription showing the minutest variation in sounds. Hence the difference between the transcripts in slanted brackets such as /pɪl/ *pill* and those in square brackets such as [pɪɫ] are that the former are given in a 'broad' transcript showing phonemes, the latter in a 'narrow' transcript showing different allophones.

The number of phonemes varies greatly from one language to another. The smallest number found in UPSID is the 11 of Rotakas, an Indo-Pacific language, the largest the 141 of !Xu, English coming somewhere in the middle of the range with around 44. The average for a language is in fact 31, with 70 per cent of languages having between 20 and 37.

The traditional way of establishing the phonemes of a language is to look for pairs of words known as 'minimal pairs'. The linguist asks native speakers of English whether *pin* is different from *pig*. If they agree, two phonemes of English have been established – /n/ and /g/. Then they are tried with [pɪl] and [pɪw]. They may recognize these are different accents of English and even regard the [w] pronunciation of /l/ as an abomination. But they will still say both words are *pill*. Next they are tried with *peat* and *pit*; then with aspirated [pʰɪt] and non-aspirated [pɪt]; and so on, till all the likely sound contrasts have been tested. In principle this 'minimal pairs' technique establishes the repertoire of phonemes in a language.

It is, however, difficult to find minimal pairs for the phonemes /θ/ and /ð/. In the middle of words *either* /iːðə/ can be paired with /iːθə/ *ether*, if, of course *either* is not pronounced /aɪðə/. At the end of words, there are a few pairs like *sooth* /suːθ/ and *soothe* /suːð/. It is very hard, however, to find minimal pairs to contrast the initial voiced /ð/ sound of *the* with the voiceless /θ/ of *three*, the only candidate seeming to be *thigh* /θaɪ/ versus *thy* /ðaɪ/. The reason is that the initial /ð/ sound occurs in 'grammatical' words like *this* and *then*, rarely in 'content' words, as was seen in Chapter 3, and there are only a handful of such words in the language. Ask someone to pronounce the name of a place they are unlikely to have heard before (unless they live in Essex), namely *Theydon Bois* and they will pronounce it /θeɪdən/, not /ðeɪdən/, although the only other word with similar spelling they are likely to have encountered is *they* /ðeɪ/. Because *Theydon* is not a grammatical word, it cannot have /ð/. Like intonation, the sounds of a language cannot be divorced from its grammar. It would be difficult to pronounce the sounds of English unerringly without knowing grammatical information about which words are nouns and which are grammatical words.

Similar problems in finding minimal pairs arise accidentally with other phonemes of English. As we have seen, the English phoneme /h/ of *hot* only occurs at the beginning of syllables, i.e. the first C in the CVC syllable structure; the phoneme /ŋ/ of *sang* occurs only at the end of syllables, the second C in CVC. It is therefore impossible to find a pair of words where the two can be contrasted and definitely established to be different phonemes. By analogy with the two forms of /l/, arguably /h/ and /ŋ/ are one phoneme with two different sounds.

The common-sense solution is to insist that two sounds as different as /h/ and /ŋ/ are unlikely to be variants of the same phoneme, even if this contrast cannot be shown through minimal pairs; sounds have to be similar to belong to the same phoneme. This solution does not work for languages that have a large range of allophones for some phonemes. Kabardian, a language spoken in the north-west Caucasus, has a single high vowel that has six variants running all the way from front [i] to back [u]. Tamil has a single plosive consonant that may be spoken as [p], [t] or [k] and furthermore is voiced before final vowels; if this were true of English, *Poe*, *toe*, *Coe* and *go* would all be the same word. Only the sound system of a language can decide whether two sounds belong to the same phoneme or not.

Minimal pairs in fact became a favourite tool for teaching English to foreigners. One textbook was called *Ship or Sheep?*; its sequel was *Tree or Three?* Exercises in some books test the students on whether the teacher has said /iː/ or /ɪ/, *bean* or *bin*, or /g/ or /k/, *good* or *could*. My favourite tests the difference between *It's nice*, *It's rice* and *It's lice*; it is hard to imagine a real world situation where these sentences are equally possible.

Sometimes the teaching materials put the minimal pair in a sentence which the student is asked to repeat: *Jean likes gin but gin doesn't like Jean.* Or longer stretches of speech are used that have liberal examples of a sound: *Don't you know Rover's got no bone? What, no bone for Rover? Rover won't stay at home unless Rover's got a bone. Joe, go to Jones . . .* and so on for another 18 memorable lines. The fallacy in using minimal pairs for teaching is that they are a linguist's technique for establishing the phonemes of a new language, not the natural means through which children learn their mother tongue or adults a second language.

However, paying too much attention to the phoneme makes speech seem a sequence of separate sounds rather than the continuous process it is. One solution is to break the phoneme up into smaller elements called 'distinctive features'. Instead of each sound being an entity of its own, it is seen as a bundle of elements, rather like a molecule made up of different atoms. Each difference between one sound and another is reduced to a yes/no, + or −, choice, called a 'distinctive feature'. These two-way choices have already been slipped into this chapter several times. Voiced versus voiceless sounds for example were given as +voice and −voice. The sound /b/ of *rib* is +voice, the /p/ of *rip* is −voice. Vowels are specified as +voice by definition almost automatically. Other distinctive features that have been used are ±high and ±back. The English /i:/ vowel of *see* is +high −back, the /ɒ/ sound of *fog* is −high +back, and so on for all the other vowels. And the ±tense feature distinguishes +tense sounds like /t/ (*tart*) from −tense sounds like /d/ (*dart*). Distinctive features are a binary code, like that used on computers or CDs, which can capture all possible sounds of speech.

VII Alternatives to speech sounds

Spoken sounds are only one of the means through which language can be expressed. There are forms of language that do not involve sounds produced by the vocal organs. The most obvious is written language, whether using an alphabet based on sounds or a character system based on meanings, as seen in Chapter 6. In Zaïre, however, there are drum languages in which the sounds are conveyed on a wooden drum called a *boungu* tuned to give two notes, Low (male) and High (female), when hit on different sides. Any word can be converted into a sequence of High and Low notes, rather like the Long and Short of Morse Code, and broadcast for up to seven miles on a still night. Thus in Kele a word such as *sango* (father) is a sequence of two High notes ˙˙ HH; *nyango* ('mother') is a Low followed by a High ˙ LH; and *wana* ('child') is a High followed by a Low ˙. To arrive at the drum expression for 'orphan' means adding some grammatical words:

English	child	has	no	father	nor	mother
Kele	wana	ati	la	sango	la	nyango
Drum sequence	H L	L H	L	H H	L	L H

A further alternative to speech sounds is whistling, which is used to communicate across distances of up to 5 km across thinly populated country, for example by shepherds or by hunters, in parts of the globe ranging from Mexico to Burma to the Canaries. Whistle languages do not convert speech sounds to high and low notes, but substitute particular notes for each vowel with consonants given by transitions between the vowels. Both drumming and whistling convert spoken language into a different medium rather than being an independent form in their own right. In other words, they are like Morse Code or shorthand in being parasitic on spoken language.

A true alternative to speech is, however, found in the languages used by the deaf, which involve gestures rather than sounds and are capable of communicating as complex ideas through as complex structures as any other human language. Take two signs from British Sign Language (BSL). The sign for 'woman' is the index finger of the right hand stroking the right cheek; the sign for 'England' is the two hands in front of the chest with the two index fingers stretched out horizontally moving to and fro, from left to right.

These gestures are just as difficult to describe in words as the sounds of speech. For the gestures of deaf language are organized in the same way as the sounds of speech. Just as the organ making the speech sounds, such as the tongue, needs to be specified, so does the shape of the hand, with 51 different handshapes possible in BSL. Then, as for plosives and fricatives and diphthongs, the types of movement need to be described, some 37 for BSL. As with the vowel space inside the mouth, the location where the sign is made needs to be specified, including in BSL nine positions on the face and four on the neck and trunk. Sometimes the same sign has different meanings if produced at a different level, just as a /p/ is different from a /k/. Thus sign language has all the normal possibilities of the phonological system of human languages.

Sign languages should not then be confused with natural gesture systems based on mime. Many deaf language signs may have originated in 'natural' gestures: the BSL sign for 'bird' is the finger and thumb of the right hand opening and closing at nose level, clearly representing a beak. Most signs have, however, become purely arbitrary: the sign for 'England' mentioned above, for example, is a remote descendant of a finger-spelling sign rather than any recognizable shape. Sometimes fanciful origins for signs have been devised. The BSL cheek-stroking sign for 'woman' has been explained variously as 'curls on a woman's cheek', 'bonnet strings' and 'soft cheek'. Yet a hundred years ago the sign was stroking the lips, showing that none of these explanations can be right.

While there may be some visual links between some signs and what they mean, these are not much closer than those between natural sounds and the sounds of speech. Indeed, otherwise there would not be large differences between the different sign languages of the world, whether Chinese Sign Language, British Sign Language or French Sign Language. Even within a single country such as France or England there are strong dialect differences. Sign-users from different regions may not understand each other completely. Deaf members of a theatre audience in Manchester, for example, complained that they could not understand the BSL interpreter of a play because he was not using the signs current in that city.

This chapter has shown that the sound system of a language consists on the one hand of particular intonation patterns, on the other of a certain number of phonemes. The actual sounds are limited by what the organs of speech can do and by universal factors such as distinctive features and sonority. Even when languages have the same sounds, they use them in specific ways according to their own systems. It is the meaningful contrasts between the sounds that are important – `John versus 'John or *got* versus *cot* – not the sheer sounds themselves.

Sources and further reading

General

Well-written introductions to phonetics and phonology in general, from which many of the examples in this chapter are taken, can be found in: D. Abercrombie, *Elements of General Phonetics* (Edinburgh: Edinburgh UP, 1967); J. Laver, *Principles of Phonetics* (Cambridge: CUP, 1994); J.D. O'Connor, *Phonetics* (Harmondsworth: Penguin, 1973). An extensive discussion of RP can be found in J.C. Wells, *Accents of English* (3 vols, Cambridge: CUP, 1982). The classic description of the RP accent of English is A.C. Gimson, *An Introduction to the Pronunciation of English* (London: Edward Arnold, 1962).

Sounds and meanings

A collection of articles on sound symbolism is L. Hinton, J. Nichols and J. Ohala, *Sound Symbolism* (Cambridge: CUP, 1994), which has a paper by John Ohala putting forward the Frequency Code.

Intonation and its functions

A standard introduction to intonation is A. Cruttenden, *Intonation* (Cambridge: CUP, 1986). English intonation in particular is covered in J.D. O'Connor and G.F. Arnold, *Intonation of Colloquial English*, 2nd edn (London: Longman, 1973). Rises in New Zealand intonation are described in D. Britain and J. Newman, 'High rising terminals in New Zealand English', *Journal of the International Phonetic Association* 22 (1992): 1–11. The football results examples are based on A. Cruttenden, 'An experiment involving comprehension of intonation in children from 7 to 10', *Journal of Child Language* 1 (1974): 221–31.

Producing the sounds of speech

The UPSID statistics for different languages are presented in I. Maddiesen, *Patterns of Speech* (Cambridge: CUP, 1984). Slovak is described in P. Balász, M. Darovec and H. Trebaatická, *Slovak for Slavicists* (Bratislava: slovernské pedagogické Nakladatel'stvo, 1976). Details of English vowels around the world are based on J.C. Wells, *Accents of English* (see above). Clear diagrams of the RP vowels and consonants are given in D. Crystal, *The Cambridge Encyclopedia of the English Language* (Cambridge: CUP, 1995). The sources for tongue-twisters are: A. Schwartz, *A Twister of Twists, a Tangler of Tongues* (Philadelphia: Lipincott, 1972); M. Sanquillet and E. Peterson (eds.), *The Essential Writings of Marcel Duchamp* (London: Thames & Hudson, 1978).

Air and speech

The original article on VOT is A.M. Liberman, F.S. Cooper, D.S. Shankweiler and M. Studdert-Kennedy, 'Perception of the speech code', *Psychological Review* 74 (1967): 431–61.

Combining sounds into syllables

Epenthetic vowels in L2 learners are discussed in E. Broselow, 'Prosodic phonology and the acquisition of a second language', in S. Flynn and W. O'Neil (eds.), *Linguistic Theory in Second Language Acquisition* (Dordrecht: Kluwer, 1988).

Sounds and phonemes

Estuary English is described in a popular book, P. Coggle, *Do You Speak Estuary?* (London: Bloomsbury, 1993). English pronunciation exercises can be found in: A. Baker, *Ship or Sheep?* (Cambridge: CUP, 1981); M.D. Mackenzie, *Modern English Pronunciation Practice* (London: Longman, 1967); L.A. Hill, *Drills and Tests in the English Sounds* (London: Longman, 1961).

Alternatives to speech sounds

The source for drum language is J.F. Carrington, *Talking Drums of Africa* (London: 1947). British Sign Language is described in: B. Woll, J. Kyle and M. Deuchar, *Perspectives on British Sign Language and Deafness* (Cambridge: CUP, 1981); J.G. Kyle and B. Woll, *Sign Language* (Cambridge: CUP, 1985). Hand gestures themselves are covered in D. McNeill, *Hand and Mind* (Chicago: University of Chicago Press, 1992). Whistle languages can be found in: R.G. Busnel and A. Classe, *Whistled Languages* (Berlin: Springer, 1976); A. Thomas, 'Whistled Languages' (1995), e-mail summary THOMAS@arts.uoguelph.ca.

5   Words and Meanings

To many people the most obvious fact about language is that it consists of words. Parents rejoice at the child's first word, not at their first speech sound or their first sentence. Newspapers have columns about words, some aimed at improving people's vocabulary, others making wry comments on current usage. Progress in a foreign language is counted by how many words the students have mastered. Without words there would indeed be little to say. But the earlier chapters have already made it clear that language is far more than words strung together. Without the systems of grammar, pronunciation and writing, words would convey little more than a series of labels.

This chapter looks at some of the properties of words and their meanings. The main emphasis is to demonstrate that the meanings of the words of a language form a system. Words are not isolated units with separate meanings of their own, to be learnt one at a time, but connect with each other in highly intricate relationships of meaning. This chapter first takes universals of human life, illustrated from colour words. Next it turns to the psychological approaches to the mental storage of meaning through the concepts of levels, components and fields of meaning. It ends by looking at the process of derivation through which new words can be constructed. One of its threads is that meaning has to be looked at from many different angles and analysed in many different ways to begin to approach its complexity in human language.

I Lexical entries and the dictionary in the mind

To understand speech or to produce it, speakers need to store the words of the language in their minds. Processing language fluently means having virtually instantaneous mental access to information about thousands of words. In this sense the mind has a dictionary that includes all the information a speaker needs about vocabulary. This is not to say that there is an actual list tucked away somewhere in the mind like that in the printed book. Nevertheless much of the information in the mind must overlap with that in the book; most of what is in a dictionary reflects what speakers already know about words. One of the uses of printed dictionaries is indeed to record the way that people use words, which in turn reflects the mental dictionary they have in their minds.

Linguists often prefer the word 'lexicon' to 'dictionary', perhaps because it provides a convenient adjective, 'lexical,' to use in phrases such as 'lexical entry'. Printed dictionaries have entries; mental lexicons have lexical entries that store parallel information, even if in a different way. To see the content of a lexical entry let us look at the noun *help*. Speakers of English know that *help* is pronounced /help/: they know its pronunciation and probably its spelling. When *help* is a noun, they know that it is usually 'uncountable'; that is to say, it is impossible to say *he gave me two helps*; and they know that it can be followed by the preposition *with*: *he gave me some help with my car*; in other words, they know grammatical information about how *help* may be used in sentences. They also know that, as a noun, *help* can be preceded by the adjective *great* in some uses when it is countable, *Mark was a great help*, but not by *large*, as in *Mark was a large help*: they possess information about the words that can occur close to it, technically called 'collocation'. *Help* also enters into certain set phrases such as *There's no help for the wicked*, and certain extended expressions, *to be of help*, etc.: speakers know the idioms of which *help* forms part. Putting these elements together, the lexical entry in the mind contains the information:

> *help*: /help/ noun, uncountable, + *with*, + *great*, not *large*, no help for the wicked,
> to be of help . . .

This entry is close in content, if not in form, to the skeleton of an entry in a standard printed dictionary. All of this information must be stored in the lexical entry in the mind in one way or another.

Detailed as the lexical entry for *help* already is, it has not mentioned anything about the meaning of the word in the conventional sense. The speaker's knowledge of a word is not only its 'meaning' but also the way that it is pronounced, and the way it relates to the structure of the sentence. The meanings are only one aspect of what speakers know about words.

II Colours and linguistic relativity

However much words in different languages seem to refer to the same 'thing', the meaning of a word is relative to the whole system of other words in the language. Languages do not just have different words for the same thing; they have different meanings for different things. Words do not connect directly to objects in the world; they connect indirectly via our minds. So they express the speakers' attitudes towards the world they see and the way that they interpret it in their culture.

Hence anybody who learns another language is in for some surprises. Arabic speaking learners of English, for example, complain that they do not know how to express whether a cousin is male or female and whether an uncle comes from their mother's or their father's side of the family. English speakers have problems in mastering the degrees of respect with which Japanese relatives are referred to when talking to someone within the family and to someone from outside. Within the family the respectful forms are used, with the ending *-san*. A mother might be formally addressed within the family as *okaasan*, more usually as *okaachan*; outside the family the word for 'mother' is usually *haha*.

Let us take a case in which there is little doubt that the objective facts of the world are the same for all human beings. The colours of objects seem to be a straightforward fact, expressible in precise physical terms of wavelength, luminosity, hue, etc., down to the 16 million colours claimed in advertisements for computer monitors. Colours are the same everywhere because they are part of the physical makeup of the world. So languages might be expected to have the same range of words for colours. This section tackles the thorny issue of the similarities and differences between colour words in different languages.

The Welsh colour term *glas* includes part of English *green* and *grey* as well as *blue*; Japanese traffic lights have a colour *awo* that is known as *blue* rather than *green* and is also used for the sky. Russian has two colours for *blue*, *sinij* ('dark blue') and *goluboy* ('sky blue'). Hungarian has two colour words for red, *piros* and *vörös*, the difference, according to a Hungarian, being that *piros* is the red in the Hungarian flag, *vörös* the red in the Russian flag. Speakers of different languages do not see the world in a uniform way; some see colours where others do not.

Celebrated research by Berlin and Kay, however, revealed an underlying pattern to colour words across languages. The basic colour terms can be grouped on a scale, shown in Figure 5.1. All languages have the first two colour terms on the scale, namely 'black' and 'white'. In Dani, spoken in New Guinea, the only colour terms are indeed *mili* ('dark-cool', i.e. black) and *mola* ('light-warm', i.e. white). Next on the scale comes the colour term 'red'. Some languages, such as Tiv, spoken in Nigeria, have a three-term system of 'white', 'black' and 'red'. Next along the scale come 'green' and 'yellow', yielding the five-term colour system found in Navajo. The progression continues through languages that also have 'blue', 'brown' and a final group of 'purple', 'pink, 'orange' and 'grey'. The full scale of basic colours is shown in the Figure. Each language exploits this scale by using all the colour terms to the left of a particular point but none to the right. Hununoo, spoken in the Philippines, goes as far as 'green' and 'yellow'. Ancient Egyptian had eight terms, including 'purple' but excluding 'brown' in favour of 'gold'. Hebrew has terms for all eleven.

Obviously English has many more colour words than the eleven basic colour terms, such as *burnt ochre*, *avocado*, *roan*, *lovat green*, and so on. Basic terms have to be single words (thus excluding *electric blue*), must not be included in the meaning of other terms (*scarlet* is a kind of *red*), and are not used exclusively for a single object (thus excluding *avocado* but including *orange*). The most extensive range of colour terms is used by cosmetics manufacturers. *Cayenne Red*, *Rare Orchid* and *Innocent Rose* are

```
  ┄┄┄┄┄┄┄┄┄┄┄┄┄┄┄┄┄┄┄┄┄┄┄┄┄┄┄┄┄┄┄┄┄┄┄┄┄┄┄┄┄┄►

  black      red       green      blue      brown     purple
  white                yellow                         pink
                                                      orange
                                                      grey
```

Fig. 5.1 The universal colour scale, according to Berlin and Kay

colours of lipstick, for instance. Seventy per cent of these advertising terms do not figure in standard dictionaries. A clothing catalogue advertises a shirt in *Cypress*, *Vintage Rose*, *Copenhagen Blue*, *Classic Navy*, *Russet Red*, *Black*, *Sunwashed Purple*, *Golden Sand* and *Ivory*. At the opposite extreme, the language of artists and art historians tends to be sparing in colour terms: they restrict themselves to basic terms with some modification, for example *warm red*. Even Turner's amazing colours are talked about by critics as *blues*, *reds* and *yellows*.

The order of acquisition to some extent reverses the scale of basic terms, with *black* and *white* being learnt rather late. By about the age of 4 years, children recognise about 73 per cent of the colour terms tested, suggesting that there is no necessity to spend much time on basic colour terms in primary school.

One reason why colours may be structured into the set of basic terms in human languages is that certain ways of looking at the world are determined in part by how the human senses work. An experiment by Berlin and Kay asked speakers of different languages to look at a set of colour chips, similar to the paint charts available in DIY stores. They first had to point to all the chips that could be called a particular colour – which chips are blue? which red? – then to the 'best' example of each of the basic colour terms – which is the best red? the best blue? Whatever their native language, people by and large agreed on the best example of each colour, called the 'focal colour'. Figure 5.2 shows how different shades of blue relate to one focal blue.

Furthermore, even when there are no basic terms for a colour in a language, chips in focal colours are nonetheless easier to remember than those in other colours. Dani speakers, with a two-term colour system, recognized the same focal colours as English speakers with an eleven-term system. Three-year-old American children, whose colour system is not yet complete, preferred focal colours to the others. A central concept of 'blue' applies across languages: there is a universal colour 'blue' regardless of whether a language even a word has for it.

One explanation may lie in how the human eye works. Vision in the retina depends on rod cells, which are sensitive to dark versus light, and on three types of cone cells, which are sensitive to red, green and blue. The first five colour terms on the scale are

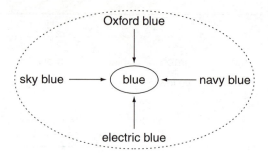

Fig. 5.2 Focal blue and other blues

then, hardly surprisingly, *black, white, red, green, blue*. Other colours are perceived by combinations of these cells. The mind processes the information from the cone cells in terms of two oppositions: red versus green, and yellow versus blue. This explains why it is possible to say *greenish blue* or *yellowish red* but not *bluish yellow* or *greenish red*. The same colour terms occur in different languages because human beings see the world in the same way, not because the outside world is structured in a particular way. Creatures whose eyes are differently constructed see different colours.

Colour words, then, show not only the similarities between languages in the meanings that they express because of the nature of human perception, but also the difference between languages in the meanings they choose to express, going from a minimal number of basic terms, such as Welsh, up to the maximum, as in Hebrew. This does not take into account other types of meaning that may be grafted onto a colour word: *blue* can be applied to a sad mood, a kind of musical note, or a risqué story.

III Levels of meaning

The hunt has been on to find universal meanings common to all languages. Noam Chomsky once suggested that, while concepts like 'carburettor' are hardly likely to be universal, concepts like 'table' or 'person' are common to all human minds. Another linguist, Anna Wierzbicka, pointed out that Polish has two words, *stoł* for a 'small or low table' such as a coffee table, and *stolik* for a 'dining-room table'. Poles do not have the single concept of 'table' which Chomsky took for granted but two separate concepts: they divide the world up in different ways. The Hebrew verb *lidchot*, for example, means both 'postpone' and 'reject', something which is hard for English speakers to grasp. Genuinely universal meanings true of all languages are hard to come up with. This section looks not so much at individual word meanings as at how the human mind thinks of the objects in the world in a particular way.

It is not the human eye that sees the world in a particular way so much as the human mind. The concept of 'basic' terms can be extended to other areas of vocabulary than colours. If English speakers are asked to name a bird, the odds are they will name a *sparrow* or a *blackbird*, not a *great crested grebe* or a *penguin*. The birds that came to the minds of the *Inside Language* panel were, in order of frequency, *sparrow*, *robin*, *crow*, *thrush*, *blackbird* and *magpie* (Q1). Like the colours, certain types of bird seem 'birdier' than others. A penguin swims; an ostrich runs; a dodo is extinct: they are not 'proper' birds because they differ from the prototype concept of 'bird' in our minds in one way or another, even if they are indeed called *birds*. A robin is a 'proper' bird; a penguin is not.

The human mind has a central meaning for a concept and relates variations to this central meaning. Switching to other vocabulary areas, the words that come to mind for 'tree' are *oak* or *apple* rather than *holm-oak* or *crab-apple*; for 'clothing', *vest* or *trousers*, not *belt* or *dinner jacket*. Human beings have certain concepts they treat as archetypes, like *oak*; other concepts are seen in relationship to these central concepts.

The 'prototype theory' proposed by Eleanor Rosch develops this idea by claiming that the mind puts objects into three levels of vocabulary. The 'basic' level consists of those objects that strike people immediately when they look at the world around them, such as *table* or *car*. These basic-level terms are the central prototypes already encountered: looking round a room we tend to see objects as *chairs*, *tables*, *lights*, etc., not as sheer shapes and forms; these are the basic ways in which we organize our world in our minds. Above this basic level, the mind builds a second, more general level at which objects are grouped together into 'superordinate' terms; the basic-level terms *tables* and *chairs* are included within the superordinate term *furniture*; *cars* and *trucks* are grouped into *vehicles*. Superordinate terms are not directly available to our eyes; they are abstractions that place things in general categories.

As well as building upwards from the basic level, the mind also builds downwards into more specific categories. At the third 'subordinate' level objects break up into more specialized terms; the basic-level term *car* is now *sports car*, the basic *red* is *pillarbox red*, and so on. The mind sees the world in three levels of abstraction going from the most general to the most specific, with the basic level coming in the middle as the most useful everyday term. Returning to colours, the abstract superordinate

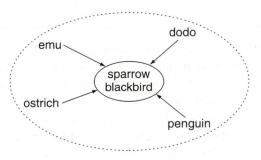

Fig. 5.3 Degrees of 'birdiness'

level is the word *colour* itself, which relates to the more concrete basic-level terms *blue, red* and so on, which in turn relate to the subordinate terms *sky blue*, *pillarbox red*, and so on. The superordinate-category *vehicles* in a sense consists of basic terms *cars* and *lorries*, etc., which consist of subordinate terms *sports cars*, *four-wheel drives*, etc.

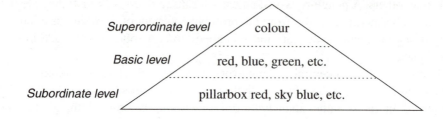

Superordinate level	colour
Basic level	red, blue, green, etc.
Subordinate level	pillarbox red, sky blue, etc.

This three-way division in people's minds has been confirmed by several experiments. In word association tests, people usually think of basic-level terms such as *hammer* and *drum* before they think of superordinate terms like *tools* and *instruments*, or subordinate terms like *claw hammer* or *tom-tom*. In reaction tests, people react to the basic-level terms more quickly than the others; they recognize pictures of objects called by basic-level terms more easily. There are sometimes grammatical differences between the three levels of terms. In English, subordinate terms are often uncountable in grammatical terms, *furniture*, rather than countable, *a furniture*, while basic-level terms are countable, *a chair* rather than *chair*. In German, basic-level terms may have both masculine and feminine gender: *der Hammer* ('the hammer', masculine) and *die Säge* ('the saw', feminine); superordinate-level terms, however, chiefly have neuter gender: *das Werkzeug* ('the tool', neuter).

Levels of meaning in English

Superordinate level	fruit	tools	fish	reading matter
Basic level	apple	hammer	salmon	books
Subordinate level	russet	claw hammer	wild salmon	novels

The growth of advertising this century introduced consumers to subordinate levels that they had never previously dreamt of. *Butter* and *tea* were what people bought in the grocer's, not *Kerrygold* or *PG Tips*. Only *sugar* remains a basic term with hardly any brand-name differentiation. It is the kiss of death for a product to become a basic-level term in its own right, such as *Hoover*, *Xerox* and *aspirin*, since this suggests that other makes exist. Conversely, a company that tries to divide its product into subordinate terms may be asking for trouble, as manufacturers such as Coca-Cola and Persil found when they tried to launch sub-varieties of product.

Though some generalizations about these levels can be made that are true for a whole language, the division into three levels varies slightly according to the individual. Rosch found that aircraft mechanics treated *wing* as a basic-level term with many subordinates, where to the layperson it has none. At some level everyone experiences the same world, yet the things they see depend in part on the ways they have been influenced by their society and their personal experiences. I go for a walk and see something I call *trees*; other, more expert people may see *holm-oaks* or *Scottish pines*.

The relationship between these levels is technically called 'hyponymy'. The words are related through a tree structure like those for grammar, where one superordinate word includes a group of hyponyms. The test for whether two words are hyponyms is whether you can say 'An X is a kind of Y'. So a *dog* is a kind of *animal*; a *car* is a type of *vehicle*; *Glenmorangie* is a brand of *whisky*. Hyponomy is only one of the types of meaning relationship between words. Words can also be 'synonyms' if they have the same meaning, *truthful/honest, munch/chew, powerful/strong*, though it is hard to find 'absolute' synonyms that always have the same meaning in all contexts: *That car is very powerful/strong*. Words can be 'antonyms' if they have opposite meanings, as seen in the box below. Words are then linked to each other in networks of meaning relations.

Opposites

One of the most complex areas of meaning is opposites. Here are some of the categories of opposites found by D. Cruse in his book *Lexical Semantics*.

Complementaries. These divide up an area into two mutually exclusive areas: *A door is either shut or open.*
Interactives. These have a stimulus/response relationship: *If you command someone, they obey.*
Satisfactives. One is an attempt, the other is successful: *If at first you don't succeed, try, try again.*

Antonyms: A pair of words with a gradation between two extremes: *He was blowing hot and cold.*
Antipodal. These indicate two extreme ends of a dimension: *They searched the house from top to bottom.*
Counterparts. Two objects with reverse dimensions: *concave, convex.*
Reversives. Motion in opposite directions: *rise, fall. He ascended the Jungfraujoch over the glacier and descended by train.*
Converses. Relationship of one direction to another: *above, below.*

This section has again demonstrated the diverse ways in which languages use words based on the same underlying properties of the human mind. At some level all human beings perceive things in the same way. The way that they organize vocabulary will be similar even if the words and meanings differ.

IV Language and thinking

The discussion of categorization leads in to the vexed question of how language relates to thinking. On the one hand, differences in the way people think might lead to differences in their language: I can't see blue so I don't have a word for it. On the other, differences in language might lead to differences in thinking: I have a word for 'blue' so I recognize it when I see it.

1 The Sapir–Whorf hypothesis

This section explores the area called the Sapir–Whorf hypothesis after the two researchers who first stated it clearly, Edward Sapir and Benjamin Lee Whorf. When Whorf worked as an insurance inspector, he was struck by the problems caused by language. For example, a pile of drums might be classified as 'empty gasoline drums' by a garage and treated with no special care. Yet such drums are extremely dangerous, as they contain explosive vapour. The way the workers labelled the situation was at fault, that is to say, their language. Whorf was mostly concerned with the ways that language restricted thinking in American Indian languages. Hopi has one word, *pahe*, for 'drinking water' and another word, *keyi*, for 'natural water in lakes,' where English has one. Hopi, he claimed, also has no indication of time, whether past, present or future; the mental organization of time in Hopi speech has a different basis from that in what Whorf called 'Standard Average European'. Whorf's most famous example is the seven words that he alleges Eskimos have for 'snow', compared to the single word *snow* in English, showing that the speakers of the two languages perceive snow differently.

Considerable controversy has raged over the substance of these claims. For example, Hopi speakers are perfectly capable of expressing time concepts. So far as 'snow' is concerned, there is a dispute on the one hand over how many words Eskimos really have for 'snow', on the other over whether English vocabulary is so deficient, having at least *sleet, slush* and *hail*. An interesting commentary on perception of snow is found in Peter Høeg's novel *Miss Smilla's Feeling for Snow*, whose eponymous heroine is a Greenland Inuit who is indeed the world's authority at distinguishing types of snow.

The relationships between language and thinking have chiefly been examined through vocabulary rather than grammar. As well as the multiple Inuit words for 'snow', Bedouins have many words for 'camel', aboriginals many words for 'kangaroo' and, according to Peter Mühlhäusler, 'Many New Guinea languages ... make dozens of distinctions between different types of cordilyne leaves, according to whether such leaves are used for dressmaking, decoration, magic, or other purposes.'

Languages also have particular lacks. English, for example, has no everyday gender-free word for children of the same parents, apart from the academic term *sibling*: it must be *I have two brothers and a sister*, not *I have three Xs*. German, however, has a plural noun, *Geschwister*, meaning 'sisters, brothers, brother and sister, brothers and sisters', as does Bahasa Melayu, with *suadara*. Another unsurprising gap is that Quechua-speaking Indians living in the Andes have no word for 'flat'.

If one language has more words for a specific area than another, does this mean that its speakers see the world differently, or just talk about it differently? In terms of colours, Dani speakers should see a very different world, divided into black and white, compared to Tiv speakers, who see red, white and black, Hebrew speakers with eleven colours, and so on. Yet, as we have seen earlier, people everywhere nevertheless distinguish the same focal colours regardless of how many colour words they know. The limitations or richness of their basic colour vocabulary have not affected their perception of colour. As with the levels theory mentioned earlier, it may be a question of how 'expert' one becomes on a topic, whether aircraft wings, colour or snow; English-speaking skiers can doubtless recognize a range of types of snow going from powder to avalanche snow, even if they do have only a single word to label them by.

What about other senses? An experiment was carried out with speakers of Bahasa Melayu, one of the languages of Malaysia, which reflects Malaysian cooking in recognizing several degrees of saltiness such as *masin kitchup* 'salty like soy sauce', *masin ayer laut* 'salty like sea water', *masin garam* 'salty like salt' and *masin maung* 'horribly salty'. Sure enough, Malaysians were able to make much finer distinctions between solutions with different amounts of salt than were English speakers. In this case their experience, whether of cooking or language, had clearly influenced their perception of taste.

Leaving vocabulary for a moment, two lines of experiments have tested whether grammar too affects thinking. People were asked to sort out objects consisting of red squares, blue triangles, etc. Speakers of languages with adjective + noun word order, as in English (*black cat*), would sort the objects out first by colour. Speakers of languages with noun + adjective order, as in Spanish (*gato negro*), would first sort them out by shape. Language influenced the way they put objects into categories.

The second line of experiments explored the grammar of conditional 'if' clauses. English and many other languages have a type of conditional clause for describing things that are untrue: *If pigs had wings, they would fly* is one example where, even if everyone knows that pigs do not have wings, they can nevertheless speculate about what might happen if they did. Chinese, however, is said not to have such clauses; at best it can express their meaning in a long-winded fashion. The prediction is therefore that Chinese speakers would have difficulty in conceiving of such hypothetical situations. Indeed, when they were given a long chain of such hypothetical statements, 98 per cent of Americans responded with contrary-to-the-facts answers, but only 7 per cent of Chinese. However, later experiments contradicted this finding by showing that, when one hypothetical statement was involved rather than several, bilingual Chinese scored the same as English speakers; if there is in fact any difference, it lies in how they deal with a chain of logical consequences, not a single sentence. These lines of research, then, suggest that, while the grammar of a particular language may make certain ways of thinking more difficult, presumably because they are less usual, it does not prevent them from happening altogether.

2 *Metaphors of meaning*

George Lakoff and Mark Johnson have claimed that a human being looks at the world through particular metaphors. A typical metaphor concerns emotions. We may be *on an emotional high* or *feeling very low*; *on cloud nine* or *in the depths of depression*; *over the moon* or *down in the dumps*; our spirits *rise* or *sink*. In other words, happiness is metaphorically 'up', sadness is 'down'. Indeed, 'up' is the metaphor for good things in general, 'down' for bad things: everything's *looking up*, everything's *going downhill rapidly*, *going up in the world*, *looking up to someone/looking down on someone*. Or, indeed, *high-minded* versus *low-spirited*. Though there is no intrinsic reason why 'up' should be better than 'down', it is a universal metaphor among human beings.

Other common metaphors suggested by Lakoff and Johnson are:

- 'Time means money'. You *save* time; you *spend* it; you *waste* it; and you *use* it.
- 'Love is war'. You *make a conquest, capture someone's heart* or *surrender*.
- 'An argument is a building'. It *hangs together*, is *well constructed*, and is *supported* on a *foundation*, so that it doesn't *fall apart*.
- 'More is better'; *a big man, large-hearted, megabucks*.
- 'Illness is a fight'; *conquer disease, fight against cancer, the war against diphtheria, battle for life, attacked by malaria, gave up the fight, a new weapon in the armoury against cancer*. Children who bravely fight against illness are given prizes for courage.

In some ways the debate over the relationship of language and thinking is like the chicken and the egg; human beings think through language and they use language to express their thoughts: who can separate the dancer from the dance?

V Components of meaning

This section and the next describe two complementary ways of looking at the meanings of words. This section analyses their meaning into smaller 'components' of meaning, rather like breaking a molecule up into its separate atoms.

1 Drinks

One example is the area of vocabulary for drinks. Anything that one drinks is normally liquid; anything that one eats is normally non-liquid; hence English speakers dispute whether soup is eaten or drunk and have to say *liquid food* for a liquid with the nourishing properties of food. One component of the meaning of any word for drink is 'liquid'. So the noun *drink* has a component [+liquid]; the noun *food* has a component [−liquid], meaning non-liquid.

Drinks may also be hot or cold. The meaning components are [+hot] for *tea* or *soup*, [−hot] for *cola* or *Pimms*. Again, any breach of the convention is usually remarked upon; *cold soup* and *cold tea* are unusual enough to need specifying; *hot cola* would be extraordinary. Adding the two components together, part of the meaning of *tea* is then [+liquid] [+hot], of *cola* [+liquid] [−hot].

Next, drinks can be divided into alcoholic and non-alcoholic: *beer* is [+alcohol], *lemonade* [−alcohol], *cola* [−alcohol], *whisky* [+alcohol], etc. Any breach needs to be spelled out: *non-alcoholic beer* is a possibility even if *non-alcoholic whisky* is unthinkable. There has been considerable controversy over whether UK manufacturers should sell *alcoholic lemonade*. The choice of alcoholic or non-alcoholic is usually confined to cold drinks, with the exception of *Irish coffee* and *mulled wine*: any deviation has to be mentioned, as in *hot rum* and *hot whisky*. So a main part of the meaning of *whisky* is the components [+liquid] [+cold] [+alcohol].

More details can be added according to the level of expertise of the drinker. *Tea* may be [±China], [±Indian], or [±herbal]. Of course, not everybody knows all of the components of meaning of each word. It is not every speaker of English that knows the difference between *China tea* and *Indian tea*, or between an *Island whisky* and a *Lowland whisky*. But all speakers use the components to distinguish one word from another at their own level of knowledge.

2 Family relations

The meanings of words for family relations can also be partially captured through components. Taking English as the example, [+male] represents part of the meaning of *father*, *son* and *uncle*; [+female] is a component in the meaning of *mother*, *daughter* and *aunt*; [+previous generation] is part of *mother* and *uncle*; [+same generation] is included in the meaning of *sister*, *brother*, *cousin*, and so on. Components in the meaning of *brother* are then [+male] [+same generation], of *uncle* [+male] [+previous generation]. A speaker of Japanese has an additional component, [±respectful].

Needless to say, such components do not sum up *all* the meaning of the word; there is more to the meaning of *brother* than 'a male relative of the same generation'. Nevertheless, a sizeable proportion of the meaning of a word is contributed by the components it shares with other words. Sometimes the difference between two words indeed comes down to a single component; *fox* versus *cub* is a difference of [±mature], just as the difference between two words can be a single phoneme, *box* and *fox*.

It is not always obvious how to describe these components best. The question of sex has been treated here neutrally as a matter of two components, [±male] and [±female], rather than as a single component of maleness, [±male]. Some of the dispute over sexist terms concerns the nature of these components and the priority between them. A person who believes that the word *man* is always [+male] will take exception to general remarks about the human species phrased in terms of *man*, say *The earliest man lived in Africa* (particularly when a crucial skeleton happens to be that of a woman, Lucy).

Those who defend such remarks are essentially claiming that the component [+male] is not present in the meaning of the word *man* when it is used generally, only the component [+human]. The same with the discriminatory overtones of *girl* compared to *woman*. If *woman* has the component [+mature], *girl* the component [−mature], as no one would dispute for *man* versus *boy* or *adult* versus *child*, an adult female should be called a *woman* not a *girl*. The derogatory implications of *girl* were stunningly revealed in a television discussion in which a noted feminist writer was addressed as *my dear girl* by the eminent linguist present, who had just been claiming that her allegations of discrimination through language were totally unjustified.

3 Cookery terms

English cookery terms have particularly noteworthy components of meaning, described by Adrienne Lehrer. What are the differences between *baking* and *roasting*, between *boiling* and *frying*, or between *stewing* and *simmering*?

- Is water used or not? *Boiling, simmering,* and *poaching* imply the use of water [+liquid +water]; *frying* and *sautéing* imply the use of fat or oil [+liquid +oil]; while *baking* and *grilling* imply no liquid at all [−liquid]. So it is not possible to poach or simmer in oil, nor to boil in oil (at least for culinary purposes), even if boiling and deep-frying are the same activity apart from the liquid concerned.
- How is the heat applied? In *grilling, barbecuing,* and *toasting*, the food is exposed directly to the heat, i.e. [+direct heat]. In *baking* the heat is indirect [−direct heat], and in *boiling* heat is transmitted via the liquid.
- How vigorous is the cooking action? *Boil* and *reduce* are [+vigorous]; *simmer* is [−vigorous]. So it is possible to say *It was boiling violently* but not *It was simmering violently* and, in reverse, *I simmered it slowly* but not *I boiled it slowly*.
- What utensils are used to contain it? *Frying* takes place in a *frying-pan*; *boiling* of water takes place in a *kettle* in England, though in much of the rest of Europe a *saucepan* suffices; *wokking* takes place in *woks*. The meaning of various processes may be marked [+frying pan] or [+wok].

The meaning of each cooking term is made up of a certain number of components. Woe betide the cook who does not know that *simmer* and *stew* are [−vigorous] compared to *boil*. As always, there are areas of doubt and confusion. *Roast* has two senses, in one of which it means 'to expose to a direct flame' (*roast an ox on a spit*), in the other 'to bake in an oven' (*Sunday roast*). What the British call *grill* the Americans call *broil*, and so on. Cooking vocabulary relies on components whose differences of meaning are crucial to the tradition of cooking in English.

The same is true of other languages. A major component of meaning in Japanese cuisine is [+uncooked] for food such as *sashimi*. Japanese has many words for rice, including *ina* when it is growing, *kome* when it is uncooked, *gohan* when it is cooked and eaten as part of a Japanese meal, and *raisu* when it is eaten with Western dishes.

Components are, then, a useful way of describing the meaning of words, which can be related to children's acquisition of vocabulary, as we see in Chapter 7. However, they do not cover all aspects of meaning of all words. Family relations and cookery

---

Special tasting vocabularies

Wine-tasting: words used by wine-tasters
High frequency: *dry*
Medium frequency: *acidic, aromatic, clean, fruity, light, refreshing, smooth*
Lower frequency: *astringent, balanced, bitter, bland, bouquet, common, delicate,*
  developed, flowery, fragrant, full-bodied, gentle, lovely, ordinary, perfumed,
  pungent, scented, soft, sour, sweet, tangy, tart, young

Apples: the most frequent adjectives used by professional tasters tasting Cox's
  Orange Pippins (with peel) in order of frequency
  juicy, crisp, chewy, acidic, tough, astringent, floury, sweet, green, sharp,
  stringy, bitter, Cox-like, estery, fruity, sugary, musty, alcoholic, scented,
  core-like, pear-like, pineapple-like, phenolic, spicy, fatty, sulphurous,
  banana-like

Malt whisky adjectives: a sample taken from two issues of the Scotch Malt Whisky
  Society's bottlings list
  assertive, astringent, biscuity, bitter, bronze, buttery, chewy, clean, complex,
  crisp, damp, dry, equinoctial, filling, fine, fruity, full, gentle, heavy, intense,
  large, malty, mellow, medicinal, mild, mouldy, oleaginous, pale, peaty,
  peppery, phenolic, pungent, powerful, red-gold, rewarding, rich, robust, salty,
  sharp, sherried, shiny, simple, smokey, smooth, sour, spicy, spirituous,
  stalwart, straw-coloured, strong, sulphurous, sweet, tart, uncomplicated

Sources: Lehrer, 'Talking about wine'; Williams and Carter, 'Sensory assessment of Cox's Orange Pippins'.

are often used as examples precisely because such limited areas of vocabulary easily show components. But the search for universal components that apply to large numbers of words has not been very successful, as seen in later chapters; nor have many vocabulary areas yet been described in this way.

VI Words and the mind

This section now raises the central issue of how words are stored in the speakers' minds and how they are integrated into the stream of speech during speaking or listening. The mental lexicon does not take the form of a straight alphabetical list of words, each with a separate meaning, like the printed dictionary. Instead the words are tied together in intricate networks; *blue* is related to *red*, *father* to *son*, *boil* to *bake*. The meanings are furthermore linked to the ways that speakers see the world, each language existing in a world of its own, whether of family relations or of ways of cooking.

How speakers carry out tasks with vocabulary provides some hints how it is treated in the mind. The fact that speakers can select words to put in their sentences at a rate of 150 or so per minute shows the speed with which they can access their lexical knowledge. Chapter 3 showed that content and grammatical words have different access times, as shown by pauses: a grammatical word like *the* is found more readily than a content word like *desk*. The mind is organized in a way that makes function words easier to get at than content words.

Word length supplies a further clue to mental processes. Experiments have required people to remember lists of countries such as *Chad, Burma, Greece, Cuba, Malta* and *Czechoslovakia, Somaliland, Nicaragua, Afghanistan, Yugoslavia*. The list of short words is far easier than the polysyllabic list, even if it is not said aloud. On average, people can remember 4.17 out of 5 countries for the list of short words, 2.80 for the polysyllabic one. The length of the word affects how it is processed in the mind, unlike a book dictionary, in which word length is more or less irrelevant.

Other clues come from the well-known feeling of having a word on the tip of the tongue. For some reason I have a problem with the word for the type of novel written in the eighteenth century such as Fielding's *Tom Jones* whose structure derives from the travels of the hero. I know the word begins with 'p', I know it is polysyllabic and that it is something like *picturesque*. Eventually I retrieve the word *picaresque*. This phenomenon is called the tip-of-the-tongue experience.

An influential experiment by Brown and McNeil induced the tip-of-the-tongue sensation by getting people to find words to match definitions such as:

- a navigational instrument used in measuring angular distances, especially the altitude of sun, moon, and stars at sea

If this example did not suffice to induce a tip-of-the-tongue experience, try these definitions from various dictionaries; the answers are in the next box. All the words come from the original experiment but the definitions have been taken from different dictionaries:

- semi-circular or many-sided recess, with an arched or domed roof
- an underground conduit for drainage, a common sewer
- a fragrant drug, that melts almost like wax, commonly of a greyish or ash colour, used both as a perfume and as a cordial
- a small boat with oars that is used especially in China

In a tip-of-the-tongue experience, people typically remember the first letter of the word, say 's' in the case of the navigational instrument, then how many syllables it has,

---

Tip-of-the-tongue results

Here are the answers the *Inside Language* panel (48 people) gave to the tip-of-the-tongue definitions (Q3). The correct answer is in italic.

Definition	Answer supplied
a navigational instrument used in measuring angular distances, especially the altitude of sun, moon, and stars at sea	*sextant* (18), compass (14), telescope (20), sexton (2), protractor (2), radar, pergonometer
semi-circular or many-sided recess, with an arched or domed roof (Advanced Learners)	alcove (15), *apse* (8), igloo, bay, dome, portico, auditorium, niche, cavern, cathedral, church, cloister conservatory, cupola, grotto, nave
an underground conduit for drainage, a common sewer (Oxford)	drain(s) (20), pipe (5), cesspit (2), culvert (3), sewer (2), main (2), tunnel, University of Essex, water table, viaduct, *cloaca* (0)
a fragrant drug, that melts almost like wax, commonly of a greyish or ash colour, used both as a perfume and as a cordial (Dr Johnson)	incense (4), opium (3), quinine (3), frankincense (3), peppermint (2), *ambergris*, scented candle, musk, soap, resin, hashish
a small boat with oars that is used especially in China (COBUILD)	junk (15), *sampan* (11), canoe (5), coracle (3), gondola (2), dhow (2), rowboat, dinghy, kayak

say two, and perhaps that it ends in 't'. They may come up with a word, say *secant*, that seems to fit, and they may be satisfied with this incorrect solution. Two of the *Inside Language* panel thought of *sexton,* for example (Q3). Or they may go on to think of the right word itself, *sextant*, as did 37.5 per cent of the panel. Sometimes people may hit on the right word but find it still does not sound right; I am never very satisfied with *picaresque*, but have a nagging feeling that a better word is lurking somewhere.

The storage of vocabulary in the mind therefore relies on the basic shape of a word. There is a pattern in the speakers' minds for the word 's - - - - - t', the beginning being most readily available, the end less so, and the middle hardly at all. Even in spelling, only 7 per cent of mistakes occur on the first letter of the word. Five of the *Inside Language* panel came up with *alcove* for *apse*, getting the first letter right. It is comparatively easy to name some words that begin in *gh*, slightly more difficult to name words ending in *gh*, and harder still to name words that have *gh* somewhere in the middle, as crossword puzzle addicts will confirm. The Speaker of the House's confusion of *Paddington Bear* with *Postman Pat* mentioned earlier shows the classic signs of a tip-of-the-tongue mistake. Both are characters in children's books whose names consist of two words beginning with bilabial plosives /p/ and /b/. This will be discussed further in Chapter 9. The form of the lexical entry in the mind is, then, beginning to emerge.

VII The structure of content words

The last chapter saw how words are made up of morphemes, for example how a word such as *books* consists of a content morpheme, *book*, and an inflectional ending for the plural morpheme, -*s*. The present section investigates how content words may be built up through the complementary process called 'derivation'. The starting-point can be a much-quoted sentence from the O.J. Simpson trial, which illustrates many of the ways in which English forms words:

We the jury in the above-entitled action find the defendant Orenthal James Simpson not guilty of the crime of murder in violation of the Penal Code section 187A, a felony, upon Nicole Brown Simpson, a human being.

There are five main methods for forming new words in human languages:

*   One method is to add a morpheme to the end of an existing word – a 'suffix'. Most languages use suffixes both for grammatical inflections and for forming new words. A word such as *defendant* is derived from a base form, *defend*, by the addition of the suffix -*ant*. The same base, *defend*, can lead to different words according to the suffix that is added: *defender* by adding an -*er* suffix, *defence* by adding -*ce* (and omitting the *d*); *defensible* by adding -*ible*, and so on. Similarly, *felon* leads to *felony* and *felonious*; *violate* to *violation* and *violator*; *guilt* to *guilty*.

These new words can in due course combine with the usual grammatical inflections: *defendants*, *violations*, *felonies*, and so on. The different suffixes have particular meanings. The *-ant* ending shows a person carrying out the action: someone who defends is a *defendant*, someone who assists an *assistant*, someone who immigrates an *immigrant*, etc. The *-tion* ending shows that the word is an abstract noun of a general kind, *violation*, *operation*, *affliction*, *revolution*; the *-y* ending shows an adjective meaning 'full of the quality': *guilty*, *windy*, *spicy*. None of these outcomes is guaranteed, since many suffixes have several meanings' – *-ant* in *important* hardly means a person who imports – and may also form part of the base of some nouns – *city* has a *y* though it is not an adjective. A word may have more than one suffix: *organisationally*, for instance, is built up from *organise* + *ation* + *al* + *ly*.

In English these suffixes often change the class of the word concerned from noun to verb, verb to adjective, and so on. That is to say, *-ant* and *-tion* change the verbs *defend* and *violate* into the nouns *defendant* and *violation*; *-y* changes the nouns *guilt* and *milk* into the adjectives *guilty* and *milky*. A single base form of a word can play many roles in the grammar by using these additional morphemes. Typical suffixes for turning verbs into nouns are *-er* and *-ation*, as in *reader* and *information*; for turning adjectives into nouns, *-ness* and *-ity*, *blackness* and *reality*. However, these endings cannot necessarily be applied to every word: the result has to be *blackness* not *blackity* and *reality* not *realness*. Native speakers do not always agree about which new words can be derived; not everyone was happy with John Major's term *additionality*.

- A second method for forming new words is to add something to the beginning of an existing word – a 'prefix', as in *entitle* with *en-* or *asleep* with *a-*. Many English prefixes came originally from Latin, such as *pro* or *anti*, and are still active in other Latin-influenced languages as well as English. Often English prefixes seem to have more definable meanings than suffixes. The prefixes *anti-* and *pro-* in the sense of 'against' and 'in favour' can be added to almost any noun – *anti-war*, *Anti-Christ*, *anti-washing up*, *anti-linguistics*, *pro-life*, *pro-vegetarianism*. Similarly, *re-* in the sense of 'do again' can be found added to verbs in e.g. *repay*, *replay*, *retake*, *refer*, *reconstitutionalize*. In many cases the prefix has become so much part of the word that the original form has ceased to exist; apart from a few witticisms, no one uses *gruntled* and *shevelled* from *disgruntled* and *dishevelled* or *kempt* and *couth* from *unkempt* and *uncouth*.

- A third method is to create a word out of two or more other words, a process called 'compounding'. The examples in the OJ sentence are *above-entitled* and *human being*, both of which are made up from other words, as are *tea-time*, *motorway* and *disc jockey*. Considerable uncertainty still surrounds whether particular compound lexical items should be written as one word, two words or linked with a hyphen. The publishers of my last book wanted to know whether I preferred *babytalk*, *baby talk*, or *baby-talk*; Chapter 7 will reveal what the decision was for this book. Compounding is a common way of forming words in other languages too; in Maori, for example, the act of buying a lolly becomes a new verb 'to lolly-buy', *hoko rare*. In German the 'Danube steamship travel company' is *Donau-dampfschiffahrtsgesellschaft*.

- The fourth method of forming words is to change their word class without altering anything else, called 'conversion'. So *head* is usually a noun but it becomes a verb in *He headed the ball* and *She headed the committee*. *Say* is a verb, but in *He had his say* it is converted into a noun. *Up* is a preposition, but in a student slogan of the 1970s *Up the grant* it became a verb; in *Life has its ups and downs* it is converted into a noun. Recent examples of computer jargon converting nouns into verbs with *-ed* include *He was flamed/e-mailed/spammed/creamed*.

- The fifth method of word formation used in some languages is to add or change material in the middle of the word, called 'infixes'. In English the base form of the word is seldom broken up; *abso-blooming-lutely*, and *kanga-bloody-roo* are rare exceptions.

Some of these processes are effectively dead in English, some are still productive. The *-ard* ending of *bastard*, *coward* and *niggard* hardly leads to new words nowadays. Suffixes are often still available. *-ism* can be meaningfully added to any thing or any person that has an identifiable idea attached to it: *Thatcherism, linguisticism, anti-Europeism,* etc., as can *-wise, language-wise, situation-wise, politics-wise,* etc. Each decade finds itself new productive morphemes. The 1990s seems fond of *mega-*, as in *megabucks, Megadog, megadegeneracy, Megalab, megazine, mega-elated*, of *Brit-* as in *Britprop* and *Britmusic*, and of *-gate* as in *Watergate, Irangate, Squidgygate*, to cite forms observed recently. It is hard to predict which morphemes can be used productively. Until one heard the Stevie Wonder song 'Yesterme, Yesteryou, Yesterday', one would hardly have anticipated that *yester-* was productive in English. Part of the knowledge of words is, then, how to build them into other words, and which prefixes and suffixes can be used.

To bring this chapter together, the lexical entry in the mind contains a variety of information about a word:

- how it is pronounced and spelled, strongest at its beginning and end, weakest in the middle: *sextant*
- how it is used in the sentence in terms of phrase structure, etc.: *John fainted him*
- how it relates to other words through systems of meaning: *grandfather, grandson*
- how its meaning shares features and divides up fields: *blue, red*; *grill, barbecue*
- how it may be built up or decomposed into other words: *defendant, yesterme*.

Comparatively little of the meaning of a word can be stated as a straightforward link to a single object in the world.

The conclusion is that words do not so much have individual meanings of their own as enter into complex systems of meaning shared with other words, whether in terms

Writers and derivation

Here are some sample new words produced by English writers, using the standard processes of derivation, mostly for comic, witty or poetic effect.

Adding a suffix

obscurism, lessness, me-ism, Brazilification	Douglas Coupland
Omnianism, exquisitor, scalbie	Terry Pratchett
swimmy eyes, her eyes became a bit soup-platey	P.G. Wodehouse
gorgeosity, heighth, howly, rabbiter	Anthony Burgess

Adding a prefix or morpheme

teleparablizing, ethnomagnetism	Douglas Coupland
ambi-sinister, cumulo-dynamic	Terry Pratchett
resuffered	Dylan Thomas
ultra-violence	Anthony Burgess

Combining words

underdogging, café minimalism, downnesting	Douglas Coupland
stoning-of-suspected-adulteresses rotas, black-on- *black eyes*	Terry Pratchett
star-gestured, year-hedged, star-flanked	Dylan Thomas
dream-dimmed eyes, that gong-tormented sea	W.B. Yeats
horrorshow kick-boots, flatblock (n.)	Anthony Burgess

Changing word class

upping with the lark, handkerchiefing my upper slopes, *he righthoed, he trousered the key*	P.G. Wodehouse
the one with the snake-pit hairdo	Terry Pratchett
fellowed, do you not sister me?	Dylan Thomas
we upped in the lift, I fisted him	Anthony Burgess

Adding an infix?

emallgration, survivulousness	Douglas Coupland

of components or levels or the relationships of synonyms, antonyms, etc. While this point might seem obvious, many experiments ignore it by testing the learning of pairs of new and old words as if there were a single constant link between words and things. Language students too have to learn vocabulary lists of pairs of words matched with their translations in the second language, a very small aspect of their meaning in the light of the discussion here. Such pairings are untypical of language, where it is rare to find an identical match in meaning between two words both within one language and across different languages. The Dane Otto Jespersen provided the example of the word for 'bat' having slightly different overtones in each language. In French *chauve-souris* emphasizes the bat's baldness and its resemblance to a mouse; in Latin *vespertilio* suggests the evening when the bat is out, and in Danish *flagermus* suggests its flapping. A word contrasts with all the other words in a language rather than having a single definite meaning of its own; the meaning of words can be broken up into components, levels and fields, as well as many other aspects, none of which gives a full account of their meaning by itself. Yet the languages of the world make use of the same resources for creating meaning, and the same ways of making new words from old, another case of similarity in diversity.

Sources and further reading

A general book on meaning is J. Lyons, *Linguistic Semantics* (Cambridge: CUP, 1995).

Lexical entries and the dictionary in the mind

A popular account of the mental lexicon is given in J. Aitchison, *Words in the Mind* (Oxford: Blackwell, 1987).

Colours and linguistic relativity

The original book is B. Berlin and P. Kay, *Basic Color Terms: Their Universality and Evolution* (Berkeley: University of California Press, 1969). A book which provides much information is S. Wyler, *Colour and Language* (Tübingen: Gunter Narr, 1992). The stages of child development come from E.G. Johnson, 'The development of colour knowledge in pre-school children', *Child Development* 48 (1987).

Levels of meaning

The original source is E. Rosch, 'Human categorization', in N. Warren (ed.), *Studies in Cross-Cultural Psychology* (New York: Academic Press, 1977). An account of the whole area is given in J.R. Taylor, *Linguistic Categorization* (Oxford: Clarendon Press, 1989). The categories of opposites are based on D. Cruse, *Lexical Semantics* (Cambridge: CUP, 1986).

Language and thinking

Whorf's ideas on language and thinking can be found in the readable collection edited by J. Carroll, *Language, Thought and Reality: Selected Writings of Benjamin Lee Whorf* (Cambridge, MA: MIT Press, 1956). New Guinea languages and much else are described in P. Mühlhäusler, 'Babel revisited', *UNESCO Courier* (Feb. 1994). Malaysian terms for tasting were tested in M. O'Mahoney and H. Muhiudeen, 'A preliminary study of alternative taste languages using qualitative description of sodium chloride solutions: Malay versus English', *British Journal of*

Psychology 68 (1977): 275–8. The experiment on word order and setting is described in A.B. Hooton and C. Hooton, 'The influence of syntax on visual perception', *Anthropological Linguistics* 19/8 (1977): 355–7. The Chinese hypotheticals are discussed in R.F. Cromer, *Language and Thought in Normal and Handicapped Children* (Oxford: Blackwell, 1991). The main work on metaphors and thinking is G. Lakoff and M. Johnson, *Metaphors We Live By* (Chicago: Chicago University Press, 1980).

Components of meaning

The original work on features was E. Clark, 'On the acquisition of "before" and "after"', *Journal of Verbal Learning and Verbal Behaviour* 10 (1971): 266–75. Her more recent ideas are in *The Lexicon in Acquisition* (Cambridge: CUP, 1993).

Cookery vocabulary is analysed in A. Lehrer, 'Semantic cuisine', *Journal of Linguistics* 5 (1969): 39–55; her later article applying this to wine is 'Talking about wine', *Language* 51/4 (1975): 901–23. The adjectives used by professional apple-tasters are described in A.A. Williams and C.S. Carter, 'A language and procedure for the sensory assessment of Cox's Orange Pippin apples', *J. Sci. Fd Agric.* 28 (1977): 1090–1104.

Words and the mind

The tip-of-the-tongue phenomenon is described in R. Brown and D. McNeill, 'The "tip of the tongue" phenomenon', *Journal of Verbal Learning and Verbal Behaviour* 5 (1966): 325–37.

The structure of content words

The processes of derivation are described in books on morphology such as A. Spencer, *Morphological Theory: An Introduction to Word Structure in Generative Grammar* (Oxford: Blackwell, 1991). The examples of word formation given in this chapter come from: D. Coupland, *Generation X* (1992); P.G. Wodehouse; T. Pratchett, *Small Gods* (1992); D. Thomas, *Collected Poems* (1952); A. Burgess, *A Clockwork Orange* (1962).

6 The Writing Systems of Language

All human languages have a sound system, the only exception being the equivalent gesture system of sign languages. However, not all languages have written scripts. In a sense the sound system of a language is 'natural', the writing system of a language is 'unnatural'. Speech evolved within human society over millennia, with no single person taking the credit for designing it. Writing systems, however, often came into being at a particular moment of history, sometimes indeed as the invention of a particular individual. For example, in 1820 Sequoyah invented a writing system for Cherokee, spoken in Tennessee, which is still used for traditional texts. Speech is learnt naturally by virtually all children; children are not taught to speak. Nearly all children, however, have to be taught to read and write; they rarely pick it up by themselves without help.

This chapter looks at the diversity of the writing systems used in human languages, particularly at the contrast between meaning-based systems and sound-based systems. It starts with visual signs, goes on to the character systems of Chinese and Japanese and then looks at the evolution of the alphabet. Finally it considers some of the bases for the English writing system. As always, it is easy to gain the impression that the system one uses oneself is best, whatever its imperfections. Yet writing systems correspond to the different sounds and grammar systems of the languages they were invented for. Given that languages vary in many ways, there is probably no ideal writing system that could do justice to all of them.

I Signs and language

The starting-point for any discussion of writing has to be the relationship between written signs, whether letters or characters or pictures and the meanings that people want to express through language. While the sounds of all languages come from a fixed set, however much the sounds themselves differ, writing systems are fundamentally divided over what the written signs represent. One type of system links signs directly to the spoken language so that written symbols correspond to the sounds of speech, that is to say phonemes or syllables. In an English word the written letter *t* corresponds to the phoneme /t/ in *top*, *l* to the /l/ in *like* and so on. Or one letter stands for two or more phonemes: *s* stands for /s/ in *sign* or /z/ in *visit*, *a* for /æ/ in *pat* or /ɑ:/ in *spa*. Or two letters stand for one sound, such as *ng* for /ŋ/ in *leaving* and *th* for /ð/ in *the*. Languages as diverse as English, Russian and Zulu have sound-based writing systems.

The other main type of writing system uses symbols that correspond with words or meanings rather than with sounds, as in Chinese and Japanese. To some extent, all of us employ this system everyday. The symbol 3 would be read as *three* in English, as *drei* in German, as *san* in Japanese and so on. But it has exactly the same meaning whatever the language: it stands for a concept, not a set of sounds. The writing of numbers and other mathematical symbols is international, indeed almost universal. You can read the times of departures in airport lounges almost anywhere in the world, even if you cannot decipher the names of the destinations.

Such signs can be understood by speakers of different languages because they are unrelated to the sounds or words of any particular language. A computer keyboard includes £ $ % & − + as well as the numbers 1 to 9. All of these have the same or similar meanings in many languages, despite corresponding with quite different words. Other signs have slightly different functions in different languages but are still widespread, for example the punctuation marks ! ? . ; ,"'.

Signs can convey full messages without reference to a particular language. A no smoking sign ⊗ is unmistakable in almost any country, even if the penalties for disobeying it vary widely – don't even think of smoking in a lift in Singapore. The signs for male and female toilets 🚹 🚺 are also international, although by no means unambiguous. Jung Chang, the author of *Wild Swans*, reports: 'I had no idea why the little figure in trousers was supposed to be a mań, because that's exactly what women looked like in China.' It is just as hard for the foreigner to know that in Poland men's toilets have a triangle ▽ on the door, women's a circle ○. International manufacturers of consumer goods have contributed many new signs. Tape-recorders have >, >> and the rest; cameras have sun-signs ✳; washing machines have spirals for fast spin; car dashboards light up with little petrol pumps when fuel is needed; and so on.

These signs exploit the visual similarity between a real object and a symbol. A drawing of a cigarette has something to do with cigarettes; double arrows with double speed >> . The signs mimic the world we see to some extent. Roman numerals partly exploit this correspondence for counting: I II III correspond to one, two or three objects; even IV was once IIII. Computer makers have littered their screens with icons of wastepaper baskets or scissors in the belief that these are more user-friendly than mere words. The advantage for manufacturers of electronic or household equipment is precisely that icons are *not* written language and so not tied in to the sounds of any specific language. Hence they are universal for speakers of all languages – if they can work them out.

Decorative English in Japan

Written language has a variety of uses of its own – for keeping permanent records of contracts, etc., for labelling objects and providing notices, and so on. Here are some examples of a more unusual use, which can be called 'decorative language' – the use of language just because it looks good, with little or no meaning. An interesting use of decorative language is seen in the Japanese custom of using English for brand-names and advertiser's slogans. Here are some examples mostly collected by students at Temple University, Tokyo, brand-names deleted.

Chocolate bars: a heroines' treasured chocolate born is cozy for the heroines in the town

A lovely and tiny twig is on the forest. The sentimental taste.

A coffee cup: **Coffee.**
Relax and have a nice coffee break. So you can meet the something wonderful happen

A milk shake: Nice day good day man and women's drink Delicious and my drink

Jackets: REVOLTING FASHION FOR MEN

Marathon race your life will never be the same after SCENES WE'D

In my childfood the world was fulled over with the dreams. I was very good at finding the dreams from everything. Having dreams is the best way to get happiness, doesn't they?

Carring on the wind in the light my heart is filled with the feelings

We send you fiery winter fun for your life

Sports bags: *TOUCH DOWN I basically feel you should sports for yourself*
To all players aiming at success supporting you

A truck ad: Whenever and everywhere we can meet our best friend – nature. Take a grip of steering.

The equivalent in spoken language is 'decorative speech' as in some kinds of singing: *ree boop a doodee doo doo deee doo dertee doodee . . .* (Louis Armstrong, *Heebie Jeebies*); *Praised amazed kinda dazed when I plays From the time inclined I used to rhyme I went for mine . . .* (the Goats)

For there is no guarantee that people interpret these pictures in the same way. Anybody can recognize that a picture of a cigarette has something to do with smoking; ⊗ but what? The meaning depends on some convention other than the picture of the object itself, in this case the meaning of the diagonal line. There is no intrinsic reason why a line or a cross over a cigarette should mean 'don't', ■ mean 'stop' or ○ 'Women's Toilet'. These conventions cannot be deduced from the pictures alone. A running man sign 🏃 does not mean 'There are men here' but shows which way to go in an emergency: if you don't know what a running man represents, the sign is not going to save your life in a fire. The sign may appear to be a recognizable picture, but the message it conveys depends on particular conventions of interpretation.

Signs do not, then, make a writing system in themselves. They have no direct link to language, even though conventions can be added that make them carry more complex meanings. Writing systems usually connect directly to the system of language itself, whether through the sounds or the meanings or in other ways we shall see later, rather than to objects in the world.

II Non-sound based writing systems

A system for writing language can start from the icons of the previous section. Simple drawings of the objects in our environment together with signs for concepts like negation could provide us with a form of written communication. This link to the real world is indeed one of the sources of the Chinese writing system. This section, then, looks at Chinese and Japanese writing systems that primarily use 'characters' rather than 'letters'.

1 Chinese

Chinese employs a large set of 'characters' rather than a small set of letters. Many Chinese characters were based originally on drawings of the most striking features of various objects. A sheep is shown by its curved horns 羊 ; a mountain by its peak 山 ; a person by two legs 人 ; a river by its banks 川. Over thousands of years these drawings have often changed out of recognition. The shape of an elephant can hardly be recognized in the modern character 象.

To cover the whole of a language, rather more is required of a writing system than stylized pictures of thousands of objects. Characters are needed for abstract concepts that require a non-literal interpretation, like the superimposed cross for negation. Chinese, for instance, devised non-literal characters for 'large' 大 , i.e. a person with arms and legs spread wide, and for the abstract concepts of 'up' and 'down', 上／下 .

The set of characters can be amplified in several logical ways. One is to combine characters to get other meanings. The character for 'person' 人 put together with the character for 'base' 本 becomes the character for 'body' 体. The character for 'tree' 木 repeated twice 林 means 'wood', repeated three times 森 means 'forest'. A second method is to extend the meaning of characters to related concepts so that 樂 *yue* ('music') also stands for *le* ('pleasure'). A third method exploits the pronunciation of a word rather than its meaning by 'lending' a character to another word that happens to sound the same. So 來 once meaning 'wheat' could also stand for 'to come', since both were pronounced *lai*.

90 per cent of Chinese characters are, however, formed by combining two types of character: one of 214 'radicals' that have a particular meaning combined with a 'phonetic' character that shows its pronunciation. For example, the phonetic character 苗 *miao* ('sprout') goes with a radical for 'animal' to get 猫 *mao* ('cat'); the same phonetic character goes with the radical for 'metal' to get 錨 *mao* ('anchor'). Since the phonetic characters have been linked to the pronunciation of Chinese from its early days in the Shang dynasty in 1766 BC, this connection is not much help with modern Chinese. Nor is it simply a matter of one character equalling one word. Chinese also combined sequences of characters to create new 'words'. For example, 火山 ('volcano') graphically combines 'fire' with 'mountain'. 英國 *ying guo* ('England') is a fortunate combination of 'smart/bright' and 'country'. Indeed, the characters for all foreign countries are formed in this way.

Some modifications to the character system have been put forward this century. A form of 'basic' Chinese was suggested in 1927 called *Common People's Thousand Character Lessons*. Nowadays 90 per cent of a Chinese newspaper indeed uses the most common 1000 characters. Since 1956 the shapes of many characters have been officially simplified in mainland China. Nevertheless an educated Chinese may still have to know around 5000 characters, a dictionary going up to 40 000.

The Chinese character system mirrors particular characteristics of the Chinese language. The meaning of 'past' in English is conveyed by the ending of the verb, *-ed*, as in *looked*. In Chinese the nearest equivalent to 'past' is the idea of an action being completed, which is shown by the addition of the word 了 *le* to the sentence, not by adding a word-ending. One language conveys the meaning through an ending, the other through a word.

In general, English uses word-endings to show concepts such as 'past' and 'plural', while Chinese shows them through whole words. Each Chinese character links to a word. Or, to be more precise, a character is linked to a unit of meaning called a 'morpheme', as seen in Chapter 3. The morpheme 'past' in English is expressed through a word-ending alone, *-ed*, in Chinese through a word, *le*. Hence the different writing systems for English and Chinese suit the different ways in which these languages are organized. The character-writing system works particularly well for the Chinese language, as the form of the word never changes. The character 走 *zou* ('walk') is the same whether it conveys the equivalent of *walks*, *walked* or *walking*.

While outsiders marvel how people learn the thousands of Chinese characters, this apparent complexity does not present particular problems to its users. Indeed, printing with metal type first took place in China in the twelfth century AD. Children find it as easy to learn characters as an alphabetic script. Though character typewriters were cumbersome to use, computer technology makes word-processors and printers using Chinese characters comparatively straightforward.

An important advantage of the Chinese writing system is that the script is universal, in the same sense as the number system is universal. For it is misleading to speak of Chinese as if it were a single language. There are around eight Chinese languages originally spoken in different areas of China, though now spread around the world, such as Cantonese (Yue), spoken by many Chinese in England because of their links with Hong Kong, and Fukkianese, spoken by many Chinese in Malaysia and Taiwan. The language taught in schools in China is Putonghua (Standard Chinese), descended from Mandarin and from northern dialects; this differs slightly from the official forms of Mandarin used in Singapore and Taiwan. It has more speakers than the other languages, about 70 per cent of the population of China, and is spread across a greater area of China. It also has higher status, having been the language of government in China for thousands of years, though not in its modern form.

Even if they were related in the distant past, these eight are as different from each other as any languages in Europe. A Chinese who speaks Cantonese would probably

Direction in writing

The main directions of writing in human languages use the two dimensions of left-to-right and top-to-bottom. Several languages can be written in different directions in special circumstances, e.g. vertical shop names in English-speaking countries.

Top to bottom (lines)

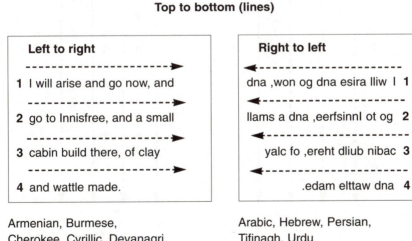

Left to right

1 I will arise and go now, and

2 go to Innisfree, and a small

3 cabin build there, of clay

4 and wattle made.

Right to left

dna ,won og dna esira lliw I 1

llams a dna ,eerfsinnI ot og 2

yalc fo ,ereht dliub nibac 3

.edam elttaw dna 4

Armenian, Burmese,
Cherokee, Cyrillic, Devanagri,
Ethiopic, English, Greek, Korean,
(Han'gul), Thai, Tibetan,
Japanese (modern), Chinese (mainland)

Arabic, Hebrew, Persian,
Tifinagh, Urdu
(Note: in many cases the forms of
the letters also face to the left)

Top to bottom (columns)

Note: as these are character languages, the alphabetic script of English does not give a proper impression.

Left to right

1	2	3	4
I	g	c	a
	o	a	n
w		b	d
i	t	i	
l	o	n	w
l		b	a
	I	u	t
a	n	i	t
r	n	l	l
i	i	d	e
s	s		
e	f	t	m
	r	h	a
a	e	e	d
n	e,	r	e.
d	a	e,	
	n	o	
g	d	f	
o			
	a		
n	c		
o	l		
w,	a		
	s	y	
	m		
a	a		
n	l		
d	l		

Right to left

4	3	2	1
a	c	g	I
n	a	o	
d	b		w
	i	t	i
w	n	o	l
a	b		l
t	u	I	
t	i	n	a
l	l	n	r
e	d	i	i
		s	s
m	t	f	e
a	h	r	
d	e	e	a
e.	r	e	n
	e,	a	d
	o	n	
	f	d	g
			o
	a		
	c		n
	l		o
	a		w,
	y	s	
		m	
		a	a
		l	n
		l	d

Chinese (Taiwan), Japanese
(traditional), Korean (characters)

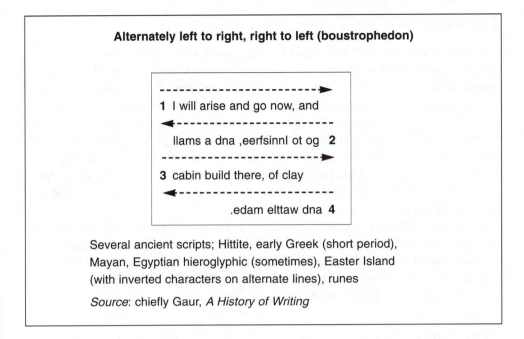

Alternately left to right, right to left (boustrophedon)

1 I will arise and go now, and

llams a dna ,eerfsinnl ot og 2

3 cabin build there, of clay

.edam elttaw dna 4

Several ancient scripts; Hittite, early Greek (short period),
Mayan, Egyptian hieroglyphic (sometimes), Easter Island
(with inverted characters on alternate lines), runes

Source: chiefly Gaur, *A History of Writing*

no more understand a Chinese speaking Hakkanese than a speaker of English would understand someone speaking Greek. The Chinese regard these eight as 'dialects' rather than as 'languages', in a sense of the word 'dialect' different from that used later in Chapter 8. The justification for calling them dialects rather than languages is precisely that the eight languages share the same set of written characters. While they are distinct languages in their spoken form, in the written form they can be thought of as 'dialects' of one language. There are of course other powerful political and cultural reasons for unifying Chinese people through a common 'language'.

As Chinese characters stand for meanings rather than sounds, it does not matter how they are pronounced. The characters could be used to represent English or Maori or any other language, provided that the meanings existed in those languages. The same written text can be understood in many parts of China by speakers of different 'dialects'. (Nevertheless, as about 6 per cent of the population of mainland China are from non-Chinese ethnic minorities, it is still necessary for Chinese banknotes to use Mongolian, Tibetan and other minority languages as well as Chinese.)

Though in principle speakers of Chinese can understand the same written text, this may not work so well in practice. The direction of reading in a newspaper varies from left-to-right in mainland China to right-to-left in Taiwan, creating problems for younger people in Taiwan. There is also variation between the characters. Mainland China uses the simplified characters, Taiwan the older, unsimplified forms. The sign *ge*, which acts as a 'counter' showing that a number is involved, is 個 in Taiwan (unsimplified), but 个 in mainland China (simplified).

2 Korean

Chinese characters came to be used as a writing system in several countries within the Chinese sphere of influence, such as Vietnam, Korea and Japan, though the languages spoken in these countries are not related to Chinese. The Chinese character system took advantage of the fact that Chinese words have a single unvarying form. Korean words, however, resemble English in being made up of a base form plus one or more inflections: adding *chee* and *da* to the Korean stem *de* ('glare') yields *chee-de-da* ('glaring'); adding *chee* and *da* to *sort* ('flood') yields *chee-sort-da* ('rapidly flood out'). The stock of basic Chinese characters needed to be amplified to represent these Korean forms. Eventually an entirely new sound-based script called Han'gul was invented for Korean, as we see later.

Nevertheless Chinese characters continued to be used in Korea until well into this century. In South Korea, many Chinese words that have become part of Korean are still represented through characters, though this practice is frowned on in the North. Indeed, to this day most Korean names are Chinese, though now spelled in Han'gul – *Lee*, *Kim* and *Park,* for example.

3 Japanese

The most enduring adaptation of the Chinese characters has, however, been to Japanese and was already well established by the seventh century AD. A series of changes was necessary to accommodate the differences between Japanese and Chinese. This process has resulted in three types of Japanese writing system, which coexist often in the same document, not to say sentence.

Japanese kanji

The Chinese characters themselves were taken into Japanese as a system called 'kanji'. One method of transferring characters from Chinese was to borrow both the Chinese character and the Chinese word itself. The character 人 means 'person' in Chinese. It was taken over into Japanese together with the Chinese word for 'person', *jin*, for example in *jin-ko* ('population'), represented by the kanji characters for 'man' and 'mouth', i.e. 人口. This technique was so popular that more than 50 per cent of modern Japanese words are derived from Chinese.

Sometimes, however, the Chinese character was attached to a Japanese word with the same meaning. Thus the character for 'person' 人 stands not only for the Chinese-derived *jin* but also for the Japanese word, *hito*. One and the same character can represent two different words with more or less the same meaning. The sign for 'mouth' 口 was given above as the Chinese-based word *ko*, but the same sign also stands for the equivalent Japanese word, *kuchi*. A kanji character may stand for different words depending on whether it is used with its Chinese-based value or its Japanese value.

For example 行 ('to go') can be said as *iku* with its Japanese-based form or *gyo* with its Chinese-derived form.

To add to the complexity, kanji characters were also used to represent the sound of a word, ignoring its meaning. The Chinese character *ma* ('horse') 馬 is used as the first character of *ma rei* ('Malaysia') 馬来 because it has the same sounds *ma* although Malaysia has no particular association with horses. The connection between character and sound became eroded as the pronunciation of both Chinese and Japanese changed. Today the same character can have alternative pronunciations in Japanese according to the Chinese pronunciation of different periods. For instance 行 ('to go') can be pronounced not only as *gyo* and *iku* but also as *ko* and *okonau*. The same character can not only stand for different things but can also represent different pronunciations.

As with Chinese, the number of Japanese characters is very large, in fact uncountable. A popular dictionary has 14 924 Chinese-derived kanji, the most elaborate dictionary 48 902. An approved list of 1850 kanji was issued in 1946, which has been more or less adhered to in newspapers; it has now been extended to 1945. A Japanese child has to learn 46 characters in year 1 of school, including 一 *ichi* ('one') and 口 *kuchi* ('mouth'); in year 2 105 characters, including 天 *ten* ('sky') and 小 *sho* ('small'); in the sixth year 969 characters still remain to be learnt to complete the basic set.

But most texts are bound to use rarer characters. Place-names, for example, often have characters outside this range of the set, such as *Sapporo* 札幌, famous for its skiing and its beer. A place-name such as 行谷 could be read in at least three different ways as *yukigayya*, as *gyoya* and as *namegaya*, the last and most unexpected one being correct. When I was hiking on a Japanese mountain accompanied by a highly educated Japanese, we became lost because she could not read the local place-names on the signposts. In England too place-names present problems for the uninitiated – *Leicester* and *Greenwich* are still pronounced /lestə/ and /grenɪtʃ/ even if *Cirencester* or *Holborn* are now mostly /saɪrənsestə/ and /həʊlbən/ respectively rather than the older /sɪstə/ and /həʊbən/.

Japanese kana

In addition to the kanji character system, Japanese evolved two other writing systems called 'kana'. Both build on the sound-based principle of using signs to represent the pronunciation of Japanese syllables. Kana characters adapted kanji characters from different sources to produce signs for around 47 syllables. Most kana signs represent a syllable of Japanese consisting of a Consonant Vowel (CV) *ka*, *mu*, *wo* and so on. Others stand for vowels alone, such as *a*, and one for a single 'syllabic' *n*. The kana systems rely, then, on the basic CV syllable of Japanese outlined in the last chapter.

The 'hiragana' system simplified whole kanji characters from handwriting rather than using parts of them. Thus: た *ta*, な *na* and ま *ma*. The whole sentence can be written in hiragana, not just isolated words; it can substitute completely for kanji characters, particularly in children's books. However, the main use of hiragana is to

---

Japanese scripts (and Arabic numerals)

Here is a heading from the front cover of a Japanese computing magazine showing four scripts in operation: kanji, hiragana, katakana and Roman alphabet (romaji).

340MB ハード・ディスクを選ぶ、買う、使う
Select, buy and use 340MB hard disks

ハード・ディスク	を	選	ぶ
katakana	**hiragana**	**kanji**	**hiragana**
hard disc	object marker	*select*	present tense marker

---

show the grammatical forms – particles, verb-endings and so on – that are as important to Japanese as they are to Korean and English but not to Chinese. A writing system devised for a language without inflectional endings, namely Chinese, had to be adapted to a language with such endings.

The alternative 'katakana' system exploited small sections of the kanji characters that stood for sounds. The same syllables are now タ *ta*, ナ *na* and マ *ma*. Katakana is used nowadays as a way of representing foreign words from Western languages, such as *Pepsi* ペプシー and *London* ロンドン.

A written sentence in Japanese usually combines the kanji characters for the nouns, verbs and so on with the hiragana characters for the endings and particles which are vital to the grammar of Japanese. For instance the hiragana for the verb *mi(ru)*, meaning 'see', combines a kanji character with the present tense ending *ru* 見る to get the present tense 'sees'. The same kanji character combines with the hiragana sign for the past tense inflection *ta* 見た to get the past tense *mita* 'saw'. Sometimes katakana or hiragana are used in parallel with kanji to provide a 'translation' of characters outside the basic set.

To the outsider, the complexity of the Japanese writing systems is daunting, particularly since a character can represent up to seven different things and since the modern system is partially based on the pronunciation and meanings of ancient Chinese. However, English speakers are mostly not aware that a single word such as *table* has 21 meanings, according to the *Oxford English Dictionary*, or that a spelling such as *gh* represents the /x/ sound of Middle English rather than any sound of modern English. Native speakers do not usually have particular problems with the Japanese writing system. As with Chinese, the practical problems of typing or printing a large set of symbols have been effectively solved by modern technology. Though it is difficult to compare countries, the literacy rate in Japan is one of the highest in the world; dyslexia is said to be unknown in Japanese children.

III Sound-based writing systems

The rest of this chapter deals with systems which relate written signs to spoken sounds. Though Chinese and Japanese characters are the best-known examples of writing systems in which written signs correspond not to sounds but to meanings, as we have seen, even in these scripts, characters that show meaning were from the outset mixed with those that show some aspect of sound, however remotely. One way of making writing correspond systematically to sounds is to match each separate sound of a language with a letter, as in a phonetic alphabet, and is therefore called an 'alphabetic' writing system. In its pure form, an alphabet-based system would require as many written signs as there were different sounds in the language.

1 Syllable-based systems

Alternatively, each written sign could represent a syllable in the language, a system known as a 'syllabary'. Examples are the Japanese kana scripts already encountered and the 85-symbol Cherokee script. The 50 or so characters of the Japanese kana are enough to convey all the sounds of Japanese because of its comparatively simple consonant–vowel CV syllable structure, as mentioned in Chapter 4. Only a small group of syllables falls outside the system and these too are included through additional marks. While in principle a syllabary can be more economical with symbols than a character system, this depends on how many syllables there are in the language. A syllable-based system would be easy to use for Hawaiian, with 162 different syllables, less easy in Yoruba, with 582, and very difficult in Thai, which has 23 638 syllables.

Apart from the Japanese kana, syllable-based writing systems are rare, although they have been invented separately in many parts of the world. One of the earliest syllabaries was the Linear B used in 1400–1200 BC in Minoa, in which 88 symbols represented CV syllables of Greek. As Greek permitted more complex syllable structures than CV, the system had to be extended in various ways, for example by treating diphthongs as two signs, as is done in kana.

Korean Han'gul

Most sound-based systems have been based on the individual phonemes of the spoken language rather than on its syllables. The Han'gul system devised for Korean as an alternative to Chinese characters is unique because it was designed to represent sounds as diagrams of the ways in which they were produced, a phonetic alphabet where the shapes of the letters themselves suggest the sounds. In English, there is no particular reason why the letter *m* should correspond to the labial sound /m/; it is simply a convention. In Han'gul, however, the sign for /m/ is **ㅁ** , an abstract drawing of the lips.

Chapter 4 showed how the crucial element in producing many consonants is the point where the tongue makes contact in the mouth – the teeth, the teeth ridge, the roof of the mouth or the back of the mouth. Consonants are symbolized in Han'gul as diagrams of the mouth from the left side. In an /n/ sound the tongue touches the alveolar ridge behind the teeth, which could be drawn as ㄴ, the Han'gul sign for /n/. Adding a convention that a stop consonant is shown by a bar, a /t/ sound with the same alveolar contact is ㄷ. In the sound /k/, the tongue contacts the soft palate at the back of the mouth, drawn in the Han'gul sign ㄱ, the stroke again showing a stop rather than a fricative.

The signs for vowels also systematically reflect the sounds of Korean. Front vowels are distinguished from their back equivalents by having a small version of the back vowel on the left. Thus the back vowel /a/ has the sign ㅏ, its front equivalent /æ/ is ㅐ. And the same applies to the signs for the other 12 consonants and 10 vowels. The major sound differences are signalled directly in the sign. While Korean in fact has 21 consonants and 18 vowels, additional marks can represent any sound needed. To get the forms of the actual script, the signs for consonants and vowels were combined together to get distinctive shapes for 140 syllables, such as 가 for *ka*. Each compound CV sign was adapted into the square shape of the Chinese characters also used in Korean. In one way, then, Han'gul is a syllabary in that each printed sign corresponds to a syllable; however, the internal components of each syllable sign show the sounds that make it up, not arbitrarily but in a systematic fashion.

The Han'gul system reflects a sophisticated linguistic analysis that separated consonants from vowels, recognized the syllable as a unit and used a concept similar to the modern idea of distinctive features. While Han'gul is flexible enough in principle to accommodate changes in pronunciation, the spelling was standardized in 1933, leading to the signs being slightly further removed from actual pronunciation. Above all, it is a rational system that can be learnt logically. Given the information supplied so far, what does the sign ㅍ correspond to? Obviously something to do with both

Korean Han'gul

Here are the back and front of a Korean visiting card, showing the Han'gul script and its Roman equivalent.

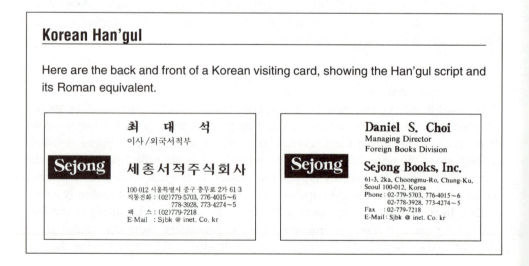

lips but less firm contact than /m/ in ㅁ ; in fact it stands for /p/. It has been claimed that the system can be mastered in a day.

2 Alphabet-based writing systems

This section turns to sound-based writing systems that make use of alphabets in which letters correspond to phonemes of the spoken language rather than to whole syllables. Writing systems emerged for particular languages by invention or by transfer from other languages, rather than by being devised for language in general. Hence they reflect the idiosyncratic properties of the original language for which they were used, whether in terms of its grammar – characters suit the lack of inflectional endings in Chinese – or its pronunciation – the kana syllabaries fit the CV syllables of Japanese. Using a writing system for another language may change its character, for instance transforming the meaning-based characters of Chinese into the sound-related kanji of Japanese.

Consonant-based systems

The alphabetic writing system likewise shows traces of its origins, and has changed as its scope was extended to other languages. The first alphabetic system that represented sounds directly by letters arose in the Semitic languages of the eastern Mediterranean around 1750 BC, leading eventually to scripts for Hebrew, Arabic and Phoenician. The grammar of Semitic languages differs from those described so far in one crucial way. English conveys concepts such as 'past' through word-endings, Chinese through words such as *le*. A third possibility is to change the vowels within the word through infixes, as we saw in Chapter 5. English uses vowel-changing to a minor extent, *ring/rang*, *blow/blew*, *crisis/crises*, *man/men*. Changing the word internally to show meaning is, however, a basic characteristic of Semitic languages. In Egyptian Arabic the root form of the word *k*t** becomes *kataba* ('he wrote') and *kutiba* ('it was written'), changing *-a-a-* to *-u-i-*. A change of tense involves a change of vowel.

In these languages the root of a word is a sequence of consonants, usually three, rather like its permanent skeleton. The vowels come and go according to fleeting aspects of meaning. Arabic and Hebrew can then represent the word using only consonants. If English *No smoking* were written on this principle, it would be *N smkng*, *Back to basics Bck t bsics*. The Hebrew word /davaʁ/ 'something' is written from right to left as דבר with letters for the consonants /d/, /v/, /ʁ/ but not for any vowels. In Arabic, also written right to left, the word /laʔiba/ لعب ('he played') has signs for the consonants, but not for the vowels.

The lack of vowels in the written language does not handicap Semitic speakers, since vowels can be predicted from the context, as they are part of the grammar, not of the structure of the words themselves. This lack of vowel signs again relates to the syllable structure of the language. A CV-syllable language can be represented easily in a consonant-only alphabet since the reader knows that each pair of consonants must be separated by a vowel and the last consonant must be followed by a vowel: 'bb' expands to 'baba' not to 'ebb'. A language that allows complex consonant clusters poses more difficulty for this vowel-less system. How would an English reader know whether 'bl' stood for *able* or *blue*, 'stry' for *stray*, *story* or *estuary*?

Nevertheless the absence of vowels still poses a problem even in CV languages. There are four Hebrew words, /diːʁ/ /daʁ/ /doːʁ/ /daːʁ/, each with a different meaning ('stable', 'mother-of pearl', 'generation', 'dwell', respectively), all spelled with *dr* דר. Hebrew and Arabic have come up with similar solutions to this problem. In 800 BC certain Hebrew consonant signs started to be used for vowels, so that 'dir' could become 'djr', 'dur' become 'dwr' and so on; thus in practice 'dr' for 'stable' (/diːʁ/) and for 'generation' (/doːʁ/) are distinguished by vowel letters. This system is still used in Hebrew for most everyday purposes, such as writing letters. It does not, however, indicate all vowels.

A second system in Hebrew, called 'pointing', uses dots to show the different vowels, nowadays only when great clarity is needed, as in poetry, the Bible or books for teaching reading. Thus a ן sign with a ㅜ below it, ‖ , means 'and'. Arabic uses bars and hooks rather than dots for the same reason. For example /laʔiba/ ('he played') without vowel signs is لعب, with vowel signs is لَعِبَ .

Both Hebrew and Arabic have retained their classical written forms because of their use in sacred texts. Since all languages change over time, contemporary spoken Arabic has thus diverged more and more from written Arabic and has evolved into different local varieties in the various countries in which Arabic is used, such as Egypt, Morocco, and Saudi Arabia. The pronunciation of Hebrew too has changed since its revival as a spoken language in the early part of this century after centuries of virtual oblivion. However good the intention to base writing on the spoken language, a script soon separates from the current pronunciation of its speakers, whether Hebrew or English.

The crucial historical contribution of the Semitic scripts was a set of letters which corresponded to sounds, strictly speaking phonemes, rather than to objects, words or meanings, in other words an alphabet. Much of Western culture takes for granted that the main function of a writing system is to represent speech. A writing system fails if it does not show how each and every word is pronounced. Non-alphabetic scripts are seen as inefficient or illogical, despite the fact that they have been used successfully for thousands of years by highly sophisticated societies, are learnt, if anything, more easily by children and are now handled readily by modern technology.

Alphabets are no more immune to problems when transferred from one language to another than other writing systems. The major problem with sound-based systems is that the range and number of sounds in the new language alters the number of letters that are required and what they stand for. A language with only three vowels, like Moroccan Arabic, places different demands on a writing system from those of a language with 13 vowels like French.

Consonant and vowel systems

The alphabet used for modern English is the result of the adaptation of the original Semitic alphabet via circuitous routes. The Greeks took over a version of the Semitic alphabet from the Phoenicians, adapting many of the consonant shapes and using many of the letter names while ignoring their original meanings. The original sign ∀ meant 'ox', based on the shape of the horns. The Phoenician letter 'aleph' ⟨ rotated the letter one step to the left. The letter came into Greek as the letter 'alpha' A, rotating again so that in the classical form the ox is now upside down. The Phoenician 'beth' for 'house' became 'beta' in Greek and so on. In the original Phoenician the word *alphabet* therefore meant 'ox'+ 'house'.

Greek was, and still is, an inflectional language that depends on word-endings to indicate meanings, for example *vlepo* ('I see') vs. *vlepoume* ('we see'). Vowels are not generally changed within the word to show differences of meaning. So the Greek writing system had to introduce letters for vowels. The method was to adapt consonant letters from Phoenician that were not needed in Greek such as A (alpha); hence 'A' started its life in the alphabet as a consonant. The Greek alphabet became a complete phoneme-based system rather than being restricted to consonants.

The Greeks passed one version of their alphabet, in which 'H' was a consonant rather than a vowel and 'V' was a letter for /u/, to the Etruscans, who in turn passed it to the Romans by about 650 BC. The Roman alphabet was modified in various ways to accommodate not only the structure of Latin but also the borrowing of Greek words into Latin, for example by reinstating 'Y' for the vowel [y] in Greek loanwords such as *Phrygian*. Then, as the Roman alphabet spread across Europe, it adapted to the local peculiarities. 'W' and 'V' were needed to show the difference between /v/ and /w/ that evolved in Germanic languages, as in English *went* and *vent*. 'J' separated from 'I' in English much later to show the syllable initial /dʒ/ sound in *judge*.

Many other sound-based alphabets and syllabaries are used in the languages of the world. Gaur's *History of Writing* lists about 65 main writing systems, though many are not in use now. India alone has 19 different scripts for its 14 or so official languages. The most familiar alphabet other than the Roman is perhaps the Greek because of its use for scientific symbols, etc., π (pi) or θ (theta). The Cyrillic alphabet, adapted from Greek in the ninth century, allegedly by St Cyrillus, is widely used for Slavic languages such as Russian and Serbian. A wide variety of other scripts also exists, ranging from those for specific languages, such as Burmese, to those for several languages, such as the Devanagari syllabic script used for Bengali, Hindi and Kashmiri. Provided the principles of sound-based writing are known, the choice of actual symbols does not matter.

English spelling

The English writing system is, then, an example of an alphabetic system. This section outlines some of its characteristics, before the next section goes into some of its well-known difficulties. The long historical chain from Greek onward has meant that the

A brief history of A

The historical relationship between the different alphabetic scripts can be seen in the following diagram, illustrated with some of the different shapes of the letter A, based on inscriptions or manuscripts.

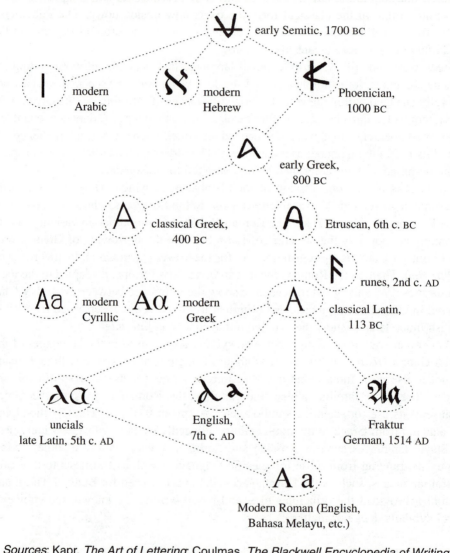

Sources: Kapr, *The Art of Lettering*; Coulmas, *The Blackwell Encyclopedia of Writing Systems*; Tubaro and Tubaro, *Lettering*; etc.

English writing system does not accurately represent the sounds of English. Both Greek and English, for instance, have two sounds that are rare in the world's languages, the 'th' dental fricatives /θ/ and /ð/ in *theme* and *them*. Greek has preserved letters for both of these, Δ (delta) in ΔΕΝΤΡΟ ('tree') and Θ (theta) in ΘΕΑΤΡΟ ('theatre'). But these were not transmitted to English across the intervening languages that lacked these sounds.

To start with, Old English represented the 'th' sounds as the Roman letters *th*, copying the Latin method of dealing with Greek 'th' sounds. Then, after a period during which Old English tried out Irish *d*, from the eighth century on, English used two letters, 'ð' formed by crossing the ascender of Roman d and þ , borrowed from the early runic alphabet, also ultimately derived from Greek. Old English did not, however, make use of the different letters to represent the two different sounds. The 'ð' letter in *monað* ('month') soon died out, apart from its reinstatement in phonetic script. The þ in *broþor* ('brother') survived to the sixteenth century and lingers on, in shape if not pronunciation, in fake antique names such as the pub in Shenfield in Essex called *Ye Olde Green Dragon*, where *Ye* is doubtless pronounced as *ye* /yi:/ rather than as *the* /ði/. When these two letters died out, English went back to the *th* combination to represent both 'th' sounds, /θ/ and /ð/.

The development of the modern English spelling system created two main problems. One is that English has gone through major changes in pronunciation since the fourteenth century. The long vowels, for example, moved around the vowel space in the mouth in the Great Vowel Shift, to be described in Chapter 10. In Chaucer's day *wine* would have been pronounced /wi:n/ with the /i:/ vowel of *teen*, *house* /hu:s/ with the /u:/ of *ooze*. Since English spelling by and large has not changed, the relationship between the spoken sounds and the written spellings became increasingly arbitrary and has stranded certain words with odd spellings. For example, *great* /greɪt/ is not pronounced the same as *greet* /gri:t/; the *i* in *police* /pli:s/ does not stand for the same sound as that in *nice* /naɪs/.

The second problem was the persistent attempts to change the spelling, mostly with the best of motives. The typesetters of the early Caxton Bible were speakers of Flemish and so introduced, more or less by accident, the initial *gh* spelling to words such as *ghost* and *gherkin* which had previously been spelled with *g*. Scholars who respected Latin tried to make English words borrowed from French conform to their ultimate Latin origins. Hence *perfit* became *perfect* by adding a *c*, *aventure adventure* by adding a *d*.

Sometimes these changes were simply wrong: *island* from German acquired an *s* as if it came from French; *admiral* from Arabic *amir* acquired d as if it were Latin. A change in the spelling led to a change in the pronunciation of some words: *perfect* is indeed now pronounced with an added /k/ and *adventure* with a /d/. Mostly this meddling separated English spelling further from a straightforward representation of sounds, leading to such oddities as *subtle* /sʌtl̩/ with silent *b* and *hiccough* /hɪkʌp/ with *gh* corresponding to /p/.

Letter frequencies

English lower case

Printers used to store the individual pieces of type in two trays, called the upper and lower cases; the lower-case tray is shown below. The sizes of the lower-case sections in English therefore provide a good guide to the frequency of the letters. Special printers' symbols and punctuation have been omitted.

				k		1	2	3	4	5	6	7	8
j	b	c	d		e	i		s		f	g		9
													0
z	l	m	n	h		o		y		p	w		
x	v	u	t			a		r					
q													

Codebreaking

Even if the same written letters are used in different languages, they have different frequencies, which are highly consistent and which are obvious in quite small samples of text. This information is used by cryptographers as a method to break secret codes. Depending on the language suspected to be used in the message, one technique is to assume the top ten code symbols stand for the top ten letters, based on frequency charts such as the following.

	1	2	3	4	5	6	7	8	9	10
English	e	t	a	o	n	i	s	r	h	d
French	e	a	i	s	t	n	r	u	l	o
German	e	n	i	r	s	a	d	t	u	g
Spanish	e	a	o	s	n	i	r	l	d	u

So, while there may be an ideal sound-based system in which each letter stands for a single phoneme, this has rarely occurred in the history of writing systems and inevitably lasts for only a short time. On the one hand, alphabets adapt imperfectly from one language to another: the Greek alphabet may have fitted Greek adequately at a particular point of history, but it does not necessarily suit other languages with different sound systems or indeed later periods of Greek. On the other hand, languages add and lose sounds continually as they develop so that the match between letters and sounds seldom stays intact for very long. The advantage of using virtually the same Roman alphabet for a range of languages is that people at least recognize the actual letters of many contemporary languages, not to mention those from the past, a weaker version of the advantage claimed for Chinese characters. English people learning another language have problems with new scripts, as in the Cyrillic script for Russian, or with character-based systems, such as Japanese and Chinese, which they do not have when learning to read Italian or Spanish.

Problems with English spelling

Any discussion of the English writing system sooner or later comes down to the problems of English spelling. This section mentions some of the well-known difficulties; the next section suggests that English may have some hidden advantages.

The battles over English spelling usually concern its incomplete correspondence with pronunciation. The discrepancy between the 44-odd sounds in the spoken language and the 26 letters of the alphabet in itself accounts for many of the problems. The main complaint is the inconsistent link between sounds and spellings. George Bernard Shaw complained that *fish* could equally well be spelled *ghoti* (*gh* = /f/ in *enough*, *o*= /i/ in *women*, *ti*= /ʃ/ in *nation*). This example ignores the position of the letters in the English CVC syllable: *gh* at the beginning of a syllable always corresponds with /g/, never with /f/. Nevertheless *ghoti* gives some idea of the slippage between letters and sounds in modern English. Further examples are the different ways of spelling the phoneme /eɪ/, as in *lake, aid, foyer, gauge, stay, café, steak, weigh, ballet, matinée, sundae* and *they* and, in the reverse direction, the many ways of pronouncing the letter *a*, as in *age, arm, about, beat, many, aisle, coat, ball, canal, beauty, cauliflower* and so on.

English-speaking people indeed have severe problems with spelling. John Downing found that British students learning German made more spelling mistakes in English than in German. An analysis of children's written work found *scissors* spelled in 37 ways, ranging from the popular *sissors* and *siccors* to *cezzous, sisore* and *sisscors*. Bad spellers made the same types of mistakes with grammatical words as good spellers, but had a higher proportion of mistakes with homophones where the same sounds can be spelled in several ways such as *where/wear, court/caught* and *righting/writing*.

Other languages with alphabet-based systems are not immune to the types of problem found in English. In French the sequence of three sounds /pɛʀ/ corresponds to at least seven written words: *père, pères, pair, paire, pers, perd* and *perds*, as seen in the spellings of /ɛʀ/ in the tongue-twister quoted in Chapter 4, *Le ver vert va vers le verre vert* ('The green grub goes to the green glass'). French too has different pronunciations for the same letter: *en* is pronounced differently in *vent, vient* and *viennent*. Spanish has a single sound /b/ spelled in two ways, *tubo* ('pipe') and *tuvo* ('had'). In

German the vowel /o:/ is spelled in five different ways: *Not* ('need'), *Sohn* ('son'), *Boot* ('boat'), *Sauce* ('sauce') and *Trikot* ('stockinet').

The archetypal sound-based writing system would faithfully represent every sound of the language; that is to say, it would be a phonetic alphabet. The logical conclusion is that the same word would be spelled differently whenever the speaker pronounced it differently. *Better* is often pronounced /beʔə/ in my casual speech but /betə/ in my formal speech and would thus need two spellings. Novelists would spell words in dialogue differently from those in prose, as is occasionally done now to label non-standard speakers, *missiz* for *Mrs* or *duzn't* for *doesn't*, as will be seen in Chapter 8.

Speakers of different dialects would also have to spell the same word in different ways, as was once true in English. The dialect of a Middle English text, for example, can be deduced from whether it spells *loving* as *lovande* (Northern), *lovende* (Midlands) or *lovinde* (Southern). Australian English spelling would differ from British spelling or from Indian spelling to a much greater degree than is the case with British and American. Tying writing into local pronunciation would create difficulties for many people.

Using a truly sound-based system would also cut us off, not just from speakers with different accents, but also from those from earlier ages. To read texts other than those of the present day would either mean transforming them into current pronunciation or getting the reader to master the pronunciation of earlier periods. In Shakespearean English *clean* was pronounced as /kleɪn/ to rhyme with *lane* rather than modern /kliːn/, *good* was pronounced /guːd/ rhyming with *mood* /muːd/ rather than /gʊd/, and so on. Would modern editions need to reflect Elizabethan pronunciation, which would make them unintelligible to most readers, or would they be based on contemporary pronunciation, which would distort them in many ways and require new editions every few years?

However, it may be misleading to consider the modern English writing to be totally based on sound. First of all, a letter-based writing system is more than a way of recording speech, a primitive form of tape-recorder. Much writing is not a record of speech but an alternative version of language, with its own grammatical peculiarities and vocabulary. Traffic signs use words or grammar that would seem strange in spoken English: *Blind summit* proclaims a road sign before a hump-back bridge in Hertfordshire; *A14 was A45* announces a sign after a main road junction in Essex; *No parking on the greensward* is to be found on a notice on the edge of a Colchester road. Those who do read aloud, such as conference presenters, news broadcasters or parents of small children, are furthermore well aware that English has to be written in a special way to be read aloud easily and rehearsed in advanced to be successful. Indeed, the act of silent reading takes place at speeds far faster than speaking.

Writing is used in ways that speech cannot be. Skimming an article to find the one or two facts of interest, going back to look again at something one has not understood or spending a day poring over the details of a house survey: none of these is possible in speech. (Nor indeed is the use of the colon as part of the grammar of the last sentence.) Children who keep too rigidly to treating English as a straight representation of sounds have problems with learning to read, as we see in Chapter 9.

Writing as the representation of words

Some linguists feel that it is misleading to think of writing as representing only sounds or meaning. Instead it may provide other useful information about words. In the English word *nation*, the letter *a* corresponds to the vowel /eɪ/; however, in words derived from this base, *a* corresponds to /æ/, that is say *national*, *nationalist*, *nationalistic* and so on. Spelling the word and its derivatives in the same way preserves the connection between them in the reader's mind. In the word *sign*, the *g* does not correspond to any sound in the pronunciation; in words derived from *sign*, *g* corresponds to /g/, as in *signature* and *assignation*. Again, useless as the *g* may be as a representation of sounds, it helps the reader to connect the forms to the same root. Keeping the spelling of a word the same in all circumstances enables the reader to see the common factor. The plural inflection -*s* is pronounced in three distinct ways as /s/ *cats*, /z/ *girls* and /ɪz/ *niches*. But spelling all three variants as *s* indicates they are the same morpheme, even if they differ in pronunciation.

Hence the spelling of English corresponds in part to the words and morphemes in the language, not to their pronunciation. A word has a fixed form that remains constant. In many words the consonant changes according to particular phonological rules: /k/ > /s/ in *electric/electricity*, /t/ > /tʃ/ in *right/righteous*, or /z/ to /ʒ/ in *revise/revision*. The English writing system provides a single form for the spelling of each of these words regardless of their variant pronunciations in different contexts. The unvarying spelling is a clue to the identity of the word as well as to the sounds that make it up in speech. Other languages also keep the same spelling for a word despite its different pronunciations. In German, for instance, the word *König* is spelled the same although the *g* in *König* ('king') corresponds to a final /ç/, in *königlich* ('royal') to a /k/, and in *Könige* ('kings') to a /g/.

The form that the word has in the mental lexicon may, then, differ from the way it is pronounced in a given sentence. However, these differences depend on the sound system of the language. English speakers know that /k/ changes to /s/ in *critical/criticize* and *medical/medicine* because that is a rule of English pronunciation. They do not need the spelling to remind them of this fact. It is more helpful if the spelling shows the involved word structure of English rather than the phonology.

The main advocates of this style of analysis, Noam Chomsky and Morris Halle, claimed in a famous book, *The Sound Pattern of English*, that 'conventional orthography is . . . a near optimal system for the lexical representation of English words'. In other words, writing relates to the lexical entry in the mind, not just to pronunciation. The base form of the word remains the same despite varying in pronunciation. The word *telegraph* is spelled the same regardless of whether the *a* is pronounced /ɑ:/ as in *telegraph*, /æ/ as in *telegraphic* or /ə/ as in *telegraphy*. Using different spellings for predictable variations in pronunciation is redundant for a reader who knows spoken English.

This link between spelling and the base form of the word helps native speakers of English who have a firm grasp of its pronunciation system but is no use to the foreigner approaching the spelling system from a different first language. The theory covers only a small proportion of English words, with many exceptions. Nevertheless it is pleasant to find people paying compliments to the English writing system for a change rather than throwing brickbats at it.

To sum up, there is not just a single relationship between spoken sounds and written signs, but several.

Written language may be linked to the spoken form via a syllabary representing whole syllables, as in Japanese kana, or via an alphabet representing individual sounds, whether the consonants alone, as in Arabic, or all the sounds, as in Italian; the form of the letters can attempt to represent the sounds themselves, as in Korean Han'gul, or be arbitrary, as in most other languages. Or written language may be linked to meanings through a character system, such as those in Chinese and Japanese kanji, where signs stand for elements of meaning. Or written language may reflect the base form of the word independently of its sounds. However pure they may be to start with, all writing systems end up as a mixture of these separate elements. Chinese characters incorporate elements of pronunciation; Roman letters become 'silent' or change values arbitrarily. Chapter 9 will suggest that becoming a fluent silent reader in English involves progressing beyond the stage of treating letters as sounds to seeing them as representing words. English writing turns out to be a little closer to Chinese than first appearances suggest!

Often the features of a writing system derive from the characteristics of the language for which it was first devised. The lack of inflections in Chinese contributed to its use of a character script, since the word always had the same unchanging form. The fact that words in Semitic languages have a consonantal skeleton contributed to the use of an alphabet that did not show vowels. Greek, however, with an inflectional system, needed an alphabet with vowel signs. Transferring the system from one language to another often creates difficulties, whether using characters with inflectional languages, as in the use of Chinese characters in Korean and Japanese, or using alphabets that do not have the right number of sounds, as in the case of English.

Languages also change their pronunciation and their grammar over the years. The written language tends to be static in its forms, particularly since the invention of printing. However perfect a sound-based writing system may be when it is first devised, it gets more and more out of step with the spoken language as time goes by, examples being the different pronunciations of Chinese characters in Japanese according to the time when they were adapted, and the slippage in English due to the change in pronunciation of English vowels. As we have seen, character-based systems

Some patterns of English spelling

Despite its notoriety, the English spelling system has a number of set spelling patterns, even if they cover far less than 100 per cent of the spelling. Here is a sample of those that have been described.

Surnames are often distinguished from ordinary nouns with the same pronunciation by having a final *e* or by doubling the final letter:

Clarke/clerk, Moore/moor, Paine/pain, Trollope/trollop, Rowe/row, Carr/car, Parr/par, Chubb/chub, Hogg/hog, Bunn/bun, Tripp/trip, Nott/not, Hogg/hog, Greene/green

Content words such as nouns usually have more than two letters; grammatical words such as pronouns and prepositions have one or two (the distinction between content and grammatical words is explained in Chapter 3):

inn/in, bye/by, eye/I, two/to, ore/or, sew/so, know/no, bee/be

th corresponds to the voiceless /θ/ in nouns such as *third* or *Thetford*, but to the voiced /ð/ in grammatical words such as *the* and *their*.

thistle/this, thespian/these, Thanet/than

'Silent' final *e* is used:

– at the end of a word after a final VC sequence consisting of a 'long' vowel (spelled with a single letter) followed by a single consonant:

late, mete, debate, tune, fine, bone

– after a final /s/, /z/ or /ð/ following a 'long' vowel digraph (combination of two written vowel letters corresponding to a single speech sound) or 'short' vowel plus consonant:

crease, house, maize; else, tense, cleanse

– after a stressed ending consisting of a 'short' vowel and a double consonant in words borrowed from French:

brunette, cassette, rosette, giraffe, gaffe, programme, cigarette

[Note: in these rules 'long' and 'short' do not have the phonetic meaning given in the last chapter.]

i before *e* except after *c*, when *i* is pronounced /iː/

receive, ceiling, conceit (but *caffeine, counterfeit, seize, Neil*, etc.)

Source: mainly adapted from Carney, *A Survey of English Spelling*.

too are not immune to effects of change, China having modified many characters, Japanese transforming them radically.

IV The relationship of speech and writing

Speech and writing differ in many ways, some of them obvious, some more surprising. For example, the grammars of speech and writing are slightly different. Writing tends to use more prepositional phrases with *for*, *to*, etc., and to have more 'nominalizations', that is to say, noun-based phrases such as *The NCP long-term off-airport car park courtesy pick-up point* seen at Gatwick airport. Some of the main differences between speech and writing, illustrated in the box below, are:

- Speed. The mind processes spoken sounds differently from written signs. Ordinary speech takes place at about 150 words per minute, reading at about 350.
- Permanency. Writing stores the information on paper or disk, speech in the memory. All of a written text is accessible at once; speech can only be accessed through the fleeting present.
- First and final drafts. Writing can be worked over time and again. Speech is always in a sense a first draft, having repetitions, false starts and redundancies that are eliminated from writing. Often writing is one-way, speaking is two-way, with the exception of broadcasting.
- Writing and formality. Writing is an authority to be trusted in a way that speech is not. Speech in a literate society is used for reasons that are more immediate.
- Density of content. Writing has a proportion of about 1 grammatical word to 1.2 content words; speech about 1 to 0.6. In other words, writing is much denser in its content words.
- Neutrality of social roles. Writing is more impersonal than speech, particularly in types of written language such as reports of scientific experiments.

These differences can be checked against the two texts given in the box below.

Spoken and written English

Here are two texts, one a spoken transcript, one a newspaper article, from the same day on roughly the same topic.

Part of a radio interview in a daily news programme with a worker in the National Health Service.

Interviewer (male): Now Joan tell me what what do you get paid and for what working what sort of hours.

Nurse (female): I I get about five hundred and fifty pounds to six hundred and fifty-six hundred pounds a month for thirty hours a week.

Interviewer: Now the the prospect we've been hearing of a pay freeze seems to be receding but tell me first, if there was to be a pay freeze, what would that mean for you?

Nurse: Well it just means that you have to cut the cloth back a little bit more. It would be all right er freezing pay if you could freeze inflation.

. . .

Interviewer: And what about the the mood among other nurses in the hospital that you work with?

Nurse: Well the mood amongst other nurses in the hospital, erm most of it is erm unrepeatable. Their their morale is very low. There are other things and other issues in the hospital that are causing low morale at the moment and this even makes it mor – worse for the nursing staffs here.

Newspaper report

Labour claims 2.3 million in 'hidden' queues that belie Bottomley claims
True hospital waiting lists 'double official figures'
Chris Mihill
Medical Correspondent

About 2.3 million patients in England are waiting either for their first appointment to see a consultant or for hospital treatment, more than double official figures, the Labour Party said yesterday.

The 'hidden' waiting list, covering the time from a GP referral to seeing a consultant, undermines the Government's claims that no one now waits more than two years for an operation, said the shadow health secretary, David Blunkett.

Some people have been waiting as long as 182 weeks – 3½ years – just to see a consultant, according to figures compiled by Labour.

The 182 weeks is the maximum waiting time for ear, nose and throat appointments at Burton Hospital Trust, Burton upon Trent, Staffordshire. The official waiting list, from seeing a consultant to having treatment, is about a million.

The Labour researchers looked at the Mersey region, which says no one waits longer that a year for treatment, finding 57,256 people waiting for hospital care. However, a further 75,558 were waiting for their first consultant appointment – some 132 per cent more than the official list.

The researchers found similar ratios in the North Western and South West Thames regions, and calculate that if the figures were extrapolated across England it would mean a true waiting list of 2.3 million.

Mr Blunkett said: "These figures are the waiting lists the Government refuses to reveal.

"Virginia Bottomley has been trotting out misleading statistics about waiting lists at every opportunity. The one thing she and her ministerial colleagues have always claimed is that nobody has to wait longer than two years for treatment. That is clearly untrue."

Source: *The Guardian.*

Sources and further reading

General

Source books on the writing systems that provided much of the information in this chapter are: F. Coulmas, *The Blackwell Encyclopedia of Writing Systems* (Oxford: Blackwell, 1996); A. Gaur, *A History of Writing* (London: British Museum, 1984); G. Jean, *Writing: The History of Alphabets and Scripts* (London: Thames & Hudson, 1992); G. Sampson, *Writing Systems: A Linguistic Introduction* (London: Hutchinson, 1985).

Japanese

A useful book on Japanese is R.A. Miller, *The Japanese Language* (Chicago: University of Chicago Press, 1967). Japanese kanji dictionaries include: A. Foerster and N. Takamura, *Kanji ABC* (Rutland, VT: Tuttle, 1992); A.N. Nelson, *The Modern Reader's Japanese–English Character Dictionary* (Rutland, VT: Tuttle). The original research on the absence of dyslexia in Japanese, now looked at somewhat sceptically, is reported in K. Makita, 'The rarity of reading disability in Japanese children', *American Journal of Orthopsychiatry* 38 (1968): 599–614.

Alphabet systems

The development of the actual forms of writing and printing is covered in: E. Johnson, *Writing, Illuminating, and Lettering* (John Hogg, 1906; repr. London: A. & C. Black, 1994); A. Kapr, *The Art of Lettering* (Munich: K.G. Saur, 1983); J. Tschichold, *Treasury of Alphabets and Lettering* (London: Lund Humphries, 1992); A. Tubaro and I. Tubaro, *Lettering: Studies and Research on the Evolution of Writing and Print Typefaces* (Milan: Idea Books, 1994).

English spelling

The history of English spelling is covered in general books such as A. Baugh and T. Cable, *A History of the English Language*, 4th edn (London: Routledge, 1993); and in more specialist books such as: D.G. Scragg, *A History of English Spelling* (Manchester: MUP, 1974); J.W. Clark, *Early English* (London: Deutsch, 1957). The source for cryptography is H. Gaines, *Cryptanalysis* (American Cryptogram Association, 1940; repr. New York: Dover, 1956). The most detailed modern account of English spelling is E. Carney, *A Survey of English Spelling* (London: Routledge, 1994). An account of spelling mistakes in English can be found in R. Mitton, *English Spelling and the Computer* (Harlow: Longman, 1996). Downing's survey is reported in J. Downing (ed.), *Comparative Reading* (New York: Macmillan, 1973). A useful and novel approach to spelling is to be found in A.G. Rollings, 'The Spelling Patterns of English' (PhD thesis, University of Essex, 1996).

Writing as the representation of the lexicon

The idea that spelling reflects lexical entries is described in C. Chomsky, 'Reading, writing and phonology', *Harvard Educational Review* 40/2 (1970): 287–309. The underlying phonological theory and the claim that English spelling is optimal come from N. Chomsky and M. Halle, *The Sound Pattern of English* (New York: Harper & Row, 1968).

Speech and writing

Useful books on the relationship between speech and writing are: M.A.K. Halliday, *Spoken and Written Language* (Oxford: OUP, 1985); M. Stubbs, *Language and Literacy* (London: Routledge and Kegan Paul, 1980); D.R. Olson, *The World on Paper: The Conceptual and Cognitive Implications of Reading and Writing* (Cambridge: CUP, 1994); D. Biber, *Variation Across Speech and Writing* (Cambridge: CUP, 1988).

7 Children Acquiring Language

The earlier chapters have demonstrated the complexity of the language system stored in the human mind. Using language means choosing from a vast set of words with an intricate system of meaning, forming sentence structures of high complexity using a large number of 'rules', and putting the results into a sequence of sounds or written symbols with precise articulation. Yet, with the exception of the writing system, the vast majority of human beings manage to construct this system easily and without effort from the samples of ordinary speech they hear. One of the greatest mysteries about language is how children manage to acquire all this with such ease in so few years.

This chapter explores some of the ways in which children's acquisition has been investigated in recent years, concentrating on the very young child. Mostly it draws on aspects of language already outlined in earlier chapters. Section I describes the earliest stages of children's acquisition of the systems of sounds, words, and grammar. Section II looks at how adults speak to children. Section III describes three rival theories that have tried to explain language acquisition. Some of the examples of children's language come from the Bristol project directed by Gordon Wells, which followed the development of 128 English children from the age of 15 months onwards, recording them for one day every three months by means of an ingenious radio system.

I Ways of acquiring language

1 Perceiving speech sounds

At what age can babies tell their mother's voice from somebody else's? Six months? A year? In fact babies already prefer their own mother's voice at three days old, perhaps because of the familiarity of hearing it while in the womb. It has even been claimed that newborn babies relax better to the signature tunes of soap operas than to other music because their mothers had relaxed to this music during pregnancy.

When can the child distinguish one language from another? Two years? Six months? The answer is that French babies react differently to the same person speaking French or Russian at four days old.

In English the difference between /b/ and /p/ is a Voice Onset Time delay of about 70 msec in vibrating the vocal cords, as we saw in Chapter 4. When can children perceive this minute difference between /p/ (*par*) and /b/ (*bar*)? Surprisingly, babies distinguish /bɑ:/ from /pɑ:/ at one month old. Children can distinguish other pairs of sounds during the first months of life: two months for /d/ (*dull*) versus /g/ (*gull*), and for /f/ (*fin*) versus /θ/ (*thin*); six months for /s/ (*sap*) versus /z/ (*zap*), and so on. It is not that babies understand the difference in meaning between *bar* and *par*, or even know that these are words; it is the sheer difference in sound that they are sensitive to.

Needless to say, the methods of establishing that babies can perceive speech sounds have to be highly ingenious. The technique is to play them one sound in a CV structure, say *par*, several times till they are used to it, and then to change to the other sound, *bar*; the baby hears a sequence of *par, par, par, par, bar, bar*, say. If the change from one sound to another has a discernible effect on the babies' behaviour, they must be able to hear the difference. The effects that are measured are the rate with which they suck on a bottle, changes in their heartbeat, and whether they turn their heads towards the sound.

The precise ages at which babies can distinguish sounds do not matter so much as the general point that they are capable of hearing subtle differences between speech sounds from the first few months of life. Telling /p/ from /b/ may not seem an enormous achievement until one remembers that the difference is a matter of less than a tenth of a second. Nor has this basic ability to distinguish the sounds of speech yet been duplicated by a computer with the efficiency of a month-old baby.

This ability to distinguish speech sounds seems to be built into the human mind. It is a manifestation of the human mind's propensity to categorize sounds as one sound or the other rather than as a continuum, discussed in Chapter 4. One support for its built-in nature is the miraculous speed with which babies would otherwise have to pick up this ability from the speech they hear during the first few days of life. A more concrete piece of evidence is that babies can hear differences in speech sounds that do not actually exist in the language used by their parents. Babies living among Kikuyu speakers could distinguish the *par/bar* contrast even though this does not occur in Kikuyu and they would never have heard it from their parents. Babies exposed to English could hear the difference between nasalized and non-nasalized vowels in /pa/ and /pã/, which are contrastive elements in French, that is to say phonemes, but marginal to English, at best allophones; they could also distinguish Zulu clicks not used in any European language. Up to about six months old, children have the ability to distinguish any speech sound, whether or not it occurs in their first language. But, by a year old, there is a decline in the ability to deal with sounds that are not part of the language the child is hearing. One exception is that adult English speakers can still tell Zulu clicks apart.

Producing speech sounds

This section switches to the child's ability to produce sounds, which occurs later than their ability to hear them. The first 'word' comes much later than the ability to distinguish *par* and *bar*. A child called Tessa was recorded every two weeks from the age of 18 months and the Voice Onset Times for all the words she said with /p/ and /b/ were measured in milliseconds, with the results shown in Figure 7.1.

In speaking, at 17 months Tessa still did not distinguish between /p/ and /b/ in the 75 words she knew. The VOT for /p/ grew month by month from 0 to 95 msec at the age of two, about the adult figure. The VOT for /b/, however, increased only slightly, so that by two years she was using about 15 msec VOT, again close to the adult norm. She was getting closer to the adult month by month. However, she was the only one of the three children tested in this study to show such a clear-cut pattern of development: one child overshot the mark with a VOT of 130 msec for /p/ at 21 months but reverted back to 75 msec by two years. To start with, children make no difference in production, like Tessa at 17 months. Then they make a contrast between the sounds that is still within the bounds of one of the adult sounds rather than separating them, and so adults do not notice that they are doing it. Gradually they acquire something close to the adult contrast. Rather than acquiring the contrast all at once, the child extends it bit by bit until it matches adult speech.

This section has then shown how skilful human babies are at acquiring the sounds of language. From almost the first moment it is possible to test them they can distinguish VOT and by the age of two they can produce it in their own speech. This is not to say that the acquisition of all speech sounds is as rapid: many English children still have problems with the /ʃ/ sound at the age of seven. Nevertheless, it shows how the sounds of language are uniquely suitable for the human mind to acquire.

2 *Acquiring words*

The child's first recognizable word is an important milestone to the parents. Children go through a phase where they produce single-word sentences – the one-word stage –

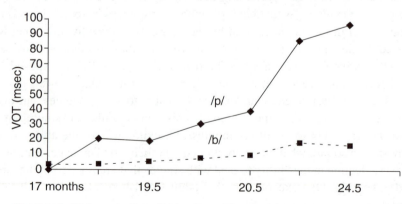

Fig. 7.1 A child's production of Voice Onset Time for /p/ and /b/

before they combine them into more complex sentences. Here is a selection of the sentences produced in one day by a 15-month-old boy from the Bristol group called Gerald:

wowwow, bub, Ee, lorry, peg, car, hop hop, weewee, yes, potty, Oh, Teddy, cheese, a box, a peg, bye baby bunting, door, man, look, mm, me, down

Gerald produces words one at a time as single units, such as *peg* or *cheese*. Sometimes he may seem to use phrases such as *bye baby bunting* or *a box*. But in fact these are unvarying formulas that function like single words rather than variable phrases. The article *a* apparently seen in *a box* and *a pet* is probably for Gerald part of the 'word' it precedes, on a par with the /ə/ sound at the beginning of *Ernie* or *early*.

Parents often think of the child's activity at this stage as 'naming'. The child looks at a lorry and says *lorry*, or at a door and says *door*. Some children, particularly firstborn children in educated families, may indeed be 'object-namers'. Yet a high proportion of children's words are not names at all, *down* and *yes*, for example. Many children use language more to express their desires and emotions; they are 'emoters'. So they may say *look* to draw someone's attention, *potty* to express a need, or *bye baby bunting* to make a pleasant noise. Some children use words in both ways, like Gerald. Emoters therefore tend to use formulas more often than object-namers.

A child saying *lorry* is no more naming the lorry than an adult saying *Half a pint of Guinness* is naming some beer. Language is used for a serious purpose: both the child and the adult are trying to get something for themselves rather than idly naming things. From the first, children use language for a reason; they are trying to get something through language rather than using it for its own sake. The child's words are not elaborated into sentences; it is a matter of a single word, *Teddy*, not a complex sentence, *Would you mind passing me my Teddy please?* The child is using language effectively for his or her own purposes, but is still only producing one word at a time rather than utilizing the grammar of word order and inflections available in English. The number of words the child uses expands rapidly, from an average of 10 at 13 months to 310 by 24 months. However, the number of words the child can understand is at least 10 times greater than this total at each stage.

Chapter 5 showed that there is far more to the meaning of a word than a link to a single object or action. Take the word *man*, for instance. Part of its meaning is the feature [+male]. Children have to learn that *man* means a male adult person [+male +adult], rather than a person with a beard or a tall person wearing trousers, say. They also have to learn that *man* is a basic-level term linked to a superordinate term, say *human being*, to which *dog* does not belong. The basis of many children's stories and cartoons is precisely the assumption that people and animals share the same characteristics. While children may use the same words as adults, they do not necessarily mean the same things by them; they may say *man* pointing to a woman because they think it applies to all human beings. My three-year-old son announced *I have a headache*; when I asked *Where is it?* he replied *In my tummy*. If the question had not been asked, I might not have realized that *headache* to him was a non-specific word for 'pain', rather than one restricted to pain in the head. To say that children have acquired a word is not just a matter of whether they actually use it, but of whether they have acquired the full meaning that goes with it.

Some odd discoveries were made when the components of meaning theory outlined in Chapter 5 were applied to children's acquisition by Eve Clark. Scottish children go through a stage when they think that *wee* and *big* have the same meaning. In other words they have acquired a feature of [size] for both words but have not discovered that there is an additional feature of [+large] for *big* and [−large] for *wee*. The same was true of the acquisition of *before/after* and *more/less*: there is a disconcerting stage at which children know both words but do not know the difference between them. In practice components theory has been hard to apply because it has proved difficult to define the range of semantic features that the child is acquiring. Eve Clark's more recent theory is that children base their acquisition of words on two principles: a new word must contrast with words the child already knows (or there is not much point in learning it); any object is likely to have a name.

Prototype theory, mentioned in Chapter 5, has also been applied to children's language. Children acquire basic-level terms like *dog* before superordinate terms like *animal* or subordinate terms like *poodle*. Basic-level terms are learnt first because they stand out in the child's perception of the world. There is a typical 'dog' for chil-

---

One child's words

Here is a sample of the groups of words produced by one child up to the age of two, showing the typical areas children talk about and the range of vocabulary they possess by this age.

Animals. *doggie, dog, mouse, cat, horse, cow, rabbit, goat, bear, lion, alligator, gorilla, seal, bird, duck, chicken, goose, turtle, fish, frog, snake, crab, ladybug, animal*

Food. *bottle, cup, meme* (=food), *banana, cheese, nut, cracker, bread, egg, pea, cereal, carrot, cookie, apple, ring* (Cheerio), *raisin, orange, jam, rhubarb, crumb, yoghurt, sugar, flake, salt, graham-cracker, toast, cornflakes, juice, tea, milk, orange juice, apple juice, food*

Vehicles. *car, plane, truck, train, bicycle, airplane, bike, cat, helicopter, sled, fire truck, bus, garbage truck, motorcycle, fire engine, boat, choo-choo train, birthday-you-you car* (toy Rolls-Royce), *race car, push chair, baby-bus*

Source: Clark, 'Later lexical development and word formation'.

dren, even if it differs from the typical 'dog' for adults. Again, however the studies of prototypes in the development of the vocabulary have been limited in number.

This section has shown how hard it is to disentangle the links between words and use. It is not enough to know that a child says *teddy*; instead it is vital to know when and why he or she says it. As with the description of adult vocabulary in Chapter 5, children's vocabulary is an intricate network of meanings and relationships, not just a set of one-to-one links between words and objects in the world.

3 Acquiring early grammar

Missing grammatical morphemes

Soon children start producing sentences more than one word long; they enter the two-word stage of development. Here is a small selection of sentences spoken by a two-year-old called Steven, studied by Martin Braine, whom we shall encounter several times in this section.

baby doll, daddy do, it ball, want high, there doggie, more book, want car, find bear, beeppeep car, bye-bye car, that doll, want do, here doll, two checker, see Stevie, there trunk

These sentences look like pairs of content words strung together minus the grammatical morphemes that link them together in adult speech: *it ball* presumably equals the adult *It is a ball* with the addition of the grammatical morphemes *is* and *a*, and *want car* relates to *I want the car*, with the addition of *I* and *the*. The main characteristic of the two-word stage is, then, the lack of grammatical morphemes, whether words such as *the* or inflections such as *-s*.

The reason why children leave out grammatical morphemes might be that they are usually unstressed, while content words are stressed. English speakers say *The cow jumped over the moon* not *The cow jumped over the moon*. The children might simply leave out unstressed elements, which happen to coincide with grammatical morphemes. It is impossible to disentangle whether the grammar or the stress is the cause, since these two elements are bound together inseparably in English. A psycholinguist once suggested, not too seriously, that the only way to distinguish between these explanations would be to teach children reverse English, in which content words were consistently unstressed and grammatical items were stressed!

A more abstract explanation has been put forward in recent years by researchers working within the Universal Grammar theory. To describe this means expanding the notion of phrase structure presented in Chapter 3, which showed how a Noun Phrase is built round a noun head: that is to say, *a dog* is based around the noun *dog*; a Verb Phrase is built round a verb head: *attacked the rat* is based around the verb *attacked*. Further types of phrase are the Prepositional Phrase, such as *in the morning*, based around the preposition head *in*, and the Adjective Phrase, such as *afraid of shadows*, built around the adjective *afraid*. These four are called 'lexical' phrases because they are built upon 'lexical' items, i.e. content words such as nouns and verbs that belong to the lexicon rather than the grammar. The structure of the sentence *A dog attacked the rat* can be shown in the following diagram.

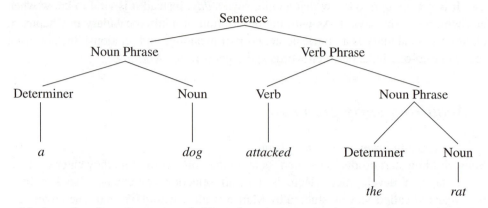

Modern theories of grammar believe that the grammatical morphemes also have phrases of their own, called 'functional phrases'. To make the tree diagram less cumbersome, the example sentence can be simplified to *A dog barked*. A determiner such as *a* is the basis of a Determiner Phrase. So *a dog is* 'really' a Determiner Phrase built around the head *a*, which includes a Noun Phrase built around *dog*. A past tense form such as *-ed* has a Tense Phrase of its own, within which the Verb Phrase and the verb *bark* nestle. These new types of phrase are seen in the tree for the sentence.

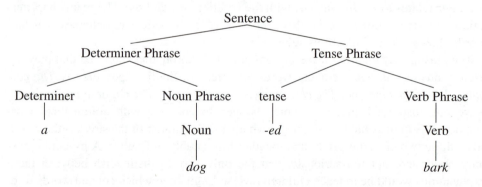

Functional phrases provide a neat explanation for the children's two-word sentences. If children do not have Determiner Phrases, they are likely to leave determiners out, so they will say *dog* rather than *a dog*. If they do not have Tense Phrases, they will not have tense endings such as *-ed* and will produce *bark* rather than *barked*. The above sentence stripped of its functional phrases would be *dog bark* rather than *a dog barked*, exactly what a child at the two-word stage might say.

Without functional phrases, and therefore grammatical morphemes, the children's sentences consist of strings of lexical phrases, such as Steven's *want car*, *see Stevie*, and the like. Until a particular time around the age of two, children's minds can cope with lexical phrases but not with functional phrases. In other words, children's first grammars consist only of lexical phrases built around content words – a Noun Phrase *dog* rather than a Determiner Phrase *a dog*, or a Verb Phrase *bark* rather than a Tense Phrase *barked*. Instead of having an overall tree for a sentence, they have isolated lexical phrases unconnected to the higher functional phrases of the sentence (see diagram). Around the age of two they acquire functional phrases built around grammatical morphemes within which they can fit their lexical phrases to arrive at the structure of the adult sentence. The single explanation that accounts for all the missing grammatical morphemes in children's two-word speech is the lack of functional phrases. This will be expanded below.

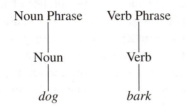

The sequence of acquisition of grammatical morphemes

Once children start to use grammatical morphemes, they add them to their speech in a fairly fixed order, first established by Roger Brown. The first five grammatical morphemes they acquire, illustrated with examples from several children, are, in order of appearance:

1. the *-ing* ending of the verb: *Playing. No singing song.*
2. the prepositions *in* and *on*: *On the table. In the field.*
3. the plural *-s* ending on nouns: *With hands. Records. Three cats.*
4. the past irregular form of verbs: *That fellow went.*
5. the possessive *'s* ending on nouns: *Jonathan's dinner.*

(Attentive readers will note that, in Brown's theory, prepositions are grammatical morphemes, not content words as assumed here; indeed, many people regard them as on the border-line between the two categories, having some properties of both.) Though some English-speaking children progress faster, some slower, they all pass through more or less the same series of stages in acquiring these morphemes. Children with various forms of language impairment pass through the same stages at a slower pace, as we shall see in Chapter 9.

The reason for the consistent order of development is far from certain. The missing functional phrases theory only explains why they are all missing or all present, not why they appear in a particular developmental sequence. The cause might be frequency; perhaps children hear verbs ending in *-ing* more often from their parents than possessive *'s* , say. Or it might be the complexity of their meaning; a continuous action shown by *-ing*, *I am driving*, is simpler for the child to grasp than the complex idea of possession shown by *'s, John's book*. Or the various types of functional phrase might not come 'on line' in the child's mind at the same time: the phrase for *-ing* is available before the phrase for plural *-s*, and so on.

One problem in studying child language is the lack of straightforward methods of comparing one children with another. Age is hard to use as the main basis of comparison, since two three-year-olds may be at different stages of language development but both may still be progressing normally through the same stages; in other words, there is too much variation between normal children of the same age for age itself to be much help. The consistency with which children acquire morphemes can be used as one measure of language development, called 'Mean Length of Utterance' (MLU). This measure involves working out the average number of morphemes that a child uses in each utterance. The method is to obtain at least 100 utterances by the child and then to count the total number of morphemes, counting both complete words and grammatical inflections, according to the rules given in the next box.

MLU provides a good measure of the stage children are at during the first few years of life, while the various grammatical morphemes are being added to their speech. It

---

How to work out MLU (Mean Length of Utterance)

1. Record a child's natural speech for long enough to get at least 100 consecutive utterances after stages 2–3 have been carried out.

2. Transcribe the child's speech.

3. Eliminate from consideration:
   all utterances where it is unclear what the child said;
   exclamations, *mm*, *oh*, etc., except when they form the entire child's utterance;
   false starts, *want – want drink*.

4. Count the number of morphemes, both content words and grammatical morphemes, in 100 consecutive utterances, counting as a single morpheme:
   compound words, *choo-choo*, *birthday*, etc.;
   words with *ie/y*, *mummy*, *doggie*, etc.;
   irregular past tense, *went*;
   but including as separate morphemes:
   auxiliaries, *will*, *can*, *is*, *'s*, *have*, *'ve*, etc.;
   all inflected endings, *-ing*, *-s*, *-ed*, etc.

5. Work out the average MLU for the child.

Note: it does not crucially matter whether words, morphemes, or whatever, are counted, provided it is consistent and the results are only compared with other children measured in exactly the same way.

Sources: Brown, *A First Language*; Fletcher, *A Child's Learning of English*.

loses its usefulness with older children, since a long sentence is not necessarily a complicated sentence, and vice versa. In other words, the sheer number of morphemes is no longer the chief measure but the complexity of the sentence structure. The comparatively late acquisition of passive sentences like *John was hit by a car* or relative clauses like *The man who was hit by a car was John* is not because they contain many morphemes but because of their complex grammatical relationships. After all, Einstein's sentences are allegedly simpler than Hemingway's.

Averaged across many children, MLU gradually expands with age. The graph in Figure 7.2 gives average MLUs derived by the Bristol survey for children between 15 months and 5 years, MLU being calculated for all the sentences recorded in a day rather than for a sample of 100. Obviously these figures cover up the wide variation between children. While the average three-year-old uses sentences with a MLU of 3.9, some were as low as 1.4, some as high as 5.5. The flattening of the curve after 4 years is a sign, not that language acquisition is slowing down, but that MLU is no longer a valid way of measuring their speech.

Rules of two-word speech

Many of the child's two-word sentences still could not be expanded into adult sentences by any stretch of the imagination. *Want high* from my children, for example, meant 'lift me up high in the air', but it cannot be converted into a possible adult sentence by filling in 'missing' items. *More book* too was a common request, meaning 'I want more . . .' , as were *more up*, *more Babar* and *more Marmite*. While the meaning of these *more* sentences is clear, many have no adult equivalent; *more up* could not be modelled on any adult sentence. This section describes some of the characteristics of the first grammars that underlie these sentences.

In the 1960s Martin Braine discovered a pattern to these sentences, based on the speech of Steven and other children. Many of the sentences combine a content word like *ball*, which he called an 'open' word, with a word of a different type like *it*, which became known as a 'pivot'. Looked at in these terms, Steven's sentences have a

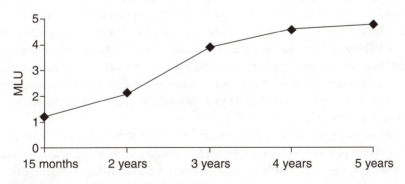

Fig. 7.2 Mean Length of Utterance (MLU) up to 5 years

consistent structure: a pivot is always followed by a content word. So, as well as the combination *it ball* with *it* pivot and *ball* content word, the child varies the content word and arrives at *it daddy, it doll, it Kathy, it bang, it shock*. Or the child varies the pivot, *get ball, see ball, it ball*. While children's open words correspond roughly to adult content words, the group of pivots includes rather more than the adult grammatical words; for example, *want* is a pivot to Steven but a content word to an adult.

The child therefore constructs sentences according to a simple rule: put a pivot word in front of an open word. The majority of Steven's sentences are explained by this rule. It can also be predicted with confidence that Steven could say *see daddy* or *see Kathy*, even if he never happens to do so. Though the pivot/open division would not work for adults, it allows the child to produce a vast number of sentences from a limited vocabulary. Some of them, like *it horses*, resemble reduced versions of adult sentences; some, like *whoa card*, are different from any conceivable adult sentences. Braine's pivot/open rule for the two-word stage was an important insight into children. They were not speaking an inefficient version of the adult language but a language of their own – two-year-old.

The difficulty is that this approach still does not take account of what the child means by the sentence; researchers may read things into the sentence that are not actually there. A famous two-word sentence, *Mommy sock*, was produced by a 20-month-old girl called Kathryn, who used the sentence on two separate occasions, once when her mummy was putting the child's sock on her, the second time when they were sorting out socks together and came to one belonging to mummy. *Mommy sock* had two meanings for the child, paraphrasable as '<u>Mummy</u> is putting my <u>sock</u> on me' and 'This is <u>mummy's</u> <u>sock</u>'. While the two sentences sound just the same and appear to have the same structure, they mean different things. Treating them as identical in pivot/open terms conceals important information about the child's grammar.

This evidence led Martin Braine to revise his theory so that, rather than a single overall pivot/open rule, the child has several distinct 'formulas', each expressing one type of meaning. One formula, for drawing attention to something, consists of *see* or *look* plus an open word: *see Stevie, see record*, and so on. A second formula, for expressing the plural, is made up of a number plus an object, *two checker*. A third is a noun followed by a verb, as in *daddy do*, used by Steven to talk about someone doing something, i.e. an 'actor' and an 'action'. Overall the set of formulas appears like combinations of pivot and open words, but each formula has different pivots and expresses a different need. *Mommy sock* is an example either of a formula expressing possession ('Mummy['s] sock') or of one showing an 'actor' plus 'object affected by the action' ('Mummy [puts on] sock').

This raises the general point that much of what children say is not just imitating adults' speech but has a system of its own. Children have in a sense invented a language that corresponds roughly to adult speech but that differs markedly in vocabulary, pronunciation and grammatical rules. Here is a short extract of adult–child interaction, to demonstrate the extent to which children speak a language of their own. The speakers are a Bristol girl called Melanie aged 3¼ and her mother.

Mother: When you were a baby.
Melanie: Yeah. When I was a lickle baby again.
Mother: Mm. You're getting a big girl now though, aren't you?
Melanie: Yeah. I eat up all that grows eggs up by where. Up by the where you walks.
Mother: You ate what?
Melanie: Eh. 'er egg where you walks.
Mother: Oh grow?
Melanie: Yeah.
Mother: You ate all 'er egg up?
Melanie: Yeah.
Mother: Yes. (*corrects*)
Melanie: (*stammers*) Where you walks.
Mother: Oh yes; that's right.
Melanie: That will make me big.
Mother: That's right.
Melanie: (*clucks*)
Mother: All the food you eat up will make you big. You've got to eat all your cab-
    bage, haven't you really?
Melanie: (*sighs*)

The girl's grammar differs from the adult version of English (*up by the where you walks*), as does her pronunciation (*lickle*), but this difference does not prevent her getting her meaning across – or the adult from getting in a correction of *Yeah* and from drawing a moral lesson about eating up your cabbage. Children are not imitation adults but children in their own right, in language development as much as in other areas.

Sentences without subjects (pro-drop)
To a large extent, the study of early child language is the study of what is absent: many of the children's sentences resembled adult sentences minus the grammatical words, grammatical endings and so on. One feature that is often conspicuously absent is the subject of the sentence. Children's two-word sentences *want car* and *find bear*, for example, look very much as if they have a missing subject *I*. English children feel free to leave the subject out, not only the first person *I* sometimes left out by adults in casual speech but also *he* and *they*.

Chapter 2 contrasted pro-drop languages such as Italian, Chinese or American Sign Language, where no subject is needed in the sentence, with non-pro-drop languages such as German and English, which require a subject. The English children are behaving like speakers of a pro-drop language. In Italian *Sono di Torino* ('am from Turin') and *Parla* ('he speaks') are perfectly unexceptionable sentences. Initially English children assume that English does not need a subject, as Italian children do for Italian. However,

English children have to go on to learn that a subject is always needed; Italian children do not. English children have an extra learning task in discovering that the subject is always needed.

Children may find the existence of the subject difficult to establish from the speech they hear. For, while Italian speech has far more examples of sentences without subjects, English still has a fair number. *Can't buy me love* comes from a Beatles song, *Will complement the taste of meat and game* from a Valpolicella label, *Next morning whilst in library queuing, am surprised by sudden case of standing-up colic* from the fictional diary kept by Dulcie Domum in the *Guardian*. While these are not addressed specifically to children, subject-less sentences nonetheless represent a reasonable proportion of what children hear around them. How do native speakers of English come to believe firmly that *He likes beer* is an acceptable sentence but *Likes beer* is not, when they actually hear both to some extent?

One possibility is that the child finds other clues in speech. In English, sentences such as *It's raining* and *There's some milk in your cup* have to have a subject, albeit a meaningless dummy *it* or *there*. Since such sentences do not need to have subjects in Italian, the child deduces from the fact that *it* and *there* are unnecessary that a subject must always be present, not just in these sentences but in all other sentences as well.

An alternative possibility harks back to the point mentioned in Chapter 2 that pro-drop languages have a fuller system of verb-endings than non-pro-drop languages; the invisible subjects of the sentence can often be pinned down by the forms of the verb. The Italian present tense, for example, has an inflectional ending for each grammatical person: *dormo* ('I sleep'), *dormi* ('you sleep'), *dorme* ('he or she sleeps'), *dormono* ('they sleep') and so on. English has only two inflections, *I/you/we/they say* and *he/she/it says*. Perhaps children listen out for verb-endings. If every present-tense verb form they hear has an inflection, they know that the language is pro-drop. If some of the present-tense verbs lack inflectional endings, they discover it is non-pro-drop, like English. While the proposal works neatly for English and Italian, it falls down with Chinese, which has no verb inflections yet is a pro-drop language, contrary to expectation; *shuo* ('speak') is the same form for each of the persons in the present tense. If children need to hear plenty of verb inflections to discover a language is pro-drop, then Chinese would definitely have to be non-pro-drop.

A current explanation for the children's null-subject sentences builds on the idea of missing functional phrases discussed earlier in this chapter. At the top of the earlier tree diagrams was something called 'sentence', which can be seen as a functional phrase built round a grammatical morpheme. The obvious candidate for its head is the inflection that shows agreement between Subject and Verb, described in Chapter 3, as the effects of agreement influence much of the sentence. The whole sentence is then an Agreement Phrase, inelegantly abbreviated to AgrP. The sentence *A dog barked* should have the tree shown opposite.

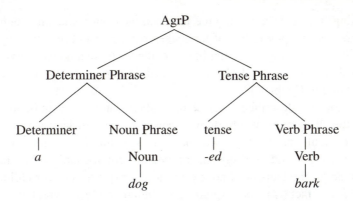

When children start speaking, they do not have any functional phrases in their grammar. There is consequently no overall phrase to make the sentence hang together, no AgrP. Hence the best they can do to make a sentence is to string lexical phrases together, such as the Noun and Verb Phrases.

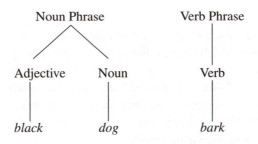

Since AgrP is absent, the Noun Phrase is not linked to the Verb Phrase; children may produce *bark*, *dog bark* or *black dog*, or indeed, memory permitting, *black dog bark*, but they do not have the Agreement Phrase that makes them both compulsory in adult speech. Young children leave out subjects because they lack the necessary functional phrase to put them in; they could not have subjects, since the phrase structure to fit them in does not exist. Missing subjects therefore have the same explanation as missing grammatical morphemes such as *-ed* or *-s*: there is no phrase to put them in. Once children acquire functional phrases, they will be able to put all of these in their rightful place in the sentence. At about two years of age, these phrases start to appear in the children's minds, and so they can fill in the missing elements, whether they are subjects or *-ed* endings.

The common factor to these explanations is what the children themselves bring to language acquisition. Spotting that *there* and *it* are the clues that English is a non-pro-drop language implies that this option is programmed in their minds for any language they encounter; children have to treat all languages as either pro-drop or non-pro-drop. Something that linguists only came across in the 1980s is known to any three-year-old. Children use the presence of dummy subjects *it* and *there* and the consistency of present-tense inflections to decide whether they are learning a language like Italian or one like English, again a subtle clue to a complex phenomenon. Their minds must include, not just the possibility of languages having or not having subjects, but also the necessity for spotting particular bits of evidence to distinguish between them. This type of explanation is typical of the Universal Grammar theory, to be developed further below and in Chapter 11.

This section has described a set of facts about language acquisition about which there is little disagreement: children's speech appears to lack various grammatical essentials of adult speech; their sentences are structured in various ways; they have systems for using sounds and systems of meaning for vocabulary. Yet this lack of disagreement about the facts does not extend to the explanations for children's acquisition. The same facts can be explained in innumerable different ways, as will be demonstrated in section III.

II Speaking to children

1 Babytalk

Children in some sense learn language from their parents. It is important then to consider how the ways in which adults talk to children affect the growth of their language. Some parents vow that they will speak to the child in the same way that they speak to an adult. However, whether experienced parent or total novice, everyone adapts their speech to children in one way or another, despite their best intentions. This section looks at the modifications that are made when speaking to children, and considers the effects of these on language acquisition.

What these parents presumably mean is that they will avoid 'babytalk' words such as *gee-gee*, *moocow* or *bow-wow*. To find out which babytalk words are most familiar today, the *Inside Language* panel were asked which words they had heard used to children (Q7). Setting aside the inevitable *-ie/y* endings of *mummy* and *auntie*, and the like, over 70 per cent were familiar with *pussy*, *sweetie*, *tummy* and *bunny*; over 50 per cent had heard *bow-wow*, *peepee* and *geegee*. Then, in order of frequency, came *puffpuff*, *wops* ('wasp'; according to the Survey of English Dialects *wopses* is still used in rural dialects in 20 counties), *biccy* ('biscuit'), *weewee*, *choo-choo*, *moocow*, *jimjams* ('pyjamas'), *doggie*, *dindins*, *poohpooh* and *yumyums*. Finally there were single individuals who spoke up for *hotty botty* ('hot water bottle'), *horsey*, *coupcoup* ('chicken'), *flutterby* ('butterfly'), *tumtum*, *moomoo*, *froggy*, *piggy* ('toes'), *bobos*, *lala*, and *sweetpea treacle* (meaning unknown).

There is indeed a range of words that are conventionally used for speaking to children. *Wops* and *bunny* go back to older stages in the English language. *Wops* was the original form of *wasp,* with the *s* and *p* changing places. *Bunny* comes from the word *coney*, the usual word for 'rabbit' in England till a sound change in the eighteenth century meant that it accidentally coincided with the pronunciation of a taboo word. *Puffpuff* and *choo-choo* have long outlived the steam engines their sounds suggested.

Many of these words have something in common. Most are two syllables long, such as *puffpuff* and *jimjams*. Many have a particular structure in which the same syllable is repeated twice, whether the two syllables are identical as in *choochoo* and *tumtum*, or the first consonant changes in the second syllable, as in *bow-wow* and *hotty botty*, or the vowel changes, as in *jimjams*. These words mirror some of the pronunciations that children themselves use at early stages, such as doubling syllables. The *ie/y* ending can be extended to almost any word, as in *sweetie*, *biccy*, *piggy*. Any sentence

---

Babytalk in different languages

WORDS FOR THE FAMILY

mother: *mummy*, *mama* (Moroccan Arabic), *mama* (Swahili), *ma* (Berber), *mutti* (German), *mamá* (Greek), *maman* (French)

grandfather: *jiji* (Japanese), *babu* (Swahili), *habo* (Arabic), *kong kong* (Chinese), *papi/pépé* (French), *papú* (Greek)

WORDS FOR PART OF THE BODY

stomach: *tummy*, *pompon* (Japanese), *umbo* (Swahili), *bumbuls* (Latvian)

foot: *anyo* (Japanese), *rejel* (Arabic), *peton* (French), *podaráki* (Greek)

WORDS FOR ANIMALS

cow: *moocow*, *moo* (Swahili), *moomoo* (Japanese), *baâ* (Arabic)

cat: *pussy*, *nyau* (Swahili), *nyannyan* (Japanese), *myow* (Arabic), *minou* (French)

dog: *bowwow*, *wan wan* (Japanese), *hawhaw* (Moroccan Arabic), *uu* (Swahili), *toutou* (French), *vau vau* (Latvian), *waw-waw* (Greek)

bird: *birdie*, *ku:ku* (Arabic), *poppo/piipii* (Japanese), *deedy* (Arabic), *pulaki* (Greek), *zozio* (French)

WORDS FOR ACTIONS

urinate: *wee wee*, *make peepee*, *kojooa:jojoa* (Swahili), *shii shii-sura* (Japanese), *hammam kicha* (Arabic), *faire pipi* (French), *káno tsísa* (Greek), *ssi* (Moroccan Arabic and Berber)

walk: *anyo suru* (Japanese, 'do footie'), *hada-hada* (Arabic), *čāpāt* (Latvian), *daddush* (Berber)

go to sleep: *go beddy byes*, *faire dodo* (French), *lala:lal* (Swahili), *nenne suru* (Japanese), *namy mama* (Arabic to a girl), *namy baba* (Arabic to a boy), *nanákia* (Greek), *nah nah* (Moroccan Arabic)

Source: mostly Essex students, and Ferguson, 'Babytalk as a simplified register' can be paraphrased in these terms: *Blairy-wairy will losey-boozy votey-woteys*. At least one English comedian has made a career out of the comic effects of this type of speech.

Babytalk words in many languages have been produced through similar processes. Japanese too adds a diminutive ending *-ko* as in *dakko* ('hug'), German *-li*, *Peterli* ('little Peter') and Greek *-aki* as in *podaráki* ('little foot'). Syllable doubling is found in babytalk as far afield as Berber *bubu* ('lump of sugar'), Latvian *pȩki pȩki* ('duck') and Japanese *meme* ('bad'). Adults everywhere believe that such syllables are easier for children to understand and to learn, whether or not this belief is right. Babytalk words are also used to speak to creatures that do not speak human language, such as dogs and cats; they are found in places where people are cared for by others, such as hospitals; and they are commonly used for endearment among adults, as the messages in the newspapers on Valentine's Day show: *Little snookum ookums wants to snuggle up to his babbit*. Babytalk is a virtually universal genre in human language, as can be seen from the box on page 151.

2 *Modifications in language spoken to children*

Apart from the oddities of babytalk, adult speech to children is adapted in other ways. This section extends the idea of adaptation to children to other areas of language than babytalk vocabulary. Because of the first-draft nature of speech, adults make 'mistakes': they get sentences muddled up; they stop in mid-stream; and so on. However, in speech directly addressed to children, virtually all the sentences are fully formed and correct. One experiment found that only one out of 1500 sentences addressed to children by their mothers was ungrammatical. Children get a tidied-up version of speech from adults, though not of course in the speech they overhear. Adults make their speech more grammatical for the children's sake. Language acquisition would be wellnigh impossible if children had to discover which sentences they heard were grammatical and which were not.

Most people also feel that they use the simplest structure they can to communicate with children, avoiding complex relative clauses or passives. Adults are also more directive in their speech to children than they are to fellow adults. One adult speaking to another tends to use mostly statements of one kind or another and comparatively few questions or commands. Speaking to children, however, adults use twelve times as many questions, and nine times as many commands, but only one third as many statements. This change in the proportion of different sentences is a by-product of the kinds of conversation adults have with children. Many adults see their conversational role as asking children questions (*What colour's that, Jimmy?*) or giving commands (*Put your coat on, Brenda*), not as discussing things with them – talking at them rather than to them.

Adults are particularly conscious of pronouns when speaking to children. Parents often use nouns rather than the first or second person pronouns *I* and *you*: *Mummy's here*, *Does Baby want to play?*, whether in English, Japanese or Romanian. The defining characteristic of pronouns seen in Chapter 2 is that they refer to different things from moment to moment according to who is speaking, who is listening and other factors. The person referred to by *I* and *you* changes from one speaker to the next, while the meaning of *Mary Robinson* remains constant. Parents might feel they are helping the child by removing the problem of deciding who is being referred to through the third person. In Japanese, however, there is an unusual use in which the first person pronoun is used to refer to the child addressed, *boku* for boys, *atashi* for girls; the logic is more concerned with the system of respect in Japanese pronouns than with whom they refer to.

Conversations with children are linked to what is going on around the speakers at that moment. To adults, speakers talk about politics, sport, their jobs and so on; to children, they talk about what they are doing at that moment and what they can see around them. Speech with children is rooted in the 'here and now'. Even adults who try not to talk down to children nevertheless instinctively make this change. Conversation tied to the concrete situation is clearly going to help children comprehend, if not acquire, language. Even if they do not understand exactly what adults say to them, children know that it is linked to the situation in which they find themselves, and so they can hunt around for the most likely meaning.

Some speech patterns may also be used by adults to show how the sentences are constructed. An experiment asked adults to read the following sentences aloud:

'You're a really BAD ball,' said Pete.
'You're really BAD, Ball,' said Pete.

The first *BAD*, which is part of the same phrase as *ball*, is said with a much shorter vowel than the second *BAD*, which is in a different phrase from *Ball*. This difference is exaggerated when an adult is speaking to a child. Children are presented with clearer clues to the structure than those in normal adult-to-adult speech. Adults are demonstrating the phrase structure by exaggerating differences that would be minimal in speech to adults.

So speech to babies does not consist just of a specialized vocabulary but has other characteristics of grammar and pronunciation. It does not seem that babytalk words themselves actively hinder the child to any great extent, or that any of these adaptations make a great deal of difference to acquisition. After all babytalk is also used to dogs, who still have not succeeded in learning to speak. There are many conventions of speech peculiar to particular speech situations – the courtroom with judges called *milud*, the hospital with surgeons called *Mr*, and so on. These special genres of speech have the same kind of importance as deciding whether to wear a pullover or a jacket: they are appropriate dress for particular situations. Most languages have a conventional style of speech for speaking to children. Some of its characteristics may slightly help the child to acquire language; none of them probably hinders. The parents' decision to refrain from this form of speech is unlikely to have a major effect on their children's language

– far less than the decision to have an au pair girl who hardly speaks the child's first language.

Some adaptation of speech to children by parents may nevertheless be helpful. One activity that correlates with children's success is being read to. Children's speed of language development can almost be predicted from the number of books that are read to them per week. It is not so much the language of the book itself that helps as the continual discussion of the book's content with an adult.

An experiment by Rick Cromer accidentally highlighted the large effects of quite small events on children's acquisition. Its basic aim was to test children's understanding of the sentences *The dogs are easy to chase* and *The dogs are eager to chase*. The first sentence implies that the dogs are chased by something, the second sentence that the dogs chase something, only one out of the 48 people in the *Inside Language* panel dissenting (Q10). This difference in grammatical meaning is not present in the phrase structure of the sentences themselves but hidden in the underlying structure, even if all native speakers make use of it. The sentences in fact come from the 1960s version of Chomsky's UG theory, where they were used to show that two sentences which appear to differ only in choice of adjective, *eager* versus *easy*, in fact have different grammatical structures. Not surprisingly, children misunderstand these sentences till about the age of seven, and assume that the first noun is always the subject, i.e. that *The dogs are easy to chase* actually means the dogs are chasing something rather than being chased. The basic point of the experiment had been achieved.

One group of children had been tested on sentences with these structures every three months for a year, without being told whether they were right or wrong. Surprisingly, this group were way ahead of children who had not been tested at all. In other words, the experience of listening to ten sentences once every three months was enough in itself to set off the children's acquisition. A small amount of language – ten sentences – from an adult had had remarkable consequences. This effect was particularly conspicuous when Princess Diana visited the research unit. A girl had been selected the week before who made the usual mistake. A week later she was tested in the royal presence to demonstrate the experiment, and she performed completely correctly. Doing the test once was enough to enable her to acquire this complex grammatical point. Minute amounts of appropriate language may be all that the child needs for some features of language. Rick Cromer in fact called this the 'Princess Di effect'.

This section has shown that there are consistent changes made by adults to child-directed speech. It is nevertheless still hard to tell if these adaptations are necessary for language to be acquired, or are simply optional extras. The problem with seeing children's acquisition as driven by specially adapted language is that conversations with children vary greatly from one culture to another. While most English-speaking parents take pains to provide language adapted to what they perceive as the child's needs, this adaptation would not be done by Samoans, Javanese or Kaluli, who may instead simply limit the kind of topic they discuss with children. Yet all children learn human language, with very few exceptions, despite the variation in their parents' behaviour. The method they use for acquisition must either be infinitely adaptable to a variety of situations or it must be so robust that the type of language and social interaction the child receives makes no difference to acquisition.

For the most part, children do not need special speech from adults in order to acquire language. Children are resilient enough to learn language more or less independently of their parents. Clearly this does not extend to total neglect and deprivation of language. The most famous case of recent years is Genie, a girl who spent the first 14 years of her life strapped in a chair in a bedroom without being spoken to. At the time she was rescued, she hardly spoke at all; but she managed to acquire a limited language ability for a few years though this was later lost. However, so strong is the human capacity to acquire language, it takes extreme conditions such as these to prevent a human child from acquiring a human language.

III Three views of language acquisition

Everyone accepts that it is an amazing achievement for a child to acquire the language system in the short space of a few years and a great deal is now known about the stages that children go through. However, there is still little agreement how acquisition takes place. This section contrasts three views of the process of language acquisition. The first is *associationist*: children learn language by forming associations in their minds, derived from sentences they hear and from the way their parents treat them. The second is *interactionist*: children learn by building up complex patterns of give-and-take with their parents. The third is *Universal Grammar*: much of language is not acquired but reflects the Universal Grammar present in the mind of every human being.

1 The associationists: 'language is learnt by forming associations in the mind'

The associationist view claims that children learn language by forming associations between sounds and objects. In Leonard Bloomfield's classic formulation, children first make the noise /da/ by chance when there is a doll near them, presumably /dɒ/ from British children. *Wow!* say the parents in one way or another. The children hear from their praise that they have done something right, and so they produce the sounds *da* the next time they see a doll. Then they learn that, if they say *da* when the doll is not visible, someone will get it for them: speech works even when the object is not there. Names for the other objects they encounter are learnt in a similar fashion. Language is then a matter of accidentally producing speech sounds and getting them shaped by parents till they correspond to the adult language.

The more sophisticated rejigging of this theory sees language as a chain of stimulus and response. The object 'doll' acts as a stimulus for the child to respond *da*. This link between stimulus and response is reinforced by the parents saying *Good girl!* or the like. Language is closely linked to the physical stimulus of the situation: language acquisition requires the parents to reinforce the child's responses till she is right. Language is then a form of behaviour, vastly more complicated than other forms, but behaviour nonetheless. Consequently language is learnt in the same way as any other behaviour. Acquiring the first language is in principle no different from learning to ride a bicycle: you have to fall off, you have to practise, and you have to be helped back on by a friendly adult.

Take the following dialogue between the Bristol child, Mark, aged 15 months, and his father:

Father: Want some?
Mark: Want some.
Father: Want some more?
Mark: Want some more. More.
Father: Ta.
Mark: Ta.
Father: Good boy.
Mark: Good boy.
Father: Good boy.
Mark: Good dad.

This dialogue is a classic example of how the child might learn language through imitating adults. Each of Mark's replies repeats his father's preceding remark: *Ta – Ta*. Only in the last remark, *Good dad*, does he vary the phrase he hears, even if it sounds slightly odd. Adults, in the associationist view, provide a model of speech which the child imitates. Children learn by getting closer and closer to the adult model.

If parents provide the right kind of language experience and the right kinds of feedback, children will acquire language. In this view, parents are incredibly good at teaching language, far better than any professional language teacher. Children are equally adept at picking language up from them. When parents provide feedback, they have to make clear to the child which sentences are wrong and which are right. This process requires exchanges such as the following dialogue between a 3¼-year-old girl and her father:

C: You read it . . .You read it to me.
Father: . . . And there was a lovely yellow chrysanthemum.
C: Chrysankinum.
Father: 'S what love?
C: Sankinun.
Father: What's that there?
C: Flower.
Father: What?

The father draws attention to the child's mispronunciation of *chrysanthemum*, so she has another attempt, before taking the easy way out and calling it a *flower*.

The chief problem with this theory is that studies of parent–child interaction have found few examples of parents giving downright praise for correct language or correcting sentences that are wrong. The father does not say *Don't say Sankinun* directly but simply makes it clear that he has not understood: *'S what love?* If reinforcement from the parent were vital to language acquisition, it would have to occur constantly rather than being a rare event.

Furthermore, the sentences that parents choose to correct are mostly politeness formulas of the *Say please and thank you* type. Other sentences that get corrected are factually wrong rather than grammatically incorrect. When a child said *Draw a boot paper*, the mother did not correct the sentence directly by saying *You mustn't say 'boot paper' but 'a boot on the paper'* but replied *That's right. Draw a boot on paper.* An encouraging response to children's speech is far more typical than discouraging correction. Parents are indeed five times as likely to express disapproval of a well-formed sentence as of an ill-formed one; it is what the child is talking about they notice, not his or her grammatical 'mistakes'.

Nor is correction very successful on the few occasions when it has been caught on tape. David McNeill reported the following, now famous, conversation:

Child: Nobody don't like me.
Mother: No, say 'nobody likes me'.
Child: Nobody don't like me.
(*eight repetitions of this exchange*)
Mother: No, now listen carefully; say 'nobody likes me'.
Child: Oh! Nobody don't likes me.

After all this effort, the mother has succeeded in getting the child to produce something that is just as peculiar as his first remark. Children seem insensitive to correction of their language mistakes. Indeed the Bristol project found that the more parents believed they corrected their children's speech, the slower their children's language developed.

The associationist theory of language has been powerful in psychology, and undoubtedly fits many parents' views of how their children acquire language. It seems obvious to them that they actively teach children language, and that it is through the continual shaping of their behaviour that children come to be adults. Much of the language training of children with learning disabilities, indeed, uses careful progressive shaping of this type. An example provided by Morag Donaldson is how to teach children to use pronouns. First the children are shown a picture and asked the question *What is the girl doing?* They are prompted *Say 'she is swimming'*, and they are praised when they say it correctly. Children are expected to learn by hearing the right form, imitating it, and then being reinforced for getting it right. The problematic issue is whether children can generalize from the limited sentences they are trained on with this technique to other new sentences, whether in fact they are learning a general use of language or limited tricks.

Acquiring the English past tense

A test case for different theories of language acquisition in recent years has been the acquisition of the English past tense. Chapter 3 contrasted the regular forms of a grammatical inflection, which are made by rule, with the irregular forms, which are often idiosyncratic. The regular form of the past tense is formed by adding a grammatical inflection *-ed* to the base form, pronounced according to the last sound of the verb as /t/ *liked*, /d/ *played*, or /ɪd/ *waited*. But the past tense can also be formed in several irregular ways, mostly reflecting earlier historical periods of English. Some verbs change their vowel: *dig/dug*, *find/found* or *eat/ate*. Others change the final consonant: *lend/lent*, *have/had*. Some change both the vowel and the final consonant, *think/thought*, *teach/taught*. Some change nothing at all, *hurt/hurt*, *let/let*, *put/put*.

English-speaking children commonly go through three stages in the acquisition of the past tense. First they tend to produce the common irregular forms such as *came* and *went*. Then they learn the regular past tense rule of adding a form of *-ed* to get *played*, *looked*, *wanted*, etc. Next they enter a period when they make irregular verbs conform to the major rule: *comed*, *goed*, *wented*. Finally they can handle both regular and irregular past tenses correctly. So they start by learning the irregular forms, but lose them as they acquire the regular forms, only to regain them in due course.

This evidence suggested that the associationist view of practice making perfect was inadequate. The children had associated the past tense morpheme with the correct irregular forms such as *came* and had produced them many times. They should therefore have improved more and more with time and practice. Instead, just as they acquire the regular forms in *-ed*, they get dramatically *worse* at the irregular forms by over-regularizing them to make them conform to the regular pattern: *comed*. Sheer improvement through practice cannot explain this temporary deterioration. The anti-associationist explanation is that, once children know a rule, it takes precedence over all their previous habits. Children acquire a rule for regular past tense forms which they then apply to every verb they know. Regardless of how successfully *come* has been associated with the right past tense, *came,* in the child's mind, it still gets converted to *comed* by the child's new rule.

If this claim is true, the associationists must be wrong: gradually building up associations through practice, imitation, and correction is unimportant compared to the power of acquiring a rule. The proof that native speakers have a rule for regular past tenses rather than simply separate habits for each verb can be seen in the ability to coin new past tenses for verbs. On an Australian soap I heard the sentence *You mustn't dob your mates.* Without hearing anything more, I know that the past tense of *dob* is *dobbed* with *-ed* pronounced /d/. A gardening programme talks about *seed-chitting*; without having to know in the slightest how to chit seeds, everybody knows that the past tense is *I chitted some seeds yesterday.* Or, to take computer jargon, people have no problem in creating past tenses for *ftp*, *fax*, *cache*, or *ungroup*.

More modern versions of associationism have challenged the need for rules by modelling acquisition on a computer. A computer program can learn the range of

English past tense forms through networks of associations. A 'connectionist network' is fed with examples of English verbs, including both regular verbs such as *play/played* and irregular verbs such as *go/went, see/saw* and *sleep/slept*. After many encounters with these, the computer 'learns' which verbs take *-ed* and which have the different irregular forms. The process consists of strengthening the connections between the forms and the verbs without the need for an abstract rule. The sequence of acquisition through which the computer progresses resembles that seen in the real-life child. Since computers do not need 'rules', there is no need to postulate them to explain children's acquisition.

Modern-day proponents of associationism do not deny that the child's mind has a structure that it employs for learning language, or indeed for learning everything else; but this structure is no more than an enormous web of connections, at the lowest level between the actual cells of the brain. The experience the child encounters builds up the strength of particular connections, and so leads to the acquisition of language. This theory proves its model of acquisition essentially by analogy: a computer program is set up that 'learns' from an English language input. A real child does not necessarily learn in the same way. Such a model of acquisition has to show that it works for languages other than English and that it applies to other areas of grammar than the past tense. Joseph Stemberger has indeed applied a connectionist model to the development of phonology in his two children.

The theory proposed by Stephen Pinker represents something of a compromise between the alternatives. Some verbs are treated by the child as covered by the regular past tense *-ed* rule. Other verbs are taken to belong to a different system of irregular verbs, consisting not just of one-off pairs such as *is/was*, but also of subsystems for particular types of verbs, such as *ring/rang, sing/sang*, or *grow/grew, throw/threw*, as in fact they are usually listed in grammar books. Hence there are two separate learning processes, one for the regular *-ed* rule, one for the irregular forms. The irregular forms are not learnt as isolated exceptions to rules but are processed in an associationist way. Pinker's theory maintains that the two learning processes in these types are very different, and that people are therefore acquiring two types of knowledge. Partly the evidence for the division between regular rules and irregular forms is that some children with language difficulties have problems with regular past tense forms but not with irregular, as we see in Chapter 9. Partly the isolation of irregular forms is seen in people's reluctance to use them for deriving a compound verb from a noun: turn the noun *grandstand* into a past tense verb and you get *grandstanded* not *grandstood*; turn *input* into a verb and it becomes *inputted*, not *input*.

2 The interactionists: 'language is learnt by interacting with people'

The interactionist view of acquisition sees the child's interaction with the environment in social terms, as the development of patterns of interaction between the child and the adult. Children learn language as part of particular social routines. A familiar example is the peekaboo game where the mother hides something and then pops it out at the child, as in the following conversation between 15-month-old Timmy and his mother:

Mother: Boo to you. Yeah. Bee bee bee bee. Bo Peepo Timmy.
Timmy: (*laughs*).
Mother: Peepo. Boo.
T: (*laughs*) . . . Mummy.
Mother: Timmy. Bee Bee beep. Bo.
Timmy: (*laughs*)
Mother: Bo.
Timmy: (*laughs*)
Mother: Bo.
Timmy: (*laughs*)
Mother: Bo.
Timmy: BO.
Mother: Ah bee bee bee bee bee BO.

In the earliest version of this language game, the mother simply hides the toy and brings it out while saying *Boo!* The game becomes more elaborate with the mother first getting the child's attention – *Look what I've got here!* – then hiding it – *He's gone!* – and announcing its imminent arrival – *He's coming to see you!* At each stage of elaboration, there is a pattern of give and take between child and adult, initially putting small demands on the child but gradually building up the child's involvement in increasingly complex chains of interaction. Similar games are played in every culture at a particular stage in the child's development.

The psychologist Jerome Bruner sees these 'formats' as the driving force in language acquisition. The child's day is made up of many such interchanges – being fed, being bathed, being dressed, having nappies changed, getting in a baby buggy, and so on. Each event is accompanied by remarks from the parent, which build up into more and more elaborate routines and thus grow into the full range of language forms and use.

To the interactionist, the crucial factor in language acquisition is taking part in the give and take of dialogue. The adult is not a mere provider of language to imitate, nor a stern judge of whether a sentence is correct, but a continuously flexible training machine building up the child's performance. According to Bruner, it is not that children are good at acquiring language, but that parents are good at adapting formats to the child's needs and thus creating language in the child's mind.

One difficulty with this approach is the variation in how children are treated in different cultures. In Java, mothers do not speak to their babies because 'they do not yet understand'; in the southern USA, some adults think it rude to talk to a child when another adult is present. In such cases children must learn, not by participating in the formats themselves, but by overhearing others using them, which puts a very different complexion on their learning. Children must be sufficiently adaptable to profit from a large variety of interaction styles, rather than from a single universal way of child–adult interaction. While linguists feel that the use of language in everyday life must be learnt in some such way, there are many elements of language that they insist could not be learnt by interaction because the clues for them are not provided by the language that children hear.

3 Universal Grammar: 'essential features of language are already built into the human mind'

The Universal Grammar model claims that neither of the other theories adequately explains how children acquire the central systems of grammar and sounds described in earlier chapters. Take the example of word order. Though children's sentences are often bizarre, they are almost always in the appropriate order for the language they are learning. For example, virtually all the examples of children's sentences used in this chapter have had the right word order for English, as can be seen if the word order in the sentences is reversed. *Baby doll*, *daddy do*, and *want car* are clearly a version of English while *doll baby*, *do daddy*, *car want* are not. Children rarely make mistakes with the word order of their first language. English children always use the Subject–verb order, *mum drive* not *drive mum* – and the preposition–noun order, *in car* not *car in*. An English child says *pretty car*, never *car pretty*. If the driving force of acquisition were trying things out and getting mistakes corrected, they would have to try out different possible word orders and choose whichever one their parents approved of. Everywhere in the world, it is rare for children to make mistakes with word order. Word order is evidently not learnt by trial and error and reinforcement of the correct order by parents.

If children were imitating adult sentences, they would be confused by the different word orders that are possible in English, for instance the question *Is John here?* alongside the statement *John is here*. But they have no problem in avoiding this verb–Subject order, even if they do not produce questions themselves for some time. The Universal Grammar theory believes that the explanation is that much of language is already present in the human mind, ready to be activated by exposure to sentences. If the child gets the right sentences, he or she will acquire the grammar. Hearing a sample of English sentences with Subject–Verb order rather than Verb–Subject order turns a particular switch in the mind. The complexity of language is not outside, waiting for the child to discover; it is inside, waiting to be revealed.

Much of the language system is therefore believed to be already latent in the human brain; it needs to be brought to life by hearing enough sentences of a human language. Noam Chomsky's recent version of the Universal Grammar theory claims that language knowledge consists of a number of universal principles that do not vary and a number of parameters that differ from one language to another, as mentioned briefly in Chapter 3. Structure-dependency, the reason why *Is Sam is the cat that black?* does not occur, is one of these principles. The presence or absence of subjects in the sentence, as outlined in Chapter 2, is one of the parameters, called the pro-drop parameter. The child's mind has the built-in expectation that a language either has subjects or does not. The samples of language the child hears from its parents 'trigger' the pro-drop parameter in the mind into one or other of these possibilities. Rather than being developed further here, the consequences of this position will be explored in Chapter 11.

Though these three theories have been presented as alternatives, none of them could contain the whole truth. Some parts of language are indeed learnt by practice and correction, some by interacting with people, some from within the mind itself. To an extent, the theories deal with complementary areas of language, rather than being in opposition. Linguists are only beginning to understand how children acquire a human language. A broad perspective on acquisition is necessary for the present rather than an all-encompassing theory, as not enough is still known about many areas. Anybody could make a major discovery tomorrow by listening to a child they know. Find a child that breaches structure-dependency and the world would beat a path to your door.

One overall theme that comes out of this chapter is, then, the enormity of the child's achievement in acquiring the system of human language in the space of a few years. Children manage to extract the whole system of pronunciation, the complexities of grammar, the chains of meaning of words, out of the simple sentences and exchanges they get from their parents. They have mastered an overall language system that linguists have still to describe in detail and that cannot be duplicated by any other being or machine. Nor is it the exceptional child that achieves this feat, but virtually every human child. As we see in Chapter 9, problems with language not associated with other developmental problems are encountered by only 1.5 per cent of children.

Sources and further reading

A very useful overall source is P. Fletcher and B. MacWhinney (eds.), *The Handbook of Child Language* (Oxford: Blackwell, 1995). The Bristol study is described in C.G. Wells, *Language Development in the Pre-school Years* (Cambridge: CUP, 1985).

Perceiving speech sounds

The work on distinguishing languages is J. Mehler, P.W. Jusczyk, G. Lambertz, N. Halstead, J. Bertoncini and C. Amiel-Tison, 'A precursor of language development in young children', *Cognition* 29 (1988): 143–78. One of the original articles on children's perception of VOT is

P.D. Eimas, E.R. Siqueland, P. Jusczyk and J. Vigorito, 'Speech perception in infants', *Science* 171 (1971): 303–6. Other papers include P.W. Jusczyk, 'Developing phonological categories from the speech signal', in C.A. Ferguson, L. Menn and C. Stoel-Gammon (eds.), *Phonological Development: Models, Research, Implications* (Timonium, MD: York Press, 1992): 17–64.

Producing speech sounds

Tessa's acquisition of VOT is described in M.A. Macken and D. Barton, 'The acquisition of the voicing contrast in English: a study of voice onset time in word-initial stop consonants', *Journal of Child Language* 7 (1980): 41–74.

Acquiring words

The original division of children at the one-word stage into two types was described in K. Nelson, 'Structure and strategy in learning to talk', *Monographs of the Society for Research in Child Development* 38/143 (1973). The discussion of growth in vocabulary is based on L. Fenson et al., *The MacArthur Communicative Development Inventories* (San Diego, CA: Singular Publishing, 1993). Meaning components were first discussed in E. Clark, 'On the acquisition of "before" and "after"', *Journal of Verbal Learning and Verbal Behaviour* 10 (1971): 266–75; prototypes in E. Rosch, 'Human categorization', in N. Warren (ed.), *Studies in Cross-Cultural Psychology* (New York: Academic Press). Clark's more recent ideas are presented in 'Later lexical development and word formation', in Fletcher and MacWhinney, *The Handbook of Child Language* (see above).

Acquiring early grammar

A clear introduction to the acquisition of grammar is H. Goodluck, *Language Acquisition: A Linguistic Introduction* (Oxford: Blackwell, 1991).

Grammatical morphemes

The original work on sequences of acquisition of grammatical morphemes and on MLU is R. Brown, *A First Language: The Early Stages* (London: Allen & Unwin, 1973). A book which builds on this is P. Fletcher, *A Child's Learning of English* (Oxford: Blackwell, 1985). Missing functional categories are proposed by A. Radford, *Syntactic Theory and the Acquisition of English Syntax* (Oxford: Blackwell, 1990).

Rules of two-word speech

The original paper on pivot/open is M. Braine, 'The ontogeny of English phrase structure: the first phase', *Language* 39 (1963): 1–13; his later theory is explained in *Children's First Word Combinations* (Chicago: Monographs of the Society for Research in Child Development, 1976). *Mommy sock* is discussed in L. Bloom, *Language Development: Form and Function in Developing Grammars* (Cambridge, MA: MIT Press, 1970).

Sentences without subjects (pro-drop)

The original work on pro-drop was reported in N. Hyams, *Language Acquisition and the Theory of Parameters* (Dordrecht: Reidel, 1986). Some later views are presented in O. Jaeggli and K.J. Safir, *The Null Subject Parameter* (Dordrecht: Kluwer, 1989).

Babytalk

The original paper was C.A. Ferguson, 'Babytalk as a simplified register', in C.E. Snow and C.A. Ferguson (eds.), *Talking to Children: Language Input and Acquisition* (Cambridge: CUP, 1977): 209–36.

Modifications in language spoken to children

The experiment with *easy/eager to chase* and the 'Princess Di effect' are described in R.F. Cromer, 'Language growth with experience without feedback', *Journal of Psycholinguistic Research* 16/3 (1987): 223–31. A popular account of Genie's life is R. Rymer, *Genie: A Scientific Tragedy* (Harmondsworth: Penguin, 1993). The 'bad ball' experiments are described in D. Morgan, *From Simple Input to Complex Grammar* (Cambridge, MA: MIT Press, 1986).

View 1: the associationists

The original account is L. Bloomfield, *Language* (New York: Holt, 1933). The extreme behaviourist position that linguists love to hate is set out in B.F. Skinner, *Verbal Behavior* (New York: Appleton-Century-Crofts, 1957). Some training techniques are described in M.L. Donaldson, *Children with Language Impairments* (London: Jessica Kingsley, 1995).

Acquiring the English past tense

The main work on connectionism and the past tense is J.L. McLelland, D.E. Rumelhart and the PDP Research Group, *Parallel Distributed Processing*, ii: *Psychological and Biological Models* (Cambridge, MA: MIT Press 1992). Phonology is covered in J. Stemberger, 'A connectionist view of child phonology: phonological processing without phonological processes', in Ferguson et al., *Phonological Development* (see above). See also S. Pinker, *The Language Instinct* (Harmondsworth: Penguin, 1994).

View 2: the interactionists

The general approach is accessible through J. Bruner, *Child's Talk* (Oxford: OUP, 1983). Peek-aboo games are described in J. Bruner and V. Sherwood, 'Peekaboo and the learning of role structure', in Bruner, A. Jolly and K. Sylva (eds.), *Play: Its Role in Development and Evolution* (Harmondsworth: Penguin, 1976).

View 3: Universal Grammar

An accessible Chomsky book is N. Chomsky, *Language and Problems of Knowledge: The Managua Lectures* (Cambridge, MA: MIT Press 1988). A detailed introductory account of UG as a theory of language acquisition is in ch. 3 of V.J. Cook and M. Newson, *Chomsky's Universal Grammar: An Introduction* (Oxford: Blackwell, 1996); see also Chapter 11 below.

8   Varieties of Language

You turn on the radio and you hear someone speaking. After a few words you can probably tell their sex, their approximate age, their social background and the region of the world or part of the country they come from. In an experiment, speakers of American English could tell whether someone was black or white after hearing a vowel lasting one second. The present chapter explores some of the wealth of information conveyed by subtle differences of accent, vocabulary and grammar. Some of it is based on answers by the *Inside Language* panel to Questions 5, 6 and 8 on the questionnaire. Much of it derives from the work of William Labov, who essentially founded modern sociolinguistics, the study of language and society.

The earlier chapters give the impression that a language is a unified phenomenon. However, this is misleading in that a language varies to suit the many types of people who use it and the diverse circumstances in which they find themselves. This chapter looks at the following broad areas of variation:

*   *Individual variation*. Language varies from one person to another. Older people speak differently from younger people; women speak differently from men. Partly this variation is one aspect of the social grouping seen below, partly it is the inevitable effect of the biological differences between the sexes and of the ageing process.
*   *Region*. People in different areas who speak the same language use different versions of the grammar, vocabulary or sounds: there are differences, for instance, between the Arabic of speakers who come from Morocco, Jordan and Gaza. Regional variation in sounds is called 'accent'; variation in grammar and vocabulary is called 'dialect'. Thus educated speakers of English from many parts of the world differ in accent but not in dialect; Australians, Texans, Canadians and Dubliners are marked out by accent but share virtually the same grammar. This is particularly evident from written language, where the accent is in effect removed.

- *Social group.* Human societies are made up of all sorts of groupings, many of which manifest themselves in distinctive language. One grouping is by language itself; for example, the group of French speakers in Switzerland is different from the group of German speakers. A second grouping is by social class; in many countries, though not all, upper-class speakers speak a prestige variety of the language compared to lower-class speakers.
- *Function.* Language is used for many different functions. An individual has to master a range of language functions and to be able to switch between them when appropriate. Proficient speakers know how to manage speaking round a family dinner, in a business meeting, to a stranger in the street, and in any of the other situations of daily life.

These differences matter deeply to the speakers of a language. The way that someone speaks proclaims their membership of particular groups, whether age, sex, class or whatever. Hence the discussion of such differences is sensitive, since it raises an issue about which many people have a strong unacknowledged belief: there is an ideal correct form of language that people *should* speak, not a free choice between arbitrary alternatives.

Factor 1: gender

Suppose you heard someone say *Absolutely gorgeous, isn't it!!!* What gender are they? The first clue is the pitch of the speaker's voice. The larynxes in men's throats are on average larger than in women's – hence the greater visibility of the male Adam's apple. So their longer vocal cords vibrate more slowly and their voices tend to be deeper. To be exact, a man's vocal cords vibrate on average 129 times a second, i.e. a pitch of 129 hertz, a woman's 225 times (225 hertz). To accommodate the growth in the vocal cords during the teens, male voices 'break', that is to say adjust their pitch downward. It appears, however, that voice-breaking is not entirely a biological necessity but may be partly conventional, since the voices of deaf boys do not break. Indeed, pitch can vary from one language to another: one experiment found American men were 20 hertz lower than Polish men.

As always, different cultures overlay such physical facts with different interpretations. For an English speaker, the basic pitch of the voice is taken as a sign of gender, conveying many overtones. Deepness may mean male authority – Mrs Thatcher apparently felt it necessary to have her voice lowered through speech training to compete with male politicians in obedience to the Frequency Code, as discussed in Chapter 4. A man adopting female gender needs extensive speech therapy, *inter alia* to raise the overall pitch of the voice towards the woman's range.

A second clue to the speaker's gender is the words they use. The sentence *Absolutely gorgeous, isn't it!!!* caricatures what English women are supposed to sound like – 'gushing' vocabulary (*gorgeous*), use of tag questions (*isn't it*), use of modifiers (*absolutely*) and exaggerated intonation (here conveyed with multiple exclamation marks *!!!*). The title of the TV programme *Absolutely Fabulous!* parodied these characteristics. Ninety per cent of the *Inside Language* panel thought *Absolutely gorgeous* and *It's nice, isn't it?* (Q5) came from women, even if one commented, 'What rubbish!'

Thirdly, women are stereotyped as chattering gossips, who talk far more than men. In the BT commercials an invisible male played by Bob Hoskins patronizingly observed how good women are at networking on the phone, with the slogan *It's good to talk!*

Though such differences between the sexes are often claimed to occur in English, mostly they have not stood up to closer investigation. Adjectives such as *gorgeous* sound like British films of the 1930s rather than contemporary language. Tag questions like *isn't it* and modifiers like *absolutely* are used by both sexes, at least in England. The sheer quantity of speech used by women also seems to be a myth. In situations ranging from staff meetings to husband-and-wife conversation, men actually speak more than women.

There are nonetheless languages which have clearcut differences between men's and women's speech. In Cocama, a language spoken in the Amazon basin, men and women have different pronoun systems. The first person 'I' is *ta* from a man but *etse* from a woman; the third person 'he' or 'she' is *uri* from a man, *ai* from a woman. Indeed, the men and women in some Amazon tribes speak different languages, because the wives have to come from tribes which have another language.

Women also often have slightly different vocabularies from men. For example Dyirbal and other Australian languages have the convention that a married woman may not utter words that sound like her husband's name. If this applied to English, the wife of a man called *Ben* would have to avoid words such as *bend* or *Benetton*. The wife of an *Ed* would have the more severe problem of finding substitutes for past tense *-ed* in *wanted*, etc. Warlpiri, another Aboriginal language, has a sign language used only by women when they are forbidden to speak, say, during periods of mourning, or to accompany storytelling, perhaps the only example of a true sign language used by non-deaf people.

Language differences between the sexes reflect their different social roles. In Dholuo, a language spoken in Kenya, the verb *kendo* ('marry'), needs an active sentence when a man is involved, *John married Yoko*, but is passive when a woman is involved, *Yoko was married by John*. Men are often said to interrupt women in English, rather than vice versa: they have different roles in the conversation. At one extreme, transcripts of mixed-sex conversation have shown 23 male interruptions for every female interruption; other research, however, shows a far more even proportion. The relationship of language with gender is taken further below in the discussion of class.

All in all, the established differences between the language of the two sexes are few and far between. Most come from anecdotes rather than strong evidence, apart from

Opening remarks and speaker's gender

Here are the first remarks by speakers on an Essex phone-in programme dealing with listeners' problems. If there are clear differences between the sexes distinct from the qualities of the voice itself, it should be immediately apparent which are men, which women. Answers at the end of the chapter.

1　I always have problems with my thighs.
2　One question I'd like to ask you know I'm a larger type you know and I've got one heck of a job to buy clothes from anywhere.
3　My question is I've had a disastrous fire in the garden and all my shrubs now are blackened.
4　Hwere [sic] did you get your accent from? It's so soothing.
5　Ken, we was in the garden centre on Saturday but you was too busy to answer this question . . .
6　Ken, I'm sorry I don't want to throw any flowers at you like that lady did . . .
7　Good afternoon. I have a query for the insurance broker . . .
8　Good afternoon to you both. Last August twelvemonth I was unfortunate enough to be driving my car when it burst into flames.
9　Hello good afternoon I wonder if you can help me. For about the past fifteen years I've run a social club . . .
10　Hello Steve. How's your throat?

those influenced by physical makeup, such as the pitch of the voice. The more intriguing aspect to be discussed below is how the sexes represent certain types of value by using particular forms of speech.

Factor 2: age

Variation in language with age may be due partly to the inevitable biological effects of ageing. The pitch of the voice usually gives away whether an adult or a child is speaking, since the child's shorter vocal cords and overall smaller body size lead to a higher-pitched voice, an average of 265 hertz. It is thus easier for women to imitate children than for men.

The apparent age of an adult speaker's voice has an effect on the listener. One experiment tested people on an interview script recorded by an actor playing an old person and a young person, and using standard and non-standard accents. The older-sounding voice with a standard accent came across as 'egocentric, living in the past and talking of trivia', the young voice as 'arrogant and pompous'. The remark *I didn't know what to think* read in the elderly voice with a standard accent was taken to show confusion, in the young voice was taken to be refusing judgement. The elderly voice with a non-standard accent fared worst of all: 'stupid, and losing his grip' was the verdict.

But many differences between generations are not caused by physical ageing as such. People tend to retain the speech that they identified with in their early years; they go forward from the cradle to the grave bearing the speech they grew up with. Take the links between vocabulary and age. The *Inside Language* panel were asked which age groups they associated with particular words (Q6). Figure 8.1 concerns three words for 'radio', showing how many out of 48 people gave a particular response. A sample of 48 people can only suggest a trend rather than proving a point, and the association of words with age is based on opinion, not on observation of what people actually say. Nevertheless *wireless* is clearly associated with old people; *tranny* with those between 25 and 64; *radio* with young people. It is interesting that *radio,* first used for a radio receiver in 1913, is associated with young people while *tranny,* introduced with the transistor radio in the 1960s, is now for the middle-aged.

The words for 'man' show a less clear distribution for age, as seen in Figure 8.2. *Mush* is not known by many people, though characterized as slightly more Working

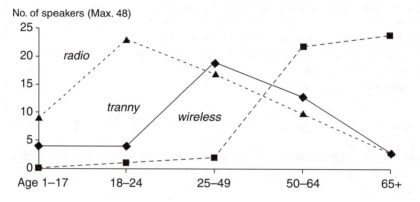

Fig. 8.1 Words for 'radio' associated with different ages

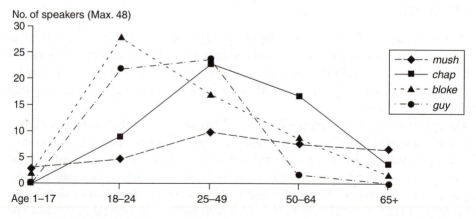

Fig. 8.2 Words for 'man' at different ages

Class (WC) than Middle Class (MC); this low recognition figure may underestimate the prevalence of the word as, never having seen it in print, I spelled it as *mooche* in the *Inside Language* Questionnaire, only to discover later that the *Oxford English Dictionary* spells it as *mush*, and regards it as 'slang'. *A nice chap* peaks with the 25-49 group and is regarded as MC by 98 per cent; *a good bloke* is associated most with the 18-24 age group and is 90 per cent WC, while *a pleasant guy* is restricted to those between 18-49 and is 94 per cent MC. It is surprising that *bloke* is thought to be WC, *guy* MC, though this result may have been biased by the adjectives *good* and *pleasant*. Speakers of English therefore have definite opinions about the vocabulary that goes with certain ages and certain classes. Similarly, older speakers of German talk of 'breakfast' as *Kaffee*, younger as *Frühstück*; older Israelis speak of a telephone as *sah rahok*, younger as *roshem kol*.

Older speakers can thus be a repository of forms of the language that are in the process of dying out. Regional speech is more common in older people, whether in France, Germany or England. Language stays still for no man, or woman, as seen in Chapter 10. Some speakers may, however, feel that they should adopt a type of language suitable for older people as they grow older. The word *bloke* may not feel right as one advances in years and so older people may feel *chap* is more appropriate, just as in the stereotype insurance commercial old men put on cardigans and potter in the garden.

Particular vocabulary items change from generation to generation, as seen with the words for 'radio'. An *LP* becomes an *album* and in turn gives way to *CD*, while *vinyl* arrives to describe the LP. Courses for teaching English as a Foreign Language readily reflect the changing use. A popular course in the 1960s still had the example sentence *My boyfriend Cyril made love to me last night*, an old meaning that now gives an unintended twist to many 1940s light comedy films.

Some speakers move with the times; others retain the older form or meaning. Each generation of teenagers, each new wave of music, proclaims its uniqueness through its vocabulary. Somebody who does not know the meaning of *harmolodics*, *M-base* or *jungle* is obviously not part of the crowd. Similarly with *ftp*, *e-mail*, and *gopher*. When Fats Waller was asked 'What is rhythm?' he answered 'If you have to ask, you ain't got it'. These factors of variation are an important part of the speaker's identity. In a sense it is hard to say whether language reflects social differences or language differences are social differences, a chicken and egg problem.

Particular pronunciations also tend to go with certain ages. As mentioned in Chapter 4, several contemporary shifts in England are associated with the so-called Estuary English of younger speakers in areas around London, for instance the use of a glottal stop [ʔ] for /t/ and of a /w/ sound for /l/, combined together in /bjuːʔɪfʊw/ for *beautiful*. New Yorkers under twenty pronounce *bird* as /bɜːrd/; New Yorkers over sixty have a diphthong /əɪ/ as in /bəɪrd/; those in between show a gradient between the two pronunciations. Chapter 10 will expand the question of how language changes over time.

Factor 3: region, dialect and standard

One of the crucial aspect of one's identity is where one comes from, both in the literal sense of actual area and in the metaphorical sense of social background. Language reveals this identity in almost everything one says. This section explores the different regional varieties of language, going from non-regional standard languages to local dialects.

1 R-dropping in English

No sooner has an English-speaking person opened their mouth to speak than another English speaker knows more or less where they come from, even if they cannot describe or imitate their speech. This section concentrates on the clue to region provided by the /r/ sounds and then expands into the question of prestige accents. It is not a matter of how /r/ is pronounced, though this varies to some extent, but of where it is used within the syllable structure. In General American English the sound /r/ occurs before vowels, as in *red* and *right* (rV), between vowels, as in *torrid* (VrV), before consonants, as in *bird* (rC), and before silence, as in *fur* (Vr). In English English the /r/ sound occurs before and between vowels in the same way (rV, VrV), but *never* occurs before a consonant (rC): *earth* is /ɜ:θ/ with no /r/ and *Oxford* is /ɒksfəd/, not /ɒksfərd/. Nor does /r/ occur as the final sound in a syllable said on its own, i.e. before silence (Vr): *fur* is /fɜ:/, not /fɜ:r/; *door* is /dɔ:/, not /dɔ:r/. A memorable example is the American who was asked in Singapore if she wanted *barley water* and was puzzled why the water had had to come all the way from *Bali* (/bɑ:rli/ versus /bɑ:li/). The same hesitation noise, /ə/, is spelled *er* in English books, *This is er very er embarrassing*, and *uh* in American books, *This is uh very uh embarrassing*. The English spelling *er* corresponds to a (Vr) combination /ər/ on one side of the Atlantic, to the vowel /ə/ alone on the other. American English is known as a 'rhotic' dialect which permits /r/ before vowels or silence; English English is a 'non-rhotic' dialect which does not have /r/ in these positions.

Rhotic varieties of English that use /r/ in the American way also occur in India, Ireland, Canada, Scotland, Barbados and the extreme south of New Zealand. Non-rhotic varieties that drop the /r/ in the English fashion occur in Australia, Africa, England and Wales, in Caribbean islands other than Barbados and in most of New Zealand. Whether /r/ is dropped or not depends on whether English arrived in these countries before or after *r*-dropping happened in England in the eighteenth century. Ireland and the USA spoke English before this date and so have the older pronunciation; New Zealand, and African countries such as Nigeria, did not and so have the newer, *r*-less pronunciation.

There are nonetheless still rhotic speakers in the British isles who say /bɜ:rd/ and /fɜ:r/. TV commercials often caricature them as stereotyped rustic yokels asking for cider or animated wooden dolls advertising varnish. That is to say, a rhotic accent is an instant code for the West Country and for the virtues of the rural life. The main rhotic areas where /r/ is found before consonants and silence are now in the west of England, that is to say, Cornwall, Somerset, and Devon, and in western cities such as Exeter and Bristol. Within the British Isles, Scotland and Ireland are also rhotic areas, but not Wales.

Rhotic /r/s are still heard from some speakers from rural areas in other parts of England, for instance in Essex, Sussex and Lancashire, showing their isolation from mainstream life. Phone-ins to Essex Radio often betray that there are rural /r/ users lurking in the remote villages of the county. Indeed 17 per cent of the *Inside Language* panel claimed that they pronounced the *r* at the end of *door* (Q8), per-

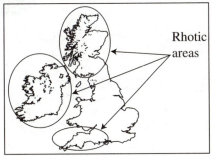

Rhotic areas

haps showing that a surprising number of people from the Essex area genuinely use *r*, perhaps showing they had misunderstood the question.

The rule in non-rhotic dialects that /r/ was dropped before silence did not apply if the next word in the sentence started with a vowel and the word itself ended with the vowel /ɑ:/, say *bar,* or any diphthong ending in /ə/, such as *beer* and *fire*. Many words therefore have two pronunciations depending whether the next word starts with a vowel. In English English the word *where* is pronounced /wɛə/ with no /r/ in *Where?,* but as /wɛər/ with an /r/ in *Where is it?*; *beer* is /bɪə/ in *A beer?* but /bɪər/ in *Your beer is here*; *bore* is /bɔ:/ but *boring* is /bɔ:rɪŋ/. This is called 'linking' /r/ as it links words together.

The habit of adding /r/s to these words has, however, spread to words that have never been pronounced with /r/ but which end in the vowels /ɔ:/ and /ə/. Examples are phrases like *law enforcement*, pronounced as /lɔ:r ɪnfɔ:smənt/ though there is no *r* in the spelling of the word *law,* and *the idea of it* /ðɪ aɪdɪər əv ɪt/ with no *r* in *idea*. Names such as *Australia* and *Madonna* are particularly prone to gain an /r/ when followed by a vowel, as any news bulletin will confirm. *Australia and New Zealand* is /ɒstreɪlɪər ən . . . /, and *Madonna is . . .* is /mədɒnər ɪz . . . /. Most non-rhotic accents of English have this so-called 'intrusive' /r/. Fifty-two per cent of the *Inside Language* panel admitted to using it in *Russia is big* (Q8), again perhaps showing lack of awareness of their own speech rather than their true pronunciation.

The letter *r* in English spelling goes back to the era before it was dropped from the pronunciation in the eighteenth century. A written *r* therefore does not correspond to any speech sound in non-rhotic dialects when it precedes a consonant, as in *orb* /ɔ:b/, or silence, as in *tenor* /tenə/. Some people insist that linking /r/ is justified when the spelling includes an *r* (*a pair of* /ə pɛər əv . . . /) but intrusive /r/ is not justified because there is no *r* in the spelling (*drawing* /drɔ:rɪŋ/). In this view, spelling is the basis of speech. If taken to its logical conclusion, this argument would logically mean restoring many English words to the pronunciation of earlier times, for example

What to call your 'grandmother' in England

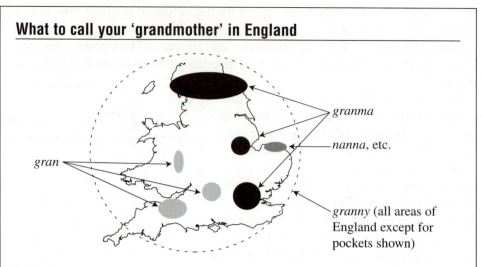

Main forms

While these show some of the main regional distribution of words for 'grandmother', there are many pockets of other forms within these areas.

granny: the most widely distributed from north to south, east to west (but given by only 4 of the *Inside Language* panel of 48 people)

granma: London and surrounding areas, pockets in the Midlands and north (6 of the panel)

gran: Devon, Somerset, Gloucestershire (9 of the panel)

granmam: north Shropshire (none of the panel)

nanny, nan (7 of the panel), *nana* (3), *nanna* (11): north Norfolk coast

Rarer forms

baba: south

gammy: north

grammer: West Midlands

grandmam: northern and West Midlands

grammy: East Midlands

gram: (1 of the panel, from Essex)

The proportions of answers from the *Inside Language* panel partly show that most of them came from Essex and East Anglia. However, *nanny* and its variants *nana* and *nanna,* which were supposed to be confined to speakers in Norfolk, in fact were confirmed not only from East Anglia (2), but also from Essex (4), south London (2) and east Sussex (1). *Nan* also is found 7 times; one is indeed from East Anglia, but 3 are from Essex and 1 each from Staffordshire, Bucks and south-east England. These forms may well be more widespread than was believed.

Sources: Upton et al., *Word Maps*; Orton et al., *Survey of English Dialects*

putting the /ç/ fricative sound back in *night* /nɪçt/, or restoring the 'silent' /k/ to *knot*. Regarding writing as the true form of language is also implausible, even if the very term '*r*-dropping' implies that speech leaves out something from writing.

Other languages supply parallel cases of a historical change creating backwaters of regional accents. The standard French accent has a 'uvular' /r/, that is to say one produced by contact between the back of the tongue and the far back of the mouth. Regional varieties within France such as Burgundy, however, have an 'alveolar' /r/ produced by the tongue tip contacting the alveolar ridge at the front of the mouth. This alveolar /r/ is regarded as 'rural and backward'.

Uvular /r/ spread from Paris in the seventeenth century, gradually driving the alveolar /r/ into the remote regions of France. Amazingly enough, this change appears to have had a strong effect on the languages of neighbouring countries. Over 300 years, many speakers of German, Dutch and Danish have come to use a uvular /r/, particularly around major cities like Berlin and Copenhagen.

2 *Regional and standard forms of language*

An accent is a matter of whether speakers drop their /r/s and so on, that is to say of pronunciation. A dialect, on the other hand, is a matter of whether they say *I never done it* or *I didn't do it*, and call a rubbish-collector a *dustman* or a *binman*, that is to say of grammar or of vocabulary as well as of accent. While an unfamiliar accent can be understood eventually, an unfamiliar dialect may be impossible, since the outsider does not know what the words mean, as in the following:

* *The mugger escaped down the folly* (Colchester, Essex, for 'alley')
* *See you at the station* (Australasian for 'stock farm')
* *That was bold of you* (Irish for 'naughty')
* *Give your form to the peon* (Indian English for 'office clerk')
* *James Ellroy writes mysteries* (American English for 'detective stories', though occasionally met in England, for example *the Ruth Rendell mysteries*)

At one level the differences of accent and dialect between people are straightforward: they are ways of showing where people come from. However, like much of language, straightforward geographical information plays only a small part in a tangle of social roles and values.

One way in is through the concept of standard language. Standard English has the same grammar and vocabulary everywhere it is spoken. But it may be spoken with an accent from Toronto, Karachi or Liverpool. A crucial accent in England, encountered in Chapter 4, is RP, which is not attached to any region. Historically, RP has been the prestige accent in England although spoken by few people. Instead, most educated people in England speak standard English with some regional variation – a modified RP. They differ from dialect speakers of, say, Yorkshire or Somerset, who have major differences in vocabulary, grammar, etc., as well as accent. On another dimension, people may speak standard English with a non-standard lower-class accent rather than RP, or they may have lower-class features of grammar and vocabulary, as we find in section V of this chapter.

	RP	Standard English	Non-standard (dialect/class)
	←——————————————————————→		
Standard grammar	✓	✓	✗
Standard vocabulary	✓	✓	✗
Prestige accent	✓	✗	✗

There is, then, a continuum in England between standard English spoken with an RP accent and non-standard English spoken with regional or class accents, grammar or vocabulary. There are comparatively few speakers at either extreme, speaking purely RP or solely dialect; indeed, some speakers may switch between these. Most English people, however, are somewhere in the middle, neither strictly RP nor strictly dialect. There are perhaps more speakers with class features, particularly in large towns.

In many countries the standard language carries the highest status, spoken with a prestige accent. It originates from a favoured section of society (London 'society', 'public school English', etc.) or from a prosperous geographical area ('Parisian French'). Hence the standard form is self-reinforcing as it spreads through the educational system and the media. In 1757 James Buchanan wrote: 'it ought to be indisputably the care of every teacher of English, not to suffer children to pronounce according to the dialect of that place or country where they were born or reside, if it happens to be vicious.' This position is not very far from the UK Secretary of State for Education in the 1990s lamenting that teenagers speak in grunts. Attempts to introduce regional accents or dialect forms into the schools and the media in England have met with a stony reception, the most famous historical incident being the uproar that followed the wartime use of a northerner, Wilfred Pickles, to read the BBC radio news. The reasons for the prestige of the standard language are historic and economic. Though the non-regional RP accent grew out of a southern accent, during this century the speech of educated people has increasingly incorporated features of London speech, reflecting its political and economic dominance.

The prestige of the RP accent, however, convinces people that it is inherently more beautiful, and that other versions deviate from it or corrupt it. People lament the ugliness, slovenliness or downright wickedness of those who speak with other accents, for example using rhotic /r/s or glottal stops [?]. Experiments demonstrate that it is arbitrary which form has the higher status. Those who are outside the language situation itself find no aesthetic difference between standard and non-standard accents. Although European French is the status form among French speakers, speakers of Welsh find European and Canadian French equally attractive. Nor do English speakers see a difference between Athenian and Cretan Greek, despite Athenian being the prestige form among Greeks.

One and the same sound can have a different value in different systems. *R*-dropping is high-status in England, low-status in the US. *H*-dropping, frowned on in England, is standard in France. The glottal stop [?], present in my own usual pronunciation of *better* as /be?ə/, is non-RP in England, and thought ugly. Nevertheless 25 per cent of the *Inside Language* panel owned up to saying [?] (Q8). In Jordanian Arabic, however, the glottal stop [?] is a prestigious allophone of /g/ and /k/ and is thought softer and more feminine. Though certain sounds have minor psychological associations, as seen in Chapter 4, these are not more likely to occur in prestige accents.

The down-side to prestige accents is that their speakers may be seen as effete, posh or artificial in some way. Pronouncing rhotic /r/ in England has its positive side in suggesting rural values and integrity. In France, Parisians are thought of as ambitious, but people from Provence are thought more hospitable. In Australia, defendants with RP accents are more likely to be thought guilty in cases of embezzlement, speakers with Australian accents more likely to be thought guilty in cases of assault. In England a doctor is more likely to diagnose a psychosomatic illness if the patient speaks with an RP accent. An experiment showed that in Wales it is three times more effective to appeal to somebody in Welsh than in English, and three times as effective in English spoken with a Welsh accent compared with RP English.

In other words, local accents have strong positive values that counteract the pull towards the prestige accent. The Beatles' accent, for example, spread a stereotype of the witty, cheerful Liverpudlian contrasting with the dull standard speaker. Low-status speech can show solidarity with the low-status group, who would scorn someone who spoke 'posh', as we see more in connection with class below. On the other hand, speakers can adopt other types of speech to identify with another group. The Beatles, for example, have far more rhotic /r/s on their records than is typical of a Liverpool accent, showing their fondness for American singers. Some of the complexities of the interaction between different personal qualities and accent can be seen in the box overleaf.

3 Dialect words

Vocabulary is probably the aspect of regional dialects of which people are most conscious. A single word can give away a region. A French speaker who says *nonante* ('ninety') rather than *quatre-vingt-dix* comes from Belgium or Switzerland; a German who calls 'Saturday' *Samstag* rather than *Sonnabend* comes from southern Germany

Status and accents

Australian English

Australians were asked to rate which accents they found the least and most competent and attractive and which accents seemed most and least full of confidence and integrity.

Least *competent/* ←——————————————————————→ Most *competent/*
  attractive   Broad   General   Cultivated   *attractive*

Least *confidence/* ←——————————————————————→ Most *confidence/*
  integrity   Cultivated   General   Broad   *integrity*

British English

British people were asked which accents they found had the lowest and highest status.

Least *status*   ←——————————————————————→ Highest *status*
              Urban   Regional   RP
              (e.g. Birmingham) (e.g. Scottish)

English women

English people were asked to rate English women with different accents as having more or less of certain qualities.

Least *warmth*   ←——————————————————————→ Most *warmth*
              RP   Northern

Least *competent* ←——————————————————————→ Most *competent*
              Northern   RP

Least *communicative* ←——————————————————————→ Most *communicative*
  skills   Northern   RP   *skills*

Least *social*   ←——————————————————————→ Most *social*
  attractiveness Northern   RP   *attractiveness*

French

French people were asked how much of an accent was shown by various regional accents and whether they had social appeal.

Least *degree*   ←——————————————————————→ Most *degree*
  of accent   Paris   Brittany   Alsace   Provence   *of accent*

Least *social*   ←——————————————————————→ Most *social*
  appeal   Alsace   Paris   Brittany   Provence   *appeal*

Source: mainly Giles, 'Evaluative reactions to accents'

or Switzerland; an Arab speaker who calls 'bread' *khubiz* comes from Jordan, one who calls it *eesh* comes from Egypt. The present section looks at words from different English-speaking regions. Of course it is hard to separate regions neatly in this way, since the people who live in towns in different areas often have more in common with each other than with the villagers only a few miles away from them.

A familiar divide in English is between English and American pairs of words like *tap* and *faucet*, *dirt* and *earth* or *chips* and *crisps*. English watchers of Australian soaps are also familiar with *chook* and *chicken*, *crook* and *sick*, and *dob* and *sneak*. Varieties of English within the British Isles have nearly as much variation. In 1959 the Opies recorded the diverse names for the game in which one child chases all the others. The word *tig* shows that the speaker comes from anywhere north of Cambridge or from Cornwall, *he* from the south-east of England or the home counties, *touch* from south Wales, Cornwall or Devon, *tick* from

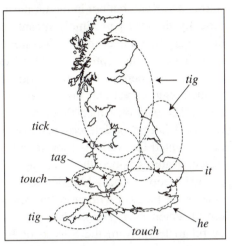

north Wales and the Midlands, *it* from the West Country or Midlands, *tag* from the area around the Severn estuary. The map above gives a crude outline of the divisions, complicated still further by differences between the state educational system and the fee-paying sector, which often has boarding-schools drawing children from other regions.

The *Inside Language* panel showed there may have been a change in the distribution of these words over the past three decades (Q8). The favourite response was *tag* (54 per cent), with speakers coming from East Anglia, London, Birmingham and Bristol, that is to say going from east to west across England apart from the north, rather than being solely the Severn estuary in the west. The next popular response was *it* (31 per cent), mostly from London and surrounding counties rather than further west; one person, indeed, commented that they switched to *it* when they moved 'down south'. Three examples of *catch* came from Essex and Surrey, though the Opies assigned it to Norfolk, and there were three examples of *tig*, one from Staffordshire, two from Leicestershire, that is to say from areas above the south as before, and two examples of *kiss chase*, both from East Anglia. In addition there were single examples of *tongue chase* (Bristol), *mob* (Essex), *tick* (north-west), *had*, *catch kiss* (north-west) and *lurgies*. The term *he*, surprisingly, did not occur, given that the Opies found it in the south-east or home counties, where most of the panel came from. The apparent richness of terms from Essex again reflected the origin of most of the *Inside Language* panel. *Lurgies* derives from a phrase in the 1950s Goon Show comedy programme *the dreaded lurgy*, which was a mysterious disease that swept England and that could only be cured by tuba-playing. Lurgies immediately became a playground game all over England, and survives to this day.

The distribution of other words in traditional dialects has been mapped across England. The word *noseholes* is used instead of *nostrils* in counties south of London, and in an area of central England stretching from east to west as well as a pocket in Surrey and Kent, but not in the far north or the rest of the south and west. Indeed, historically the *-tril* part simply meant 'hole' in Old English. The word *lug* for 'ear' occurs north of a line from Merseyside in the west to Yarmouth in the east, apart from a small area in the centre around Derbyshire and Nottinghamshire, where the word is *tab*. Even southerners have the informal word *lugholes* in their vocabulary.

Such regional variants do not necessarily represent everyday speech in these areas today. The data on which they are based usually come from the massive Survey of English Dialects, which took place over thirty years ago. The classic dialect methodology hunted for NORMs (non-mobile older rural males). This tended to exaggerate dialect features, since they are more likely to be used by men, older people and country people. Local libraries are full of lists of dialect words for quaint rustic objects. In Essex a *willum* is 'the space under a bridge across a trench', as in such useful sentences as *The fox has gone to ground in the willum.* It is doubtless equally useful to learn from the Survey of English Dialects that a *muckfork*, the tool for spreading dung, is a *muck-shovel* in the south but a *sheppock* or a *yelve* in the West Midlands.

Most people in England use standard English vocabulary, with a modicum of dialect words that occasionally creep into their speech. My own vocabulary includes *shrammed* ('very cold'), which is restricted to the south-west of England. My wife sometimes says *peon* meaning 'clerk' rather than 'peasant', giving away that she was born in Burma. But the variation in the vocabulary of standard speakers in England amounts to only a small proportion of the words they use.

4 Dialect grammar

Differences in grammar are harder to find in present-day regional dialect than differences of pronunciation or vocabulary. This section develops some aspects of grammar that vary from place to place. As with pronunciation, this variation usually means that more people use a form in one area than in another rather than all or none of the people in an area use it; it is a question of frequency of use.

Pronouns

The pronoun system discussed briefly in Chapter 2 is one source of variation in many languages. Standard English, for example, lost the second person distinction between singular *thou* and plural *you* three centuries ago, apart from peripheral archaic uses as in *O wild West Wind thou breath of Autumn's being; ye gods and little fishes; thou swell.* Everyday Irish English, however, still employs a singular *you* and plural *youse* or *yiz*, as does New Zealand English. In Barrytown, Roddy Doyle's fictional suburb of north Dublin, scene of *The Commitments*, the greeting to one person is *Howyeh* as in *Howyeh gorgeous!*, the greeting to several is *Howyis*; this distinction has also spread to Merseyside. Scottish English too preserves a plural, *yous* or *yous yins*, though this usage is shunned by educated speakers. Some Tyneside speakers contrast *ye* singular with *yous* plural, as in *Ye can get lost, Kevin!*; others now use *yous* for both singular and plural. Singular *thou* occurs occasionally in the north of England, while singular *thee* is sometime found in the West.

The case system, which demonstrates the grammatical relationship of words in the sentence, also provides a rich source of dialect variation, as we saw in Chapter 2. In modern English, case is confined to the pronouns, *she, her, hers,* and so on. While standard German has a system involving four cases, regional varieties of German often have simpler pronoun systems in which one or more of the four cases is lost. Standard German uses the masculine pronoun *ihm* ('him') when someone receives something (the dative case), as in *Ich gab ihm das Buch* ('I gave him the book') but another form, *ihn,* when someone is affected more directly by the verb (the accusative case) as in *Ich sehe ihn* ('I see him'). Northern German speech, however, uses *ihm* for both, so that *Ich sehe ihm* is possible.

A further clue to region in German speech is how the speaker uses the article *der* ('the'), as in *der Mann* ('the man'). Standard German has different forms not only for the singular *der*, as in *der Mann* ('the man'), and the plural, *die Männer* ('the men'), but also for the subject, *der Mann,* versus the object, *den Mann.* South German speech, however, uses *de* for both subject *der* and object *den*; north German uses *de* for both singular *der* and plural *die*.

Verbs: be *in English*

The forms of verbs can also vary from one dialect to another, particularly in English the verb *be*. The West Country traditionally had only a single form of *be*, as in *I be thirsty, we be thirsty*, etc., with an alternative plural in *'m, we'm thirsty*. Hardy's characters in *Under the Greenwood Tree*, written in 1872, make remarks such as *Here you be* and *If I be hot week-days, I must be hot Sundays.* As late as the 1980s these were found in Somerset speakers, though restricted to certain kinds of sentence.

Some dialects of English also leave *be* out of the sentence. Some psychologists and educationalists claimed in the 1960s that Black American children produced forms that were 'illogical', such as *He not American* or *Some say you gonna die*, because they were deprived of language. This lack would deprive them of proper access to education. So compensatory programmes were set up, Sesame Street being one of the longer-lasting consequences.

Standard English has a rule that the 'contracted forms' of *be*, that is to say *'s* (*he's*), *'re* (*they're*), *'m* (*I'm*), cannot occur in questions, *Is he French?* not *'S he French?* (with the exception of the father seen in the last chapter who said *'S what love?*), or in short answers, *Yes, he is*, not *Yes, he's*. The sociolinguist William Labov found that *be* was left out in American Black English only when the verb may be contracted in the standard language, as in *She real nice*, rather than the full form seen in questions, such as *Is she real nice?*

The circumstances when *be* is left out in Black English correspond to when it may be contracted in Standard English. Both Black English and Standard English have essentially the same rule, except that where one leaves something out, the other uses a contracted form. One version of the rule is no more illogical than the other; they are simply dialect variations. Indeed, *be* is left out in other regional dialects of English, such as Singapore English (sometimes known as Singlish) where it does not occur preceding an adjective, as in *John happy*. Many languages have no *be* in such sentences at all, for instance British Sign Language and Bahasa Indonesia *Ali guru* ('Ali is a teacher').

The remedial programmes for American Black children were not tackling the child's cognitive disadvantage so much as helping them change from one dialect to another. Missing *be* was unconnected to the child's ways of thinking; the rules of their dialect of English had a minor difference from the standard language. In itself, using *be* or leaving it out could have no direct effects on their education, apart from the social disadvantage of speaking a low-status dialect. The value of the remedial programmes was in encouraging the children to switch dialect, not in helping them to think.

Negation in English

Standard English differs from most non-standard dialects in its forms for negation. One sign of non-standard language is supposedly the use of *never* as an all-purpose negative form with the past tense, *I never done it*, or the short denial *I never!* The Second Drowned Man in Dylan Thomas's *Under Milk Wood* says *Tell my missus no I never* and the Third Drowned Man continues, *I never done what she said I never*. This use of *never* is now so widespread in England that people question whether it is still non-standard.

A further social marker is a phenomenon called 'multiple negation'. Where a standard speaker says *I didn't like any of the books*, marking negation once in the sentence by *n't*, non-standard speakers of several dialects say *I didn't like none of the books*, marking negation several times, here *n't* and *none*. To take three examples: *We ain't never had no trouble about none of us pullin' out no knife* from a black Detroit speaker; *She never lost no furniture nor nothing* from Irish English; *You couldn't say nothing bad about it* from Tyneside English. Multiple negation is indeed a long-standing practice in English. In the fifteenth century Chaucer's *parfit gentil knight . . . never yet no vilanye ne said in all his life unto no manner wight* ('never said anything rude to any kind of person in all his life'). To a certain extent modern standard English is the odd one out in lacking multiple negation, which is also common in other languages.

Traditional school grammars have been worried by multiple negation. In arithmetic two minuses turn into a plus; by the same logic *I didn't like none of the books* must mean 'I liked all of them'. William Cobbett in 1819 claimed 'two negatives, applied to the same verb, destroy the negative effect of each other. "I will not never write". This is the contrary of "I will never write"'. But it is doubtful whether a speaker of any variety of English would really interpret the sentence in that way. There is no necessity for negation to behave like a minus sign in mathematics; schoolchildren's lives would indeed be easier if arithmetic followed the rules of grammar.

Multiple negation normally has the effect of making the negation more emphatic. Easy Rawlins, the hero of Walter Mosley's books, says *She don't know nuthin'* or *She didn't have no accident?* but everybody knows what he means; the same applies to Mick Jagger's *I can't get no satisfaction*, as Deborah Cameron points out. While it is possible to imagine someone saying *I never said nothing to no one noway and nohow* with five negatives, a listener would not need to work out whether the end result mathematically is positive or negative, but would interpret it as vehement denial. Labov found multiple negation prominent in Black English, as in the following sentence *It ain't no cat can't get in no coop*. Taking multiple negation as emphasis, only one negative is in fact intended, meaning in standard English 'There isn't any cat that *can* get into any coop'. Nevertheless, however comprehensible the use of multiple negation may be, it can still label the speaker as non-standard.

The most extreme type of variation is when there are two distinct forms of the same language which are used in different circumstances, a situation called 'diglossia'. In the German-speaking areas of Switzerland, for example, there are two forms of German: High German, which is used for official purposes, and Swiss German, which is used for everyday purposes. The differences between them are primarily in pronunciation but also in vocabulary, High German *etwas* ('something'), Zurich Swiss *oppis*, and in grammar, where *Egge* ('corner') and *Bank* ('bench') are feminine in High German but masculine in Zurich Swiss. The High form of a language has the highest prestige, the low form may not even have a written literature. In Switzerland the odd consequence is that speakers of French are not taught the Swiss German spoken by their neighbours but the High German that is the prestige form. So they may be able to follow parliamentary speeches but not everyday conversation. Having spent some time as a child in Switzerland, the only form of German I can understand to a limited extent is Swiss German, but Swiss people talking to a foreigner automatically switch to High German, which I can hardly follow.

Factor 4: social class

As well as age, sex and region, the speaker's social class and role can also be apparent from their speech, partly through accent, partly through grammar and vocabulary. As with dialect, there are social variants by class ranging from accent to non-standard grammatical forms and vocabulary, amounting to what are effectively dialects based on class rather than region. To quote Shaw again: 'Whenever an Englishman opens his mouth another Englishman despises him'. *I never!*, for example, is a marker of social class in England as well as of region.

1 R-*dropping and class*

In the UK, as we have seen, lack of *r*-dropping is a sign of regional, and hence of a non-RP accent. In the United States, however, the reverse happens: *r*-dropping is a marker of lower class, being also associated with the south and with Black English, even though the prestige Boston accent was non-rhotic until comparatively recently. The classic studies of *r*-dropping were carried out by William Labov in New York, who found that New Yorkers who were higher in terms of socioeconomic group were more likely to use /r/.

In one memorable experiment Labov spent two afternoons in 1962 going round three New York stores asking casually for a department he already knew to be located on the fourth floor: *Excuse me, where are the women's shoes?* Then he would lean forward and say *Excuse me?* and get the answer a second time spoken in a more careful way. He managed this exchange 264 times. He then noted whether the shop assistant pronounced the pre-consonant /r/ in *fourth* and the pre-silence /r/ in *floor*, in both answers. The shops he went to ranged from luxury Saks on Fifth Avenue through medium-priced S. Klein to downmarket Macy's on the Lower East Side. The shop assistants in high-class Saks preferred to reply with the high-status form /fɔːrθ flɔːr/ *fourth floor* with both /r/s 60 per cent of the time; those from lower-class S. Klein used the high-status form only 20 per cent of the time, preferring /fɔːθ flɔː/ instead, that is to say, the English *r*-less pronunciation. Macy's came in the middle. The shops reflected the likely class of their customers, not just the class or age of their workers (see Figure 8.3). Chapter 10 discusses how this picture has changed over time.

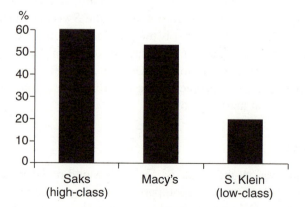

Fig. 8.3 Percentage of /r/s supplied by shop assistants in three New York department stores in 1962

An interesting issue arising from Labov's study of New York speech is the peculiar behaviour of the lower middle class. Though the number of /r/s increased according to class, the lower middle class were an exception in that they in fact used more /r/s in some situations than did the upper class. In other words, they were more high-class than the upper-class itself. A similar effect was found in Norwich in East Anglia. Here the vowel in *hell* varies between a front vowel /e/ /hel/ for higher-class speakers and a further back vowel /ʌ/ /hʌl/ for lower-class speakers, making *hell* almost rhyme with *hull*. But the upper working class in Norwich are out of step, exceeding the upper middle-class frequency of /e/ most of the time.

The name for the phenomenon in which the speaker overshoots the high status target is 'hypercorrection'. The word *price,* for instance, is pronounced as /praɪs/ in RP, rhyming with *rice,* but sounds closer to /prɔɪs/ in some non-standard speech, i.e. the *oys* in *oyster*. Speakers who are determined to avoid /ɔɪ/ may exaggerate the diphthong and end up saying /preɪs/, to rhyme with *ace*. A hypercorrect speaker goes over the top, ending up as 'refined' or 'genteel'. Or, as the children's graffiti announce in the folly behind my house, *Cately has a fake accent.*

2 H-*dropping in English*

Particular varieties of a language are, then, associated with higher or lower class. The familiar test of lower-class speech in England is *h*-dropping – pronouncing *hat* as *'at*, or *Harry* as *'Arry,* parodied in the *My Fair Lady* speech-training exercise *In Hertford, Hereford and Hampshire hurricanes hardly happen*. *H*-dropping means using spoken words without /h/ that correspond to written words with /h/, for example /ærɪ/ versus /Hærɪ/. Like *r*-dropping, the term is misleading since it implies the primacy of writing. *H*-dropping can only be seen as actually dropping the *h* from *Harry* if the written spelling takes precedence over the spoken sounds /ærɪ/ rather than being two alternative forms in different mediums.

Again like *r*-dropping, *h*-dropping is believed to have spread from south-east England since the eighteenth century, leaving only a few pockets unscathed in East Anglia and the extreme north-east. Certainly by 1856 the periodical *Punch* was poking fun at it: *It ain't the 'unting as 'urts 'un, it's the 'ammer, 'ammer, 'ammer, on the 'ard 'igh road*. So *h*-dropping occurs in England, Australia and parts of the West Indies, but not in the USA or in Scotland, depending whether English was established before the main *h*-dropping period in the eighteenth century. There are, however, signs that *h*-dropping existed in England as far back as the fourteenth century. A medieval scribe wrote *ate* for *hate, ostel* for *hostel* and *eld* for *held*, classic examples still found today.

In content words such as *hurricane* or *Hertford,* /h/ is rarely dropped in standard English speech, apart from a small group of words taken from French (where *h*-dropping was total), *heir, hour, honest* and so on. /h/ is, however, normally dropped from unstressed grammatical words in speech, such as *he* and *has*, even if most speakers are unaware of it. In my informal pronunciation of the sentence *I wonder if he's done it* there would be no /h/ in *he* or in *'s* (*has*), at any rate.

If some *h*-dropping had not been permitted in the past, the standard language would not have the pronoun *it* but *hit*, its original form, found at least up to Chaucer. Nor could modern speakers say *'em* for *them* – *give 'em hell*, since *'em* is an *h*-dropped form of the original *hem,* later replaced by *them*. The /h/ would still be universally present in the pronunciation of *wh* words such as *what* and *why* as /hwɒt/ and /hwaɪ/ instead of /wɒt/ and /waɪ/, rather than being restricted to certain actors.

The crucial factor is not so much whether the speaker drops *h* itself, since dropping of /h/ is widespread with grammatical words such as *have* and *he*, but whether the /h/ is dropped from content words like *hurricane* and *Hampshire*. Indeed, a characteristic of some conservative RP accents is dropping the /h/s in a small group of words, such as *an historical change,* and *an hotel*. Many people in England have no /h/ phoneme, saying *hat* as *'at* /æt/, *heaven* as *'eaven* and so on. John Wells tells of an American on a English train who asked for an *egg* and was surprised to be given a whisky (*Haig*). They sometimes add /h/ for emphasis alone, *haitch* /heɪtʃ/ being an emphatic form of *H* (*aitch*) /eɪtʃ/, *hedge* /hedʒ/ of *edge* /edʒ/, rather than different words. The same medieval scribe was writing *halle* for *all* and *hunkinde* for *unkind* in the fourteenth century, just as a caller on Radio Essex in the 1990s offered to sell his *hornaments*.

H-dropping has been consistently associated in England with lower class. In *Lady Chatterley's Lover* Lady Chatterley says *hut*, Mellors the gamekeeper *'ut*. In London, working-class boys *h*-drop 81 per cent of the time, middle-class boys 14 per cent. In Norwich in East Anglia, lower working-class speakers drop 61 per cent, middle middle-class 6 per cent. In Bradford in the north, the lower working class drop 93 per cent, the upper middle class 12 per cent. The difference between the classes in the use of /h/ is marked and widespread across the country (see Figure 8.4).

English people have always been acutely conscious of *h*-dropping. Gossamer Beynon says in Dylan Thomas's *Under Milk Wood, I don't care if he does drop his*

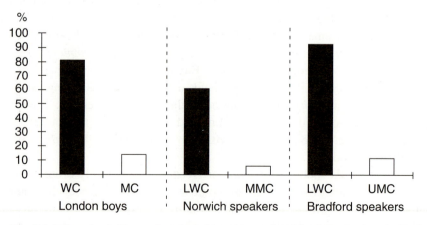

Fig. 8.4 *H*-dropping by (upper/lower) working-class and middle-class speakers in England

Novelists' spelling of English accents

A conventional way of reflecting non-standard accents in novels is to use 'phonetic' spelling. Often this creates an illusion of non-standard speech rather than accurately capturing the dialect, since the odd spellings are semi-phonetic attempts at conveying the *standard* pronunciation. Here are three examples of novelists' dialect.

Modern London dialect (Jerry Cornelius's mother in Michael Moorcock's *The Condition of Muzak*, 1977)

Wot's 'appenin'?
Wot's 'e want?
Nosy bloody parkers ther lot of 'em.
Sorry I'm shore.
I 'eard 'e corled 'isself somefink else.
It woz nuffink forin'.

Spellings that in fact represent something close to standard speech: *wot, 'e, shore, ther, corled, woz, forin', 'em*; spellings that show general non-standard *h*-dropping and final /ɪn/: *'appenin', 'eard, 'isself*; spellings that show features sometimes found in London speech: *nuffink, somefink* (/f/ for /θ/, /ŋk/ for /ŋ/).

Traditional Nottingham dialect (D.H. Lawrence, *Sons and Lovers*, 1913)

An' he'll be satisfied if he gets his 'lowance.
An' so yer see, I knowed it was.
Tha mucky little 'un.
'Appen not it'ud dirty thee.
I ham that, said Morel.
I sh'll come to thee in a minute.

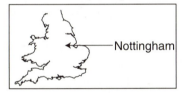
Nottingham

Spellings that in fact represent standard speech: *yer, sh'll, 'ud*; spellings that show general non-standard *h*-dropping and *h*-adding: *'appen, ham*; spellings showing dropping of final consonants, perhaps an actual Nottingham feature, but found elsewhere: *an'*. Note also the use of dialect grammar: *knowed, tha, thee*.

More recent Nottingham dialect (Alan Sillitoe, *Saturday Night and Sunday Morning*, 1958)

I don't know where 'e puts it all. It just goes in and in and you wonder when 'is guts are goin' ter go bust all over the room but 'e duzn't even get fatter.
There's nowt wrong wi' me.
'Ark at who's talkin'
I give 'im money because I was lucky to get a ha'penny when I was a nipper.
If it 'ad summat to do wi' me bein' wi' Winnie at the fair, it didn't mean owt ...

Spellings that in fact approximate to standard speech: *'is, ter, 'e, duzn't, 'im, ha'penny*; spellings that show general non-standard *h*-dropping and final /ɪn/ for *ing*.

'ark, talkin', bein'*; spellings that show final consonant dropping, perhaps a Notting-ham feature, also given in Lawrence: *wi'*.

This use of 'dialect spellings' to suggest the speech of non-standard speakers is dis-tinct from the systematic use of spelling to show the whole book is written in a non-standard English, as in the following example of Shetland English:

Onywye, Up-Helly-Aa duy kem roond, in we riggat wiz athin wir sunday suits in polished wir shön, in stöd raedy for Wullie Aervin's bus ti pick wis up. (*Source*: Melchers, 'Spelling and dialect'.)

aitches, so long as he's all cucumber and hooves. Like *r*-dropping in department stores, *h*-dropping is affected by the class of the person who is being addressed. Travel agents in Wales have been found to use more /h/s to upper-class customers than to lower-class customers. The *Inside Language* panel were asked whether a person who said *He lost his 'at* would be middle class (MC) or working class (WC) (Q6). Ninety per cent chose working class, one person said 'either', and the rest did not answer.

Since *h*-dropping first occurred it has been widely condemned, particularly by teachers, and identified with Cockney, Brummy or other undesirable accents. A scholar writing in 1873 suggested 'Few things will the English youth find in after life more profitable than the right use of the aforesaid letter'. The two developments of *r*-dropping and *h*-dropping have thus had diametrically opposed social consequences in England, *r*-dropping becoming the prestige form, *h*-dropping the stigmatized form.

In England, Estuary English, alias lower middle-class home counties speech, has become more widely heard in the 1990s, particularly from television presenters such as Jonathan Ross, to the extent that it attracted the scorn of one minister of education, herself an ex-teacher. But, despite its adoption of /w/ for /l/ and [ʔ] for /t/, Estuary English does *not* drop *h*s, unlike the London dialect out of which it sprang. Upwardly mobile speakers of Estuary would still find it dangerous to be tainted by *h*-dropping. Indeed, non-English accents that formerly had *h*-dropping, like Australian and New Zealand, now seem to be restoring /h/ to their pronunciation.

Prestige is in the ear of the listener. There is no intrinsic link between *h*-dropping and slovenliness or carelessness of pronunciation. *H*-dropping is a social marker in England but is unknown in the United States and other areas; obviously the rest of the world is less slovenly than the English themselves. The sheer fact of *h*-dropping is not a sign of lower class, but has become associated with social class in England. *H*-dropping has indeed become part of the standard form of other languages. The Latin *homo* ('man') had an /h/; its descendants in French *homme* and Italian *uomo* do not. French /h/ has retreated to remote rural regions, such as parts of Normandy, Lorraine and Alsace, in the same way as English /r/.

3 Ne-*dropping in French*

Negation in French demonstrates how class goes not only with region but also with sex, and age. The French negative consists of two words *n(e) ... pas* with the verb in between: *Il ne peut pas aller* ('he can't go') or *Ce n'est pas vrai* ('that's not true'). In fact *ne* is often omitted in French speech, so that the common forms are *Il peut pas aller* and *C'est pas vrai*. Age is one factor that goes with *ne*-dropping; young people omit *ne* 81 per cent of the time, older people 48 per cent of the time: the older the speaker the more *ne*s they are likely to use. This difference may reflect a historical change in which the older people are clinging to the form they grew up with, in which case *ne* will eventually disappear as its speakers die out. Or French speakers may feel that using *ne* is as much part of growing old as grey hair and it will be adopted by each new generation of old people. Evidence for this view is that, despite *ne*-dropping being part of French for centuries, it has still not taken over as the norm.

The second factor in *ne*-dropping is sex. *Ne* is left out by women 57 per cent of the time, by men 69 per cent of the time. Women thus use the full form, *ne ... pas*, slightly more than men. Thirdly, *ne*-dropping goes with social class. The lower class drop *ne* 84 per cent of the time, the higher 55 per cent of the time; higher-class speakers are more likely to use *ne*. Putting these factors together, a person who uses the maximum number of *ne*s should be an upper-class old woman, a person with the minimum a working-class young man (see Figure 8.5).

There are deeper and subtler differences between regional forms of grammar than those described here. Yet to some extent deep differences only matter to the linguist: it is whatever speakers notice that counts in their assessment of others. The pronouns, forms of *be*, and negation seen in this chapter are valuable indicators of region, even if in grammatical terms they are fairly superficial.

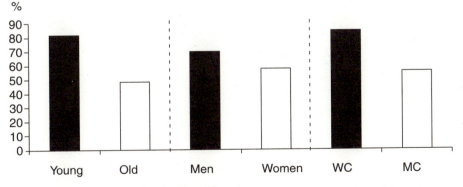

Fig. 8.5 Omission of *ne* by French speakers

4 Class and women's language

A hotly debated issue in language variation is the interaction between class and gender, already encountered with *ne*-dropping in French. The initial research linking class and gender carried out in Detroit found that multiple negation was used less by women in each of four social classes, ranging from lower working class (LWC) to upper middle class (UMC), as seen in Figure 8.6. In terms of *r*-dropping, too, Detroit women used more /r/s than men in each class. The same effect occurred for the sound /θ/ as in *bath*, which has non-standard US pronunciations of /f/ and /t/. Again the women in each social class used more /θ/s than the men.

The interaction between sex and class also shows up in the *-ing* inflection in English words such as *taking* or *looking*. The pronunciation of *-ing* varies between /ɪn/ produced with the tongue tip nasal /n/, as in /teɪkɪn/, and /ɪŋ/ produced with the back of the tongue nasal /ŋ/, as in /teɪkɪŋ/. With due respect to the English *huntin'*, *shootin'* and *fishin'* set (who preserve the prestige eighteenth-century pronunciation), the RP version is now /ɪŋ/. In Norwich /ɪŋ/ was used 69 per cent of the time by the 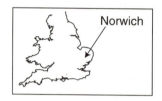 higher-class speakers, but 0 per cent by the lower class. However, 70 per cent of Norwich women used more of the RP /ɪŋ/ then men. Indeed, 77 per cent of the *Inside Language* panel felt that *Jane's walkin' to work* was more likely to be said by a man than by a woman (Q5). A characteristic of English around the world is that women use more /ɪŋ/s than men, whether in Canada, Australia, the US or Yorkshire, the only exception being South Africa, where everyone uses the /ɪŋ/ pronunciation. Even second-language learners of English soon learn which form is appropriate to their gender; in one study male learners produced five times as many /ɪn/ forms as women.

But, as well as this upwards pull towards the prestige accent of higher classes, there is also a downwards pull towards the lower-class forms. A lower-class accent does not just have negative associations of low status but also positive overtones of male soli-

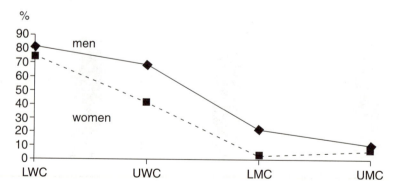

Fig. 8.6 Multiple negation in four classes in Detroit

darity. Expressions like *rockin' and rollin', finger-lickin' good, a sippin' whisky, lovin' 'n likin'*, or a T-shirt proclaiming *NOTRE DAME FIGHTIN' IRISH* give an impression of no-nonsense toughness. Women are not usually affected by the downwards pull to the same extent as men. However, one study of US teenage girls found that the most rebellious dropouts had more of the lower-class forms than boys of the same age.

There are problems in defining social class within this area of research, particularly when women are defined by their husband's class rather than in their own right. Nevertheless the same generalization appears time and again in different research and with different languages: women tend to use more upwards prestige forms, men more downwards lower-class forms. Many reasons for this difference have been suggested. Women's extra facility with language may be one factor, woman's conventional child-rearing role another, their range of possible occupations a third. To explain differences between working-class and middle-class speech, Basil Bernstein claimed that small girls are asked to be substitute mothers for other siblings, while small boys are not; hence girls develop a greater range of social roles. Or it may be that women have more facility with language in general; at Essex University only one in four language students is a man, a similar proportion to that in most countries. Labov suggested that hypercorrection by women is due to their greater social mobility. In many studies the women in the lower middle-class group are the most hypercorrect, for example with the /ɪŋ/ form in Norwich. Some male speakers correct themselves *downwards* from the standard, as in the Sydney man who corrected *we were skating around* to *we was skating along*.

Whatever the reason may be, in many languages women use the prestige version more than men. French-speaking women in North Africa, for instance, are closer to the prestige uvular /r/ than men. A much-discussed exception is Arab women, who use less Classical Arabic forms than do men. For example, Arabic men from several countries use the uvular plosive [q] to a greater extent than do women, who prefer its glottal stop allophone [ʔ]. The position of Arabic is, however, highly complex, since as well as being an international language it has local forms in different countries. Classical Arabic is reserved for formal occasions and is used internationally for religious purposes, rather as Latin used to be in the Catholic Church. It is not spoken by anyone as a first language, so that everyday life makes use of the local standard Arabic, whether Moroccan, Jordanian or whatever. Arabic is, then, an example of diglossia, with High and Low forms of the language used in different circumstances. But, because of its international nature, in addition to the prestige form Classical Arabic, there is also a local standard form which carries prestige within a country compared to regional or lower-class dialects. In the case of Jordan, it is indeed true that Jordanian women use less of the Classical Arabic forms than men. However, they use *more* of the local standard forms which have their own local prestige. Arabic women are not therefore exceptions to the rule but have more upward forms than the men, as women do everywhere else.

Factor 5: style

The four factors looked at so far imply that, while the language varies, a given speaker always behaves in the same way. A woman uses the woman's type of language; a pensioner from Somerset speaks an old West Country form; and so on. A moment's reflection shows that each person's speech varies from one moment to the next according to a network of social relationships and purposes. A greeting for a relative at breakfast might be *Up at last?*, for a neighbour at the bus stop *Good morning*, for a friend at work *Hello*, and so on. Asking after someone's health might be *Well?* to one person, *How are you?* to another, *What's the verdict then?* to a third. Speech is adapted to the person who is being spoken to and to the occasion of speaking. Part of the speaker's knowledge of language is knowing which styles are appropriate to a particular moment of speaking.

One dimension of variation is the degree of formality. Chapter 6 showed that the formal nature of written language increases the proportion of content words. But speech too has a range between the most formal and the most casual, between, say, a speech in court and a conversation in a pub. The dimension of formality was divided by Labov into four distinct 'styles'. The most formal style is reading single words aloud, the most informal style casual conversation. Using aspects of English already encountered here, a formal style of English speech will have:

- more /h/s
- more /r/s if American, fewer if English
- more /ɪŋ/s, fewer /ɪn/s
- more standard forms of *be,* i.e. not *I be, they was,* etc.
- more standard negation, *I didn't* rather than *I never*

Similarly a French speaker uses more *ne*s in a formal style; a German more standard pronoun forms.

The factor of style intermeshes with the factors of age, sex and class. In the department store study of *r*-dropping, Labov asked the assistants for the fourth floor in two ways, one designed to get an answer in casual style: *Excuse me, where are the women's shoes?*, the other an answer in formal style: *Excuse me?* Sure enough, the formal answers had more /r/s than the casual style. In informal conversation, lower-class New Yorkers hardly use /r/ at all, even the upper class to the extent of only around 20 per cent. But, in the task of reading words aloud, the lower-class use increases to 10 per cent, the upper class to around 50 per cent. In other words, both groups raise their level of /r/s according to the formality of the style. New Yorkers are alive to the fact that formality means increasing the number of /r/s. As always, this effect is felt particularly keenly by the lower middle class, who exaggerate the number of /r/s to 60 per cent in the word-reading task, above the level of the upper class, as can be seen in Figure 8.7.

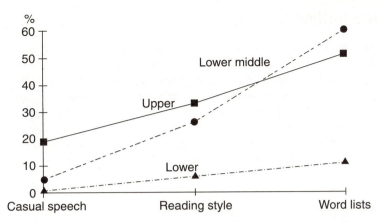

Fig. 8.7 The pronunciation of /r/ by three New York classes in three styles

The chapter has confirmed that many of the factors that distinguish groups of speakers are not questions of either/or but matters of degree. Men use more /ɪn/s; upper-class US speakers use more /r/s; English speakers use more /h/s when speaking formally, rather than any of them having exclusive features they use all the time. Speakers give away their class or sex or nationality by using more or less of a particular feature. A feature is seldom unique to a particular kind of speaker. Instead, they vary continuously from one dialect, class or sex to another. It is not that English speakers are incapable of using the other forms – nobody (probably) drops *all* their /h/s.

In a sense, much variation in language is like clothes. People proclaim their age by their tweed jacket, their jeans, or their use of *wireless*; their region by their kilt or their Scottish 'tapped' [ɾ]; they flaunt their Arsenal strip or their glottal stops; they dress for an occasion by putting on a suit or not dropping their /h/s. But language goes deeper, in that they are seldom aware of the distinguishing badges they wear. Consequently they are at the mercy of their unconscious attitudes to language when judging people, if only for first impressions. We may be almost incapable of changing our own speech in one direction or another beyond a small limit.

Answers to openings (page 169)
1. F   2. M   3. M   4. F   5. M   6. M   7. F   8. F   9. M   10. F.
The *Inside Language* panel were tested on 2 and 4 (Q5) and produced the answers: 2: 44%F, 54%M; 4: 58% F, 35%M, showing that only a few of them could distinguish the sexes more accurately than by chance.

Sources and further reading

General introductions to sociolinguistics include: P. Trudgill, *Sociolinguistics: An Introduction* (Harmondsworth: Penguin, 1974); S. Romaine, *Language in Society* (Oxford: OUP, 1994). The experiment with Black vowels is described in J.H. Walton and R.F. Orlikoff, 'Speaker race identification from acoustic cues in the vocal signal', *Journal of Speech and Hearing Research* (1994): 37, 738–45. The original work of William Labov, which forms the basis for the research tradition discussed in much of this chapter, can be found in: *The Social Stratification of English in New York City* (Washington, DC: Center for Applied Linguistics, 1966); and *The Study of Non-Standard English* (Champaign, IL: National Council of Teachers, 1970).

Factor 1. Gender

The clearest brief outline of language and gender is J.K. Chambers, 'Linguistic correlates of gender and sex', *English World-Wide* 13/2 (1992): 173–218. Useful books here and for Factor 4 are: D. Graddol and J. Swann, *Gender Voices* (Oxford: Blackwell, 1989); D. Cameron, *Feminism and Linguistic Theory* (Basingstoke: Macmillan, 1992); W. Majewski, H. Hollien and J. Zalewski, 'Speaking fundamental frequencies of Polish adult males', *Phonetica* 21 (1972): 119–25. R.M.W. Dixon, *Searching for Aboriginal Languages* (Chicago: Chicago UP, 1989). Warlpiri sign language is described in D. McNeill, *Hand and Mind* (Chicago: Chicago UP, 1992). Amazon customs are described in A.P. Sorenson, 'Multilingualism in the North-West Americas', *American Anthropologist* 69 (1967): 670–84.

R-*dropping in English*

An account of attitudes to English can be found in L. Mugglestone, *'Talking Proper'* (Oxford: Clarendon Press, 1995).

Regional and standard forms of language

The major source for English accents across the world is J.C. Wells, *Accents of English*, I–III (Cambridge: CUP, 1982). A short account of dialects in England is P. Trudgill, *The Dialects of England* (Oxford: Blackwell, 1990). An account of US dialects is given in W. Wolfram, *Dialects and American English* (Englewood Cliffs, NJ: Prentice-Hall, 1991). An account of French can be found in C. Sanders (ed.), *French Today* (Cambridge: CUP, 1993), particularly J. Durand, 'Sociolinguistic variation and the linguist' (257–86).

Work with attitudes to accents can be found in: H. Giles and N. Coupland, *Language: Contexts and Consequences* (Milton Keynes: Open University Press, 1991); H. Giles, 'Evaluative reactions to accents', *Educational Review* 22 (1970): 211.

Sources used in the box (p. 178) were O. Elyan, P. Smith, H. Giles and R. Bourhuis, 'RP-accented female speech: the voice of perceived androgyny?', in P. Trudgill (ed.), *Sociolinguistic Patterns in British English* (London: Arnold, 1978), 121–31; G. Melchers, 'Spelling and Dialect', in P.A. Luellsdorff (ed.), *Orthography and Phonology* (Amsterdam: John Benjamins, 1987), 187–214. The Buchanan quotation is from J. Buchanan, *Linguae Britannicae Vera Pronunciatio* (London, 1757).

Dialect words

The survey of English Dialects is presented in H. Orton et al., *Survey of English Dialects* (Leeds: E.J. Arnold, 1962–71). A selection of dialect maps based on it can be found in C. Upton, S. Sanderson and J. Widdowson, *Word Maps: A Dialect Atlas of England* (London: Croom Helm, 1987). Children's games are described in I. Opie and P. Opie, *The Lore and Language of Schoolchildren* (Oxford: OUP, 1959).

Dialect grammar

Sources for German are: S. Barbour and P. Stevenson, *Variation in German* (Cambridge: CUP, 1990); R.E. Keller, *German Dialects* (Manchester: Manchester UP 1990). Some features of current English dialect grammar are described in: Trudgill, *The Dialects of England* (see above); J. Milroy and L. Milroy, *Real English* (Harlow: Longman, 1993).

Verbs: 'be' in English. Labov's work with *be* is described in W. Labov, 'Contraction, deletion, and inherent variability of the English copula', *Language* 45 (1969): 715–62.

Negation in English. The study of Detroit speech used here and for Factor 5 originates from W. Wolfram, *A Sociolinguistic Description of Detroit Negro Speech* (Washington, DC: Center for Applied Linguistics, 1969). Cobbett's grammar is: W. Cobbett, *A Grammar of the English Language* (1819; repr. Oxford: OUP, 1984). The term 'diglossia' was coined in C. Ferguson, 'Diglossia', *Word* 15 (1959): 325–40.

Factor 4. Social class

A comprehensive account of *h*-dropping is in J. Milroy, 'On the sociolinguistics of *h*-dropping in English', *Odense University Studies in English* 4 (1983): 37–43. The work on Norwich, here and elsewhere, derives from P. Trudgill, *The Social Differentiation of English in Norwich* (Cambridge: CUP, 1974).

Ne-dropping in French

The main source on French negation is W.J. Ashby, 'The loss of the negative particle *ne* in French: a syntactic change in progress', *Language* 57 (1981): 674–87.

Class and women's language

This is discussed in the main references (above). L2 learners were tested in H.D. Adamson and R. Regan, 'The acquisition of community speech norms by Asian immigrants learning English as a second language: a preliminary study', *Studies in Second Language Acquisition* 13 (1991): 1–22.

Factor 5. Style

The main source consists of the works by Labov cited at the top of page 194.

9 When Language Goes Wrong

Despite the complexity of the language system described in previous chapters, it rarely goes wrong. The vast majority of people acquire spoken language without any problem, even if reading and writing present more difficulties. A few may have problems with certain speech sounds, rarely with the grammar or vocabulary of speech. Some also have problems caused by illness or injury of various types. The overall argument for the biological basis of language is indeed that human minds acquire and use it with such ease, as already seen in Chapter 7. This chapter describes the few occasions when the language system goes wrong, starting with children's early difficulties, going on to the problems of adults with various disorders and finishing with difficulties in learning to read.

The study of when things go wrong provides important evidence for many aspects of language. Looking at how a system malfunctions tells the observer about the system itself. In particular, the analysis of language disability not only suggests ways of helping people whose language is deficient in one way or another, but also reveals how language is built into the human mind and brain. As the coverage in this chapter is selective, readers should not relate it to any specific person they know but should seek specialized advice if necessary.

I Children's difficulties with language development

1 Language and disability

The percentage of children that have difficulty in acquiring language is small. Many physical disabilities do not affect language, as witness Helen Keller or Steven Hawking. Other physical disabilities can be associated with language problems, for example Down's Syndrome. Chapter 7 introduced the technique for measuring children's speech called MLU (Mean Length of Utterance), based on the average number of morphemes for a particular child. Children typically reach an MLU of about 4.6 by the age of 4, after which MLU is no longer a relevant measure. The MLU for Down's Syndrome children, however, goes up from about 1.00 at the age of 4 to 3.4 at the age of 11½ to 6.0 as adults, as seen in Figure 9.1. Hence their MLU is way behind other children, at 11½ still below the typical 4-year-old.

The language of Down's Syndrome children is not, however, identical with that of younger children. They have more problems with grammatical morphemes such as pronouns and past-tense inflections than is usual for their apparent stage of language development. They also continue to progress long after acquisition in other children comes to a halt, as seen in the improvement in MLU up to adulthood. The language of one person, in fact, continued to improve up to the age of 30.

The language of autistic children presents a different picture. Take the following conversation recorded by David Crystal:

Teacher: What are you going to do with that car now?
Child: I like my car (*pushing it on floor*).
Teacher: Look. I've got one like that.
Child: In here it goes (*pushing car into garage*).
Teacher: Don't forget to shut the door.
Child: Find the man now.

While the child is undoubtedly having a conversation, little of what he says relates to the teacher's remarks; there is no social link between them. Speech therapists call this 'monologue tendencies'. One overall cause for the condition of autism is that the children affected do not realize that other people have minds of their own. They lack a 'theory of mind', as it is usually termed. They do not need to tell people things because they assume other people already know everything they do. Their problems with conversation are a consequence of their general inability to relate to other people rather than specifically to do with language.

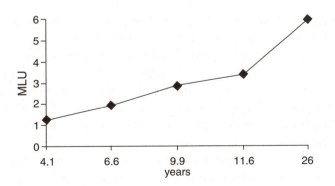

Fig. 9.1 Mean Length of Utterance in Down's Syndrome children

2 Specific Language Impairment in development

This section concentrates on a phenomenon in language development that has been fascinating researchers recently, namely difficulties with language acquisition that are not apparently associated with any other developmental difficulties, a condition usually called Specific Language Impairment (SLI). The question is whether there are otherwise totally ordinary children whose language is strange in some way. Should these exist, they would provide powerful evidence that language is distinct from the other cognitive processes of the mind.

A typical case is a boy known as PB, who produced the following sentences: *You make one points*; *They put present under the Christmas trees*; *Red Riding Hood arrive at his grandma's house*; *Now they say 'Oh what big eyes you got'*. At first sight the outside observer could think that PB was backward and had little idea of grammatical number. Plural *-s* is supplied unnecessarily on *one points* and *Christmas trees* but is missing from *present* where it was clearly needed; Red Riding Hood is referred to as *they* rather than as *he* (in his version of the story she seems to be a boy). Yet this child is top of his class in mathematics, that is to say well aware of number in other circumstances. It is his language that is odd, not his cognitive development in general.

Some researchers have argued on the basis of such evidence for the existence of SLI, in which language alone is deficient, rather than language deficiency going along with other disabilities. Controversy surrounds the existence and nature of SLI, and the question whether it is a single condition or a cover term for several conditions. Though it is hard to estimate how many children fall into this category, the number of children with severe SLI is put by some at 1.5 per cent, a very small proportion and a further tribute to the automaticity of language acquisition for most children. SLI affects more boys than girls, in a ratio of 2.8 boys for every girl. Many of these children continue to have language problems, an estimated 60 per cent still showing peculiarities at the age of 10.

3 Deficiency in grammar

While most of the children with SLI have deficiencies in vocabulary, it is their grammar that has interested researchers. Speakers with SLI tend to leave out grammatical words, such as the English prepositions *to* and *for*, the articles *the* and *a*, and the auxiliaries *will* and *is*. A typical sentence from a 16-year-old is *That boy climbing a rope to get to the top the rope*, with the grammatical words *is* and *of* both missing. They also leave out the grammatical inflections such as past tense *-ed*. In other words, children with SLI have particular problems with the grammatical morphemes described in Chapters 3 and 7.

The samples of PB's speech given above included the singular *one points* and the plural *present*. One of his problems is the inflectional endings for English nouns and verbs, in particular the plural *-s* inflection for nouns – *a cat, a dog and a fox* versus *two* *cats, two dogs and two foxes*. In most children, plural *-s* is learnt quite soon, as we saw in Chapter 7, although the /ɪz/ ending seen in *foxes* /fɒksɪz/ comes later than the rest.

Children with SLI might simply be passing though the same stages as normal children, but at a slower pace. In this case their grammar would correspond to that of younger children without SLI, but not to that of other children of the same age. On the other hand they might be developing in distinctive ways of their own. In this case their grammar would differ both from their own age group and from children of any age without SLI. Usually, then, the children with SLI are compared with two different groups: *age-matched*: children without SLI who are the same age; *language-matched*: children without SLI who are at a similar stage of language development regardless of age, i.e. usually much younger children.

In a 1992 study Laurence Leonard and his colleagues compared English children with SLI, not only with language-matched children aged 3–3½ who were at about the same stage of language development measured by MLUw (MLU measured in words), but also with age-matched children aged 3½–5. The children had to describe a picture of a ball or a picture of balls. The children with SLI supplied an *-s* ending 69 per cent of the times it was needed. But the age-matched children scored 97 per cent; the language-matched younger children 96 per cent (see Figure 9.2). In this instance the SLI children were behaving neither like children of the same age nor like younger children at earlier stages of language development, but following a distinctive pattern of their own. SLI seems to be a difference of kind, not just a slower rate of progress.

It might be that children with SLI are incapable of hearing the final *-s*, that is to say, their deficiency is a matter of speech perception. However, they hear the *-s* ending perfectly well on nouns such as *rice* and *noise* that happen to end in /s/ or /z/ by coincidence rather than being plurals. The problem might also affect all the grammatical inflections ending in *-s* equally, not just the plural. The possessive inflection *'s* has exactly the same variant pronunciations /s/, /z/ and /ɪz/ as the plural *-s*: *Pete's book*, *Sarah's house*, and *Liz's car*. At an early stage when children with SLI have an MLUw of 2–2.5 words, they nevertheless get the plural *-s* right 70 per cent of the time,

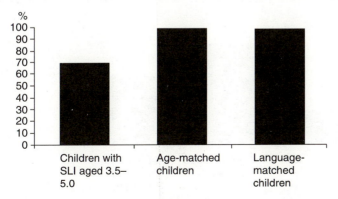

Fig. 9.2 Plural *-s* in English-speaking children

but the possessive *'s* right only 30 per cent. At the most advanced stage tested, when they are producing utterances that are 5 or more words long (MLUw = 5+), they are 98.5 per cent right on plural *-s* but still only 56 per cent right on possessive *'s*. In other words, they treat the two *-s* inflections differently, even though they have exactly the same form. The problem therefore lies in individual morphemes. It is not the final sounds /s/ and /z/ that are a problem, nor grammatical inflections in general, but specific morphemes.

Chapter 7 showed that the elements 'missing' from children's speech tend to come from a particular area of grammar, namely functional phrases. If the plural *-s* is missing, the present-tense *-s* should also be absent, since these are both part of the Agreement Phrase in which a grammatical feature spreads across the sentence. Likewise, the past-tense *-ed* inflection is part of the functional Tense Phrase and so should also be missing. The same research tested the English children on the tense endings for verbs, *-s* as in *sits* and *-ed* as in *painted*. English children with SLI scored only 34 per cent on production of *-s* compared to 91 per cent from the age-matched children and 59 per cent from the language-matched children. The past-tense *-ed* endings were also a problem: children with SLI scored 32 per cent compared with 97 per cent for the age-matched children and 65 per cent for the language-matched group (see Figure 9.3).

In general, children with SLI tend to leave things out rather than make mistakes: they make errors of omission, not of commission. But what is actually missing from their speech? If children with SLI really do not know the *-s* or *-ed* endings, they would be likely to use them in their speech more or less at random. The child PB seen above indeed omitted the plural *-s* inflection much of the time but also produced it wrongly on many occasions, as in *You got a tape-recorder̲s̲*, and *I find a cop̲s̲*.

Yet, in the Leonard experiment, children with SLI did not use plural *-s* in the wrong place more often than the other children; such mistakes made up only 1.6 per cent of their total compared with 1.9 per cent for non-SLI children. That is to say, children with SLI were no more likely to say *a bee̲s̲* or *this one cat̲s̲* than anybody else. While the children with SLI omitted the past-tense *-ed* more often, they also produced the 'overgeneralized' forms of the past-tense *-ed*, such as *drawed* and *breaked,* typical of

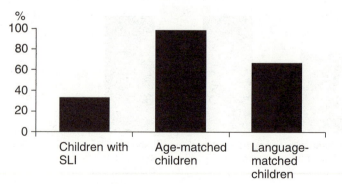

Fig. 9.3 Past-tense *-ed* in English-speaking children

other children's development. In some sense children with SLI must 'know' the inflections -*s* and -*ed* since they know when not to use them and they make errors typical of those who do know them. Indeed, even with the English children with SLI, it is difficult to argue that something is missing that is actually present 69 per cent of the time.

Nevertheless there is clearly a deficit of some kind that consistently affects the same grammatical features in children with SLI: their grammar is deficient in a distinctive way. The children do not have difficulties with other aspects of life, so their general cognitive processing is not at fault. They do not have problems with other aspects of language, so it is not language in general that is lacking. They often live in families with brothers and sisters who do not have the same problem; their deficiency cannot therefore be blamed on their upbringing or environment. The deficit is highly specific, affecting only one precise area of grammar. The problem is discovering its cause.

4 *Genetic causes of deficiency?*

The most controversial research into SLI concerns an English-speaking family known by the initials KE, which includes a high proportion of speakers with SLI. In the family tree overleaf, the speakers with SLI in the KE family are printed in bold. As can be seen, in the first generation the grandmother has SLI; in the next generation four of her five children have SLI; in the third generation 11 of the 24 grandchildren have SLI. In all, 16 out of 30 members of the KE family have SLI, with ages ranging from 2 to 74.

The family were first described in a set of case studies by Hurst and colleagues. Then two researchers, Myra Gopnik and Martha Crago, tested 20 members of the family, including 13 of the SLI speakers, for the usual group of grammatical features. The test of plural -*s,* for example, asked them to look at a picture of an imaginary animal while the experimenter said, 'This is a zoop.' Then they were shown a picture with several animals and were asked, 'These are ____?' Figure 9.4 give the average score for the two groups within the family; Gopnik and Crago's own figures are based on a more

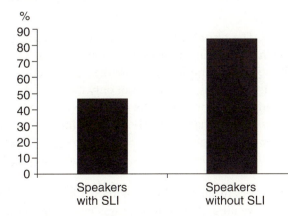

Fig. 9.4 Plural -*s* in members of the KE family

Grandfather=**GRANDMOTHER**

MOTHER	Father	**MOTHER**	**FATHER**	**MOTHER**
Daughter	Son	Daughter	Son	**SON**
SON	Daughter	Daughter	Daughter	Son
Daughter		**DAUGHTER**	**DAUGHTER**	Son
SON		**DAUGHTER**	**DAUGHTER**	Daughter
		SON		**SON**
				Son
				DAUGHTER
				Son
				DAUGHTER

The KE family (members with SLI are printed in **bold** capitals)

detailed comparison, age by age. The test clearly showed large differences between the two groups, the speakers with SLI scoring 47 per cent compared with 83 per cent for the others, though this difference was not in fact so marked on the other tests of plural -s. A second test looked at verb forms, including not only the past-tense inflection -ed and the present-tense inflection -s but also the future auxiliary will and the present continuous tense is walking. They had to supply the right form of the verb in sentences such as 'Every day he walks eight miles. Yesterday he ____?' Again the speakers with SLI scored dramatically below the others, 38 per cent compared to 92 per cent.

On both counts, then, the members of the KE family with SLI have very different scores from the others. Yet they have all grown up in the same environment and have much the same lifestyle. It cannot be coincidence that 16 out of 30 members of the same family have SLI. Gopnik found that the child PB had a cousin and an uncle with SLI. Others have found that, if one identical twin has SLI, the chances are 80 per cent that the other will, while the chances for a non-identical twin are only 35 per cent. The closer the relationship the more likely SLI is to be shared. Gopnik and Crago suggest: 'it is not unreasonable to entertain an interim hypothesis that a single dominant gene controls for those mechanisms that result in a child's ability to construct the paradigms that constitute morphology'.

In popularizations of this research, this has been called 'the grammar gene'. Grammatical inflections, however, form a small part of grammar, not the whole; at best it could be a gene for grammatical morphemes. The research has furthermore not demonstrated the gene's existence through painstaking research into the human genotype but by the kind of everyday observation that ginger cats tend to be toms or that asthma runs in families. Any family has vocabulary items that mean nothing to outsiders. For example, my family talked of *going to the hodel*, our local shop having a sign that had started life as *The Model Dairy* but had become *h odel airy* by the time we knew it. Families may well have linguistic peculiarities of their own. This research clearly demonstrates that SLI runs in families, but, as Steven Pinker points out, so do recipes and money. The research provides no clues to locating the actual gene, simply a logical presumption that it exists.

These claims for innateness differ from those made by the Universal Grammar theory, which relies on demonstrating logically that certain aspects of language must be built into the mind because they could not be learnt. The SLI research shows that the same grammatical deficits occur in members of the same family and therefore must be genetic in origin. But this explanation does not say precisely what this gene controls. It is inconceivable that a specific gene PLURAL -S exists in human beings or even a specific gene for grammatical inflections, if only because not all languages have grammatical inflections, let alone PLURAL -S, as we saw in Chapter 3. Instead, like all genes, its effects are bound to be widespread and indirect; something affects something else in the complex makeup of the human being which has the effect of causing difficulty with grammatical inflections. At best there may be a gene for 'grammatical number', say, which will manifest itself in different ways in different languages, its absence leading to lack of plural *-s* in English speakers with SLI among other consequences.

Detailed examination of the KE family also shows that the picture is not so clearcut as first presented. Vargha-Khadem and colleagues have examined the KE family in greater depth, and discovered that the members with SLI were worse at a whole range of language tasks, not just grammatical morphemes, including: sound manipulation, 'Say this non-word adding the first letter e.g. arg → varg', i.e. adding a specific initial phoneme to a word; spelling, 'Write this non-word as if it were a real English word'; rhyme, 'Tell me a word that rhymes with this word'; understanding of relative clauses; and many more. The only language tasks on which they performed the same as the other members of the family were object-naming and picture vocabulary.

What is more, the people with SLI differed in other mental processes as well as language. Their average IQ was 86 compared to 104 for the rest of the family. Their ability to imitate sequences of facial movements, such as 'Stick out your tongue, lick your upper lip, and smack your lips', was much worse. So it is not just grammatical inflections or, indeed, just language, that are affected but a whole range of mental capacities. Vargha-Khadem *et al.* claim: 'The evidence from the KE family thus provides no support for the proposed existence of grammar-specific genes.'

Furthermore, the original research also grouped children with SLI with adults and so cannot be compared with research based only on children. Most of the speakers with SLI in the KE family were women, 10 out of 16, though SLI usually affects about three times as many boys as girls. Hence, whatever the explanation for the SLI in this family may be, it does not appear to be the same as the SLI typical of children.

A further experiment with SLI children showed that their language deficiency is not confined to grammatical morphemes by testing how children made use of a range of English verbs such as *put*. In adult speech, this verb requires both a direct object and a prepositional phrase, technically called its 'arguments': *you put something somewhere*. In sentences produced by children with SLI such as *Put on there* and *Game to put on*, the children have left out the 'something', namely the direct object Noun Phrase that refers to what is being put, say *the doll* or *bottle*. In sentences such as *Put the chair* and *Put the hammer* the children have left out the 'somewhere', that is to say the phrase that states the location into which it is being put, *over there*, or *on the table*. So the children are definitely leaving out, not just a grammatical morpheme, but one of the two main elements of the sentence needed to go with this particular verb, namely one of its arguments, whether the direct object or a prepositional phrase. A language-matched group also leave out these elements on occasion, but less often than the children with SLI, and with a smaller range of verbs. So, as with the KE family, it is not just inflections that are missing in SLI.

It is premature to claim that the 'grammar gene' has been found. Though the KE family provide a fascinating source of evidence, their case becomes more blurred the closer it is examined. Nevertheless, clearly some component of language disability is inherited.

5 *Other languages*

One test case for the importance of grammatical inflections in SLI could be whether there are similar gaps in children with SLI when acquiring languages with different properties from English. As discussed in Chapter 3, some languages make a greater use of grammatical inflections, for instance by marking each of the six persons in the present-tense verb with inflections (Italian, Arabic, etc.), and by having agreement between adjectives and nouns to indicate number and case, as in Greek. Other languages, however, do not have grammatical inflections at all, for instance Chinese. If the gene primarily affects the child's learning of these inflections, SLI should show up in an exaggerated form in Italian and not at all in Chinese.

Leonard's experiment described on page 199 was also carried out with Italian children. In Italian, singular number is shown by one inflection, the plural by another, *cane* ('dog') versus *cani* ('dogs'), and *nave* ('ship') versus *navi* ('ships'); it is a matter of alternative endings, not the addition of a plural inflection to a singular inflectionless form; there are no base forms used without inflections. Those who see SLI in terms of missing inflections would predict that grammatical inflections will be absent from Italian children with SLI. In fact Italian children with SLI have comparatively little problem with the plural endings of nouns, scoring 79 per cent compared to the 89 per cent of age-matched children and 89 per cent of language-matched children.

The present-tense inflection on the Italian verb shows both the person and number of the subject – *dormo* ('I sleep'), *dormi* ('you sleep'), *dorme* ('he or she sleeps'), *dormono* ('they sleep'), and so on. The children with SLI did not make mistakes with the third person singular *dorme*, scoring 93 per cent, the same as the other groups. In the third person plural, instead of omitting the ending, the children with SLI used the wrong ending, *dorme* instead of *dormono*, leading to a score of 50 per cent compared to 91 per cent for age-matched, 82 per cent for language-matched.

The prediction that grammatical features are missing in SLI is not borne out. While the Italian children have problems with certain inflections such as third person plural, they have no difficulty with most of the others. Furthermore the nature of the problem with third person forms is that they substitute other endings rather than omit them as the English children do; in a language that has compulsory inflections throughout all the verb forms, they are less likely to be left out. The children also have grammatical problems outside this narrow area of inflections, for instance with the use of so-called 'clitic pronouns', not found in English, and French *Je t'aime* ('I you-love') with *te* attached to the beginning of the verb.

This comparison only involves English and Italian, which are not very dissimilar in grammatical inflections. It would be interesting to see how children with SLI fare in languages that have a single present-tense inflection for all the persons; *yomu* in Japanese means 'I/you/he/she/it/we/they read' even if the *-u* ending indicates the present tense. It would be fascinating to discover how SLI manifests itself in the two extremes of Vietnamese, which has no grammatical inflections, and Greenland Inuit, which has 318 grammatical inflections. A study of a single Greenland Inuit child indeed shows that verbal inflections were frequently omitted. So far, all that is known is that the phenomena of SLI are not confined to English, and manifest themselves in slightly different ways depending on the grammar of the language involved.

6 Deficiency and working memory

Researchers in the area of memory have often shown that developmental language disorder goes with poor working memory, which is the type of memory used for storing information in the mind for a few seconds. But is the children's language weak because of their poor working memory or is their memory weak because of their poor language? Susan Gathercole and Alan Baddeley made children with developmental language disorder repeat longer and longer nonsense words and then compared them with normal children. While they give no examples, the method presumably essentially builds up from *varg* to *truflag*, *ajfumig*, and *pishtrublishny*. The results are given in Figure 9.5.

With words of one and two syllables, the language-disordered children were about as successful as the others. With words of three and four syllables, they started to get dramatically worse, as can be readily seen. While they can cope with individual words, the more there are the worse they do, showing that the problem was one of memory capacity. The gap between them and the other children was larger on this repetition task than on other language tasks, putting them four years behind rather than 20 months. As seen earlier, nonsense word plurals were also a problem for the KE family.

In another experiment, children with SLI between 4 and 6 and age-matched children had to learn a new inflection, *-u* meaning 'large', with nonsense words such as *gack* and *mab*: a *gacku* is a large *gack*, a *mabu* a large *mab*. The results were that children either learnt the new morpheme or they did not; that is to say, it was a matter of all or none rather than of knowing it partially. Most SLI children belonged to the unsuccessful group. SLI children therefore clearly have a problem with handling new endings.

The part of the working memory system that is at fault is not production or perception, but the storage of speech sounds, particularly affecting the learning of vocabulary, as seen with the nonsense words. While the working memory theory has not as yet provided a precise explanation for the children's difficulties with grammatical inflections, it does give a general clue to the type of mental system affected by the 'grammar gene' and suggests where the problem may be located.

Other researchers have suggested that language disability is not as specific to language as the discussion here has implied. Some children have a hearing loss for sounds with high frequencies, which is not severe enough to constitute deafness but

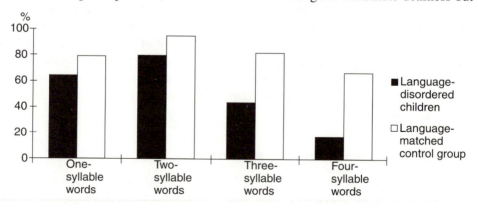

Fig. 9.5 Repetition of nonsense words by language-disordered children and a language-matched control group

may cause speech delay. Many SLI children are slow to pass other developmental milestones such as the age of walking, suggesting a more general impairment. In practical terms the importance of distinguishing between specific language impairment and language deficit associated with other cognitive problems is deciding whether a child needs speech therapy or more general therapy.

Two stories by children with language disorders

To show some characteristics of the *written* language of children with language disorders, here are attempts by two children to tell the same story they have seen acted out by a wolf, a duck and two monkeys, involving some table tennis balls and containers made of wire.

A

table tennis ball tube putting
basket bite in a wolf down.
the buck tube
look and fritened the to you cause over basket
In monkey sad here you no?
In duck no over duck two tennis ball down on happy
In to wolf see look duck duck angry wolf bad
quck good duck happy two on over no wolf you

B

The wolf is taking his table tennis ball. he is putting in the tube. The monkey is bitting the wolf's ear.
    chasing
The wolf is running the monkey. The duck is taking round the tube. The ball is in the basket. The wolf is saying oh gone the ball. Again the wolf is taking his table tennis ball in the tube. The monkey is bitting the wolf's ear. The wolf is chasing him. The duck is saying oh again ball in the tube. The duck is bitting the duck's ear.

Source: Cromer, *Language and Thought in Normal and Handicapped Children*

The criteria for spoken-language deficiency are mostly poor vocabulary and lack of grammatical inflections. These extracts demonstrate the extent to which these are true of the children's written language, and whether they have mastered the specific features of written language mentioned in Chapter 6.

II Aphasia in adults

This section describes some things that can go wrong with language in adults – 'aphasia'. Mental illnesses are occasionally associated with changes in speech. Some schizophrenics, for example, lose part of their awareness of lexical ambiguity and part of their ability to work out what a word means from the context, as well as sometimes having grammatical and phonological problems such as rhyming speech. Most aphasia in adults is, however, caused by physical damage to the brain – the consequences of strokes, tumours, car accidents or the like – rather than the structural causes of mental illness, such as the brain chemistry differences believed to underlie schizophrenia. This section introduces the main types of aphasia and their interaction with different components of the language system.

1 Types of aphasia

During the last century, it was discovered that injuries to different areas of the brain produce different types of aphasia. Conventionally the brain is divided into two sides or 'hemispheres', left and right. Broadly speaking, the language system is stored in the left side of the brain rather than the right. Research has shown a link between speech and the left hemisphere in babies from birth onwards, even in those that are premature. Damage to the left hemisphere therefore has the strongest effects on the language system. Damage to the right hemisphere has less obvious consequences on speech, affecting intonation patterns and the ability for social interaction rather than speech sounds or grammatical structures themselves.

If the first language is stored in the left side of the brain, where are other languages stored? Early research found that bilinguals use their right hemisphere more for language than do monolinguals. However, later research has found that this bias varies from one person to another, depending on such factors as the age when the second language was learnt and the situation, whether in a classroom or 'naturally'. While a second language may well be stored somewhere differently from a first, the available research tools at present do not allow this conjecture to be proved or disproved. In a classic experiment by Ojemann and Whitaker, different areas of the brains of two bilinguals were electrically stimulated while they were having brain operations. The researchers found no clear pattern to the storage of the two languages. Some small areas of the brain were clearly linked to one language, some areas to the other language; at many points they overlapped.

2 Broca's aphasia

In 1861 Paul Broca linked one type of aphasia to injury in a particular part of the front left hemisphere of the brain, known as 'Broca's area', shown in Figure 9.6. The term 'Broca's aphasia' has been used ever since for a set of aphasic impairments that seem

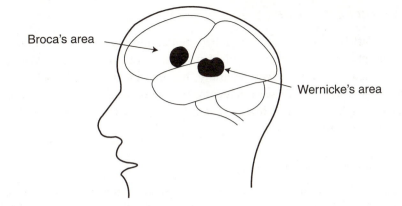

Fig. 9.6 Left hemisphere of the brain

to go together. Here is a man called FL with Broca's aphasia responding to the question 'What do you like to cook most?':

I don't know how there is any single way, there's so many thing, you know, that I like, I like meats, I have liked beef, the Germans, you know, and what, well the French you /kut/ the whole, I can't recall the words that I can't /θeI/, it was the where you make all the food, you make it all up today the keep it 'till the next day with the French, you know, uh what is the name of the word, god, public /səpinz/ they talk about, uh but I have had that, it was /raidəs/, just before the storage, you know, seven weeks I had personal friends that, that I would cook an' food the food and serve /fə/ four or six mean for an evening.

Inevitably the conventions for writing speech down make this speech appear odder than it really is. The transcriber, for example, has given *till* an apostrophe (which it has never needed, being a separate word from *until*, not a reduced form) and *an'* an apostrophe (which corresponds to a perfectly usual speech form without /d/; it would be odd, for instance, to pronounce the *and* of *Marks and Spencers* as /ənd/ with a /d/ rather than just as /ən/).

The sample from FL illustrates the main characteristics of Broca's aphasia. Patients are able to understand speech adequately: FL knew perfectly well that the question was about cookery. But they cannot speak fluently, sometimes producing unstructured strings of nouns and verbs; their gestures, too, are vague and meaningless. Grammatical morphemes are once again a major problem: *many thing* lacks plural *-s*, *meats* has an unneeded *-s*. In extreme cases Broca's aphasics produce strings of content words without grammatical morphemes, a condition known as 'agrammatism', seen in the following answer by a patient to the question 'Could you tell me, Mr Ford, what you've been doing in the hospital?', reported by Howard Gardner:

Yes. Sure. Me go, er. uh, P.T. nine o'cot, speech . . . two times ... read . . . wr . . . ripe, er, rike, er, write . . . practice . . . getting better.

3 Wernicke's aphasia

In 1874 Carl Wernicke found a link between another type of aphasia and injury in a particular part of the back left hemisphere of the brain, christened 'Wernicke's area'. The associated syndrome has, naturally, become known as Wernicke's aphasia. Its main characteristic can be seen in a conversation between a doctor and a patient with Wernicke's aphasia called Grogan, again taken from Howard Gardner's fascinating book *The Shattered Mind*:

Doctor: What brings you to the hospital?

Patient: Boy I'm sweating. I'm awful nervous, you know, once in a while I get caught up, I can't mention the tarripoi, a month ago, quite a little, I've done a lot well, I impose a lot, while, on the other hand, you know what I mean, I have to run around, look it over, trebbin and all that sort of stuff.

Doctor: Thank you Mr Grogan I want to ask you a few ...

Patient: Oh sure, go ahead, any old think you want. If I could I would. Oh, I'm taking the word the wrong way to say, all of the barbers here whenever they stop you it's going around and around, if you know what I mean, that is tying and tying for repucer, repucuration, well, we were trying the best that we could while another time it was with the beds over there the same thing.

In a way this extract seems familiar; the slips produced by Mr Grogan are those all of us make from time to time – my word processor attempted to correct *repuceration* to *recuperation*. But they occur much more often in Wernicke's aphasia. In some ways Wernicke's aphasia is the mirror-image of Broca's in that Wernicke's aphasics speak fluently but have great problems with comprehension. The first question, *What brings you to the hospital?*, gets an answer, *Boy I'm sweating . . .*, that seems more like a reply to the question *How have you been lately?* Some Wernicke's aphasics speak in a remorseless stream, as can be deduced here from the vain attempts of the doctor to direct the conversation. This characteristic is particularly noticeable in their frequent production of set phrases, such as *on the other hand*, *if you know what I mean*, *all that sort of stuff*, which gives their speech an illusion of fluency. Patients may also have severe problems with the names of everyday objects. Mr Grogan can manage *book* and *ear* but says *chair* for *table*, *knee* for *elbow*; he calls *clip plick*, and *butter tubber*. He seeks desperately for words: for *ankle* he said *ankey, no mankle, no kankle*; for *fork* he said *tonsil, teller, tongue, fung*.

So, hit your head on the right side and you lose part of your intonation; hit it on the front left and speaking will become difficult; hit it on the back left and listening will be the chief problem. The division of aphasia into two types is only a first approximation. There are many other types, and many other areas of brain injury apart from Broca's and Wernicke's areas; the syndrome called 'anomia', that is to say, impaired ability to find names, sometimes goes with injuries behind Wernicke's area in a location called the left angular gyrus. Some researchers feel that the terms 'Broca's aphasia' and 'Wernicke's aphasia' are convenient labels for making diagnoses rather than corresponding to specific brain damage as neatly as was once supposed, even if they represent two recognizably different sets of problems. Nor is it necessarily easy to fit any individual patient into one or other of these categories.

Children may also develop aphasia as a result of brain damage. It is usually accepted that children recover speech more easily than adults, though their educational progress may be affected and they may run a greater risk of psychiatric disorders. In one view, the brains of children are more flexible and can recover better from injury, with the exception of lead poisoning. Adults stop improving about six months after their injury; children can improve for several years. But the position for adults is by no means gloomy, about half of cases recovering completely. Indeed, one man who made no improvement for a year subsequently made a complete recovery.

4 Language components and aphasia

Mostly aphasia has been classified into different syndromes based on the area of the brain that is injured. Another approach is to consider aphasia in terms of the different components of language, such as vocabulary and grammar, setting aside reading to the next section.

Difficulty with vocabulary

Vocabulary is a problem area for many aphasics, which can manifest itself in diverse ways, as Mr Grogan has already demonstrated. Naming disorders are when the patient cannot summon up the word for a particular object, say the word for 'chair'. What is missing is often not just a single word but an entire set of words, flowers, animals, occupations and so on. In this case the meaning component of the word has gone.

In other cases, it is the form of the word that is elusive: Mr Grogan's *fung* for *fork*, reminiscent of the tip-of-the-tongue phenomenon encountered in Chapter 5. Though he knows most of the information about the word, somehow he cannot produce the actual sounds themselves. Here is an example of a patient S trying to describe a picture of a kite:

> S: . . . this is the sort of thing that I have trouble . . . it's on the right, it's blowing, on the right, and er there's four letters in it, and I think it begins with C goes when you start it and then goes up in the right in the air I would I would have to keep racking my brains how would I spell that word that flies, that that doesn't fly, you pull it round, it goes up with the air . . . and I can't . . . I can't just tell you what it is but I know more or less there'd be four I would think there'd be four letters and it's a . . .
>
> *Therapist*: Begins with K.
>
> S: K oh [ka] kite kite.

He knows almost everything about the word: its meaning, *doesn't fly, you pull it round, it goes up in the air*; the number of letters, *there's four letters in it*. But the actual word eludes him. It is not the word itself that has gone so much as the connection between the form of the word in the mental lexicon and actual speech.

Difficulty with grammar

Like the children with SLI, many aphasics have problems with grammatical morphemes. A French example dating from 1819 is a patient who said *Souhaiter bonjour, rester, mari venir* ('wish good morning, stay, husband come'), leaving out all the grammatical morphemes. Mr Ford showed a similar lack of grammatical morphemes, resulting in an unstructured string of content words, usually nouns. Here is a dialogue between a therapist and a patient about a picture of a cowboy breaking in a horse:

T: what's this?
P: erm
T: mmm
P: cowboys and and –
T: mm
P: cowboy and wrestler – wrestler and –
T: well the horse is tied with a rope isn't it?
P: a rope ah yes yes
T: what are they doing with the rope?
P: string
T: mmm
P: yes – mmm string string

The patient can only produce a sequence of nouns, *cowboys, wrestlers, rope, string*. All the grammar, complete with grammatical morphemes, has gone, apart from an occasional *and* or *a*; hence this is the type of speech sometimes called 'agrammatism'. A patient called ML missed out 62.4 per cent of free grammatical morphemes such as *the* and 18.5 per cent of grammatical inflections such as past tense *-ed*, but only 3.8 per cent of content words. The free morphemes that are words in their own right are missing more often than the bound inflections that have to be attached to words. Even with aphasics at a less reduced level, other aspects of syntax may pose a problem. However, many aphasics do appear to have particular problems with verbs. One man would leave out the verb from the sentence, *The woman is* [drinking] *a cup of tea*, or invent a new verb, *The child was laddering* [climbing].

Chapter 7 mentioned that one current explanation for the missing elements in children's language is the lack of functional phrases within which the grammatical inflections can be placed. They do not have plural *-s* with Nouns (*two book*) because they lack a type of functional phrase called a Determiner Phrase. They do not have third person *-s* with Verbs (*he like*) because they lack a Tense Phrase, and so on.

Yosef Grodzinsky has extended this type of explanation to the grammatical deficiencies of aphasics. He hypothesized that a single grammatical lack underlies the agrammatism of Broca's aphasia. In particular, the functional phrases called Agreement and Tense Phrases no longer have the grammatical features they normally carry, namely number, person, tense and gender. So, in English, this lack implies an inability to express number, with a consequent loss of the third person -*s* and the past-tense -*ed*, as the aphasics seen so far demonstrate abundantly. In Hebrew it means not only producing wrong agreement of number, as in *ha-yeled katbu sefer* ('the boy wrote [plural] a book'), but also wrong agreement of gender, as in *ha-yeled kotebet sefer* ('the boy writing [feminine] a book'), since Hebrew verbs change to show the gender of the subject.

This explanation runs into problems with languages that rely on grammatical inflections more than English. Section I discussed how Italian children with SLI do not leave out inflectional endings to the same extent as English children with SLI, but instead substitute the wrong inflection, because an inflection of some kind is compulsory for all verbs in Italian but not required in English. Grodzinsky claims that it is not so much a matter of differences between languages as of differences between individual words. Some Russian words are uninflected in one form, but inflected in others; the word for 'snow' is *snjeg* in the nominative case uninflected form, but *snjega*, *snjegu*, *snjego* etc. in other forms. Russian-speaking aphasics, however, omit all the case forms for *snjeg* rather than substituting a wrong form.

Grodzinsky extends this analysis to other elements missing from aphasic speech. The other functional phrases within which these belong are lacking, for example the Determiner Phrase within which the articles *the* and the plural -*s* can nestle. Aphasics are left only with the lexical phrases containing the main types of lexical category such as Nouns and Verbs. Hence aphasic speech resembles that of children at the stages when these functional phrases have still to come on line, as seen in Chapter 7.

One possibility is, then, that aphasia is the mirror-image of language acquisition. The levels of aphasia mirror the stages through which children develop: aphasia is 'unlearning' language. At the moment the evidence to test this hypothesis is slight. One intriguing argument concerns the sequence of language acquisition. Children have to learn the binding relationships mentioned in Chapter 2 between words like *himself* and their antecedents in a particular order, starting with the language with the most restrictions such as English and gradually expanding till they get to the least restricted, namely Japanese, as we see in Chapter 11. The 'subset principle' claims that it would be impossible for them to go in the opposite direction and learn English starting from the Japanese setting. Aphasics indeed go in the same direction as children; they will, for example, accept the sentence *John threatened Mary to spray bug-spray on herself* while normal speakers will not.

Finally, what happens to brain-injured people who know two languages? Is the grammar lost in one or the other, or in both? Which one is worst affected, the first or the second? Michael Paradis suggests that there is no single answer to any of these questions, since the forms that aphasia takes in bilinguals vary immensely from person to person. Some people lose the language that they learnt *last*, and so revert to their mother tongue. Some people lose the language that they use *least*, and recover the one that they were using most when they were injured. Some people retain the language that they feel most attached to psychologically. Others recover the language of the situation they find themselves in, usually the hospital ward.

Two of Paradis's case histories illustrate the complexity of bilingual aphasia. One is a trilingual speaker from Madagascar, who had learnt Gujarati and Malagasy from birth at home but had been educated in French and had used it daily in his work. His knowledge of French and Malagasy were not affected by his injury. His Gujarati, however, was severely affected, and he was unable to carry out ordinary speech movements. The second case is a bilingual speaker of French and Arabic, who lived in Casablanca. Ten days after a road accident, she could speak French but not Arabic; the next day she could speak Arabic but not French; and the next day she went back to fluent French and poor Arabic; three months later she could speak both. The diversity of aphasia cases in bilinguals thus means that the exact connections between the two or more languages in the minds of bilinguals still remain a mystery.

III Problems with reading

This final section explores the links between children's development and written language. As seen in Chapter 6, reading is not just a way of turning written marks into spoken sounds, but uses several different systems, even in a language such as English with an apparently straightforward alphabet-based system. Hence learning to read involves several processes which may vary from one language to another. Before looking at children's problems, it is necessary to have an idea of the normal processes of development. As always, there are many rival theories of reading deficiency; the following account is based mainly on the work of Uta Frith.

1 Principles of reading in children's development

Most accounts of the acquisition of reading divide it into a series of principles or levels that the child has to pass through. Frith's model involves three overall stages.

Frith's three stages in learning to read

1. Logographic	Recognizing words as wholes	*cat, zoo, dog*
2. Alphabetic	Learning correspondences between letters and sounds	*cat* = /kæt/
3. Orthographic	Words as shapes, letter combinations as rules	*to/two, yob/yobbo*

The starting-point for most children is recognizing particular words they encounter in the world around them. Advertising, for example, ensures that children recognize a Coca-Cola label, a bottle of HP sauce, or a McDonalds restaurant: the Golden Arches M is said to be the most readily recognized sign in the world. These signs consist of complexes of distinctive letters, colours and shapes thought up by some designer rather than just the letters themselves. Virtually all children can recognize some of the signs in their environment. However, this is a pre-reading stage rather than reading proper, since the child makes no real distinction between a real 'word' and a sign.

Stage 1: the 'logographic' stage

Reading itself starts when children recognize a word as a whole, called the 'logographic' stage. My children, for example, recognized *zoo*, *cat* and *dog* in their early books. London children can usually recognize *Harrods* on bags and vans. At this stage children cannot split the word into its component letters – z+o+o; it is the overall shape that counts. They have a limited reading vocabulary of a certain set of words, which they often recognize in different variations – *Harrods*, *HARRODS*, or even *hArRoDs*. But children have great difficulty with words that do not belong to this set, and are unable to read made-up words such as *vilp* or *wug*.

Teaching exploits this stage through the 'look–say' whole-word method, in which teachers hold up flashcards of words which the children have to recognize. Children respond to the words as wholes rather than to the letters that make them up. In one British whole-word method, the *Breakthrough to Literacy* scheme, the words that the children learn to read come from their own speech. The teacher constructs their reading books out of their own sentences. If children want to write *A hippopotamus is wallowing in the swamp*, then this will be their reading text.

Stage 2: the 'alphabetic' stage

Next comes the 'alphabetic' stage, when children learn that written letters correspond to spoken sounds: *cat* is read aloud as /kæt/, *zoo* as /zu:/ and so on. This stage relies on the alphabetic principle of writing that relates letters to spoken sounds discussed in Chapter 6. It is not therefore needed for acquiring non-alphabetic writing systems such as Chinese characters, since these do not have direct links between writing and pronunciation. The teaching method that stresses this stage is 'phonics'. Since at least 1912 children have learnt that /kə/ /æ/ /tə/ spells *cat*, and that *candy*, *cavities*, *calendar* and *California* all start with 'ca' /kæ/.

The alphabetic stage is straightforward for children learning many languages with alphabetic-based writing systems where each letter corresponds to a spoken sound, such as Finnish, Italian and Hungarian. Languages where the alphabetic principle combines with other principles present more of a problem for the learner, since the link between letters and sounds is less predictable, as we saw in Chapter 6, for example English,

French and Danish. In English the alphabetic rules work partially. One letter can correspond to several sounds; 'i' is /ə/ in *terrible*, /ɪ/ in *practice*, /aɪ/ in *sign* and /i:/ in *police*. In the reverse direction, one sound may be linked to several letters; the sound /k/ can be spelled 'c' *stoic*, 'k' *kind*, 'ck' *back*, 'ch' *chemist*, 'qu' *conquer*, 'cc' *soccer*, 'kk' *trekking*, and be part of 'x' *six*.

A further problem in English is the discrepancy between the names for the letters and the sounds they represent in spelling. While the letter-name 't' /ti:/ may well start with a /t/ and the letter-name 'v' /vi:/ begin with a /v/, 'm' /em/, 's' /es/ and 'f' /ef/ finish with their respective sounds; 'g' /dʒi:/, 'h' /eɪtʃ/ and 'y' /waɪ/ do not even contain an example of the sounds they usually represent, /g/, /h/ and /j/. Many children go through a stage when they invent spellings for words based on the letter-names. One four-year-old wrote YUTS A LADE YET FEHEG AD HE KOT FLEPR, meaning 'Once a lady went fishing and she caught Flipper'. The YUTS and YET become 'once' and 'went' when it is seen that 'Y' stands for the sound /w/ in the letter-name /waɪ/; LADE becomes 'lady' /leɪdɪ/ if 'E' is seen to stand for the letter-name /i:/. Children's invented spellings also reveal their difficulties with digraphs where two letters stand for one sound, H for 'sh' /ʃ/ in FIH ('fish') or T for TH /ð/ in MOTR ('mother'), and a tendency to omit nasal consonants, BOPE for 'bumpy' and CADE for 'candy', perhaps because they hear such sounds as nasalised vowels, say /ʌ̃/ rather than as vowel–consonant VC sequences such as /ʌn/, the same process that led to the loss of syllable-final /n/ in French.

The structure of the English syllable is a particular problem for phonics. Since English syllables have a compulsory vowel, as seen in Chapter 4, consonants cannot be said in isolation but have to be 'sounded' with a consonant plus a vowel. This

---

Invented spellings

Here are some examples of the spellings that children invent for themselves spontaneously at the early stages of learning to read and write.

Letter-name consonants: BLW   HAV   FAS   DESES (dishes)   SKIY (sky)
    PLEZ (please)
Other consonants: CLAS (clouds)   HED (head)   WERRE (wearing)
    YALO (yellow)   GOWE (going)
Digraphs: HRP (chirp)   FIH (fish)   SOS (shoes)   TA (they)   MOTR (mother)
Nasals: LAP (lamp)   RAD (rained)   CADE (candy)   AJLS (angels)
Long vowels: NAM (name)   PLES (police)   BIT (bite)   DOT (don't)   NTU (into)
Short vowels: FAL (fell)   HEM (him)   WIS (wants)   SOPR (supper)

Source: Temple et al., *The Beginnings of Writing*

need for a vowel affects the actual letter-names: 'k' is said as /kəɪ/ not /k/, 't' as /tiː/ not /t/. But the syllable structure also affects the way they are said in phonics; 'k' is /kə/, 't' /tə/, with 'er' /ə/ epenthetic vowels to pad them out to normal English syllables. The difficulty with phonics in English is that 'cat' is not linked directly to /kæt/ but to /kə æ tə/ (in my pronunciation, at any rate, with added glottal stops /kəʔ æʔ təʔ/). Writing systems that use signs for whole syllables do not have this drawback; for example, the Japanese katakana sign タ stands for the syllable *ta*. Nor do languages that permit syllables consisting only of a consonant, such as the Slovak word *vrch* /vr̩x/ 'summit'.

Stage 3: the 'orthographic' stage

Finally, children come to the orthographic stage where they treat writing as an independent system rather than one based on pronunciation. Here the visual shapes of words are recognized in their own right without being converted to sounds. Rather than the focus being the letters themselves, as at Stage 2, now it is words and morphemes that make up the reading units. At this stage children acquire the orthographic rules of the language that are independent of the sounds – the different spellings for content and grammatical words, *to* versus *two*, and for proper names and nouns, *Mann* versus *man*, or the rules for consonant doubling, *yob* versus *yobbo*, and so on.

Without this stage, people would not be able to read at about three times the speed they can speak. Nor would they be able to read words they cannot pronounce. Everybody will remember the reactions when they first used some word in conversation that they had only encountered in writing, say *misled* as /mɪzl̩d/, or *dishevelled* as /daɪʃevəlɪd/. Children learning a writing system such as English have to go through these three stages. Without the logographic stage, they could not get to the alphabetic; without the alphabetic, they would not get to the orthographic. Particular methods of teaching favour particular stages. But all of them are necessary to become a fluent reader.

Other writing systems may not need three principles. If a language has a character system such as Chinese, it might be possible to skip the alphabetic principle altogether in teaching children to read. Opinions about this differ. In mainland China children are first taught the sound-based system called 'pinyin' before they learn the characters. In Japan too, children start with the syllable-based kana systems before learning the kanji characters. However, in Hong Kong children go straight to Chinese characters, omitting the alphabetic stage.

One view mentioned in Chapter 6 is that the forms of spelling are close to the forms in which words are stored in the mind. Take the words *photograph*, *photographic* and *photography*. In these the letter 'a' corresponds to three distinct sounds /ɑː/, /æ/, and /ə/ (*cart*, *cat* and *asleep*), at least in southern British pronunciation. If the alphabetic principle alone were adhered to, these words would have to be spelt in three different ways, which would hinder readers from seeing that they are in fact the same word. In the same way, the differences in spelling between *metal* and *mettle*, or *flour* and *flower*, effectively obscure the fact that they were historically variant spellings of the same words.

Most of the complaints against English spelling are misconceived, in the light of the discussion of different writing systems in Chapter 6. While it is indeed not fully effective as an alphabetic system, the English orthographic system is only partly linked to sounds, with some affinity to character systems such as Chinese or Japanese. To function effectively, even English readers have to go beyond the alphabetic principle to the regularities of orthography.

Some of the difficulties associated with teaching reading may be due to over-stressing the alphabetic principle. No method of teaching reading takes the orthographic principle as its creed, even if elements of it are included in various methods. While children may have to pass through the alphabetic stage that teachers concentrate on, it is an interim stage rather than the final goal.

This is not to say that English adults cannot use all three principles. There are occasions when readers are forced back to earlier strategies. I steered my way round Tokyo by a building with a particular sign on top, which I took to be Coca-Cola but in fact meant 'earth'– a logographic strategy. I have read the phrase *oral stereognosis* (the ability to distinguish shapes with the tongue, which facilitates learning second languages!) but have never heard the word pronounced; my guess is /sterɪɒgnəʊsɪs/, an alphabetic strategy. Hearing the name /klɑːk/ on the radio I guess it is spelled *Clarke* rather than *Clark* because of the 'e' that is often added to proper names – an orthographic process. On the other hand it is very annoying when shop assistants apply this principle to my own surname and ask whether *Cook* is spelled with an 'e', since I have never yet met a *Cooke*. (Or, to be more factual, in my local phone-book *Cooks* outnumber *Cookes* by six to one.)

2 Problems with reading

The problem that has been most associated with deficiency in reading is developmental dyslexia. Many of the same research controversies surrounding SLI are also found with dyslexia. Some deny that there is any specific condition. Given any human ability such as playing the piano or mental arithmetic, some people are good at it, some are not. In this view, dyslexia is simply a term for those at the lower end of the spread of reading ability. Other researchers argue that dyslexics have a specific type of deficit like SLI, rather than just being poor readers. In this case dyslexics would experience differences from normal reading development rather than having slower than the average rate of development. Some studies of dyslexia therefore compare age-matched and language-matched samples, like the SLI research. A further dispute is whether dyslexia applies only to reading, or whether it is a sign of a more general cognitive deficit, again like SLI.

In terms of the three Frith principles used here, children's difficulties come from getting stuck at one of the early levels of reading. Few children fail to acquire the logographic principle, most managing to recognize some words as wholes. One study showed that only 10 per cent of dyslexics had problems with this principle. A higher proportion of children fail to get the alphabetic principle. About 67 per cent of dyslexics in one study were deficient in the relationship of sounds and letters. These are the true dyslexics, who are unable to 'sound out' the letters of a word but perfectly capable of learning logographically. Some children may be considered good at reading in a whole-word approach until the day comes when they have to switch to the alphabetic principle. Indeed, English-speaking children who had failed to learn to read were capable of learning to read 30 Chinese characters in only two to five hours.

The actual spatial relationships of the letters present a particular problem. One component in intelligence tests is the ability to recognize shapes in different orientations. Writing is, however, one of the cases where this ability is counterproductive; 'd' is not the same as its vertical inversion, 'q', or its horizontal inversion, 'b', or its vertical and horizontal inversion, 'p'. The letters too have to appear in a particular direction from left to right: *pat* is different from *tap* and from *apt*. Children have to learn that writing follows a consistent direction; some children alternate orders, or go in both directions simultaneously, *JJIWILL*, even with the letters in mirror-image, as here.

Since the alphabetic principle links letters to the sounds of speech, children with dyslexia may also be deficient in speech. Dyslexia of this type goes with inability to repeat unfamiliar words, mistakes with learning nonsense words, and in general with reports of delayed language acquisition. It is the sound system itself that is involved, not just reading. Consequently, this form of dyslexia is said to be unknown in Japan, since Japanese scripts are either character- or syllable-based, but not alphabetic. One bilingual child could read normally in Japanese but not in English.

The orthographic principle can also go wrong. Frith believes that the writing and reading systems are often out of step. The orthographic principle is first learnt in reading and then passed over to writing, rather than learnt in both simultaneously. Hence some children can read fluently but cannot spell. They can be detected through the 'e-cancellation' task, a version of which is given in the box overleaf. The text is given at the end of the chapter with all the 'e's marked.

Readers who have mastered the alphabetic principle will easily spot the letters that are vital to the pronunciation of the word. The 'e' in *red* is vital because it distinguishes *red* from *rod* or *rid*, as are the 'e's in *well* (*will*, *wall*) and *ears* (*bars*, *cars*, etc.), and so on. But readers who have mastered the orthographic principle will also spot those letters that are vital to the spelling rather than the pronunciation. The 'e's in some words are totally predictable or even 'silent', as in *nine*, *watched*, *those*, *little*, etc.

Everybody has occasional lapses with the orthographic principle, trying to remember whether the right spelling is *independant* or *independent*, *advice* or *advise*, *receive* or

The e-cancellation test

Cross out all the occurrences of the letter 'e' in the following set of proverbs.

A stitch in time saves nine. The early bird catches the worm. He who hesitates is lost. Look before you leap. A bird in the hand is worth two in the bush. A watched pot never boils. Red sky in the morning is the shepherd's warning. Little jugs have big ears. Seeing is believing. An Englishman's word is his bond. There's no road without a turn-ing. All's well that ends well. Those that can, do, those that can't, teach. More haste, less speed. The more the merrier. You can't make an omelette without breaking eggs. An apple a day keeps the doctor away. The child is father to the man.

(Answer at the end of the chapter)

recieve. People who are 'dysgraphic' have severe problems with remembering such spellings, shown by their inability to cross out 'unimportant' 'e's on the e-test. This is not to say that problems with the alphabetic or orthographic principles cannot be overcome by other means. The rules taught for English spelling partly compensate for failings with the alphabetic principles. My children were taught that 'fairy e' waves its magic wand over the preceding vowel to make it 'say its name' (*wine/win, mope/ mop*, etc.).

Loss of reading may also be associated with aphasia. Typically, Broca's aphasics are capable of reading for meaning but find reading aloud difficult; they are better at isolated words than connected sentences, the orthographic principle retained without the alphabetic. Wernicke's aphasics, on the other hand, are unable to read for mean-ing but can read aloud in a limited fashion without comprehending what they are say-ing; the alphabetic principle partly survives. A typical case of 'word-blindness' was a Frenchman called Monsieur C, who could recognize RF as meaning 'République Française', and could read numbers and play cards, but he could not identify letters and could not get the meaning of written words; this is then a clear case where the logographic principle alone remains. Very often the written language suffers in the same way as the spoken, rather than being out of step. Bilinguals, as always, show a diverse pattern. One polyglot could not read in English, his native language, but could still read French, Latin and Greek.

This chapter has demonstrated that disabilities with language are not random aberra-tions but reflect different aspects of the language system, in particular vocabulary and grammatical morphemes. There is still only partial understanding of their causes. While the genetic explanation for SLI may be correct, there is fairly slim evidence as yet, apart from the absence of other suggestions. Explanations of aphasia in terms of the location of injury within the brain again seem broadly correct, but it is still unclear how this reflects how language is stored in the brain. What is abundantly clear is the extreme robustness of the language system in the mind.

The e-cancellation test

A stitch in time saves nine. The early bird catches the worm. He who hesitates is lost. Look before you leap. A bird in the hand is worth two in the bush. A watched pot never boils. Red sky in the morning is the shepherd's warning. Little jugs have big ears. Seeing is believing. An Englishman's word is his bond. There's no road without a turning. All's well that ends well. Those that can, do, those that can't, teach. More haste, less speed. The more the merrier. You can't make an omelette without breaking eggs. An apple a day keeps the doctor away. The child is father to the man.

Sources and further reading

Children's difficulty with language development – background: language and disability

The discussion of MLU in Down's Syndrome children is based on J.R. Rondal, 'Language development and mental retardation', in W. Yule and M. Rutter (eds.), *Language Development and Disorders* (London: MacKeith Press, 1987), 248–61.

Specific Language Impairment in development

PB is described in M. Gopnik, 'Feature blindness: a case study', *Language Acquisition* 1 (1990): 139–64.

Deficiency in grammar

Leonard's approach can be found in: L.B. Leonard, 'Language learnability and Specific Language Impairment in children', *Applied Psycholinguistics* 10 (1989): 179–202; L.B. Leonard, U. Bortolini, M.C. Caselli, K.K. McGregor and L. Sabbadini, 'Morphological deficits in children with Specific Language Impairment: the status of features in the underlying grammar', *Language Acquisition* 2 (1992): 151–79. Other useful papers are: P.J. Connell and C.A. Snow, 'The conceptual basis for morpheme learning problems in children with Specific Language Impairment', *Journal of Speech and Hearing Research* 37 (1994): 389–98; J. Johnston and T. Schery, 'The use of grammatical morphemes by children with communicative disorders', in D. Morehead and A. Morehead (eds.), *Normal and Deficient Child Language* (Baltimore, MD: University Park Press, 1976), 239–58; R.K. Kail, 'A method for studying the generalized slowing hypothesis in children with Specific Language Impairment', *Journal of Speech and Hearing Research* 37 (1994): 418–21; M.F. Schwartz, E.M. Saffran, D.E. Bloch, and G.S. Dell, 'Disorders of speech production in aphasic and normal speakers', *Brain and Language* 47 (1994): 52–88.

Genetic causes of deficiency?

The original papers on the KE family are: J.A. Hurst, M. Baraitser, E. Auger, F. Graham and S. Norell, 'An extended family with an inherited speech disorder', *Developmental Medicine and Child Neurology* 22 (1990): 347–55; M. Gopnik and M.B. Crago, 'Familial aggregation of a developmental language disorder', *Cognition* 39 (1991): 1–50. A useful critique is in S. Pinker, *The Language Instinct* (Harmondsworth: Penguin, 1995). More critical accounts are in: F. Vargha-Khadem, K. Watkins, K. Alcock, P. Fletcher and R. Passingham, 'Praxic and non-verbal cognitive deficits in a large family with a genetically transmitted speech and language disorder', *Proceedings of the National Academy of Science* (USA) 92 (1995): 930–3; P. Fletcher and R. Ingham, 'Grammatical impairment', in P. Fletcher and B. MacWhinney (eds.), *Handbook of Child Language* (Oxford: Blackwell, 1995); G. King and P. Fletcher, 'Grammatical problems in school-age children with Specific Language Impairment', *Clinical Linguistics and Phonetics* 7 (1993): 339–52; A useful source is R.F. Cromer, *Language and Thought in Normal and Handicapped Children* (Oxford: Blackwell, 1991).

Other languages

The paper on Greenland and Inuit cited in Fletcher and MacWhinney, *Handbook of Child Language* (see above) is M.B. Crago, S. Allen and L. Ningiuruvik, 'Inflections gone askew: SLI in a morphologically complex language', paper presented at the 6th conference of the International Association for the Study of Child Language (Trieste, 1993).

Deficiency and working memory

Working memory theory is described in S.E. Gathercole and A.D. Baddeley, *Working Memory and Language* (Hove: Lawrence Erlbaum, 1993); Gathercole and Baddeley, 'The role of phonological memory in vocabulary acquisition: a study of young children learning arbitrary names of toys' *British Journal of Psychology* 81 (1990): 439–54. The other experiments mentioned are described in: L. Swisher and D. Snow, 'Learning and generalization components of morphological acquisition by children with Specific Language Impairment: is there a functional relation?', *Journal of Speech and Hearing Research* 37 (1994): 1406–13; C.A. Heywood and A.G.M. Canavan, 'Developmental neuropsychological correlates of language', in Yule and Rutter, *Language Development and Disorders* (see above), 146–58; G. Ojemann and H.A. Whitaker, 'Language localisation and variability', *Brain and Language* 6 (1978): 239–60; M. Paradis, 'Epilogue', in Paradis (ed.), *Readings on Aphasia in Bilinguals and Polyglots* (Quebec: Didier, 1983).

Adult aphasias

A useful modern account of aphasia is C. Code (ed.), *The Characteristics of Aphasia* (Hove: Lawrence Erlbaum, 1989). The descriptions of Mr Ford and Mr Grogan come from H. Gardner, *The Shattered Mind* (New York: Vintage, 1974). Mr S and the examples of verbs come from R. Lesser and L. Milroy, *Linguistics and Aphasia* (London: Longman, 1993). The cowboy dialogue is from D. Crystal, P. Fletcher and M. Garman, *The Grammatical Analysis of Language Disability* (London: Edward Arnold, 1976). The language of ML comes from A. Caramazza and A.E. Hillis, 'The disruption of sentence production: some dissociations', *Brain and Language* 36 (1989): 625–50. Also useful is Y. Grodzinsky, *Theoretical Perspectives on Language Deficit* (Cambridge, MA: MIT Press, 1990).

Problems with reading

The easiest access to Frith's work is U. Frith, 'Beneath the surface of developmental dyslexia', in K.E. Patterson, J.C. Marshall and M. Coltheart (eds.), *Surface Dyslexia* (London: Lawrence Erlbaum, 1985), 301–30. A very accessible account of reading can be found in C. Temple, R. Nathan, F. Temple and N.A. Burris, *The Beginnings of Writing*, 3rd edn (Boston: Allyn & Bacon, 1993). Also of importance is D. Mackay, B. Thompson and P. Schaub, *Breakthrough to Literacy* (London: Longman, 1970).

Dyslexia is described in E. Boder, 'Developmental dyslexia: a diagnostic approach based on three atypical reading–spelling patterns', *Developmental Medicine and Child Neurology* 15 (1973): 663–87. The use of Chinese characters is reported in P. Rozin, S. Poritsky, and B. Sotsky, 'American children with reading problems can easily learn to read English represented by Chinese characters', *Science* 171 (1971): 1264–7.

10 Language Change

In a way it is not surprising that languages change: why should language be different from any other aspect of human life? However, the principle of structure-dependency seen in Chapter 3, the basic levels of vocabulary seen in Chapter 5, are all part of language, wherever and whenever it is spoken. Any language from any period of history must conform to the constraints of human language itself, for at least as far back as the time when the human mind took its present shape. Elizabethan English, Ancient Egyptian, and Sanskrit were as much bound by the human mind as the modern languages descended from them. Whatever else happens, the grammar of English will not change by 2100 AD to permit a question *Is Sam is the cat that black?*; whatever innovations there may be in furniture, the word for 'table' will still form part of a system of vocabulary with the three levels of basic, superordinate and subordinate.

As well as the absolute requirements on language, it is also possible to make educated guesses about other features of a language, whatever period it comes from. Chapter 4 showed that it is 91.5 per cent likely that a language will have a high front vowel, 94 per cent certain that this vowel will be unrounded /i/ rather than rounded /y/; Chapter 3 showed that there is a 96 per cent probability that the Subject will come before the Object, rather than after it. So it is unlikely, though not impossible, that by 2100 English-speaking people will use a rounded front /y/ in *bean* or will have the canonical sentence order OSV *You John loves madly.*

Yet previous chapters have already mentioned major changes in language. Chapter 8, for instance, described how French dropped 'h' while RP English preserved it, and French exported uvular 'r' into German, Dutch and Danish. Even though languages are restricted by universal principles, there is nevertheless much that can change. This chapter first gives some general examples of historical change, then looks more specifically at the development of the English inflections; it goes on to consider the reasons for language change that come both from outside the language and from within, and finishes with the vexed question of whether language change can be averted or, indeed, instigated.

I Historical development of languages

There have been scholars studying language change since the beginning of the nineteenth century, some under the name of 'comparative philology', some under that of 'historical linguistics'. This section looks at some of the classic ideas about how languages develop and how earlier stages can be reconstructed.

1 The Romance languages

A familiar example of historical change is the development of the Romance languages. In the days of the Roman empire, Latin was spoken over a wide area of Europe through right of conquest, taking in Gaul, alias France. As the linguistic power of the empire declined, many of its former provinces evolved their own forms of Latin, for example, Spain, France and Italy. By the end of the eighth century AD French was sufficiently distinct from Latin to be regarded as a language in its own right, with other Romance languages following suit. The evolution of French from Latin illustrates a type of historical change in which a language is effectively imposed on a native population by an imperialist power and then develops its own character when the imperialist power leaves.

The common ancestry of the Romance languages can be seen in the similarities in their vocabulary: /ne/ in French, /naso/ in Italian, /na/ in Romanian, /naso/ in one Spanish version all show their common source in Latin *nasus*, as indeed does English *nose*. The historical relationships between languages are also reflected in the systematic correspondences between their sound systems. For example, the Latin syllable-initial /k/ phoneme became /ʃ/ in many French words but stayed as /k/ in other languages. Latin *carus* ('expensive') is *cher* in French, and *caro* in Italian, Spanish and Portuguese. The Latin word *candela* ('candle') is *chandelle* in French, *candela* in Italian and Spanish, and *candeia* in Portuguese.

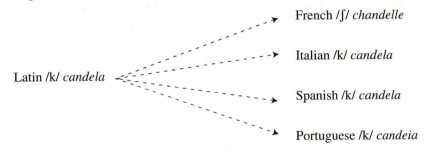

A more limited change affected the sound /k/ in front of a consonant in Latin, i.e. '/k/C'. Take the Latin word *octo* ('eight'). In French and Portuguese, /k/ merged with the preceding vowel to produce *huit* and *oito*. In Italian it merged with /t/, *otto*, and in Spanish it became /tʃ/, *ocho*. So the Latin word *lactem* ('milk' in the accusative case) also changed into *lait* (French), *leite* (Portuguese), *latte* (Italian) and *leche* (Spanish), as shown below. An underlined space /_/ means that there is no sound.

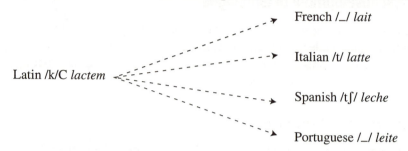

Latin /k/C *lactem*

French /_/ *lait*

Italian /t/ *latte*

Spanish /tʃ/ *leche*

Portuguese /_/ *leite*

Sound changes do not normally apply to individual words, but to the whole phonological system of a language. So it is not just *octo* and *lactem* that change, but all the words with '/k/C' combinations. Sound changes gradually differentiated the sound systems of the Romance languages, sometimes by losing a sound, as in *lait*, sometimes by gaining one, as in *leche*, sometimes by one sound changing into another, as in *cher*.

2 Trees and language families

When there are enough changes in sounds, vocabulary and grammar, these may add up to a new language. Just as it is hard to separate languages where one shades into another geographically in areas such as the French/Italian borders, so it is hard to assign languages a precise historical date of birth, since change never stops.

A common way of depicting historical change is as a family tree. The simplified tree below represents how Latin evolved into the Romance languages. Such family trees provide a convenient way of classifying languages into historically related groups. They are dangerous, however, if the analogy to a family is taken too literally. Languages do not fall into neat generations, one giving birth to another at regular intervals; they transform into something else rather than giving way to their successors. Nor do they have precise dates of death: Latin survived for centuries in marginal uses such as the seventeenth-century writings of Milton and Dryden; Hebrew came back from the dead in the twentieth century to become the language of Israel.

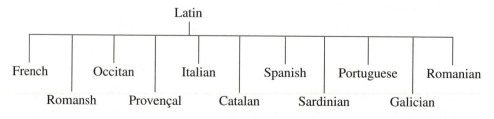

Latin

French	Occitan	Italian	Spanish	Portuguese	Romanian
Romansh	Provençal	Catalan	Sardinian	Galician	

The family tree of most languages can be extended back to languages whose existence are matters of sheer deduction, since no direct trace of them remains. Behind Latin, and indeed most of the languages of Europe, stands the Indo-European language, from which descend the Germanic family (English, German, Icelandic, etc.), the Indo-Iranian family (Persian, Hindi, etc.), the Celtic languages (Gaelic, Welsh, etc.), the Romance languages (French, Italian, Spanish, etc.) and many more, as seen in the simplified tree below. Many of the languages of Europe, the Middle East and India thus go back to the same source. The exceptions are Finnish and Hungarian, which are related only to each other, and Basque, which seems unrelated to anything else.

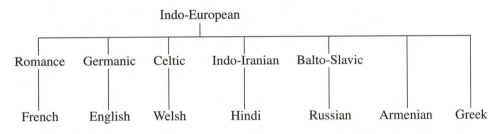

The place where Indo-European was originally spoken is uncertain. One source of linguistic evidence is shared words for particular types of flora and fauna. The similarity in words for trees such as 'beech' and 'birch' across languages shows that Indo-European speakers must have lived in an area where these grew. Put together with other ecological clues, this suggests one possible location is south Russia. Indo-European culture can be inferred too from the common vocabulary: the large numbers of words for animals compared to the small number for grains and vegetables suggests, for instance, that they were hunter-nomads. But the meanings of words change in many ways; in Greek, for instance, 'beech' and 'oak' have the same name. It is not clear that this argument is more than speculation. Ernst Pulgram, for example, shows that the same logic applied to the Romance languages would indicate, if written records of Latin had not survived, that the Romans spent their time 'guzzling beer and smoking cigars in sidewalk cafés', because equivalents to French *bière*, *tabac* and *café* are found in all Romance languages.

The archaeologist Colin Renfrew claims from the archaeological record that agriculture started in Anatolia in Turkey about 6500 BC and spread across Europe, reaching the Orkneys by 3500 BC. The Indo-European language accompanied this spread as the language of the migrating farmers, rather than by conquest, at a rate of 20–30 miles per generation. Renfrew points out that the spread of Polynesian in the Pacific fits this dispersal model even better than Indo-European, since the path from current languages back to the proto-language can be reconstructed more clearly. Yet, as Renfrew himself puts it, 'to say that the first farmers of Europe spoke an early Indo-European language is sheer hypothesis': on the one hand is the historical record of cultural dispersal, on the other the reconstructed tree of Indo-European, but there is no way of showing these are the same.

A second large group of languages is the Altaic family, which stretches from Turkish to Mongol to Japanese. Africa has many language families, such as Niger Congo, which includes Swahili and Zulu. In North Africa, the Semitic family includes Arabic, Hebrew and Berber. A major group in the Pacific is the Austronesian family, which includes Maori and Tongan. In recent decades there have been controversial attempts to reduce the indigenous languages of America into three large families: Amerind in the south, Na-Dene in Alaska and American south-west, including Navaho and Apache, and Eskimo-Aleut in the north. In Australia, the 500 or so known Aboriginal languages have so far defied attempts to fit them into families.

The development of Latin into the Romance languages is easy to follow, because written documents illustrate each period. Often, however, the earlier forms of the language have to be discovered by comparing existing languages and working back to the form from which they come, as in the case of Indo-European. The Polynesian family of languages are closely related to each other, but there are no records of the original source. So it is necessary to work out the properties of the original 'proto-language'. For example, the word for 'forbidden' is /kapu/ in Hawaiian, /tapu/ in Tongan, Samoan and Raratongan, spoken in the Cook Islands, coming into English via New Zealand Maori as *taboo*. By deduction the proto-language had a single word for 'forbidden', from which the modern words are descended with a /t/ in some languages, a /k/ in others. Putting together a range of vocabulary across the Polynesian languages helps to reconstruct the hypothetical proto-language.

The changes in the Polynesian languages reflect the migration of people around the Pacific. They are an example of language change following displacement of speakers from one place to another. One group remains in a particular island or territory and preserves the older form of the language. Another group may emigrate and change the language to meet new circumstances. Though visible in retrospect, these processes are still unpredictable: in South Africa, Dutch changed sufficiently to become a new language, Afrikaans, but in the same circumstances English only acquired a different accent and some new vocabulary.

II Changes in English noun inflections

The grammatical system is just as likely to change as the sound system. The topic of grammatical inflections has come up time and again in these pages in contexts as diverse as children's language and adult aphasia. This section concentrates on the changes that have taken place in English noun inflections over the past 1000 years, and shows how present-day anomalies often have historical explanations.

As we saw in Chapter 2, case is the system for inflecting nouns to show their grammatical function in the sentence, such as the Subject or Object. Putting pronouns to one side, modern English nouns have only two case inflections in the spoken language apart from the base form: one is the possessive *'s* morpheme in *dog's*, the other the plural *-s* morpheme in *dogs*. Old English, spoken from around 700 to 1100 AD, however, had a complex system of cases, in many ways closer to the systems in Latin or German than to current English.

An Old English noun had, then, several case forms. The singular forms of the noun *scip* ('ship') were *scip* in the nominative (subject) case, *scipes* in the genitive (possessive) and *scipe* in the dative (indirect object). In addition there were forms for the cases in the plural: *scipu* (nominative), *scipa* (genitive) and *scipum* (dative).

	Singular	Plural
Nominative	*scip*	*scipu*
Genitive	*scipes*	*scipa*
Dative	*scipe*	*scipum*

Forms of the Old English noun *scip*

Let us keep to the nominative case to simplify matters. The form of the plural morpheme in Old English varied for different groups of nouns, spelled out in the diagram on page 230 overleaf. An *-n* plural inflection occurred with nouns ending in *-a*, such as *guma* ('man', the ancestor of *groom* in *bridegroom* and related to Latin *homo* 'man'), yielding *guman*. A *-u* plural inflection occurred with neuter nouns such as *scip* ('ship'), yielding *scipu*. Some feminine nouns such as *andswaru* ('answer') had an *-a* plural inflection, *andswara*; others, such as *cwen* ('woman'), had *-e*, *cwene*. The main form for masculine nouns was *-as*, so that the plural of *cyning* ('king') was *cyningas*.

Other less common variants are spelled out on the pages of Old English grammars. One group consisted of nouns that changed their vowels to show plural, *fot* ('foot') versus *fet* ('feet'), *gos* ('goose') versus *ges* ('geese'), and *toð* ('tooth') versus *teð* (teeth). Another group made no difference between singular and plural, for example *stede* ('place', e.g. *Hampstead*), *swin* ('swine'), and *ealu* ('ale'). There were thus alternatives for the plural inflection, as well as the regular forms, depending partly on the gender of the noun, partly on its pronunciation. These forms, of necessity, come from written records, not from the spoken language. The pronunciation of Old English in the tenth century reduced unstressed final vowels to /ə/, so that *scipu*, *andswara* and *cwene* might all have been pronounced with the same final vowel. The written language was making distinctions that were already dying in the spoken language, just as verbs in modern French have five forms in the present tense in writing but only three in speaking.

By the Middle English period (1100–1500 AD), most of the case forms of nouns had been eliminated. The plural inflections were affected by the tendency for final vowels to become /ə/, spelled as *-e*, one reason for its frequency as the last letter of English words. The inflections *-e*, *-u*, and *-a* became *-e* or ceased to exist; *scipu* ('ships'), for instance, became *schippe*. The plural inflections in *-an* and other nasals became *-en*, as in *eyen*.

The main exception to the vanishing plural inflections was the *-s* inflection on nouns like *stanas* ('stone'), which was neither a vowel nor a nasal; *stan* was still different from *stanes* in Middle English. The plural *-s* could be used for nouns that had never had it before in the nominative plural. So *quen* (now meaning 'queen' and with a spelling change from *cw-* to *qu-* imitating French) added an *-s* inflection in the plural

Changes in the plural inflection of English nouns

(Minor groups are linked with broken arrows and circles; individual words may have circuitous routes and idiosyncratic spellings.)

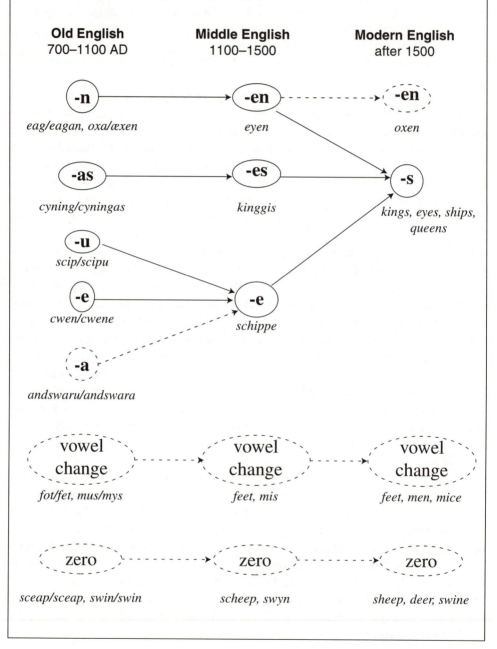

Old English
700–1100 AD

Middle English
1100–1500

Modern English
after 1500

-n
eag/eagan, oxa/œxen

-en
eyen

-en
oxen

-as
cyning/cyningas

-es
kinggis

-s
kings, eyes, ships, queens

-u
scip/scipu

-e
cwen/cwene

-e
schippe

-a
andswaru/andswara

vowel change
fot/fet, mus/mys

vowel change
feet, mis

vowel change
feet, men, mice

zero
sceap/sceap, swin/swin

zero
scheep, swyn

zero
sheep, deer, swine

quens; *schip* ('ship') had plural *schips* or *schippes*. Both of these had had -*s* endings in the genitive case in Old English, so the combination was not in itself novel.

Many plurals with vowel change also acquired this new plural -*s* ending. The plural of *boc* ('book') was *bec* in Old English, made by vowel change. It would have come down as *beech* (compare *geese* from old English plural *ges*) if the new -*s* ending had not yielded *books*. The -*s* ending then became the dominant way of showing the plural, though the -*en* form was still active. A side-effect was that words that coincidentally ended in -*s* were sometimes treated as if the -*s* were a plural ending. People felt that the singular form *pease* must 'really' be plural despite having a plural -*en* form, *peasen*, so they created a new singular word *pea*, with *peas* for its plural. The same process applied to making new singulars such as *cherie* ('cherry') from old singular *chirise*, and *riddel* ('riddle') from *ridels*.

The -*en* ending also started to be used with nouns that had formerly had other endings. For example, Middle English *deouel* ('devil') had a new -*en* plural, *deoulen*, where in Old English it had had -*as*, *deoflas*, as did *sho* ('shoe') with *shoon* and *sunu* ('son') with *sunnen*, formerly *suna*. A more complex example is *child*, which had the -*ru* plural *cildru* in Old English, but acquired the -*en* ending in Middle English to become the modern *children*. Many of the nouns that acquired -*en* later switched to -*s*, as in *devils*, *shoes* and *sons*, though not *children*.

Since Middle English, the language has maintained the difference between the singular and plural, *dog/dogs*, and between the nominative and genitive, *dog/dog's*. The written language has added the convention of the apostrophe *'s* to distinguish the possessive case from the plural, *dogs* versus *dog's*, even extended by Lowth in 1762 to *hers* and *ours*; the perennial spelling mistake of possessive *it's* follows this rationale. English has also lost the inflected forms of adjectives (with the exception of -*er*, *bigger*, and -*est*, *biggest*) and most of the different case and gender forms of the determiners, leaving just *the* and *a/an*. Rather than wearing its heart on its sleeve by indicating grammatical relationships through inflectional endings, English now displays few of these overt signals.

Nevertheless most linguists see these case relationships as still present beneath the surface of the sentence. The grammatical cases are important to English and to other languages at a deep level of the grammar. Old English had already largely lost the difference between nominative and accusative for nouns; Middle English made the loss complete, apart from the pronouns *he/him*, etc. Yet it is still useful to be able to talk about the nominative case for grammatical subjects and the accusitive for grammatical objects even if their sole appearance in English is in pronouns such as *they* and *them*. This enables all languages to be described within the same framework of Universal Grammar, so that the real differences between English and Latin or between Old English and modern English can be stated.

Each period of English, then, has a system of number for nouns, with preferred regular forms and less common irregular forms. The actual forms are different at each period; a regular form from Middle English, -*en*, may be an irregular form in modern English. But the number system goes on.

Survivals from Old English

Plural nouns. Irregular plural forms in modern English are often derived from Old English case forms, though some went through intervening changes: *geese, teeth, mice, children, oxen, sheep, men, brethren*. Rural dialects in England have even more survivals, according to the Survey of English Dialects: *childer* (Lancashire, Yorkshire, etc.); *eyen, shoon* (Northumberland, Cumberland), *kine* (Cumberland, Yorkshire).

Adjectives. The loss of inflectional endings has left a few adjectives with alternative endings for comparison: *good better best* (Old English *god betra betst*); *worse, worst*.

Past tenses. A class of 'strong' verbs in Old English made the past tense by vowel change, some of which have survived: *drove, rode; cleft; drank, ran; gave, sat; woke, swore; fell, blew*.

Vocabulary pairs. The same word in Old English sometimes had different forms because of the way the different case-endings interacted with sound changes, yielding two words that gradually acquired separate meanings: *fox/vixen, golden/gild*.

Grammar. *The more the merrier* comes from a comparative Old English sentence type 'by the more so the merrier' in which one thing was compared to another by dative forms of the article *þe*.

Spelling. The letter þ for the 'th' sound has become misinterpreted as 'y' and survives in: *Ye Olde Green Dragon* (see Chapter 6). The *gh* spelling comes down inter alia from the velar fricative /x/ in Old English and has left many words in which it is effectively silent, except in initial position, as seen in Chapter 6: *tight, weigh, caught*.

III Reasons for change

But *why* do languages change? Each period of a language has an adequate system of its own, apparently sufficient to its needs. So why should Latin turn into French, English lose most of its inflections, Hawaiian change /k/ into /t/? Some main causes of change are external to the language itself – the politics of empire, the spread of migration, and the consequent contacts between speakers of different languages and the fragmentation of one language through isolation in far-flung areas. Some reasons are based on properties of the language system itself, for example the theory that sounds form natural patterns in the vowel space and move to fill empty positions, or the idea that certain sounds are more difficult to say and hence susceptible to change if they ever arise in a language for some other reason. Two major sources of change are contact with other languages, which will be dealt with in this section, and pressures from within, which will be described in the next.

Some causes of language change are global events involving communities of language speakers taking over new places, moving into new countries or areas, and so on, as we saw with Polynesian. The vocabulary of the English language quickly betrays the other countries and languages that English people have had contact with over the past 2000 years, sometimes via intermediaries such as Latin and French. Languages that have been involved include:

- Latin, as in town names derived from Latin *castra* ('camp') such as *Doncaster, Chester, Leicester,* or *Colchester.*
- French, as in the names for cooked meat, *mutton, beef, veal.*
- Indian languages such as Urdu *pajamas* and Hindi *bungalow.*
- Native American languages, as in *moose, toboggan.*
- Aboriginal Australian, as in *kangaroo, boomerang.*
- Arabic, often recognizable from the initial *al* from the Arabic definite article, *alcohol, algebra, alkali.*
- Persian, as in *paradise, khaki.*

Modern contacts can be seen through such food names as *pasta, chapati, sushi* and *baguette.* The diversity of the sources from which English took vocabulary has led to considerable problems for the English spelling system as it tried to assimilate these words, as the words above bear witness, for example *khaki* and *alkali.*

Contacts between languages: pidgins and creoles

Contact with another language has already been implicit in the development of Old English into Middle English. The Norman French who conquered England in 1066 naturally used their own language for the business of the occupying power. Hence the strong French influence on English legal terms; *justice, jury, gaol* came from French, even if equivalent Old English forms already existed. The aristocracy of the royal court also used French: the motto on the UK royal family crest is still the Norman French *Honi soit qui mal y pense* ('Evil to him who evil thinks'). Though the record of written English is largely interrupted for two centuries, except for some religious works, the spoken language was clearly in active use in everyday life and formed the basis for working-class life; *Lewede men cune Ffrensch non* ('Common men know no French'), said one thirteenth-century commentator.

Large numbers of new words came in from French and Latin, ranging from terms for administration such as *government, subject* and *traitor* to terms for cookery such as *mackerel, sugar* and *grape.* Chaucer alone has sometimes been credited with introducing over 1000 words into English, partly reflecting simply that they are recorded for the first time in his extensive works. More recent history provides many examples of contact situations between two languages. In one scenario the speakers of the two languages concerned start by creating a 'pidgin' language that they can use with each other. Then their children start speaking this language as their own first language and it becomes a 'creole'. Though these definitions are controversial, a pidgin is usually taken to be a language used for contact purposes between two groups, for example plantation slaves and masters, or local inhabitants and traders, and a creole is taken to be a language used for a full range of language functions. A well-known modern example is Tok Pisin, which started as a lingua franca used by the inhabitants of Papua New Guinea to communicate across their many language divisions, i.e. a pidgin, but is now a recognized language with 10000 speakers, i.e. a creole.

Pidgins have a particular set of characteristics, which can be illustrated from Tok Pisin:

- a lack of variation in word order. Most pidgins have a constant Subject–verb–Object order: *Mi tokim olsem* ('I said this to them') and *Mi tok gutnait* ('I said goodnight').
- a minimal pronoun system without gender or case: *Em i go long market* means 'he, she, or it is going to market' and *Mama bilong mi lukim em* means 'My mother sees him/her/it'.
- a lack of grammatical inflections, such as genitive 's: *John's house* is expressed as a phrase, *Haus bilong John*, with the grammatical word *bilong,* rather than through an inflection.

A pidgin is a minimal language, consisting of only those features needed for dealing with speakers of another language, in a sense a glorified phrase-book for traders. The rest of the speakers' lives takes place through their first languages.

Chapter 4 described how people adapted the syllable structure of other languages to fit their own. Pidgins and creoles often rejig syllables from their contact languages into a Consonant–Vowel (CV) format. Thus Hawaiian Creole turns *volcano* into *wolokeiono* to avoid the CC cluster /lk/. Sranan, an English-based creole spoken in Surinam, turns monosyllabic *thief* into *tifi* by making the final /f/ into a syllable of its own /fi/. Guyanese Creole turns *America* into *merika* to avoid the VC first syllable /æm/.

Some of the common elements in pidgins must reflect the features of the two languages involved. Many pidgins and creoles have arisen in colonial situations where one of the languages is that of an imperialist power. Spanish forms one component of pidgins and creoles spoken in Latin America (Venezuelan Pidgin Spanish) and in the Philippines. French is involved in pidgins and creoles in the Caribbean (Haitian Creole), in Africa (Ivory Coast Pidgin) and even allegedly in Iceland (due to the presence of French fishermen!). English took part in pidgins and creoles in Hawaii, Jamaica, West Africa (Cameroon Pidgin English) and New Zealand (Maori Pidgin English).

It is hard to decide whether the features of pidgins arise from universal processes or are due to the specific features of this small set of colonial languages, which are chiefly from the Germanic or Romance groups of Indo-European languages. Sometimes other languages may be buried beneath the surface. Caribbean creoles such as Sranan are claimed to have features not only from African languages but also from Sabir, a Portuguese-based pidgin spoken in Africa, from which such widespread pidgin terms as *savvy* derive.

Pidgins do, however, arise naturally all the time. One that has recently come to light is an Italian-based pidgin used by Spanish immigrant workers in German-speaking areas of Switzerland. This situation is due to Italian speakers traditionally being a source of migrant labour in Switzerland and so influencing the new Spanish workers. The combination creates words with Spanish bases but Italian inflections, such as *serebbe* ('be'), or vice versa with Italian bases but Spanish inflections, as in *amicos* ('friends'). Pidgins are transient by nature, since they are temporary solutions to contact between two languages, and so may die when contact is lost, or when the speakers start using it as their main language. Tok Pisin has, however, lasted as a pidgin all of 80 years.

A creole is created when the children of pidgin speakers start learning it as their first language. To become a creole, a pidgin needs to acquire native speakers who use it for all their language needs rather than just for trading. Hence a creole requires the resources of a full language in terms of grammar, vocabulary and pronunciation. The characteristics of creoles show their recent emergence from pidgins. One such feature is the forms of the verb. Rather than having grammatical inflections like third person *-s*, *he smokes*, or past tense *-ed*, *he smoked*, creoles use verbal markers that come in front of the verb, that is to say, separate grammatical words rather than bound inflections.

Hawaiian Creole, for example, uses three such markers: *bin*, equivalent to past tense *-ed*: *A bin go si Toni* ('I went to see Tony'); *stei,* equivalent to the English continuous tense formed with *be* and *-ing*: *Wail wi stei padl, jæn stei put wata insai da kanu* ('While we *were* paddl*ing*, John *was* lett*ing* water into the canoe'); and *go*, which functions as the equivalent of English future tense *He go telifon* ('He will phone'). While Tok Pisin has been used as an example of a pidgin, it is in fact acquiring young native speakers and going through the types of changes necessary to become a creole, taking in verbal markers such as *bin* for past tense: *Mi bin go long taun* ('I went to town') and *bai* for future: *Bai me go long taun* ('I will go to town').

The study of creoles has more profound implications for human language. Derek Bickerton has suggested that creoles provide a unique insight into how language is built into the human mind. Children hear their parents using pidgins that lack some of the usual features of human language. From these minimal languages, they invent for themselves creoles with verbal markers like *stei*, and with the other creole characteristics. First-generation creole children have to invent these forms for themselves, that is to say, draw on the built-in properties of the human mind rather than on the properties of the language input provided by their parents. Other children do not in general need to invent new elements, since the sentences they hear come from fully-fledged languages.

Bickerton has then proposed a language 'bioprogram' to act as the default for all human children. Most children hear full languages from their parents and do not need to use the bioprogram. When children hear only a pidgin, however, they have to fall back on the innate bioprogram. This core of human language is only needed during the brief and comparatively rare situation when the child has to learn a language from the limited resources of a pidgin. Both the bioprogram and the Universal Grammar theories claim that language acquisition depends on built-in properties of the mind. The Universal Grammar theory, however, believes that all children acquire languages in this way, the bioprogram theory that only a small minority do so.

While it is obvious that languages change when they come into contact with each other, there is still no agreed explanation for the origin of pidgins and creoles. Some see them as psychological in origin, representing a common solution to the problem of communicating with someone who does not command the same language: indeed, they have sometimes been compared to the babytalk and pet-talk described in Chapter 7. Others see creoles as combinations of particular languages, with their common features derived from the underlying languages rather than universal processes. Still others insist that they represent the innermost part of the language faculty in the human mind, only activated when the child needs to create a language from the impoverished input of a pidgin.

IV Change from within the language

An everyday contact situation is between two dialects of the same language. This too involves language change, whether temporary change by individual speakers or long-term change by whole groups. Speakers of two dialects often adapt to each other in conversation, known technically as 'accommodation'. English people living in the United States soon start using US /æ/ in words such as *dance* rather than British /ɑː/, and US tongue tap [d] in the middle of words such as *bitter* rather than British [t]. Yet they do not start using /r/ in the US rhotic fashion or changing British /ɒ/ in *got* to US /ɑ/. They accommodate to the English around them in fairly consistent ways, making some changes, rejecting others.

At one time it was thought that historical change in language could not be observed in action, since the time-scale was so vast that changes would not be apparent to the contemporary observer. Now, however, methods have been devised that make it possible to study language change by repeating observations over a period of time, as is done with children's development of language. Compare English speakers from 1960 with those from 1990 and perhaps the changes will be visible.

When a mixture of speakers of particular dialects are found in one place, the phenomenon of dialect-levelling occurs. In the first half of the twentieth century the new town of Høyanger in Norway brought together local speakers of rural dialect with incomers who spoke other dialects. By the third generation the speakers started to speak a unified form that is a distinct Høyanger dialect of its own. Similarly, the new town of Milton Keynes

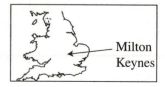

was founded in 1969 56 miles north of London, with a mixture of speakers from all over England. The majority of younger speakers there have now adopted some features of the general south-east, such as the use of glottal stop /ʔ/ for /t/ in *bitter*. They have passed over the local English in favour of the dialect of the majority of the first-comers, with children particularly in the van.

In 1962 William Labov established that social classes in New York differed in how many /r/s they used in words like *fourth* and *floor*, as outlined in Chapter 8. One of his techniques was to ask shop assistants in different stores for a department on the fourth floor. He found that shop assistants in upper-status stores like Saks used more /r/s than those in lower-status stores like S. Klein. In 1986 Joy Fowler went back to the New York stores to see what changes had taken place over 24 years. One change was that, though Saks and Macy's still existed, S. Klein had gone out of business, and had to be replaced with May's. The differences between 1962 and 1986 were that the proportion of /r/s had gone up in all the stores, as seen in Figure 10.1.

In other words, though there were still differences between social classes, New Yorkers at all levels now use more /r/s than they used to. New York pronunciation of /r/ is moving towards that of the higher-status group, as reflected in the differences for the age of the speaker. In 1962 younger speakers at Saks used 80 per cent /r/s, older speakers 50 per cent; in 1986 the comparable proportions were 90 per cent versus 60 per cent. So the younger speakers have the highest proportion of /r/ at both times; each new generation is using more /r/s. Looked at another way, the 20-year-olds are now 40-year-olds. In the intervening years their pronunciation has changed slightly, the number of /r/s rising by some 10 per cent at Saks and Macy's. The speakers themselves are not changing to any great extent: it is the characteristics of a particular age of speaker that is changing.

Internal language change does not come out of nowhere, but reflects the increasing importance of a pattern already existing within the community of speakers. Like the theory of natural selection, language change affects things that already exist rather than itself bringing new things into being. The increase in /r/s in New York is not the

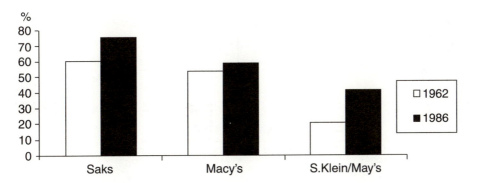

Fig. 10.1 Percentage of /r/s supplied by shop assistants in three New York department stores in 1962 and 1986

imposition of a new form from outside or a spontaneous mutation, but the gradual expansion of a form that already exists.

A further study into change over time was carried out by Peter Trudgill on Norwich speech. In 1968 he had looked at the pronunciation of the /e/ vowel preceding /l/ in words like *well*. A characteristic of Norwich speech is the use of the /ʌ/ sound of RP *cut* /kʌt/ in /el/ words rather than RP /e/, i.e. pronouncing *hell* as /hʌl/, the same as RP *hull*, particularly in spontaneous informal speech. Figure 10.2 shows how this varies with age for the people tested in 1968; the scores are based on a method in which the highest score is the furthest away from the standard accent. The younger the person the more /ʌ/ sounds they produce; hence in 1968 it appeared to be a sound change in progress. In terms of style, casual speech also has more /ʌ/s than formal speech, that is to say reading words aloud. The prediction is that /ʌ/ would become even more frequent in the future, so that by 1983 /ʌ/ should have taken over completely in the speech of young people.

However the results in Figure 10.2 show this was not quite the case. In casual speech, there was no real change between the young people of 1968 and those of 1983. Only in formal speech was there an increase in the frequency of /ʌ/. Trudgill argued that the change has effectively reached its peak. Other styles are simply catching up with casual speech.

Change may also grow out of differences within the speech of one person, that is to say, the different styles people employ in the various activities of their lives. A feature found chiefly in one style may spread to others. To go back to New York /r/s, Chapter 8 showed that these vary according to the formality of the style being used: /r/s are used more often in formal tasks such as reading words aloud than in informal tasks such as conversation. So change can mean moving features of language from one style to another, as in the case of Norwich /ʌ/.

The concept of style-shifting in the same speaker has been used in language teaching. Japanese learners have difficulty in differentiating the voiced /z/ and unvoiced /s/

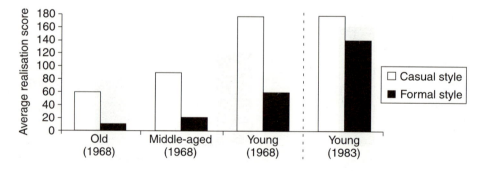

Fig. 10.2 Pronunciation of /e/ as /ʌ/ in *tell* by Norwich speakers of different ages in different periods

sounds of English, pronouncing *Sue* as /zu:/ not /su:/, and *noise* as /nɔɪs/ rather than /nɔɪz/. This problem occurs least in the formal task of word-reading, most in free speech. The more formal the task the closer their pronunciation is to English. First they achieve the right pronunciation in the formal style and then move it across to their other styles. Language students do not need to despair if their classroom performance is way ahead of their performance in the world outside. They are following a natural sequence of extending the features from their formal style across to their informal style.

The great vowel shift in English

The classic example of systematic internal change is the major change between Middle English and Elizabethan English known as the 'Great Vowel Shift'. This affected, not just a single vowel, but every long vowel in the language. Let us start with the changes to back vowels (see Figure 10.3). The Middle English /ɔ:/ phoneme in words like *goat* /gɔ:t/ (rhyming with modern English *caught*) became /o:/ by Elizabethan times, and later changed into the modern diphthong /əʊ/ of /gəʊt/. In terms of the vowel space, the back vowel /ɔ:/ moved higher to occupy the position of /o:/, as seen below. In addition the sound /o:/ in words such as *root* /ro:t/ also changed into /u:/, yielding the modern pronunciation /ru:t/.

So the direction of movement for both these back vowels was upwards. As one vowel shifts its position to get a new pronunciation, the vowel in the new position moves on to another position, and so on in a knock-on process affecting a whole chain of vowels.

However, this process of raising could not easily apply to the original /u:/, which was already at the highest position. Instead /u:/ underwent 'diphthongization' into the moving diphthong /aʊ/, heard in modern English *house* /haʊs/, shown by the dotted arrow. The cumulative changes are like a chain where each link is connected to the next.

A similar process took place with the long front vowels of Middle English (see Figure 10.4). The /a:/ vowel in *name* moved up to become /ɛ:/, later changing to the

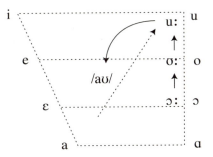

Fig. 10.3 The Great Vowel Shift (back vowels)

modern diphthong /eɪ/, other examples being *make*, *tale* and *baby*. The front /ɛ:/ vowel in *clean* moved up to become /e:/, later changing to modern /i:/, as in /kli:n/. The /e:/ vowel in *meed* also moved higher to /i:/, other examples being *seed*, and *field*. The /i:/ in *wine* /wi:n/ again could not go further upwards and became a diphthong /aɪ/, as in the modern English /waɪn/.

In both cases chains of vowels follow each other round the vowel space, displacing and replacing each other. Rather than appearing from nowhere or disappearing altogether, each phoneme moves into the place occupied by another. It is hard to say how such chains start moving. In general there seems a need for vowels to keep far enough apart to be distinguishable: they have to keep their distance. So a chain might start by 'dragging': the /i:/ starts the cycle by becoming a diphthong and drags the other sounds behind it to fill the empty space. Or the impetus might be 'pushing': one sound encroaches on the space of another and pushes it out.

Whichever the cause, there is a drastic shift between Middle English and Early Modern English, which affects a large proportion of modern words. The changes since the Great Vowel Shift have been comparatively minor compared to this upheaval. Unfortunately, much of the spelling system was established before this historical watershed. One of the chief reasons for the English writing system not being fully alphabetic, as described in Chapter 6, is indeed the Great Vowel Shift.

William Labov has recently provided principles for language change that account for the Great Vowel Shift and the changes in Norwich among many others. One is that 'In chain shifts, long vowels rise'. This principle accounts for the main upwards direction of the Great Vowel Shift for both front and back vowels. A second principle is 'In chain shifts, short vowels fall'. An example from English might be the change from /u/ to /ʌ/ in words such as *cup*, which is a lowering rather than a raising movement. Labov goes on to reduce the principles of chains to a single overriding principle that peripheral vowels rise and central vowels fall. However, this summary distorts Labov's views as peripheral and central vowels are defined in terms of sound frequencies rather than the dimensions of the mouth, a theory it is not possible to take further here.

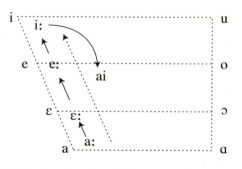

Fig. 10.4 The Great Vowel Shift (front vowels)

While the reasons for change from outside seem obvious, the reasons for change from within are more debatable. Chapter 8 described two opposing tendencies in language. One is the upward push towards prestige upper-class forms. Consequently New Yorkers over the years gradually use more /r/s. Change comes from above as lower-status people imitate those of higher status. A contrary source of change is the solidarity effect seen, for example in the downwards pull towards the working class. Sounding like a member of a particular group may give a prestige of its own. Pop groups dress and sound alike, as do media presenters, financial advisers, public schoolboys and civil servants. A group that is socially cohesive adopts its own language partly for its own defensive needs, partly to proclaim its own unique differences, as any new teenage subculture illustrates, in literature most famously in Anthony Burgess's *A Clockwork Orange*, where the teenagers call people *droogs*, *chellovecks* and *ptitsas*.

Internal language changes seem partly to be motivated by the relationships between groups in society. Large-scale changes such as the Great Vowel Shift are more difficult to explain in this way, and seem more a question of the regulatory 'pushes' and 'pulls' within the pattern of vowels in a language.

V Language in decline?

Change in language has always been an emotive subject. When was English at its best, for example? In the post-medieval period, when English was competing with Latin for status, many thought it was incapable of expressing serious ideas. A translator in 1560 complained: 'our grosse tongue is a crude and a barren tong, when it is compared with so florishinge and plentifull a tongue [as Greek]'. Arthur Golding in 1587 apologized for infelicities on account of 'the rarenesse and profoundnesse of the matters there handled, not accustomed heretofore to be treated of in our language'. However, English people were soon complaining that English was getting worse. Alexander Gil in 1620 appealed to his countrymen: 'O you English . . . retain, retain, what hitherto remains of your native tongue and follow in the footprints of your ancestors.' Dr Johnson in 1755 claimed: 'From the authours which rose in the time of Elizabeth, a speech might be formed adequate to all the purposes of use and eloquence.'

So, according to people in 1560, English is defective; according to those in 1620, English is a poor shadow of what went before; according to those in 1755, the language was at its prime in the Elizabethan era. The Golden Age of any language is always somewhere in the past. In German, according to Jacob Grimm in the mid-nineteenth century, 'six hundred years ago every rustic knew, that is to say practised daily, perfections and niceties in the German language of which the best grammarians nowadays do not even dream'. In Papua New Guinea today, students regret they cannot speak their native language as well as their parents.

It is a universal feeling that language is changing for the worse. For all our progress in science and standard of living, the people of today feel they are unable to use language as well as their ancestors. However, the only aspect of the language that is known to us directly about earlier periods is the formal written language, spoken language mostly being filtered through the dialogue of plays, at least until the invention of sound recording. The comparison between older *written* language and current *spoken* language is unlikely to succeed. Hence the present-day view of past periods of a language may be as biased as that of a future historian looking at present-day language from such surviving artefacts as a copy of *The Times* and a cornflakes packet, or Dr Johnson looking at Elizabethan English through Shakespeare's plays.

It is not clear how the present state of English could be objectively measured as worse than previous states. Such criticisms are not usually directed at the types of change described in this chapter: no one writes letters to the newspaper deploring the Great Vowel Shift or requiring people to use *shoon* or *foon* rather than *shoes* or *foes* because Shakespeare did. Mostly the discussion concerns the behaviour of a small number of words, *con<u>tro</u>versy* versus <u>*controversy*</u>, or *hopefully*, or certain areas of traditional English grammar such as avoiding split infinitives, *to boldly go*, or prepositions ending sentences. Often the criticism is aimed at the pronunciation of groups that are breaking in to the mainstream, for instance the change from /t/ to glottal stop /ʔ/ found in Estuary English.

Most commonly the charge refers to a decline in certain aspects of spelling. To quote Prince Charles, 'All the letters sent from my office I have to correct myself, and that is because English is taught so bloody badly', in itself a sentence many teachers would criticize on other grounds than spelling. As described in Chapters 6 and 9, English spelling is a complex system of alphabetic, logographic and orthographic principles. Like Chinese, it has attained a particular fixed form that is only indirectly related to changing pronunciation. This may create tensions for amateur writers, if not for professionals with their spelling checkers. A Gallup Poll in 1992 showed that 73 per cent of people spelled *accommodation* wrong – indeed, I have just used my spelling checker to make certain I am not among them. But whether this is a decline from previous generations is unclear without concrete evidence that they were actually better on some scale that can be measured. In practical terms, the solution is for Prince Charles to buy his staff word processors.

As we saw in Chapter 8, non-standard spelling does not so much interfere with people's comprehension of written English as tell them about the writer's social or educational status. Spelling, like many aspects of language, easily gets tied up with social issues. For example, Chapter 8 showed how apostrophes are used to create an image of a blunt lower-class man, e.g. *'is* for *his*, and *fightin'* for *fighting*. The social importance of spelling needs to be taken into account in education, as children have to learn to live with the language attitudes and beliefs of the society to which they belong.

A more objective measure of the decline of English might be in terms of effectiveness. Perhaps current writing in English is less able to convey nuances of meaning than it once was, Martin Amis writes less well than Kingsley Amis, Joanna Trollope

Three parliamentary speeches

These speeches were all made by MPs in the UK House of Commons in times of crisis, as recorded in Hansard. Try to put them in order of effectiveness. One name is changed to prevent too easy recognition.

A Today we were assisted by the Prime Minister at Question Time telling us that to end the war Lilliput must obey all United Nations resolutions immediately. He used the word 'immediately' and I shall examine his use of that word in a moment. When I made my notes, I assumed that only the public would be led to believe that the United Nations has further imperative demands on top of resolution 660 which must be met before the guns fall silent. Now, listening to Conservative Members, it appears that they have joined what I perceive to be the public position. The public has been led to believe that and so have they. If that is the position being put forward by the Government, it is not an honest summation of the 12 resolutions passed by the United Nations Security Council.

B In the history of nations, there is no example of such frivolity. When I have looked at this chronicle of events during the last few days, with every desire in the world to understand, I have just not been able to understand, and do not yet understand, the mentality of the Government. If the right hon. and learned Gentleman wishes to deny what I have said, I will give him a chance of doing so. If his words remain as they are now, we are telling the nation and the world that, having decided upon the course, we went on with it despite the fact that the objective we had set ourselves had already been achieved, namely the separation of the combatants.

C I say, let pre-war feuds die: let personal quarrels be forgotten, and let us keep our hatreds for the common enemy. Let party interest be ignored, let all our energies be harnessed, let the whole ability and forces of the nation be hurled into the struggle, and let all the strong horses be pulling on the collar. At no time in the last war were we in greater peril than we are now, and I urge the House strongly to deal with these matters not in a precipitate vote, ill-debated and on a widely discursive field, but in grave time and due time in accordance with the dignity of Parliament.

The examples are taken from Hansard's *Proceedings in Parliament*, speakers identified as (A) Mr Sillars on the topic of the Iraq/Kuwait war on 21 Feb. 1991, (B) Mr Bevan discussing the Suez Invasion on 5 Dec. 1956, (C) Mr Churchill on the Second World War on 8 May 1940. Does their order of effectiveness reflect their dates? If so, does this tell us that parliamentary English is declining?

than Anthony Trollope. To test the postulated decline in English properly would mean measuring, say, the effectiveness of a modern political speech compared to those of bygone days. Since contemporary listeners will not react to older speeches as did their original audience, even this measure could not be truly valid. Nevertheless it can be tried on the speeches in the box on page 243.

VI Deliberately affecting language change

So far language change has been portrayed as an inevitable process, a glacier slowly coming down a mountain that can neither be diverted from its path nor held back. Yet people have tried to influence this immense force, whether by stopping it, by changing language deliberately or by choosing which language to speak.

1 Stopping change

Those who believe in the decline of the language think it their duty to prevent it. Thus Dr Johnson's initial aim in writing a dictionary of English eventually published in 1755 was to 'ascertain', i.e. 'make certain', the facts of the English language. Academies to control a language were founded in Italy in 1581 and France in 1635. The French academy still pursues the goal of maintaining the purity of French. Language is too important to be left to itself. Those who know best must be able to tell other people what to do. In England the idea of an academy has never caught on, despite proposals by Dryden and Swift to found a British Academy that would be responsible for English usage. Of the English-speaking countries, only South Africa has seen fit to found 'The English Academy of Southern Africa' in 1961.

2 Forcing change: language and discrimination

Some believe that language should be maintained for its own sake. Others insist that the perpetuation of discrimination in society comes from language. Changing the language so that it is free of discrimination can help to cure discrimination itself. In a sense this is a benign version of Orwell's Thought Control or the Sapir–Whorf hypothesis discussed in Chapter 5. By changing language we can change the world. In Islington in 1995 a social worker was said to be unsuitable for her job because of the prejudice revealed by her use of the expressions *immigrant* and *cultural question*. In language terms this issue harks back to the unresolved debate in Chapter 5 about whether people perceive colours differently if they have different words for colour, that is to say, whether a society speaking a language without a word for 'cruelty' is less cruel than one that does have a word for it, whether a person who says *multi-ethnic* is less prejudiced than one who says *immigrant*.

Most often it is vocabulary that people have tried to change to prevent discrimination. Racially loaded language was countered with a succession of bans on use of

Some dos and don'ts

To illustrate different attitudes among those who want to change people's language, here is a selection of advice offered to native and non-native speakers of English.

Advice to native speakers of English

Another helpful thing, if you are a woman talking to a man, is to ask advice. (Emily Post, 1922)

Many women could learn from men to accept some conflict and difference without seeing it as a threat to intimacy, and many men could learn from women to accept interdependence without seeing it as a threat to their freedom. (Tannen, 1992)

It need hardly be said that shortness is a merit in words . . . particularly so in English where the native words are short and the long words are foreign. (Fowler, 1926)

If it is possible to cut out a word, always cut it out. (Orwell, 1946)

Take great care not to be too free in your use of the verb *to do* in any of its times or modes. (Cobbett, 1819)

When the sound ng . . . occurs twice in succession, as in singing, an n is always used . . . as it prevents a monotonous sound. (Batchelor, 1809)

Use the active voice. The active is usually more direct and vigorous than the passive. (Strunk and White, 1979)

Advice to non-native learners of English

You usually use *much* and *many* in negative sentences and questions. You use *many* with countable nouns. *We haven't got <u>many</u> carrots.* (Greenall, 1994)

The endings of adjectives do not change. *A different place/different places.* (Murphy, 1993)

We can leave out the word *minutes* if the number in front of it is a multiple of 5, but not if it is a number like 18 or 23. (Bald et al., 1986)

It is unusual to put adverbs between the verb and its object . . . *I very much like skiing/I like skiing very much.* (Swan, 1980)

When we want to talk about people in general (not specific people) we can use the GENERAL PRONOUN one: *One should always wait at a zebra crossing.* (Bosewitz, 1987)

Note the generality of the advice to natives, on what are chiefly matters of stylistic choice – many famous writers would fail to meet the requirements to use short sentences or words – compared with the specificity of the advice to non-natives, on what are basic matters of English grammar over which there is very little choice.

terms, *nigger, negro, coloured, immigrant.* However, often the solidarity principle asserts itself and these discriminatory terms become signs of group membership. A group may wear the detested term with pride as a badge of identity, for example the Black rap group, Niggas with Attitude or the Mikey Smith poem 'Nigger Talk'. Similarly, British war veterans are proud to call themselves the 'Old Contemptibles', and the Conservative Party does not mind being known by the name of seventeenth-century Irish bandits, *Tories.*

Gender-loaded vocabulary has also been under fire in English, as discussed in Chapter 2, particularly the use of male nouns or pronouns to include women, as in *chairman, man* (the species), which assumes that males take precedence; and *girls* for *women,* which uses an age-related term. The solidarity principle has again revived some of these terms: a group that protests against male-dominance in art galleries is called 'Gorilla Girls'.

Sometimes grammar has also been involved. To reprise Chapter 2, there has been considerable debate about the use of the pronoun *he* to cover occasions when both sexes are included: *If anyone is offended, he should leave.* People reading a text with *he* do indeed feel that it has more to do with men than with women. Substituting *he or she* or *they* may strike a small blow against discrimination. In this instance the attempt to change the language consciously seems to have had some effect, if one can credit the claim that the frequency of *he* dropped by 75 per cent in written American English during the 1970s. Writers brought up before the 1970s may feel simply that another checklist has been introduced, of the order of 'i before e except after c or before g', rather than affecting the actual meaning; writers brought up since the 1970s may avoid *he* without such conscious thought. If such a small change does have an effect on people's behaviour, then why not make it?

This chapter has shown that it is an illusion that language ever remains the same. Speakers are labelled with the speech of their generation and see that as the norm, not appreciating that the older and younger generations see their language in the same way. Now that it is possible to listen to the speech of bygone periods, it is clear that change has not come to a stop but continues apace. Any 1930s or 1940s film revived on television immediately bears witness that English has not remained static, whether in the pronunciation of dashing heroes or of cheeky Cockney flowersellers, or in vocabulary items such as the meaning of *make love* or *gay.*

Sources and further reading

General sources

An interesting book on change using unusual examples is T. Crowley, *An Introduction to Historical Linguistics* (Oxford: OUP, 1992). Other standard books are: A. McMahon, *Understanding Language Change* (Cambridge: CUP, 1994); J. Aitchison, *Language Change: Progress or Decay?* (Cambridge: CUP, 1991). The original classic on English is A.C. Baugh and T. Cable, *A History of the English Language*, 4th edn (London: Routledge, 1993). B. Strang, *A History of English* (London: Methuen, 1970) would be in the same league if it did not present history in reverse direction, from the present backwards.

Historical development of languages

The history of romance languages and Indo-European is covered in any standard source. An interesting book by an archaeologist, which includes the Pulgram quote, is C. Renfrew, *Archaeology and Language* (Harmondsworth: Penguin, 1987). The Polynesian example comes from Crowley, *An Introduction to Historical Linguistics* (see above).

Changes in English noun inflections

Information about inflections is spread over different sections of books such as Baugh and Cable, *A History of the English Language* and Strang, *A History of English* (see above), and C. Barber, *The English Language: A Historical Introduction* (Cambridge: CUP, 1993).

Reasons for change

The sources for pidgins and creoles are: Aitchison, *Language Change* (see above); S. Romaine, *Bilingualism* (Oxford: Blackwell, 1994); P. Mühlhäusler, *Growth and Structure of the Lexicon of New Guinea Pidgin* (Canberra: Australian National University, 1979). Italian pidgin in Switzerland is described in S. Schmid, 'Learning strategies for closely related languages', in B. Kettemann and W. Wieden (eds.), *Current Issues in European Second Language Acquisition Research* (Tübingen: Gunter Narr, 1993), 405–18. Bickerton's Bioprogram is described in D. Bickerton, *Roots of Language* (Ann Arbor, MI: Karoma, 1981).

Change from within the language

Dialect change, in particular Høyanger and Norwich, is described in P. Trudgill, *Dialects in Contact* (Oxford: Blackwell, 1986). The research in Milton Keynes is described in P. Kerswell, 'Babel in Buckinghamshire? Pre-school children acquiring accent features in the New Town of Milton Keynes', in G. Melchers (ed.), *Proceedings of the Stockholm Conference on Non-standard Varieties of Language* (1991). Labov's major work on historical linguistics which describes Fowler's replication of the stores study is W. Labov, *Principles of Linguistic Change*, I: *Internal Factors* (Oxford: Blackwell, 1995). The replication work on Norwich is described in P. Trudgill, 'Norwich revisited: recent linguistic changes in an English urban dialect', *English World-Wide* 9 (1988): 33–49. Japanese learners of English and style are described in L. Dickerson, 'The learner's language as a system of variable rules', *TESOL Quarterly* 9 (1975): 401–7. The Great Vowel Shift is described in any of the histories of the English language, e.g. Baugh and Cable, *A History of the English Language* (see above).

Language in decline?

A clear book on arguments about value in language is D. Cameron, *Verbal Hygiene* (London: Routledge, 1995). Historical sources in English are R.F. Jones, *The Triumph of the English*

Language (Stanford, CA: Stanford UP, 1953); T. Batchelor, *An Orthoëptical Analysis of the English Language, including an Orthoëptical Analysis of the Dialect of Bedfordshire* (London, 1809); D. Denison, *English Historical Syntax* (Harlow: Longman, 1993); J.B. Greenough and G.L. Kittredge, *Words and Their Ways in English Speech* (Basingstoke: The Macmillan Company, 1900, 1991, first published as a Beacon paperback, 1962).

Some dos and don'ts

Sorces for the quotations are as follows: Emily Post, 1922, cited in Cameron, *Verbal Hygiene* (see above); D. Tannen, *You Just Don't Understand* (London: Virago, 1992); H.W. Fowler, *A Dictionary of Modern English Usage* (Oxford: Clarendon Press, 1926); G. Orwell, 'Politics and the English Language', *Horizon* 76 (1946); W. Cobbett, *A Grammar of the English Language* (1819, reprinted Oxford: OUP, 1984); T. Batchelor, 1809, cited in L. Mugglestone, *'Talking Proper'* (Oxford: Clarendon Press, 1995); W. Strunk and E.B. White, *The Elements of Style* (Boston: Allyn and Bacon, 1979); S. Greenall, *Reward* (Oxford: Heinemann, 1994); R. Murphy, *Basic Grammar in Use* (Cambridge: CUP, 1993); W-D Bald, D. Cobb and A. Schwartz, *Active Grammar* (Harlow: Longman, 1986); M. Swan, *Practical English Usage* (Oxford: OUP, 1980); R. Bosewitz, *Penguin Students' Grammar of English* (Harmondsworth: Penguin, 1987).

11 Universal Grammar

It will have been apparent that the main influence throughout this book is that of Noam Chomsky, the key figure in twentieth-century linguistics. This chapter takes Chomsky's own theory of Universal Grammar (UG) as an example of current thinking about language. A book like this would not have done its job if readers finished it without seeing why the Universal Grammar theory is for many the central pillar in our understanding of language. The discussion that follows mostly uses syntactic terms and categories built up through this book rather than introducing a new, more technical vocabulary. It starts by outlining the principles and parameters theory of Universal Grammar, and then explores some of the issues it raises for the acquisition of language.

The Universal Grammar theory claims that languages are similar because they are all known and learnt by human beings. Language takes a particular form because of the mind that acquires and stores it, just as a computer eventually reduces any information to sequences of binary ons and offs. Language is moulded by the space that it fills in the mind. By separating those things which all languages have in common from those that are peculiar to one language, UG theory can discover the essential properties of human language. The SVO word order of English sentences such as *Stanley Morison designed Times New Roman*, for instance, is not interesting for its own sake but for difference from the SOV and VSO word orders of other languages. Bringing different languages within a single overall framework has brought to light many of the insights reported in this book.

The starting-point for Chomsky is what language actually *is*. Some linguists regard language as the sentences that people actually say, their behaviour – the fact that John Major once said *there was there was no deception there was no deception in what I said at the time of the elections* or that Yeats once wrote *The unpurged images of day recede*. Others say that the essence of language is social interaction between people – how men and women talk or fail to talk to each other and how language reinforces or establishes power relationships between people, by for example using T and V forms of pronouns. Still others say that language is the contents of the *Oxford English Dictionary* or of Fowler's *Modern English Usage* – an outside authority to be obeyed. Chomsky calls these definitions 'E-language' – external language. He rejects this view by claiming that language is knowledge. Yeats's poem or T/V pronouns or the *Oxford Dictionary* presuppose the existence of language in the mind. Grammar books and dictionaries are pale reflections of the reality inside the individual human mind. Linguistics is then closer to psychology than sociology, concerned with the contents of the mind rather than with relationships between people in the world. It is a matter of 'I-language' – internal language.

Universal Grammar can concern several areas of language. A universal view of speech sounds provides a repertoire of categories possible to human languages. The sound features of [± voice] or [± tense] introduced in Chapter 4 occur universally throughout human languages. Even the meanings of words can be reduced in part to what Chomsky calls 'a rich and invariant conceptual system'. UG theory has, however, mostly concentrated on the grammar itself as the crucial 'computational' link between the speech sounds on the one hand and the meanings in the mind on the other.

Though UG is complex, it is intrinsically no more difficult than theories of physics or areas of mathematics taught in school, with the added convenience that its evidence is all around you rather than available only through gigantic experiments with cyclotrons. Many of the ideas of grammar introduced in Chapters 2 and 3 and of language acquisition outlined in Chapter 7 can now be related to this theory. For readers who have followed the discussion in earlier chapters there should not be many new concepts; it is their integration in UG theory that is new here.

I Principles and parameters theory

Since the early 1980s, Chomsky has proposed that knowledge of language consists of universal principles and varying parameters. Principles of UG are universal and apply to all languages, specifying what they have in common at an abstract level. Parameters keep the variation between languages within tight limits. A language may have one value for a parameter or another, but it *must* have one or the other; there are no other possibilities. This section illustrates the best-known principles and parameters, most of which are familiar from earlier chapters.

Let us take the analogy of car-driving. Overall there is a principle that drivers have to keep consistently to one side of the road, which is taken for granted by all drivers in all countries. Exceptions to this principle, such as people driving down motorways on the wrong side, rate stories in the media or car chases in action movies. The principle does not, however, say, *which* side of the road people should drive on. A parameter of driving allows the side to be the left in England and Japan, and the right in the USA and France. The parameter has two values or 'settings' – left and right. Once a country has opted for one side or the other, it sticks to its choice: a change of setting is a massively complex operation, whether it happens for a whole country, as in Sweden, or for the individual travelling from England to France. So a universal principle and a variable parameter together sum up the essence of driving. The principle states the universal requirement on driving; the parameter specifies the variation between different countries. Needless to say, the analogy between language and car-driving should not be taken too far. The driving principle and the value for the parameter are laid down by law while language principles and parameters come from the speaker's own mind rather than an outside authority.

1 Principles and parameters of phrase structure

Phrase structure principles

Chapter 3 showed how a crucial part of grammar is that sentences have structure: they are built up of phrases nested within phrases. So a sentence such as *The cat licked the dish* is, to use a simplified analysis, made up of a Noun Phrase, *the dish*, within a Verb Phrase, *licked the dish*, within a sentence having a further Noun Phrase, *the cat*, as seen in the tree here. This tree illustrates something that at first seems obvious, namely that each phrase has a head of a particular type: a Noun Phrase has a head Noun, whether *cat* or *dish*, a Verb Phrase has a head Verb, *lick*. The same is true of Preposition Phrases such as *in the morning* and Adjective Phrases such as *afraid of the dark*, which have preposition heads and adjective heads respectively.

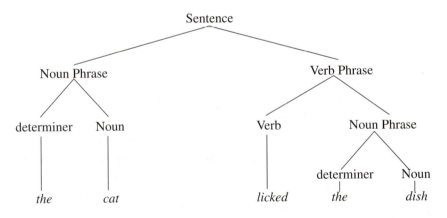

The type of grammatical analysis used not only in UG theory but also in other contemporary linguistic theories is called 'X-bar syntax'. One of its principles is indeed that the head of a phrase must be the same category as the whole phrase, so that a Verb Phrase has a head Verb not a Noun, a Noun Phrase a head Noun not a Verb, and so on. All phrases in all languages must have heads of the same type as the phrase itself. The tree of any phrase takes the shape shown below, where the X stands for the same category in both places, i.e. like an x in algebra, this being the reason for the 'X' part of X-bar syntax. Universal Grammar theory then claims that it is a property of a human language that all its phrases obey the principle that the head of the phrase is the same type of expression as the whole phrase.

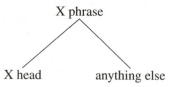

One of Chomsky's major innovations in the 1980s was to propose that the functional phrases, introduced in Chapter 7, had the same structure as lexical phrases and so had heads of the same type; a Determiner Phrase, *the man*, has a head Determiner such as *the*, a Tense Phrase, *licked*, has a head inflection such as *-ed*. The difference from lexical phrases is that heads are not compulsory in functional phrases. The principle has now become so powerful that all phrases in all languages are claimed to obey it.

Languages differ markedly in word order. Chapter 3 described the choice between Verb–Object order and Object–Verb order that distinguishes English from Japanese, French from Arabic, etc. In English the Verb is followed by an object Noun Phrase, *bought a book*. In Japanese the Verb is preceded by the object Noun Phrase, *hon-o katta* ('book bought'). In X-bar syntax this two-way choice is a parameter specifying the position of object Noun Phrases within the Verb Phrase; languages must have Verb Phrases that are either VO or OV order. The two phrases could be shown as:

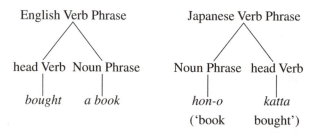

However, UG theory always tries to get the greatest possible mileage out of its parameters: why should this parameter apply only to the Verb Phrase? The word order in the Preposition Phrase also varies between languages like English that have a preposition before the Noun Phrase, *on Tuesday*, and those like Japanese that have a 'postposition' after the Noun Phrase, *kayobi ni* ('Tuesday on').

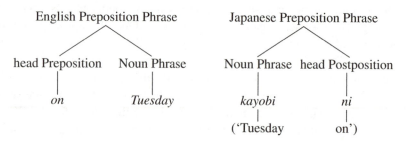

Furthermore, some languages, such as English, have Noun Phrases where the noun precedes a modifying phrase, *the claim that he's right*, others, like Japanese, have Noun Phrases in which the noun follows the modifying phrase, *jibun ga tadashii-to-iu shucho* ('self right claim').

Universal Grammar ascribes all these order variations to a single parameter. The word order differences among these four types of lexical phrase amount to whether the head comes first or last in the phrase. In the Preposition Phrase, English has the head preposition *before* the Noun Phrase, *after midnight*, Japanese has the head postposition *after* the Noun Phrase, *kayobi-ni* ('Tuesday on'). In the Verb Phrase, English has the verb before the object phrase, Japanese the verb after the object noun phrase, and so on. All these phenomena can be brought together into a single statement: either a language has lexical phrases in which the head comes first or it has phrases in which the head comes last.

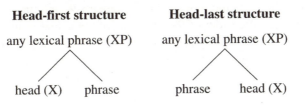

Bringing together these examples from English and Japanese yields the patterns shown below. CP here stands for Complement phrase, here consisting of a clause.

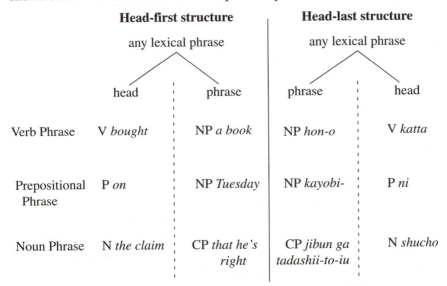

This is called the 'head' parameter because it concerns the location of the head of the phrase in relation to other phrases within it – English is a head-first language, i.e. Verb–Object, prepositions, and all the rest, while Japanese is a head-last language, i.e. Object–Verb, postpositions, etc. Different as English word order may be from Japanese, this only amounts to setting the head parameter one way in English, another way in Japanese.

Much of the phrase structure of language can therefore be reduced to a principle that heads are required and a parameter with two positions in which they can occur. Putting the analysis in this form brings the phrase structure of all languages together within one framework. The description of any single language is no longer isolated but always located within the framework of the whole of human language. Information about English leads to insights into language in general. The principles and parameters theory provides linguists with a powerful tool for investigating any human language.

2 *Principles and parameters of movement*

A central idea in grammar is the movement of elements within the sentence, encountered first in Chapter 3. The order of the elements of the actual sentence the speakers see or hear depends on an underlying order they do not actually hear. Thus the passive sentence *Keith was hit by a mugger* seems to depend on something like *A mugger hit Keith* by moving the noun phrase *a mugger* to the beginning.

> *A mugger hit Keith.*

> *Keith was hit by a mugger.*

The question *Is Greta German?* likewise derives from an underlying form similar to *Greta is German* by moving *is* to the beginning.

> *Greta is German*

> *Is Greta German?*

The structure of actual sentences thus depends on abstract forms in which the elements are not moved. To quote Chomsky, 'objects appear in the sensory output in positions "displaced" from those in which they are interpreted . . . This is an irreducible fact about human language, expressed somehow in every contemporary theory of language, however the facts about displacement may be formulated.'

Several principles of Universal Grammar limit the movement of elements within the sentence. The structure-dependency principle introduced in Chapter 3 claims that moving elements from one place to another depends upon the phrase structure, not upon the linear order of words. So the sentence *Is Sam is the cat that black?* is ruled out because the verb *is* has moved from the 'wrong' position in the structure, i.e. from inside the relative clause, shown by brackets overleaf.

Sam is the cat (that is black).

Is Sam is the cat that black?

A possible question is *Is Sam the cat that is black?* since in this case the *is* moves from the correct position inside the main clause.

Sam is the cat (that is black).

Is Sam the cat that is black?

Every human being knows the principle of structure-dependency, which is not broken in any language. Universal Grammar forces every language to restrict movement within the sentence instead of allowing anything to move anywhere.

Another principle of movement is called 'subjacency'. Questions such as *Is Casablanca hot?* come from underlying forms like *Casablanca is hot* by movement. Questions with wh-words (*who, why, where,* etc.) are also derived by movement. A question like *What will you watch?* comes from an underlying structure *You will watch what*, by moving various parts around (as well as by doing other things to it). The wh-word *what* moves from its position at the end of the sentence to the beginning.

You will watch what?

What will you watch?

More complicated wh-word questions involve the same kind of movement. *Who did Mary think John saw?* is derived from an underlying form similar to *Mary thinks John saw who*.

Mary thinks John saw who?

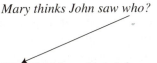

Who did Mary think John saw?

85 per cent of the *Inside Language* panel indeed accepted *Who did Mary think John saw?* (Q9). On this basis, the underlying form in *He wonders whether Sarah will play what?* ought to yield the sentence *What does he wonder whether Sarah will play?* by moving *what* to the beginning of the relative clause. Yet in an experiment 72 per cent of English speakers rejected sentences with this construction.

What is wrong with it? A brief version of the highly technical answer is that *what* has moved too far in the sentence: *what* is not free to go anywhere; it cannot cross over more than one noun phrase or clause boundary.

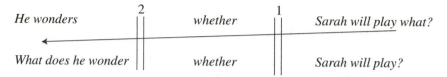

Other languages are restricted in this way as well as English. The general principle called 'subjacency' prevents items in the sentence from moving across more than one boundary. One way of thinking of subjacency is as a set of hurdles in a race; even the best of hurdlers can only manage one at a time.

The subjacency principle has proved an interesting area for researchers, even if the results are often confusing. For example, the ERP researchers found that sentences with subjacency mistakes caused different types of brain activity from sentences involving other issues of movement: they concluded that, once the speaker goes wrong with a subjacency sentence, there is no way out, while other sentence types allow them to recover after a word or two. Subjacency has also fascinated researchers into second-language acquisition: are people capable of acquiring subjacency in a new language? The results are highly controversial: some claim that second language learners never master this aspect of a new language, while others point out that they learn it less efficiently than monolinguals rather than not at all.

These two movement principles of structure-dependency and subjacency do not so much liberate language as confine it within limits. No language may have movement that is structure-independent or that crosses more than one boundary. These tight restrictions are one reason why children can acquire language in a short amount of time. A child does not have to work out all the possible combinations that could log-ically occur in a language – movement of any element anywhere – only those that could be conceived of by the human mind, that is to say restricted by structure-dependency and subjacency. The task is rather like attempting to guess someone's computer password: the infinite possibilities are limited at least by knowing that it uses the Roman alphabet, thus eliminating Japanese characters, Hebrew symbols and other written signs at one fell swoop.

The principle of subjacency nevertheless has a parameter linked to it because it operates differently in some languages. In English it is impossible to say *The task which I didn't know to whom they would entrust* because *which* has moved across too many boundaries, that is to say has broken the principle of subjacency. The equivalent sentence in Italian, *L'incarico che non sapevo a chi avrebbero affidato,* does not breach subjacency. In English the Noun Phrase counts as a boundary for subjacency but in Italian it does not. So the Italian sentence is grammatical because the Noun Phrase that is crossed does not count as a boundary. One parameter of UG is which phrases act as boundaries, whether those in Italian or those in English.

Structure-dependency, subjacency and the principle of heads in phrases are principles of Universal Grammar rather than peculiarities of English or Chinese or any particular language. So they form part of the knowledge of *all* human beings, regardless of which language they know. It is possible to imagine languages that break structure-dependency, or that allow elements to move without restriction, or that have noun phrases with verb heads. But they would not be *human* languages. The language knowledge in a human mind contains these principles, plus a handful of others that have been discovered, whatever the language. This is not to say that the principles and parameters that have been proposed by linguists are perfect and never to be changed. They represent the best guesses at Universal Grammar so far, to be superseded as more evidence comes along and language comes to be understood better, just as Newton's account of the universe stood until a better one arrived.

Indeed, principles and parameters are constantly being revised. In the most recent version of Universal Grammar theory, called the 'Minimalist Programme', Chomsky has proposed principles that are still more powerful and abstract in their effects on language knowledge. The most general is the principle of 'Economy', which ensures that there are no superfluous elements in the grammar so that the links between sound and meaning are as direct as possible, eliminating the elaborate levels of structure of previous theories. A further principle called 'Procrastinate' forces movement to be postponed as late as possible. Both of these principles are beyond the limits of this book, not just because of the levels of technicality involved but also because they are so recent that, like the theory of relativity in the early days, as yet only a handful of people understand their implications.

The knowledge of language in a person's mind consists of unvarying principles and varying parameters. A person who speaks English not only knows structure-dependency, subjacency and the other principles as they affect English but also has particular settings for all the parameters that apply to English. A person who knows Japanese differs in that they know how the principles apply to Japanese – for example, structure-dependency is not required for Japanese questions since these are not formed by movement – and they know the parameter settings for Japanese, such as head-last for the head parameter.

Principles and parameters theory is like a complex bank of switches controlling the lighting of a stage; a small number of switches can produce a variety of lighting effects by being combined in different ways. Setting the parameters in a particular way yields a particular language, English, Japanese, or whatever. Though the switches themselves are few in number, they have far-reaching consequences. After all, a phone is in a sense a switching device with ten buttons, but their combination enables the user to reach almost anyone in the world. Learning a language is, according to Chomsky, rather like completing a checklist in a questionnaire: is it head-last or head-first? do noun phrases count as boundaries or not? And so on for all the parameters of UG. A major part of the knowledge of a human language is captured by these principles and parameters, which in principle could be extended to include all human languages if information were available about them.

The problem in discussing these principles and parameters is that they are so obvious; if you ask people 'Could you say *Is French? Is Sam is the cat that black?*' they look at you as if you were asking 'Is the sky green?' or 'Do horses have eight legs?' The principles are taken for granted – that's just the way that language *is*. The same is almost true of the principles of driving. The legal section of the UK Highway Code (HMSO, 1993) cites no law that drivers should keep to the left. The only mention is one sentence of paragraph 49 of 242 numbered paragraphs in the advisory section: *Keep to the left, except where road signs or markings indicate otherwise or you want to overtake* . . . This does not even use the *MUST* found in many other paragraphs. It is so obvious that drivers keep to the left in England that it is hardly necessary to state it in a law.

3 Vocabulary

Given the strong restrictions on languages seen so far, one language still ought to resemble another very closely – the same principles, a few differences in parameter settings. Why cannot a new language be understood after a minute or two if all that is necessary is to apply principles and set parameters? The major gap so far is vocabulary. In the broadest sense, this means the various kinds of information about the meaning of words, dealt with in Chapter 5. No one can claim to be a speaker of English if they do not know unconsciously how the word *sparrow* fits in to the three levels of categories, what the components of meaning of *nephew* are, what the associations of *blue* are, and what kind of object *grass* refers to. This knowledge also includes the word's properties in terms of sounds: how it is pronounced, how it varies in form or pronunciation, whether it builds up into other words, and so on.

The aspect of vocabulary that UG theory concentrates on is how individual words connect to the structure of the sentence. Speakers of English know that *Cromwell executed Charles I* is a proper English sentence but that *Cromwell executed* is not. They know, in other words, that the verb *execute* must be followed by an object noun phrase such as *Charles I*. They also know that *Samson fainted* is grammatical but *Samson fainted Delilah* is not. They know that certain verbs such as *faint* must *not* be followed by an Object, i.e. are 'intransitive' in traditional terms. It is not that the ungrammatical sentences cannot be understood. *Samson fainted Delilah* is understood quite readily as 'Samson made Delilah faint'. Part of the speaker's knowledge of entries for particular words such as *execute* or *faint* is whether they must have Objects or not. A lexical entry in the mind must then contain information such as that in the following entries:

cat   Noun . . .
make   Verb, Object needed . . .
faint   Verb, no Object needed . . .

In addition it must have all the other information about the word's meaning, morphology and pronunciation.

So, as well as principles and parameters, knowledge of language means knowing vocabulary. All verbs, and in fact all lexical items, are used in sentences according to a set of complex specifications. In a computer study of 12 000 basic verbs of French, Maurice Gross discovered that no two verbs would fit exactly the same range of sentences. Knowing the grammar of French is no use without also knowing how each verb of French behaves in the sentence.

The structure of a sentence is an interplay between its structure, as laid down by the principles and parameters, and the individual properties of the lexical items. Learning the universal principles may not require much effort, since these are automatically imposed by our minds. Setting the values of parameters may also be straightforward, since these take only a few sentences to observe. The task of learning the idiosyncratic behaviour of thousands of words is, however, mammoth. Overall knowledge of language comes down to a combination of principles, parameters and vocabulary. Since the principles are already specified, knowledge of a particular language amounts largely to knowing the vocabulary and the parameter settings.

The Minimalist Programme claims that everything that is learnt is part of the lexicon; 'language acquisition is in essence a matter of determining lexical idiosyncracies'. So far it has been assumed that parameters are attached to principles and therefore part of the main structural component of the grammar. But, if all learning is vocabulary, parameters must also be part of the lexicon.

An illustration of this comes from the binding principles mentioned in Chapter 2. These state that in the sentence *Helen said Sarah respects herself* the reflexive pronoun *herself* is bound to *Sarah* and so refers to the same person.

Helen said Sarah respects herself

However, in *Helen said Sarah respects her* the pronoun *her* may not be bound to *Sarah*, and so refers to someone else, whether to Helen or to a person who otherwise is not mentioned.

(someone else)

Helen said Sarah respects her

The principles of binding limit the relationship between the pronoun and its antecedent by the structure of the sentence – another example of structure-dependency. So *herself* can only be bound within a certain part of the structure, that is to say the clause *Sarah respects herself*. The pronoun *her*, on the other hand, is free to go outside this limit, so it may be bound to the Noun Phrase *Helen* in the main clause *Helen said. . .* or to someone else altogether. Over 90 per cent of English native speakers agreed with these interpretations of the two sentences in an experiment of mine.

However, Chapter 2 suggested that *jibun*, the Japanese equivalent to *herself*, ignores this restriction and can be bound *outside* the clause. Is the principle therefore wrong? Instead, linguists have argued that there is a parameter about what restricts binding in a language. English has a tight restriction on *herself*, binding it within its own clause; Japanese has a far looser restriction on *jibun*, binding it within the whole sentence. This does not affect all the pronouns or all the reflexives in a language, but only particular words. In other words, it is a parameter that belongs to the individual word. Speakers have to learn which of the settings is possible for *herself* in English, for *jibun* in Japanese, and so on. The parameter is a matter of vocabulary, not of grammatical principles. Variation between languages has been put where it belongs – in the lexicon. This is termed the 'lexical parameterization hypothesis'.

Many of the parameters discussed so far are not clearly linked to vocabulary items. The word-order effects described above in the head parameter do not seem a property of individual nouns; instead, all nouns in a language behave in the same way. Such parameters are now connected to the abstract functional phrases, such as the Tense Phrase for present tense *-s* or past tense *-ed* in English, introduced in Chapter 7. The Tense Phrase in sentences like *Peter coughs* can be divided into a Tense element and a Verb Phrase:

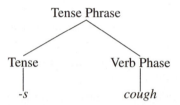

The inflection *-s* is separate from the actual Verb and has a phrase of its own.

Minimalism makes the startling proposal that the properties of functional phrases belong in the lexicon alongside the properties of nouns, verbs and so on. As well as lexical entries for all the words in the language, the lexicon also includes a set of functional phrases. Learning English means learning that the *-s* ending is the head of the Tense Phrase and that it must agree with the subject of the sentence, whether *Peter coughs* or *They cough*. There is a lexical entry something like:

> Tense Phrase: *-s* as overt head, agrees with subject

Acquiring English Determiner Phrases similarly means discovering that the head of the phrase can be *the* (*the field*), *a/an* (*a field*), or Ø (*fields*), and that these elements precede the noun phrase (*a field*, not *field a*).

> Determiner Phrase: determiner head *the/a/Ø*, head-first

In a speaker of another language the phrases would have their parameters set appropriately for that language.

Thus the lexicon is extended to include the knowledge of phrases. Alongside the section of the mental dictionary for lexical words like *cat* and *feed* is a section for functional phrases like Tense Phrase or Determiner Phrase. The properties of functional phrases are just like those of lexical phrases. The only major difference is that there is no necessity to have a head of a functional phrase in the actual surface of the sentence. *People cough* has no determiner head in the Determiner Phrase *people* and there is no tense head in the Tense Phrase *cough*, even if both these are present in the underlying structure of the sentence. The head parameter and the other parameters are linked to particular phrases in the grammar. This is called the 'functional parameterization hypothesis'.

This change in the nature of the lexicon alters the relationship between the vocabulary and the structure of the sentence. In the Minimalist Programme inflections are added to lexical items in the mental dictionary and 'checked out' against the structure of the sentence in terms of principles and parameters. The starting-point is a word such as *cat* to which an ending *-s* is added; this is checked out against the sentence structure and, if it is plural *The _____ are in the garden*, it may be used; if it is singular *The _____ is in the garden*, it may not.

To sum up this section, all variation between one language and another, or, more precisely, between the grammar in one person's mind and that in another's, whether in vocabulary or parameter settings, is in the lexicon. English differs from Japanese because of the settings for functional phrases and the lexical entries, both of which are stored in the lexicon. We are all speakers of the same language, separated only by our different vocabularies. At the moment the repercussions of this theory are far from settled. But, given the impact that Chomsky's ideas have always had, their development will undoubtedly occupy a generation of linguists.

II Universal Grammar and language acquisition

The UG-related ideas about language acquisition from Chapter 7 can now be put in the context of UG theory as a whole. To acquire a language, learners have to apply the principles of UG to the samples of speech they encounter, set the parameters of the functional phrases, and gain detailed lexical information about masses of lexical items. All of this depends on the speech heard from parents or others activating the relevant parts of the learners' minds. This section looks at how the process of acquiring the specific content of UG for one language takes place, both imposing features of the mind upon language and taking features of the input from outside.

1 The 'black box' metaphor of language acquisition

For many years Chomsky compared language acquisition to a black box. Things go in one side of a black box and things come out the other side. But there is no way of observing what is going on inside the black box itself. Suppose some industrial spies see milk going into a dairy and cheese coming out; by analysing the cheese, they can deduce what must have been done to the milk inside the dairy, a matter of working out cause from effect. The speech of adults goes into children's minds; after a few years of absorbing this input, children arrive at a complete grammar of the language. By comparing the grammar children acquire with the speech input they hear, it is possible to work out what must happen inside the children's minds. In the case of the dairy, the spies could confirm their guess by breaking and entering. With language, there is no way of getting inside the mind except by studying what goes in and what comes out.

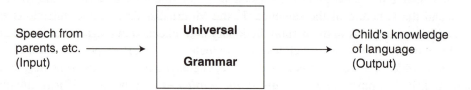

Universal Grammar is the black box responsible for language acquisition. It is the mechanism in the mind which allows children to construct a grammar out of the raw language materials supplied by their parents. Since all children end up with grammars involving principles, parameter settings and vocabulary, these must be favoured by the UG in their minds. The mind can be deduced to contain at least the means for constructing grammars with these characteristics. The mysterious black box can be partly filled in with principles and parameters. It is not coincidence that all human languages have the same principles and parameters, since these are part of the UG black box in the minds of all their speakers.

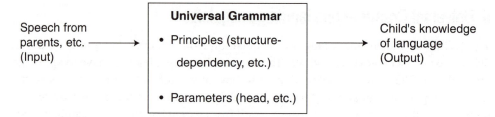

In a sense this is labouring the obvious fact that children learn language from the speech they hear. But why should all English-speaking children arrive at the same grammar in terms of principles and parameters, apart from effects of dialect? How do all human children work out structure-dependency, subjacency and the rest from widely differing sentences provided by their parents in many different languages and circumstances? Only because they are already primed to look for them by the properties of the UG in their minds.

The existence of these elements in the black box is partly demonstrated by the speed and confidence with which children master complex principles of language that have taken linguists decades to describe. The Universal Grammar in their minds cuts down on the options available to them. They do not have to explore all the logical possibilities that language could take because only a few languages are possible. The few may be numbered in many thousands, but nevertheless a restricted number, at least in terms of principles and parameters. The principles and parameters in the mind lighten the learner's load.

Suppose, however, the spies see milk going into the dairy and hamburgers coming out. There is no obvious way in which milk can be turned into hamburgers. They would assume that a supply of beef had been delivered before they started observing. Returning to the familiar example of structure-dependency, this principle is part of the grammar of all human languages: it comes out of the UG black box. So it must have gone in. But where did it come from? Children might, for example, have imitated their parents' sentences such as *Is Sam the cat that is black?* As adults never break structure-dependency, all the sentences they produce are structure-dependent. The child could learn to produce sentences with structure-dependency by imitation, as starlings learning to imitate football referees' whistles.

But structure-dependency not only accounts for the sentences people hear, it also allows them to make judgements about sentences that break structure-dependency, which they are never likely to hear in normal circumstances. The *Inside Language* panel unanimously rejected *Is the teacher who on leave is Jones?* (Q9). Yet they had never heard such a sentence before, apart from those who attended linguistics classes. Chomsky argues that the ability to reject impossible sentences could not be acquired by imitation alone since speakers would never be able to distinguish sentences that are new and perfectly acceptable from those that are new but unacceptable, certainly not with the degree of confidence they show with structure-dependency.

From the Universal Grammar perspective, children do not 'learn' this principle of language: it is already there. So, whatever language they learn, whether English, Russian or whatever, they incorporate structure-dependency into it. The reason why they never make mistakes with structure-dependency, and so never need to be corrected, is that they already know it. The sentences that break structure-dependency strike us as bizarre because they go against something that is built into the mind, as basic as the ability to recognize faces or to walk upright. There is no way children could acquire structure-dependency from the kind of speech they hear or the kinds of language activity in which they take part. Like the beef in the dairy, structure-dependency must have come in before we started observing. In other words, it is already part of the UG black box, not added in the process of creating the grammar in the mind.

2 *Innateness of language*

Chomsky therefore concludes that principles of UG such as structure-dependency are part of the innate structure of the human mind. They are not learnt from the language the child hears, nor from anything in the child's environment, but are part of the human mind itself. When babies are born they already have UG within them, just as they have ways of breathing, seeing and hearing. This is why so few children have problems with acquiring language; it is as natural for human beings to learn to speak as it is for them to learn to walk. Though a few people cannot talk, just as there are some who cannot walk, this is the consequence of disability of some kind, not of improper input or training, as described in Chapter 9. Extreme deprivation does prevent people from talking, as it prevents them from walking, as in the case of Genie, who was deprived of language until her teens. But, given some exposure to language, all human children learn to talk, just as they learn to walk, because it is programmed into them by their genetic inheritance.

Chomsky is not therefore just making vague suggestions that some parts of language are innate, but proposing that the precise contents of Universal Grammar are an inherent part of the human mind – the principles such as structure-dependency and the parameters such as the head parameter. They are not learnt but part of the innate structure of the human mind. On the face of it, it should be easy to prove or disprove his claim. Finding a language in which structure-dependency is broken or in which, say, subjacency is used according to some totally different principle would disprove Universal Grammar. Or, to be more exact, it would disprove these elements of UG as it is understood now. It would be hard to maintain the current principles and parameters model of UG if languages were found that breached all of its central claims. However, while the theory is constantly progressing to cover new languages and new facts, there are no signs that languages will be found that fall outside the scope of its principles and parameters.

The idea of language being innate has outraged many working with language, who insist that everything in language can be learnt through means already available to the child. Or, like the psychologist John Anderson, they claim that principles such as structure-dependency are general properties of the way the mind processes information, not peculiar to language. Some psychologists point to the bizarreness of the features alleged to be innate. Structure-dependency is no particular help in communicating with people; binding is an arbitrary choice that helps or hinders communication rather less than many aspects of language that are not part of UG. If innate parts of the mind were developed for their efficiency for the species, as Darwinian theories of evolution would suggest, what is the benefit for one's descendants of being able to judge that *Is Sam is the cat that black?* is not English? Piaget claims that 'this mutation particular to the human species would be biologically inexplicable'.

Chomsky's main point is, however, based, not on the history of the species, but on the logic of the black box: if something comes out that did not go in, it must be innate, however useless or useful it may be. Chomsky sometimes calls this Plato's problem: 'How do we come to have such rich and specific knowledge, or such intricate systems of belief and understanding, when the evidence available to us is so meagre?' In linguistics this is usually called 'the poverty of the stimulus argument': the 'stimulus' input going into the black box is not 'rich' enough in information to lead to the complex grammar that comes out. Chomsky's argument is that the ingredients for the complex knowledge of language in our minds are not found in the actual input we receive and so must come from elsewhere.

Chomsky's main claim for innateness is based on an argument that has three steps: first you discover a property of language; then you show that it is not available in the child's normal input; finally you conclude that it must be innate. The first step can be challenged by showing that language does not have principles and parameters of the kind he postulates. The second can be challenged by discovering some means by which the child could acquire these properties from the environment. And the third step could be refuted by insisting the knowledge does not come from the input but from a source such as telepathy, universal consciousness or some other non-physical means. In other words, to show that structure-dependency is not innate, you would have to claim either that it is not a real property of language, or that it can be easily worked out by children from their parents' speech, or that it comes from some other source than the mind itself. However, Chomsky's critics have not tried to demolish the steps in this argument; in other words, they have not tackled him on his own ground by producing evidence that contradicts the poverty of the stimulus argument.

3 Acquisition of parameter settings

Chapter 7 described the acquisition of the settings for the pro-drop parameter concerning whether there has to be a subject in the sentence or not. The group of non-pro-drop languages that includes English and French insists on a subject, *It's raining*, *Il pleut*. The group of pro-drop languages that includes Italian and Japanese allows sentences without subjects, *Piove* ('It's raining'), *Atsui* ('It's hot'). The pro-drop parameter has to be set one way or the other in every language.

To acquire the right parameter setting, the child needs to hear sentences of a language. Without a sample of English sentences like *It's hot* or *He's a pilot*, the child would not be able to tell English was a non-pro-drop language. Without hearing Japanese sentences like *Atsui*, the child would not be able to tell that Japanese was pro-drop. Hence evidence is needed to 'trigger' the parameter setting in the child's mind. The same applies for the other parameters of Universal Grammar: the child needs to encounter clues to be able to set the subjacency parameter, the head parameter, and all the others.

An interesting example is the difference between *him* and *himself* in binding, described above. A parameter specifies how far binding of reflexives such as *himself* may stretch, ranging from a clause for English, *himself*, to a whole sentence for Japanese, *jibun*. But, unlike pro-drop with its two settings, there are several alternative settings for this parameter. Italian, for example, allows a reflexive to be bound out of a Noun Phrase. The English sentence *Mary looked at Helen's pictures of herself* forces the reflexive *herself* to be bound to the Noun Phrase *Helen*, not to *Mary*:

> *Mary looked at Helen's pictures of herself*

while the Italian equivalent *Maria guardò i ritratti di sé di Mario* allows *sé* 'herself' to be bound to *Maria*.

> *Maria guardò i ritratti di sé di Mario*

Other languages like Norwegian and Icelandic allow still wider possibilities for binding the reflexive pronoun and the Noun Phrase.

Children in fact have to choose between five different possibilities for this parameter, rather than the usual binary choice. But, as they are learning naturally from the sentences they hear rather than from elaborate explanation or constructed examples, how do they sort out these possibilities?

All children, whatever language they encounter, start by assuming that it has the most restricted setting for binding, which happens to be that found for English *herself*. If they are prodded by other sentences, they go on to another, slightly more relaxed, setting for Italian, slightly more relaxed again for Norwegian, and for Icelandic, till some children get to the most relaxed setting of all, which occurs in Japanese *jibun*. The sequence goes from most to least restricted setting, permitting them to learn the right setting without being corrected by their parents. If they started with the loosest setting, they would only be able to restrict the setting by correction from their parents, which is unlikely to be forthcoming in the case of binding as binding mistakes would go unnoticed.

This is called the Subset Principle, because children start with the tightest restriction, a 'subset' of the possibilities, and then expand to more and more relaxed settings in response to the sentences of the language they encounter. The Subset Principle is a universal of language learning that supplements the UG theory itself. It enables children to select a setting with the minimum of problem, simply by hearing examples of binding, rather than requiring correction of mistakes.

While the Universal Grammar theory emphasizes the innate features of language in the mind, it also gives a precise role to language input. In a Japanese-speaking environment, the speech children hear allows them to acquire Japanese rather than English by setting the parameters appropriately and acquiring the vocabulary. Without such input, nothing at all would happen and the principles and parameters would remain latent in their minds. Exposed to language input, children can create the knowledge of a specific language in their minds, whether Japanese or English or whatever. The information from the environment is vital to acquisition.

The language input does not, however, need to possess any special characteristics beyond those of ordinary speech. The evidence for setting the major parameters has to be available in ordinary sentences that the child will encounter in everyday conversation. To set the pro-drop parameter for English, the child needs sentences both with subjects like *He's a pilot* and with dummy subjects (*it, there*) like *It's raining*. To set the head parameter, as Chomsky points out, a few sentences like *John ate an apple* are enough to demonstrate that verbs come before objects, determiners before nouns, and so on.

Setting the subjacency and binding parameters at first sight seems to need complex sentences involving a sufficient number of clauses, noun phrases, and so on. However, David Lightfoot has argued that all the evidence needed is actually present in simple movement within a single clause, such as the question *Are you happy?* While it is vital that children hear quantities of speech, parents do not have to structure or edit this in a particular way to help them acquire principles and parameters.

One justification for this view is that, despite the great variation in the speech and language interaction that children encounter in different cultures, they all manage to acquire their first language. Obviously their command of the language varies in all sorts of other ways and they may be slower or faster at learning language. But virtually all human adults possess a fully-fledged grammar of one language or another, with the exception of the 1.5 per cent with Specific Language Impairment discussed in Chapter 9 and those suffering from other disabilities that have repercussions for language.

Hence, what parents actually say to children cannot affect them greatly, however important the parents themselves feel it to be. In some cultures, for instance in Java, children are only spoken to through their parents, but they still learn language. Research in England showed that children who were talked *to* rather than talked *at* developed language better. In neither case is there any evidence that the nature of the input affects their basic knowledge of the core of language, rather than aspects of language use. It is vital to much language acquisition that the child has structured interaction with adults; for example, the benefits of reading books with young children are well proved. But none of this is necessary for the acquisition of principles and parameters grammar, which only requires exposure to ordinary sentences.

The UG theory concerns certain parts of language rather than the whole. It deals with the 'core' grammar couched in the knowledge of principles, parameters and lexical entries for vocabulary. It has nothing to say about how children learn to use language appropriately nor about the myriad other aspects of acquisition, which are bound in with the other sides of the child's maturation – social, physical, cognitive and so on. This deliberate limitation is often not appreciated by its critics, who claim it cannot deal with, say, acquisition of social interaction or the range of vocabulary discussed in Chapter 5. Why should it? No one would expect a theory of gravity to explain why people take aspirins for headaches. Language is many-sided: the UG theory tackles only one side, the principles and parameters, though needless to say it regards this as the most important.

4 Second-language learning and Universal Grammar

What about the acquisition of second languages? There is a common belief that children learn second languages easily and adults do not. An example that is often cited is the novelist Joseph Conrad, who was born in Poland. He then went to live in Marseilles at 17, where he improved the French he had started learning as a child. He started English at 20 while a seaman on a Polish ship, passing the British second mate's examination in spoken and written English two years later. He then became one of the leading novelists in English of his time. But Ford Madox Ford claimed that 'speaking English he [Conrad] had so strong a French accent that few who did not know him well could understand him at first'. For this reason Conrad is often held up as an example of the inefficiency of learning a second language after the teens. Virginia Woolf, moreover, claimed that Conrad was 'a foreigner, talking broken English'; H.G. Wells that 'he spoke English strangely'; Bertrand Russell that he 'spoke English with a very strong foreign accent'. On this evidence, UG is not available to L2 learners after the critical period.

Conrad is, however, not a good example: after all, his English can only be called poor if his written English does not count. His French, learnt in his late teens, was so good that Paul Valéry found it 'elegant' and so fluent that he spoke it with Henry James in preference to English. At most we can number Conrad among those whose accent in a third language is not very good.

Yet there is some truth to this image of the older second-language learner having greater problems. Every year I meet overseas students who come to England with small children. The students themselves start with reasonable English, the children with none. By the end of the year the children are fluent speakers; the adult students have only made slight improvements. This could be taken as a sign of the decline of language-learning ability after the early teens. Adults have to overcome their inherent lack of language-learning ability by compensating in one way or another.

The situations of children and adult are, however, seldom the same. Children playing naturally with their peers and immersed in a school class may be in a naturally good situation for learning a second language. Adults trying to cope with all the stress of organizing their lives in a new country and relying on grammar books or dictionaries may be cutting themselves off from the best sources of information. To test the Critical Period Hypothesis in L2 learning, Jacqueline Johnson and Elissa Newport compared L2 learners of English who had started learning at different ages with natives (see Figure 11.1).

Though the results from research such as that by Johnson and Newport suggests there is indeed an age difference, most other research has not endorsed the child's superiority so strongly. People who learn a language from childhood are better speakers than those who start comparatively late: an early start is an advantage in the long

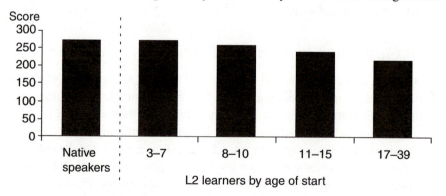

Fig. 11.1 The decline of L2 learning in adults: grammar test scores for natives and L2 users who started at different ages

term. But experiments over short periods of up to a year usually find that adults have an advantage over children. For example, researchers studied English speakers who had gone to the Netherlands. Up to a period of a year adults outperformed children who were in the same situation. A further example comes from research with the Total Physical Response method of language teaching. This consists of responding to commands from the teacher – *Stand up*, *Turn to the left*, and so on, something that might be expected to suit children. Yet adults taught by this method in fact outperformed their juniors. In the short term it is an advantage to be an adult, even if this advantage wears off in long-term acquisition.

So many other things are involved in second-language acquisition that it is perhaps not a fair test of the Critical Period Hypothesis. The issue has been formulated within the UG theory as a question of whether second language learners have 'access' to UG. The reason for the feeling that children are better than adults might be that children can apply their Universal Grammar; adults cannot.

If this were the case, however, L2 grammars could not consist of principles and parameters. Take structure-dependency, for example, which is an arbitrary fact about human language derived from UG. If a second language were acquired by some other means than UG, then L2 learners would not have grammars that included it, since, as seen above, there is no obvious way of learning such an abstruse fact, and language teachers are unlikely to have explained it to students. Figure 11.2 sets out the scores for structure-dependency for native speakers of English and for three groups of L2 learners of English, taken from an experiment of my own. Natives are 100 per cent successful at rejecting *Is Sam is the cat that brown?* and 90 per cent at accepting *Is Joe the dog that is black?* But non-native speakers are nearly as good: Japanese and Finnish users of English scored 94 per cent and 100 per cent respectively for grammatical sentences, and 67 per cent and eighty-one per cent respectively for the ungrammatical sentences. Though they are obviously not perfect, they clearly know structure-dependency. This is particularly interesting in the case of Japanese, because the Japanese language does not form questions by movement. Hence the Japanese

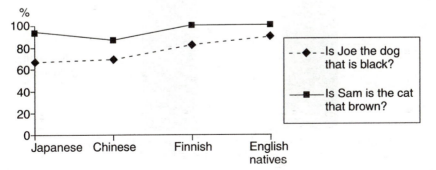

Fig. 11.2 Structure-dependency in four groups of native and non-native speakers of English

learners would never have needed structure-dependency for questions in their first language, and so could not be using it as a basis for their second.

There is more controversy over whether the parameters of UG can be reset in a second language. L2 learners tend to carry over their L1 setting to the second language. Hence French learners of English reject subjectless sentences like *Is English* more than Spanish learners. Whether the first language is pro-drop or non-pro-drop has a clear effect on the learning of subsequent languages. It is easier to go in one direction than the other; for example, English learners of Spanish do not have the same problems with leaving the subjects out of the sentence as Spanish learners of English have with putting them in. Nevertheless they all have UG present somewhere in their minds.

Other parameters such as subjacency turn out to be trickier. A sentence such as *What did John realize he could not sell?* was accepted by 97 per cent of natives but by only 65 per cent of non-natives. An impossible sentence such as *What did Sam believe the claim that Carol had bought?* was rejected by 100 per cent of natives but by only 79 per cent of non-natives (see Figure 11.3). In other words, the L2 learners had not set the boundaries for subjacency in the same way as English native speakers. Similar research with learners of different ages showed that the younger the age at which they had started English the more likely they were to know subjacency. Therefore adult learners do not have access to Universal Grammar, but acquire a second language in a totally different fashion from their first.

However, even if the second-language learners did not perform like natives, they still performed at a high level, at 65 per cent or 79 per cent in the experiment above, well above the 50 per cent that might be expected by chance. Rather than not knowing subjacency in English at all, they do not know it very well. It is a matter of partial success rather than complete failure. Though this area will doubtless remain controversial for years to come, this line of research still leaves open the question of whether second-language acquisition past a certain age is cut off from Universal Grammar.

Fig. 11.3 Subjacency in native and non-native speakers of English

Conclusion

I hope that this book has realized its goals of opening the reader's eyes to the diversity of language and of showing that language can be studied scientifically. Issues about language should not be settled by the opinions of newspaper pundits or members of the Royal Family but by recourse to the large body of research into language that has been built up over generations. Language is neither simply a collection of amazing words nor a collection of rules about split infinitives but something far deeper and far more important, the means through which we claim to be human beings and through which we express the meaning of our lives.

Sources and further reading

As well as being highly technical, the UG theory also changes rapidly. It is crucial, then, to check the date of any introductory book on this area. Both the general ideas and the technicalities of the grammar are covered in V.J. Cook and M. Newson, *Chomsky's Universal Grammar: An Introduction* (Oxford: Blackwell, 1996). Other introductions are L. Haegeman, *Introduction to Government and Binding Theory*, 2nd edn (Oxford: Blackwell, 1994); J. Ouhalla, *Introducing Transformational Grammar* (London: Edward Arnold, 1994). Noam Chomsky's own works are mostly highly technical, one exception being *Language and Problems of Knowledge: The Managua Lectures* (Cambridge, MA: MIT Press, 1988). The Minimalist Programme is presented in *The Minimalist Program* (Cambridge, MA: MIT Press, 1995), from which the quotations in this chapter are taken.

Principles and parameters theory

The original principles and parameters theory was presented in N. Chomsky, *Lectures on Government and Binding* (Dordrecht: Foris, 1981). Gross's work with French is presented in M. Gross, 'Lexique: Grammaire LADL', paper given at the AILA Congress, Thessaloniki, Apr. 1990.

Universal Grammar and language acquisition

The various references are to: J.R. Anderson, *The Architecture of Cognition* (Cambridge, MA: Harvard UP, 1983); J. Piaget, 'The psychogenesis of knowledge and its epistemological significance', in M. Piattelli-Palmarini (ed.), *Language and Learning: The Debate between Jean Piaget and Noam Chomsky* (London: Routledge & Kegan Paul, 1980). The relationship of the subset principle to the acquisition of binding is discussed in K. Wexler and M.R. Manzini, 'Parameters and learnability', in T. Roeper and E. Williams (eds.), *Parameters and Linguistic Theory* (Dordrecht: Reidel, 1987). The study of English parents is reported in C.G. Wells, *Language Development in the Pre-school Years* (Cambridge: CUP, 1985). Passives and maturation are discussed in: H. Borer and K. Wexler, 'The maturation of syntax', in T. Roeper and E. Williams (eds.), *Parameter Setting* (Dordrecht: Reidel, 1987), 123–72; E.H. Lenneberg, *Biological Foundations of Language* (New York: Wiley, 1967); H. Lane, *The Wild Boy of Aveyron* (London: Allen & Unwin, 1977); D. Lightfoot, *How to Set Parameters* (Cambridge, MA: MIT Press, 1991).

Second-language acquisition and Universal Grammar

Age effects in second-language acquisition are described in: J. Johnson and E. Newport, 'Critical period effects in second language acquisition: the influence of maturational state on the acquisition of ESL', *Cognitive Psychology* 21 (1989): 60–99; J.S. Johnson and E.L. Newport, 'Critical period effects on universal properties of language: the status of subjacency in a second language', *Cognition* 39 (1991): 215–58; J. Asher and G. Garcia, 'The optimal age to learn a foreign language', *Modern Language Journal* 38 (1969): 334–41; C. Snow and M. Hoefnagel-Höhle, 'The critical period for language acquisition: evidence from second language learning', *Child Development* 49 (1978): 1114–28. The relationship between UG and second-language acquisition is reviewed in V.J. Cook, 'UG and the metaphor of access', in N. Ellis (ed.), *Implicit Learning of Language* (London: Academic Press, 1994).

Main Languages

This includes the main features of languages used in the text about which a range of information is known. The information for each language consists of:

- *Its name.* Languages often have alternative names, the difference sometimes having political overtones, e.g. Persian/Farsi, Bahasa Malaysia/Bahasa Melayu, Inuit/Eskimo.
- *Where it is spoken* (unless obvious from the name).
- *Numbers of speakers.* Numbers of speakers are approximate and taken from a number of sources; they usually refer to the total number of speakers in the whole world, not just in one country, particularly relevant for languages such as French, English and Spanish. The information mostly comes from the series B. Comrie (ed.), *The Major Languages of East and South Asia; The Major Languages of Western Europe; The Major Languages of The Soviet Union*, Croom Helm; G. Campbell, (1991), *Compendium of the World's Languages*, London: Routledge; D. Crystal (1987), *The Cambridge Encyclopedia of Language*, CUP.
- *The usual word order* of S (Subject), V (Verb) and O (Object). Again some languages have a freer word order and it is hard to assign a single canonical order.
- *Whether it is pro-drop (PD) or non-pro-drop (NPD).* For many languages the information is not clearly available.
- *The language family to which it belongs.*
- *Its writing system.* The default writing system is, for convenience, Roman alphabet and left–right direction, so only other possibilities are specified. Writing systems sometimes have political importance, for example in North and South Korea.

Albanian (Albania and adjacent countries)   5 million
     SVO; Indo-European; Roman (since 1908)

Arabic (North African countries such as Morocco, Middle East   150 million
    countries such as Jordan, etc., widespread religious use)
    VSO; PD; Semitic; Arabic alphabet (r – l, vowel-less)
Bahasa Melayu/Bahasa Malaysia/Malay (Malaysia)   10 million
    SVO; Austronesian; Roman (since 19th c.), differing from
    Indonesian (Bahasa Indonesia) in vocabulary
Basque (Spanish–French border area)   500 000
    SOV; no known family
Bengali (Bengal, i.e. Bangladesh and West Bengal)   165 million
    SOV; Indo-European (Indic); Devanagari script
Berber (name for several closely related languages such as   12 million
    Kabyle and Shawia used in Morocco, Algeria and neighbouring countries)
    VSO; Afro-Asiatic; formerly Berber alphabet (r – l)
Burmese   30 million
    SOV; PD; Sino-Tibetan; Burmese alphabet (based on circles)
Chinese (China, Taiwan, Singapore, etc.)   1000 million
    8 main dialects (alias languages)
    SVO; PD; Sino-Tibetan; character script (see p.114 for directions of script)
Chinook
    VSO; Penutian
Cocama/Kokama (Peru, Columbia, Brazil)   10 000
    SVO; Andean–Equatorial
Czech   16 million
    SVO; PD; Indo-European (Slavic); Roman (adapted)
Dutch (Netherlands, Belgium, Surinam)   20 million
    SVO; NPD; Indo-European (Germanic)
English   230 million
    SVO; NPD; Indo-European (Germanic)
Fijian   300 000
    Verb-initial; Austronesian
Finnish (Finland, parts of Russia and Sweden)   5 million
    SVO; Finno-Ugric; Roman (only 21 letters)
French (Francophone Africa, Quebec, France, French colonies, etc.)   ?70 million
    SVO; NPD; Indo-European (Romance)
German (Switzerland, Austria, Germany, etc.)   94 million
    SOV; NPD; Indo-European (Germanic); Roman (previously Fraktur Roman)
Greek (Cyprus, Greece)   10 million
    SVO; PD; Indo-European; Greek alphabet
Hawaiian
    VSO; Austronesian
Hebrew (Israel, widespread religious use)   4 million
    VSO (SVO); PD; Semitic; Hebrew alphabet (r – l, vowel-less)

Hindi (India) 225 million
    SOV; Indo-European (Indic); Devanagari alphabet
Hungarian 14 million
    SOV; Finno-Ugric; Roman (adapted)
Indonesian 15 million
    SVO; Austronesian close to Bahasa Malaysia except for some vocabulary
Irish Gaelic 100 000
    VSO; Indo-European (Celtic)
Italian (Italy, Switzerland, neighbouring areas etc.) 60 million
    SVO; PD; Indo-European (Romance)
Japanese 120 million
    SOV; PD; kanji character scripts plus kana syllabaries
Kabardian 350 000
    SOV; Caucasian; formerly Roman, now Cyrillic alphabet
Korean 60 million
    SOV (verb-final); PD; Han'gul sound-based script (l – r)
    and characters (r – l)
Latin (dead language, formerly widespread, more latterly for religious use)
    SOV; PD; Indo-European
Maori (New Zealand) 100 000
    VSO; Austronesian
Persian/Farsi (Iran, parts of Afghanistan, Tadzhik republic) 38 million
    SOV; Indo-European; Persian alphabet (derived from Arabic, r – l)
Polish 46 million
    SVO; PD; Indo-European (Slavic); Roman (without q, v, x, but plus many
    diacritics)
Portuguese (Brazil, Portugal) 135 million
    SVO; PD; Indo-European (Romance)
Punjabi/Panjabi (Punjab border of India/Pakistan) 50 million
    SOV; Indo-European; Gurmukhi alphabet
Romansh (pockets of eastern Switzerland and northern Italy) 50 000
    Indo-European (Romance)
Russian 160 million
    SVO; PD; Indo-European (Slavic); Cyrillic
Samoan 200 000
    VSO (verb-initial); Austronesian
Scots Gaelic 80 000
    VSO; Indo-European (Celtic)
Seneca (New York State)
    Iroquoian; Roman alphabet (reduced to 12 letters plus 'œ')
Serbian 18 million
    SVO; Indo-European (Slavic); Serbian (adapted Cyrillic alphabet)

Slovak   18 million
  SVO; Indo-European (Slavic); Roman (adapted)
Spanish (Latin America, Spain, etc.)   250 million
  SVO; PD; Indo-European (Romance)
Sranan (Surinam, the Netherlands)   100 000
  Creole (English plus Portuguese and African elements)
Swahili/Kiswahili (East Africa inc. Tanzania, Kenya)   4 million
  SVO; Niger–Congo (Bantu); Roman alphabet without c, q, x
Swedish   8 million
  SVO; Indo-European (Germanic, North)
Tagalog (Philippines)   50 million
  VOS; Austronesian
Tahitian   70 000
  VSO; Austronesian
Tamil (southern India, Sri Lanka, Malaysia, etc.)   54 million
  SOV; Dravidian; Tamil syllabary
Thai   40 million
  SVO; Sino-Tibetan; Thai alphabet
Tok Pisin (Papua New Guinea)   1.5 million
  SVO; pidgin/creole
Tongan   80 000
  V-initial; Austronesian
Turkish (Turkey plus groups in adjacent countries)   51 million
  SOV; Altaic; Roman alphabet since 1928 (with no q, w, x)
Ukrainian (Ukraine and neighbouring areas)   60 million
  SVO; PD; Indo-European (Slavic); Cyrillic alphabet (adapted)
Urdu (Pakistan, India)   50 million
  SOV; Indo-European; Urdu script (Arabic derived, r – l)
Vietnamese   66 million
  SVO; Austro-Asiatic; Roman (with many diacritics)
Welsh   500 000
  VSO; Indo-European (Celtic)
Xhosa (South Africa, Transkei)   5 million
  SVO; Niger–Congo
Yoruba (Nigeria)   16 million
  SVO; Niger–Congo
Zulu (South Africa)   3.5 million
  SVO; Niger–Congo (Bantu)

Glossary

The aim is not to present complete definitions so much as quick reminders for terms that are mentioned in several sections rather than just being used once. The number in brackets refers to the chapter in which the idea is discussed most fully. Cross-references to other entries in the Glossary are printed in small capitals.

agreement Agreement consists of a change of form in one element of a SENTENCE caused by a second element, to show their common NUMBER, GENDER, etc., e.g. Subject–Verb Agreement of number in English:

One swallow doesn't make a summer/Two swallows don't make a summer.

allophone (4) Allophones are alternative pronunciations of PHONEMES in a particular language that never affect the meaning, usually predictable from their environment. For example, RP English has clear [l] at the beginning of words such as *lick*, dark [l] at the end of words such as *kill*, but these do not change the words if the wrong one is used; in Polish the two [l]s are different phonemes.

alphabetic principle (3) The writing system in which written symbols correspond to spoken sounds, contrasted with the LOGOGRAPHIC and ORTHOGRAPHIC principles.

aphasia (9) Aphasia is in general the impairment of the ability to use language, particularly GRAMMAR and vocabulary, usually caused by some form of damage to the brain, sometimes accompanied by other forms of impairment, consisting of types such as BROCA'S and WERNICKE'S APHASIAS.

binding (2) The relationship between a PRONOUN such as *herself* and its antecedent noun such as *Jane* as in *Jane helped herself, Helen said Jane helped her*, etc., is called binding – a complex area of the UNIVERSAL GRAMMAR theory.

Broca's aphasia (9) A type of APHASIA characterized by loss of ability to produce but not to comprehend speech, associated with injury to Broca's area in the front left hemisphere of the brain (left frontal lobe).

canonical order (3)   The canonical order of the sentence is the most usual order of the main sentence elements, SUBJECT (S), VERB (V) and OBJECT (O), in a language, e.g. VSO in Arabic or SVO in English. See also word order.

case (2)   Case is variation in the form of NOUNS and PRONOUNS to show their role in the structure of the SENTENCE, in English limited visibly to pronouns, SUBJECT case *he*, OBJECT case *him*, possessive case *his*, in Latin extending to nouns with 6 cases, in Finnish to 15, used nowadays for a more abstract relationship not necessarily visible in the sentence itself.

clause   A clause has the attributes of a SENTENCE but may occur within a sentence, e.g. a relative clause *who came to dinner* within the sentence *The man who came to dinner stayed too long*.

components of meaning (5)   One way of describing the meaning of a word is to split it up into separate components so that, for example, the noun *boy* can be seen as having the components [non-adult] [male], *girl* the components [non-adult] [female], *woman* the components [adult] [female], and so on.

consonant (4)   Typically, in terms of sound production, a consonant is a sound which is obstructed in some way by tongue or lip contact as in /k/ *keep* or /b/ *beep*, as opposed to the unobstructed sound of a VOWEL. In terms of the sound system, a consonant is a sound that typically occurs at the beginning or end of the SYLLABLE rather than the middle, thus contrasting with the vowels.

content words (3)   Content words such as *table* or *truth* are best explained in the dictionary (lexicon). Content words form 4 types of LEXICAL PHRASE around lexical HEADS – NOUNS, *table*, VERBS, *see*, adjectives, *pretty*, and PREPOSITIONS, *to*. They contrast with GRAMMATICAL WORDS.

creole (10)   A creole language is a new language created when children acquire their parents' PIDGIN language as their first language, e.g. Hawaiian creole and Guyanese creole.

dialect (8)   A dialect is a particular variety of a language spoken by a group united by region, class, etc. It is usually seen nowadays as a matter of different vocabulary or GRAMMAR rather than just of accent.

diglossia (8)   Diglossia is a situation where there are two versions of a language with very different uses, a High form for official occasions and a Low form for everyday life, as in the difference between High German and Swiss German in German-speaking areas of Switzerland.

diphthong (4)   A diphthong is a type of VOWEL produced by moving the tongue as it is produced from one position towards another, for example in English /ɪə/ *fear* and /əʊ/ *low*. It may correspond to one or two written letters.

distinctive feature (4)   Distinctive features are a way of analysing speech sounds in terms of a certain number of on/off elements. So the /b/ in English *bee* has the feature +voice, the /p/ of *pea* has the feature –voice, and so on.

dyslexia (9)   Children with developmental dyslexia have problems with reading but not necessarily with other areas of development.

epenthesis (4)   Epenthesis is the process of adding VOWELS etc., to make possible SYLLABLES out of impossible consonant sequences, e.g. *Rawanda* for *Rwanda*.

Estuary English (2)   This is some people's name for a recent accent of British English allegedly originating from the Thames estuary, known for its use of the GLOTTAL STOP, [ʔ], /bɪʔ/ for *bit* /bɪt/ and of /w/ for /l/, /fuw/ for *full* /ful/.

fricatives (4)   A type of CONSONANT in which the air escapes through a narrow gap created between lips, teeth and tongue, as in English /f/ *fine*, /ʃ/ *shine*, /v/ *vine*.

front/back (4)   In PHONETICS the dimension in the position of the tongue for VOWELS from the front to the back of the mouth is called front/back.

functional phrases (7, 11)   In current syntactic theory, a functional phrase is built round a HEAD consisting of a GRAMMATICAL WORD such as *the* (Determiner Phrase), e.g. *the book*, or a GRAMMATICAL INFLECTION such as present tense *-s*, as in *lives*. According to some theories, these are not available to young children.

gender (2)   Gender is a system for allocating different elements in the SENTENCE to categories such as masculine, feminine and neuter. In English gender is seen only in the link between PRONOUNS such as *she* and NOUNS such as *Susan*, in other languages it affects AGREEMENT of adjectives and VERBS with nouns. Gender is called 'natural' when it correlates with sex, 'arbitrary' when it does not, as in French *la table* (feminine, 'table') and German *das Mädchen* (neuter, 'girl').

glottal stop (4)   A speech sound made by closing the VOCAL CORDS and then releasing them, as in a cough.

grammar (2)   Grammar is the system of relationships between elements of the SENTENCE that links the 'sounds' to the 'meanings'. It is used to refer both to the knowledge of language in the speaker's mind and to the system as written down in rules, grammar books and other descriptions. The type of grammar derived from classical languages that is often taught in schools is called traditional grammar, and is more concerned with prescribing how native speakers should use language than with describing it. Main areas of grammar are WORD ORDER, GRAMMATICAL MORPHEMES, PHONOLOGY GRAMMATICAL INFLECTION and PHRASE STRUCTURE.

grammatical inflections (3)   Grammatical inflections are a system of showing meaning by changing word forms, as in the English *-ed* inflection indicating past tense, *I looked*, absent from some languages like Vietnamese.

grammatical morphemes (3)   Grammatical morphemes is a collective term for MORPHEMES that primarily play a role in the grammar of the SENTENCE, consisting in English of either GRAMMATICAL WORDS such as the articles *the/to* or PREPOSITIONS, *to/in* or GRAMMATICAL INFLECTIONS such as the past tense *-ed*, *liked*, or the possessive *'s*, *John's*. In recent UG these are the heads of FUNCTIONAL PHRASES, apart from prepositions.

grammatical words (3)   Grammatical words such as PREPOSITIONS, *by/for*, or determiners, *a/an*, express the grammatical relationships in the SENTENCE rather than meanings that can be captured in the lexicon.

h-dropping (8)   *H*-dropping refers to the presence or absence of /h/ in the pronunciation of certain words where the letter 'h' is present in the spelling, as in *Harry* versus *'Arry*. In French, *h*-dropping is part of the standard language; in English English, but not American, *h*-dropping is a strong social marker of low status in words like *hurricane* or *hit*.

head (3)   The head of a lexical phrase is a lexical head around which the phrase is built, i.e. Noun Phrases like *a good book* have a head NOUN such as *book*. The head of a functional phrase may be an inflection such as -*s* or a GRAMMATICAL WORD such as *the*.

head parameter (11)   The head parameter captures the difference between languages in which the HEAD of the phrase comes first, i.e. the PREPOSITION head comes before its 'complement' in English *on Tuesday*, and those in which it comes last, as the Postposition head comes last in Japanese *Nippon ni* ('in Japan').

hyper-correction (8)   Hyper-correction is the phenomenon whereby a speaker exaggerates the prestige pronunciation beyond that used by high-status speakers, e.g. /hɒnɪst/ for *honest*.

infix (5)   An infix is a MORPHEME that is added inside a word to get a new meaning, such as *absobloominglutely*.

International Phonetic Alphabet (IPA) (4)   Internationally agreed phonetic alphabet for writing down the sounds of languages in a consistent fashion, given on p. 286.

intonation (4)   Intonation is the change of pitch used in the sound system of language, i.e. *John?* versus *John!* Sometimes intonation refers specifically to the use of change of pitch to show attitude or GRAMMAR in a language rather than vocabulary differences, in which case it is opposed to TONE.

laterals (4)   Laterals are speech sounds produced asymmetrically in the mouth, typically /l/, in which one side of the tongue makes contact with the roof of the mouth but not the other.

length (4)   Length usually distinguishes pairs of VOWELS in a language, such as short /ɪ/ in /pɪt/ *pit* versus long /iː/ in /piːt/ *Pete*.

lexical entry (5)   A word has a lexical entry in the mind that gives all the information about it such as its pronunciation, meaning and how it may be used in the structure of the sentence.

lexical phrase (11)   A lexical phrase is built around a lexical HEAD such as a NOUN, *house* on the hill, a VERB, *cross* the road, an Adjective, *quick* to anger, or a PREPOSITION, *in* the spring. It contrasts with a FUNCTIONAL PHRASE.

linguist   In the study of language, a linguist is usually someone who studies LINGUISTICS rather than someone who speaks several languages.

linguistics   The academic discipline that focuses on language is called linguistics and is carried out by LINGUISTS.

logographic principle (6)   The writing system in which written symbols correspond to meanings, as in Chinese characters.

Minimalist Programme (11) The Minimalist Programme is the current version of Chomsky's UNIVERSAL GRAMMAR theory, as yet only partially developed, which tries to reduce grammar to the minimum possible principles.

MLU (Mean Length of Utterance) (7) MLU measures the complexity of a child's speech by averaging the number of MORPHEMES or words per utterance, useful as a measure up to about the age of 4.

morpheme (3) A morpheme is the smallest unit in the GRAMMAR that is either a word in its own right (free morpheme), *cook*, or part of a word, *cooks* (bound morpheme *-s*). GRAMMATICAL INFLECTIONS that form part of the grammar, such as the plural *-s* in *books*, are one type of GRAMMATICAL MORPHEME.

movement (3) Movement is a way of describing the structure of the SENTENCE as if elements in it moved around, typically in questions and passive constructions in English. Thus the question *Will John go?* comes from a similar structure to that underlying the statement *John will come* by movement of *will*. See SUBJACENCY and STRUCTURE-DEPENDENCY.

nasals (4) Nasals are CONSONANTS created by blocking the mouth with the tongue or lips, lowering the soft palate (velum), and allowing the air to come out through the nose, as in English /m/ *mouse* and /n/ *news*. VOWELS may be nasalized by allowing some air to come out through the nose and mouth at the same time, as in French /sõ/ *son* ('sound').

noun (3) The lexical category of Noun (N) consists of words such as *John*, *truth* and *electron*. In UNIVERSAL GRAMMAR theory, a noun is the HEAD of a lexical phrase, the Noun Phrase. It can also be thought of as a potential SUBJECT or OBJECT of the sentence, *The truth hurts*.

number (2) Number is a way of signalling how many entities are involved, e.g. through the forms of NOUNS, PRONOUNS and VERBS. English, French and German have two numbers, singular (*he*) and plural (*they*). Tok Pisin and Old English, etc. add dual (2 numbers); Fijian trial (3 numbers). Number is often used to signal other things than sheer quantity, e.g. social relationship is expressed in pronouns.

object (3) The object of the sentence is usually a Noun Phrase in a particular relationship to the VERB of the sentence acting as 'receiver of the action'; e.g. the verb *see* requires an object, *see something*; the verb *give* two objects, *give someone* (indirect) *something* (direct).

open/close (4) In PHONETICS the dimension in which the tongue position of VOWELS varies from the bottom to the top of the mouth is called open/close.

orthographic principle (6) A writing system in which written symbols have a system of their own, corresponding neither to sounds nor to meanings. Cf. ALPHABETIC PRINCIPLE.

parameter (11) In UNIVERSAL GRAMMAR theory the variation between languages is seen as a question of setting values for a small number of parameters; e.g. Italian sets the PRO-DROP parameter to have a value of pro-drop and thus allows sentences without subjects, *Vende* ('he sells'), while German sets the value to non-pro-drop and thus has subjects in all sentences, *Er spricht* ('he speaks').

person (2)   Person is a way of linking the SENTENCE to the speech situation through the choice of PRONOUN or VERB form, often in terms of the person speaking (first person, *I/je/ich*, etc.), the person(s) spoken to (second person, *you/tu/vous/du/Sie*, etc.), and other people involved (third person, *he/she/it/they/il/elle/ils/elles /er/sie/es/Sie*, etc.). Sometimes person is extended to people not previously mentioned (fourth person), as in Navaho, and to listener-included *we* versus listener-excluded *we*, as in Melanesian Pidgin English *yumi* and *mipela*. Often linked to NUMBER.

phoneme (4)   The distinctive sounds of a particular language system are its phonemes, studied in PHONOLOGY. Thus in English the sounds /p/ and /b/ are different phonemes because they distinguish /piːk/ *peak* from /biːk/ *beak*; the sounds [p] and [pʰ] are different phonemes in Hindi because they distinguish two words, but are not in English as they simply form two variant ALLOPHONES of the same phoneme without ever distinguishing two words.

phonetics (4)   The sub-discipline of LINGUISTICS that studies the production and perception of the speech sounds themselves is called phonetics and contrasts with PHONOLOGY.

phonology (4)   The area of LINGUISTICS that studies the sound systems of particular languages is phonology, and is contrasted with PHONETICS.

phrase structure (3)   The phrase structure of the SENTENCE links all the parts together in a structure like that of a family tree. So the Noun Phrase *the dog* combines with a VERB to get the Verb Phrase *chased the dog*, which in turn combines with the Noun Phrase *the cat* to get the sentence *The cat chased the dog*.

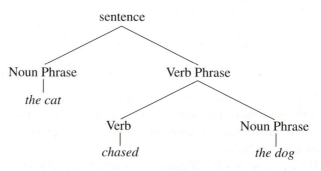

pidgin (11)   A pidgin language is created by speakers of two different languages for communicating with each other. Pidgins share similar characteristics wherever they arise, such as CV SYLLABLE structure. Examples are Tok Pisin (Papua New Guinea), Cameroon Pidgin English, Ivory Coast Pidgin. See also CREOLE.

plosive (4)   A speech sound made by blocking the air-stream completely with the tongue or lips, allowing the air to burst out after a brief moment, as in English /t/ *tea* or /b/ *bee*. See VOICE ONSET TIME.

prefix (5)   A prefix is a MORPHEME that is added to the beginning of a word to create another word by derivation, as *re-* is added to *write* to produce *rewrite*.

preposition (3)   The category of grammar called preposition (P) consists of words like *to*, *by* and *with*. In UNIVERSAL GRAMMAR theory the Preposition is the HEAD of a LEXICAL PHRASE, the Preposition Phrase. When coming before a NOUN, the category is called 'preposition' as in *in England*, when after a Noun a 'postposition' *Nippon ni* ('Japan in').

principle (11)   In the UNIVERSAL GRAMMAR theory, principles of language are built into the human mind and are thus never broken in human languages. Examples are STRUCTURE-DEPENDENCY and SUBJACENCY.

pro-drop (2)   The pro-drop PARAMETER divides languages into pro-drop languages, in which the SUBJECT of the SENTENCE may be left out, as in Italian *Sono di Torino* ('am from Turin') and Chinese *Shuo* ('speak'), and non-pro-drop languages in which the subject must be present in the actual sentence, as in English, German and French.

pronoun (2)   Pronouns such as *he* and *them* differ from NOUNS in that they refer to different things on different occasions: *She likes it* can refer to any female being liking anything; *Helen likes beer* only to a specific person liking a specific object. English pronouns have CASE (*she* versus *her*) and NUMBER (*she* versus *they*).

***r*-dropping (8)**   Some standard accents of English such as American are 'rhotic' in that they have /r/ before CONSONANTS: *bird* is /bɜːrd/, or before silence: *fur* /fɜːr/. Other accents of English such as British RP are 'non-rhotic', in that they do not have /r/ in these two positions, i.e. *bird* /bɜːd/, *fur* /fɜː/. R-dropping is a marker of low status in the USA and lack of *r*-dropping is a marker of rural accents in England.

RP (4)   The prestige accent of British English is known by the two letters RP, originally standing for 'Received Pronunciation'. It is spoken in all regions of the UK, even if by a small minority of speakers.

sentence   A sentence is the largest independent unit in the GRAMMAR of the language. It may include other CLAUSES within it.

sign language (4)   A sign language differs from other human languages only in using a gesture system rather than a sound system.

Specific Language Impairment (SLI) (9)   Specific Language Impairment (SLI) is one term for difficulties with language development in children unaccompanied by non-linguistic disabilities, possibly genetic in origin and characterized *inter alia* by missing GRAMMATICAL MORPHEMES.

structure-dependency (3)   Structure-dependency is a restriction on MOVEMENT in human languages that makes it depend on the structure of the SENTENCE, rather than on its linear order. A PRINCIPLE of UNIVERSAL GRAMMAR.

style (8)   'Style' is used by William Labov and others to refer to the dimension of formal to informal in language use.

subjacency (3, 11)   Subjacency is a restriction on grammatical MOVEMENT in the SENTENCE that prevents elements moving over more than one boundary, the definition of boundary varying as a PARAMETER from one language to another.

subject (3)   The Subject (S) is the NOUN Phrase of the SENTENCE alongside the Verb Phrase in its structure, _John_ _likes biscuits_, compulsory in non-pro-drop languages in the actual sentence but may not be present in PRO-DROP languages; it often acts as the 'agent of the action'.

suffix (5)   A suffix is a MORPHEME that is added to a word to create another word by derivation. _Felon_ thus becomes a second noun by adding _-y_, _felony_, and an adjective by adding _-ous_, _felonious_.

syllable (4)   A sound structure usually consisting of a central VOWEL (V) such as /ɑ:/, with one or more CONSONANTS (C) preceding or following it, such as /b/ or /k/ CV /bɑ:/ _bar_ and VC /ɑ:k/ _ark_. Languages vary in whether they permit only CV syllables or allow CVC syllables as well and in the combinations of C that may be used. See EPENTHESIS.

tone (4)   Usually tone means a unit of pitch change for a given language, English having about 7 tones. Sometimes tone is used to contrast a tone language, where tones are used to show vocabulary differences, such as Chinese, and an INTONATION language, where tones show attitudes, GRAMMAR, etc., such as English.

Universal Grammar (UG) (11)   Sometimes Universal Grammar refers simply to the aspects of language that all languages have in common. This book mostly uses Universal Grammar in the Chomskyan sense to refer to the language faculty built into the human mind, seen as consisting of PRINCIPLES and PARAMETERS.

uvular /r/ (4)   An /r/ pronounced with tongue contact at the uvula at the back of the mouth – the usual French /r/.

verb (3)   A Verb (V) is a lexical category in the GRAMMAR made up of words such as _like_ and _listen_. In UG theory it is the head of the lexical Verb Phrase (VP). Different types of verbs specify whether there is a need for: no OBJECT, _John fainted_, one object, _Mary phoned Peter_, two objects, _Mary gave the money to her brother_, an animate SUBJECT, _the man fainted_ not _the rock fainted_, and so on.

vocal cords (4)   'Vocal cords' are flaps in the larynx which may open and close rapidly during speech to let out puffs of air, producing a basic vibrating noise called VOICE.

voice (4)   Voice in PHONETICS is technically the vibration contributed to speech by allowing flaps in the larynx known as VOCAL CORDS to rapidly open and shut as air passes through them. Presence or absence of voice is then a DISTINCTIVE FEATURE that separates voiced sounds like the /d/ of _dime_ from unvoiced sounds like the /t/ of _time_.

Voice Onset Time (VOT) (4)   When a PLOSIVE sound is created by blocking the airway through the mouth, the moment when VOICE starts is called Voice Onset Time. If voicing starts before release (minus VOT) a voiced sound is heard, if after release (plus VOT) a voiceless sound. For example English /p/ is distinguished from /b/ by its longer VOT _inter alia_. VOTs vary from one language to another.

vowel (4)   In terms of sound production, a vowel is a single speech sound produced by vibrating the VOCAL CORDS and not obstructing the mouth in any way, as in the

/æ/ of *bank*, shaped by the position of the lips into rounded and unrounded sounds, as in English /i:/ *bee* and /u:/ *boo*, and by the position of the tongue into open/close, as in English /ɒ/ *lot* versus /u:/ *loot* and front/back, as in English /ʊ/ *foot* versus /e/ *bet*. In terms of sound structure, a vowel typically occurs as the core of the SYLLA-BLE rather than at the beginning or the end, thus contrasting with CONSONANT.

Wernicke's aphasia (9) Wernicke's aphasia is the name of a type of APHASIA involving difficulty with comprehension rather than speaking, associated with injury to Wernicke's area in the back left area of the brain (posterior upper temporal lobe).

word order (3) A crucial aspect of the GRAMMAR of many languages is the order of the elements in the SENTENCE, called word order in general. One variation is the order of SUBJECT, VERB and OBJECT, whether SVO, SOV, or whatever, the main order for a language sometimes being called its CANONICAL ORDER. Another word-order variation is whether the language has PREPOSITIONS before NOUNS in *England* or post-positions after Nouns, e.g. *Nippon ni* ('Japan in'). See HEAD PARAMETER.

THE INTERNATIONAL PHONETIC ALPHABET (revised to 1993, corrected 1996)

CONSONANTS (PULMONIC)

	Bilabial	Labiodental	Dental	Alveolar	Postalveolar	Retroflex	Palatal	Velar	Uvular	Pharyngeal	Glottal
Plosive	p b			t d		ʈ ɖ	c ɟ	k g	q ɢ		ʔ
Nasal	m	ɱ		n		ɳ	ɲ	ŋ	N		
Trill	ʙ			r					R		
Tap or Flap				ɾ		ɽ					
Fricative	ɸ β	f v	θ ð	s z	ʃ ʒ	ʂ ʐ	ç ʝ	x ɣ	χ ʁ	ħ ʕ	h ɦ
Lateral fricative				ɬ ɮ							
Approximant		ʋ		ɹ		ɻ	j	ɰ			
Lateral approximant				l		ɭ	ʎ	L			

Where symbols appear in pairs, the one to the right represents a voiced consonant. Shaded areas denote articulations judged impossible.

CONSONANTS (NON-PULMONIC)

Clicks		Voiced implosives		Ejectives	
ʘ	Bilabial	ɓ	Bilabial	ʼ	Examples:
ǀ	Dental	ɗ	Dental/alveolar	pʼ	Bilabial
ǃ	(Post)alveolar	ʄ	Palatal	tʼ	Dental/alveolar
ǂ	Palatoalveolar	ɠ	Velar	kʼ	Velar
ǁ	Alveolar lateral	ʛ	Uvular	sʼ	Alveolar fricative

OTHER SYMBOLS

ʍ	Voiceless labial-velar fricative
w	Voiced labial-velar approximant
ɥ	Voiced labial-palatal approximant
ʜ	Voiceless epiglottal fricative
ʢ	Voiced epiglottal fricative
ʡ	Epiglottal plosive

ɕ ʑ Alveolo-palatal fricatives

ɺ Alveolar lateral flap

ɧ Simultaneous ʃ and x

Affricates and double articulations can be represented by two symbols joined by a tie bar if necessary.

k͡p t͡s

VOWELS

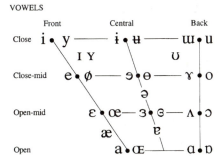

Where symbols appear in pairs, the one to the right represents a rounded vowel.

SUPRASEGMENTALS

ˈ	Primary stress
ˌ	Secondary stress
	ˌfoʊnəˈtɪʃən
ː	Long eː
ˑ	Half-long eˑ
̆	Extra-short ĕ
ǀ	Minor (foot) group
ǁ	Major (intonation) group
.	Syllable break ɹi.ækt
‿	Linking (absence of a break)

DIACRITICS
Diacritics may be placed above a symbol with a descender, e.g. ŋ̊

̥	Voiceless	n̥ d̥	̤	Breathy voiced	b̤ a̤	̪	Dental	t̪ d̪
̬	Voiced	s̬ t̬	̰	Creaky voiced	b̰ a̰	̺	Apical	t̺ d̺
ʰ	Aspirated	tʰ dʰ	̼	Linguolabial	t̼ d̼	̻	Laminal	t̻ d̻
̹	More rounded	ɔ̹	ʷ	Labialized	tʷ dʷ	̃	Nasalized	ẽ
̜	Less rounded	ɔ̜	ʲ	Palatalized	tʲ dʲ	ⁿ	Nasal release	dⁿ
̟	Advanced	u̟	ˠ	Velarized	tˠ dˠ	ˡ	Lateral release	dˡ
̠	Retracted	e̠	ˤ	Pharyngealized	tˤ dˤ	̚	No audible release	d̚
̈	Centralized	ë	̴	Velarized or pharyngealized	ɫ			
̽	Mid-centralized	e̽	̝	Raised	e̝	(ɹ̝ = voiced alveolar fricative)
̩	Syllabic	n̩	̞	Lowered	e̞	(β̞ = voiced bilabial approximant)
̯	Non-syllabic	e̯	̘	Advanced Tongue Root	e̘		
˞	Rhoticity	ɚ a˞	̙	Retracted Tongue Root	e̙		

TONES AND WORD ACCENTS

LEVEL			CONTOUR		
e̋ or	˥	Extra high	ě or	˩˥	Rising
é	˦	High	ê	˥˩	Falling
ē	˧	Mid	e᷄	˦˥	High rising
è	˨	Low	e᷅	˩˨	Low rising
ȅ	˩	Extra low	e᷈	˧˦˧	Rising-falling
↓		Downstep	↗		Global rise
↑		Upstep	↘		Global fall

Index